European Yearbook of International Economic Law

Special Issue

The European Yearbook of International Economic Law (EYIEL) is a Springer-publication in the field of International Economic Law (IEL), a field increasingly emancipating itself from Public International Law scholarship and evolving into a fully-fledged academic discipline in its own right. With the yearbook, editors and publisher make a significant contribution to the development of this "new" discipline and provide an international source of reference of the highest possible quality.

The EYIEL covers all areas of IEL, in particular WTO Law, External Trade Law of major trading countries, important Regional Economic Integration agreements, International Competition Law, International Investment Regulation, International Monetary Law, International Intellectual Property Protection and International Tax Law.

EYIEL publishes articles following a substantive review by the editors and external experts as appropriate.

The editors have published extensively in the field of IEL and European Law alike. They are supported by an international Advisory Board consisting of established scholars of the highest reputation.

Saarbrücken, Germany	Marc Bungenberg
Erlangen, Germany	Markus Krajewski
Glasgow, UK	Christian J. Tams
Lausanne, Switzerland	Andreas R. Ziegler

The European Yearbook of International Economic Law (EYIEL) is an annual publication in International Economic Law, a field increasingly emancipating itself from Public International Law scholarship and evolving into a fully-fledged academic discipline in its own right. With the yearbook, the editors and publisher intend to make a significant contribution to the development of this "new" discipline and provide an international reference source of the highest possible quality. The EYIEL covers all areas of IEL, in particular WTO Law, External Trade Law for major trading countries, important Regional Economic Integration agreements, International Competition Law, International Investment Regulation, International Monetary Law, International Intellectual Property Protection and International Tax Law. In addition to the regular annual volumes, EYIEL Special Issues routinely address specific current topics in International Economic Law.

Silvia Solidoro

Indigenous Peoples in the World Bank Group's Practice

An Inquiry in Light of International Human Rights Law

Springer

Silvia Solidoro
Law, University of Salento
Lecce, Italy

ISSN 2364-8392 ISSN 2364-8406 (electronic)
European Yearbook of International Economic Law
ISSN 2510-6880 ISSN 2510-6899 (electronic)
Special Issue
ISBN 978-3-032-05146-2 ISBN 978-3-032-05147-9 (eBook)
https://doi.org/10.1007/978-3-032-05147-9

This Springer imprint is published by the registered company Springer Nature Switzerland AG
The registered company address is: Gewerbestrasse 11, 6330 Cham, Switzerland

Silvia Solidoro

Indigenous Peoples in the World Bank Group's Practice

An Inquiry in Light of International Human Rights Law

Springer

Silvia Solidoro
Law, University of Salento
Lecce, Italy

ISSN 2364-8392 ISSN 2364-8406 (electronic)
European Yearbook of International Economic Law
ISSN 2510-6880 ISSN 2510-6899 (electronic)
Special Issue
ISBN 978-3-032-05146-2 ISBN 978-3-032-05147-9 (eBook)
https://doi.org/10.1007/978-3-032-05147-9

This Springer imprint is published by the registered company Springer Nature Switzerland AG
The registered company address is: Gewerbestrasse 11, 6330 Cham, Switzerland

To Giorgio and Pina

Acknowledgments

Writing this book has been both a challenging and enriching experience, which has ultimately broadened my intellectual horizons. As I reflect on this journey, I am filled with appreciation for the many people who have played a vital role in bringing this work to fruition.

First and foremost, I am profoundly thankful to Professors Saverio Di Benedetto, Susanna Cafaro, and Nicola De Liso. Their insightful guidance has been instrumental throughout the development of this book. Each of them, in their unique way, has contributed to shaping not only the direction of my research but also the clarity and depth of my arguments. Their expertise and encouragement have been essential in refining the focus and substance of my work.

I am equally grateful to my family and friends, whose constant presence has been a steady source of strength and inspiration. Their support reminded me of the importance of perseverance, balance, and perspective.

To all who have walked beside me on this path, I offer my sincere gratitude.

Silvia Solidoro

July 2025

Competing Interests The author has no competing interests to declare that are relevant to the content of this manuscript.

Contents

1 **Introduction** . . . 1
References . . . 10

2 **The Challenged Relationship Between Development and Human Rights in the Context of World Bank Group's Operations** . . . 11
2.1 The World Bank Group's Multifaceted Engagement with Development Financing . . . 11
2.1.1 IBRD's and IDA's Financing Activities . . . 16
2.1.2 IFC's Financing Activities . . . 20
2.2 The Contentious Political Prohibition Clauses Included in IBRD's Articles of Agreement . . . 20
2.3 The Emergence of a New Mandate Through Practice . . . 26
2.4 Recent Developments in the Interpretation of IBRD's Articles of Agreement . . . 30
2.5 The Evolution of the Framework for Managing Environmental and Social Issues . . . 37
2.5.1 The Regime Applicable to IBRD's and IDA's Investment Project Financing . . . 37
2.5.2 Other Lending Instruments: Delimiting the Scope of Inquiry . . . 43
2.5.3 The Framework Governing IFC's Operations . . . 45
2.6 Role of the World Bank Group vs the Borrower During the Project Cycle . . . 48
2.6.1 Public Sector Projects . . . 48
2.6.2 Private Sector Projects . . . 53
2.7 The Establishment of Independent Accountability Mechanisms: Preliminary Remarks . . . 55
References . . . 57

3 Relevant Practice Concerning Indigenous Peoples in Public Sector Projects . . . 63
3.1 The Interface of World Bank's Indigenous Peoples Policies with International Law . . . 63
3.2 Policy Instruments Encompassing an 'Escape' Clause . . . 77
3.3 The Inspection Panel's Mandate . . . 83
3.4 Protection of Indigenous Peoples' Rights in the Inspection Panel's Practice . . . 87
3.4.1 Early Cases (1994–2005) . . . 88
3.4.2 Indigenous Peoples Policies as a Reflection of International Human Rights Law (2006–2009) . . . 106
3.4.3 Interpretation in Light of Regional Human Rights Case Law (2009) . . . 112
3.4.4 Recent Cases (2012-Present) . . . 114
3.5 Interim Conclusions . . . 124
References . . . 139

4 Relevant Practice Concerning Indigenous Peoples in Private Sector Projects . . . 147
4.1 The International Finance Corporation's Standard on Indigenous Peoples . . . 147
4.2 Peculiarities of the Compliance Advisor Ombudsman's Mandate . . . 153
4.3 Protection of Indigenous Peoples' Rights in the Compliance Advisor Ombudsman's Practice . . . 157
4.3.1 Early Cases (2002–2011) . . . 158
4.3.2 Facilitating Access to Remedy Through Dispute Resolution (2012–2014) . . . 170
4.3.3 Free, Prior, and Informed Consent in Recent Compliance Cases (2014–2018) . . . 174
4.4 Interim Conclusions . . . 182
References . . . 192

5 The World Bank Group's International Legal Obligations Regarding Indigenous Peoples' Rights . . . 197
5.1 Attribution of Member States' Treaty Human Rights Obligations: Criticism . . . 198
5.2 Obligations Arising from the Relationship Agreement with the UN: Criticism . . . 201
5.3 The Way Forward . . . 204
5.3.1 Obligations Arising from Customary International Law . . . 205
5.3.2 Obligations Arising from General Principles of International Law . . . 213
5.4 Interim Conclusions . . . 216
References . . . 217

6 Final Remarks 223
6.1 The Emergence of a Spontaneous Commitment to Uphold Indigenous Peoples' Rights 223
6.2 The Normative Weight of the World Bank Group's Institutional Practice. 224
6.3 The Impact on State Practice 227
6.4 The Multifaceted Nature of World Bank Group's International Legal Obligations. 230
References. 232

List of Abbreviations

AfrCommHPR	African Commission on Human and Peoples' Rights
AM	(IBRD/IDA) Accountability Mechanism
BP	Bank Procedure
CAO	(IFC/MIGA) Compliance Advisor Ombudsman
CESCR	UN Committee on Economic, Social and Cultural Rights
CIFI	Corporación Interamericana para el Financiamiento de Infraestructura (non-banking financial institution)
CODE	World Bank Group's Committee on Development Effectiveness
CSOs	Civil Society Organizations
DPF	Development Policy Financing
EA	Environmental Assessment
ECOSOC	UN Economic and Social Council
EHS	Environmental Health and Safety Guidelines
ESAP	(IFC) Environmental and Social Action Plan
ESF	(IBRD/IDA) Environmental and Social Framework
ESMS	(IFC) Environmental and Social Management System
ESRPs	(IFC) Environmental and Social Review Procedures
ESRS	(IBRD/IDA) Environmental and Social Review Summary
ESS	(IBRD/IDA) Environmental and Social Standard
ETESA	Empresa de Transmisión Eléctrica S.A. (state-owned enterprise)
FAO	Food and Agriculture Organization of the United Nations
FPIC	Free, Prior and Informed Consent
GP	Good Practice
HAGL	Hoang Anh Gia Lai (business enterprise)
HRC	UN Human Rights Committee
IACHR	Inter-American Commission on Human Rights
IACtHR	Inter-American Court of Human Rights
IAM	Independent Accountability Mechanism
IBRD	International Bank for Reconstruction and Development

ICCPR	International Covenant on Civil and Political Rights
ICERD	International Convention on the Elimination of All Forms of Racial Discrimination
ICESCR	International Covenant on Economic, Social and Cultural Rights
ICR	Implementation Completion and Results Report
ICRR	Implementation Completion and Results Report Review
IDA	International Development Association
IEG	Independent Evaluation Group
IFC	International Finance Corporation
IFI	International Financial Institution
ILA	International Law Association
ILC	UN International Law Commission
ILO	International Labour Organization
IMF	International Monetary Fund
IPDP	Indigenous Peoples Development Plan
IPF	Investment Project Financing
IPP	Indigenous Peoples Plan
IPPF	Indigenous Peoples Planning Framework
ISS	Integrated Safeguards Sheet
LRIF	Latin Renewables Infrastructure Fund L.P. (private equity fund)
MAP	Management Action Plan
MDB	Multilateral Development Bank
MIGA	Multilateral Investment Guarantee Agency
NAFTA	North American Free Trade Agreement
NGO	Non-Governmental Organization
NTF	Nordic Trust Fund
OAS	Organization of American States
OD	Operational Directive
OED	Operations Evaluation Department
OHCHR	United Nations Office of the High Commissioner for Human Rights
OMS	Operational Manual Statement
OP	Operational Policy
OPCS	Operations Policy and Country Services
OPN	Operations Policy Note
PS	(IFC) Performance Standard
SEA	Sexual Exploitation and Abuse
SH	Sexual Harassment
UDHR	Universal Declaration of Human Rights
UNDP	UN Development Programme
UNDRIP	UN Declaration on the Rights of Indigenous Peoples
UNESCO	UN Educational, Scientific and Cultural Organization
UNGPs	UN Guiding Principles on Business and Human Rights
UNHCR	UN High Commissioner for Refugees

UNHRC	UN Human Rights Council
UNICEF	UN Children's Fund
UN Women	UN Entity for Gender Equality and the Empowerment of Women
WBG	World Bank Group
WHO	World Health Organization

Chapter 1
Introduction

One of the most interesting developments in international affairs since World War II amounts to the expansion of the role of international organizations. Originally designed to act for the objective of supporting member states' efforts related to international peace, security, and economic recovery, their operations have dramatically changed over time to cope with emerging global challenges. Gradually, by broadening the scope of their activities beyond the initial mandate, international organizations have begun to address an increasingly diverse range of issues. Furthermore, by overcoming the premise on which they were established, whereby their primary focus was to address State-to-State relations,[1] they have come to involve various other entities at different levels, such as non-governmental organizations, transnational corporations, and even individuals, thereby enabling these actors to play a role in defining their global agenda.

Multilateral Development Banks ('MDBs') constitute a good illustration of such changes. Established for the primary purpose of providing loans for rebuilding infrastructure, particularly in Europe, they have evolved into organizations engaged in various activities, including policy advice and technical assistance to governments and the private sector, intended to improve the conditions for attracting investment while also encouraging economic growth and development, with the effect of influencing individuals' lives and the exercise of their human rights in multiple ways.[2] This shift has had unavoidable implications regarding their impact.[3] Among the different types of existing MDBs, the case of the World Bank Group ('WBG') is of particular significance, not only because it is the only one that

[1] Bradlow and Grossman (1995).

[2] Bradlow (2019, p. 2).

[3] Suzuki and Nanwani (2005, p. 180).

S. Solidoro, *Indigenous Peoples in the World Bank Group's Practice*, European Yearbook of International Economic Law,
https://doi.org/10.1007/978-3-032-05147-9_1

operates on a global scale but also due to the fact that three of the entities constituting the organization hold the status of UN specialized agencies.[4]

Notably, as the international human rights legal landscape began to take shape globally with the establishment of the UN Charter-based system and the adoption of the Universal Declaration of Human Rights ('UDHR'),[5] the World Bank, then the sole institution of what would later become the WBG, came under growing criticism for not explicitly including human rights in its mandate.

Over time, the UN, civil society and academia have increasingly advocated for a reconsideration of its involvement in this field. Yet a formalistic reading of the so-called 'prohibition clauses', insulating the World Bank from interference in the political affairs of its member countries, has led it to exclude considerations that could raise significant concerns about sovereignty from its agenda. For a long time, the Bank curtailed the remit of human rights considerations relevant to its activities by drawing a clear distinction between social, and cultural rights on the one hand, and civil and political rights on the other hand, emphasizing the relevance of the former over the latter, with the main consequence of downplaying the interdependence of each category of rights and the inevitable political content of both.

Nowadays, it is widely recognized that the role of the World Bank Group needs to be understood in light of a modern conception underpinning reconciliation with a holistic understanding of human rights.[6] Nevertheless, the fact remains that, as the WBG generally approaches human rights from a development perspective—emphasizing the crucial relevance of the poverty reduction and sustainable economic growth objectives to its mandate—it does not frame its commitment to human rights in an explicit way. Considering that the WBG is not even a party to any human rights treaty, this study will examine its practice to assess whether any valuable insights can be drawn regarding the manner in which it carries out its core activities. Building on these premises, the analysis will seek to contribute to the ongoing debate regarding the potential human rights obligations that may bind the organization, a topic that remains highly contentious.[7]

Over the course of its evolution, although never elaborating an overarching policy on human rights,[8] the WBG has in fact adopted a number of operational instruments regulating the impact of its projects, better known as 'safeguards'. These

[4] For a comprehensive analysis of this relationship, Perinbam (1966, p. 293).

[5] UN General Assembly, *The Universal Declaration of Human Rights*, Resolution 217A (III) of 10 December 1948, UN Doc. A/RES/217(III).

[6] In this regard, Christopher Stephens, the former General Counsel of the Asian Development Bank, formulated an alternative approach by holding that «the theory that facilitating human rights constitutes interference in political affairs is misplaced. It's not the political nature of the issue that is prohibited; it's the interference. MDBs' projects are collaborative in nature. They are derived from, determined by, and implemented through extensive consultations with developing member countries». See Asian Development blog, *Why MDBs Should Include Human Rights in the Development Agenda*, available at: https://blogs.adb.org/blog/why-mdbs-should-include-human-rights-development-agenda. Accessed 23 April 2025.

[7] Neuman (2019, p. 9).

[8] Sarfaty (2012).

instruments, developed through procedures regularly involving consultations with the public,[9] which ultimately resulted in a framework meant to minimize harm to the environment and local communities, while also enhancing their participation, especially during the project implementation phase. Safeguards are relevant in two different ways for the purposes of the present analysis. First, because of their noticeable convergence with internationally accepted human rights standards. Second, because their incorporation into agreements signed with states or private entities provides strong incentives for both to abide by these commitments, ultimately ensuring that the World Bank Group's funds do not contribute to violations of the rights protected under the safeguards. Since the adoption of their first version in 1989, these instruments have spontaneously evolved into a sophisticated framework setting out the requirements that funding recipients must fulfill at every stage of a project, first to secure financial support, and later to retain it. In this regard, it is noteworthy that the past few decades have seen increased cooperation with other organizations involved in financing activities in this field, leading to the harmonization of the majority of their environmental and social policies, which represents a remarkable trend in the field of development finance. Such cross-institutional normativity might eventually assume the qualities of a *droit commun* among MDBs, allowing for the emergence of a body of common rules and procedures.[10] Notably, the World Bank Group has driven this process, which is exclusively based on practice, by pioneering the adoption of the safeguards in both the private and public sectors. Due to a massive emulative process, safeguards have progressively become widespread among other MDBs.

Furthermore, the World Bank Group has strengthened its collaboration with the UN, currently extending across a wide range of issues and encompassing nearly every region and sector.[11] In particular, after the UN General Assembly adopted the Agenda for Development in 1997,[12] which called for an initiative promoting international cooperation for revitalizing development, the Economic and Social Council ('ECOSOC') gathered the first UN International Conference on Financing for Development in Mexico in 2002.[13] The event brought together over 50 heads of state and government, and, for the first time, representatives of the WBG and the International Monetary Fund ('IMF') as well, to discuss the way development finance could facilitate the attainment of internationally agreed development goals,

---

[9] Hunter (2020, p. 441). In the case of other organizations, such as the World Trade Organization, the inclusion of environmental and social concerns in the policies dates back to the time of the institution's establishment: see Pauciulo (2017).

[10] Boisson de Chazournes (2011, p. 174).

[11] For instance, in early 2020, after recognizing the links between fragility and poverty, IBRD has massively scaled up its work in fragile settings and launched its first Strategy for Fragility, Conflict and Violence (2020–2025). Currently, the United Nations and the World Bank Group partner in almost 50 countries to address the main challenges existing in this field, following calls by Member States to enhance cooperation: see UN General Assembly (2016).

[12] UN General Assembly (1997).

[13] UN (2002).

including those contained in the UN Millennium Declaration.[14] The document that emerged from the conference, known as the 'Monterrey consensus', called for a partnership between industrial and developing countries aimed at steering globalization towards sustained and equitable development for all people worldwide. Furthermore, it emphasized the need for continued engagement with relevant intergovernmental stakeholders.[15] A second Global Conference was held in Doha in 2008, and a third one in Addis Ababa in 2015. The outcome of the latter has been a document laying out a new international agenda for financing sustainable development.[16] It mandated the ECOSOC to hold an annual 'Forum on Financing for Development Follow-up', which serves as a platform for ongoing multi-stakeholder dialogue among the leadership of major international organizations, such as the World Bank Group, the International Monetary Fund, and the World Trade Organization, as well as representatives of Member States, civil society organizations, and the private sector. The document summarizing the conclusions of the latest meeting,[17] convened from 22 to 25 April 2024 in New York, contains intergovernmentally agreed recommendations compiled by the ECOSOC President on the basis of informal consultations. It includes relevant considerations regarding the World Bank Group's evolving mission in supporting developing countries. Furthermore, it underpins notable efforts to reform the entire international financial architecture in order to accelerate sustainable development, particularly for countries which are most in need of support.

Against this backdrop, the second chapter of this book will unfold in two directions. First, it will provide an overview of the developments that have led to an extensive interpretation of the World Bank Group's mandate, whose boundaries have long been contested by the formalistic reading excluding human rights consideration from its purview. In parallel with that, it will examine the framework that the organization has developed in order to manage the environmental and social aspects associated with its projects. Among the various entities constituting the World Bank Group,[18] the analysis will take into consideration the operations supported by the International Bank for Reconstruction and Development ('IBRD'), the International Development Association ('IDA'), and the International Finance Corporation ('IFC'), by virtue of their peculiar status as United Nations specialized agencies, drawing a distinction between investments provided to public entities and those addressed to private ones.

Among the existing World Bank Group's safeguards, the subsequent chapters will focus on those devoted to the avoidance, mitigation, or eradication of adverse impacts affecting indigenous peoples in light of their cross-cutting nature, which

---

[14] UN General Assembly (2000).

[15] The World Bank (2003).

[16] UN General Assembly (2015). Notably, the UN 2030 Agenda envisages «a world of universal respect for human rights and human dignity, the rule of law, justice, equality and non-discrimination».

[17] UN Economic and Social Council (2024, para. 40).

[18] For a comprehensive analysis of the activities they undertake, see Pauciulo (2025, p. 195).

links them to many key environmental and social challenges faced by projects, such as preservation of natural habitats, sustainable development of forest ecosystems, protection of cultural heritage, and avoidance of involuntary resettlement. The case of the customary rights of indigenous peoples pertaining to lands traditionally owned, or customarily used or occupied, is emblematic. Many governments recognize only a fraction of this land as legally belonging to them. Furthermore, even when the rights of indigenous peoples to land are legally recognized, other issues may arise, such as those related to the use and exploitation of natural resources, which threaten the survival and maintenance of the ecosystems these communities depend on, or those related to involuntary resettlement, often a major source of social conflict.

Notably, in the international landscape, there exist hard and soft legal instruments protecting indigenous peoples. In 1957, the International Labor Organization ('ILO') adopted the only international treaty dealing exclusively with their rights, the Indigenous and Tribal Populations Convention no. 107,[19] subsequently replaced by the Indigenous and Tribal Peoples Convention no. 169 of 1989.[20] In its preamble, the Convention recalls that its text builds upon the terms of the International Bill of Human Rights, as well as all the international instruments on the prevention of discrimination. Furthermore, it holds that its contents were developed in cooperation with the United Nations and its specialized agencies in their respective fields of competence, such as the Food and Agriculture Organization ('FAO'), the United Nations Educational, Scientific, and Cultural Organization ('UNESCO'), and the World Health Organization ('WHO'). Although ratified by only 24 countries, it sets standards that are widely used as a point of reference at both the national and international levels.[21] More recently, in 2007, the General Assembly adopted the United Nations Declaration on the Rights of Indigenous Peoples ('UNDRIP'), a non-legally binding resolution that has been regarded as the leading instrument on the matter from the outset.[22] In the same year, the UN Human Rights Council ('UNHRC') established the Expert Mechanism on the Rights of Indigenous Peoples as a subsidiary body composed of seven independent experts,[23] entrusting it with the task of assisting Member States in achieving the goals of the UNDRIP while also providing them with advice on key matters, such as self-determination and Free, Prior, and

[19] International Labour Organization, *Convention concerning the Protection and Integration of Indigenous and Other Tribal and Semi-Tribal Populations in Independent Countries*, C107, Geneva, 26 June 1957 (entered into effect on 2 June 1959).

[20] International Labour Organization, *Convention concerning Indigenous and Tribal Peoples in Independent Countries*, C169, Geneva, 27 June 1989 (entered into effect on 5 September 1991).

[21] Xanthaki (2009, p. 91).

[22] UN General Assembly, *United Nations Declaration on the Rights of Indigenous Peoples*, Resolution 61/295 of 2 October 2007, UN Doc. A/RES/61/295.

[23] UN Human Rights Council, *Expert Mechanism on the Rights of Indigenous Peoples*, Resolution 36/3 of 14 December 2007, UN Doc. A/HRC/RES/6/36. Its mandate has been amended in September 2016: see UN Human Rights Council, *Expert Mechanism on the Rights of Indigenous Peoples*, Resolution 33/25 of 5 October 2016, UN Doc. A/HRC/RES/33/25.

Informed Consent ('FPIC'). Among other relevant UN bodies mandated to carry out similar activities, there is the Permanent Forum on Indigenous Issues, an advisory body to the ECOSOC composed of 16 independent experts, which was established in 2000 to deal with all matters related to their economic and social development, culture, environment, education, health, and human rights.[24] The Forum formulates recommendations to the ECOSOC, as well as to UN specialized agencies, through the active involvement of both regional indigenous representatives and states, and serves as a platform that ensures a systematic exchange of information. In addition, since the adoption of the UNDRIP, it follows up on the effectiveness of its implementation. Last but not least, in 2001, the then UN Commission on Human Rights decided to appoint a Special Rapporteur on the Rights of Indigenous Peoples within the system of thematic Special Procedures, for the purpose of promoting good practices among states, including new laws, government programs, and constructive agreements with indigenous peoples. This independent expert reports on their general human rights situation around the globe and provides recommendations to states on the appropriate remedies to adopt in response to violations of these rights. Its mandate has been renewed multiple times so as to include cooperation with the Expert Mechanism on the Rights of Indigenous Peoples, relevant UN bodies and treaty bodies, as well as regional human rights organizations. Notably, it currently foresees the promotion of the UNDRIP and «international instruments relevant to the advancement of the rights of Indigenous Peoples, where appropriate».[25] The mandates of the three mechanisms, which meet annually to coordinate their activities and share information with each other, can thus be seen as complementary.

At the regional level, it is worth mentioning the adoption of the 2016 American Declaration on the Rights of Indigenous Peoples by the Organization of American States ('OAS'),[26] largely building upon «the progress achieved at the international level in recognizing the rights of indigenous peoples», especially through ILO Convention No. 169 and the UNDRIP, which are explicitly referenced in its preamble. Both the Inter-American Commission on Human Rights and the Inter-American Court of Human Rights can interpret the Declaration to provide context for other instruments, such as the American Convention on Human Rights.

Based on the existing international and regional legal frameworks governing indigenous peoples' rights, the main question on which the analysis will be based is whether and to what extent the World Bank Group's practice has drawn from them in carrying out its core financing operations. In order to determine so, a first strand

[24] UN Economic and Social Council, *Establishment of a UN Permanent Forum on Indigenous Issues*, Resolution 2000/22 of 28 July 2000, UN Doc. E/RES/2000/22.

[25] The Special Rapporteur's mandate has been renewed in 2004, 2007, and, most recently, in 2022 by the Human Rights Council: see UN Human Rights Council, *Human Rights and Indigenous Peoples: Mandate of Special Rapporteur on the Rights of Indigenous Peoples*, Resolution 51/16 of 12 October 2022, UN Doc. A/HRC/RES/51/16.

[26] Organization of American States, *American Declaration on the Rights of Indigenous Peoples*, 15 June 2016, AG/RES.2888 (XLVI-O/16).

of research will investigate the drafting history and subsequent evolution of the operational policies that are aimed at minimizing harm to indigenous peoples in projects involving them. In this context, the evaluation of the role played by the World Bank Group's Independent Accountability Mechanisms ('IAMs') will be crucial. Established in the 1990s to provide individuals potentially affected by the implementation of projects funded by the World Bank Group with a means to have their voice heard, IAMs can be regarded as a forum where the entities constituting the organization are requested to act in accordance with their operational policies. A second strand of research will thus investigate how IAMs have scrutinized the World Bank Group's conduct in light of these policies. It must be noted that, since human rights are not typically discussed in the World Bank Group's policies, likewise, IAMs tend to avoid any explicit reference in this respect. Based on this twofold approach, the analysis will be developed separately in relation to funding extended to public and private recipients, respectively.

In particular, the third chapter will deal with the policies and procedures governing investment project financing provided by IBRD and IDA, the two entities that make up the 'World Bank'. It will investigate the main features of these instruments from their inception, analyzing their contents in terms of alignment with international human rights law, thus providing a comprehensive overview of the requirements that the World Bank itself has to comply with, while exerting a *de facto* conditionality when deciding whether to extend funds to borrowing countries. Under the modern version of these safeguards, after having determined whether indigenous peoples are present in, or have collective attachment to, the project area, the Bank in fact needs to ask the borrower to undertake a social assessment in accordance with the requirements set out in the policies, in order to evaluate the potential effects on them and, where the project may generate adverse effects, to engage in a process of free, prior, and informed consultation in order to ascertain whether they provide broad project support. Thus, the Bank needs to review both the terms of the social assessment and the outcome of this process, and cannot «proceed further with project processing if it is unable to ascertain that such support exists».[27] At this stage, the Bank agrees on the appropriate development component to be integrated into the design of the project, which is prepared by the borrower and may vary widely, depending on the context. Notably, operational policies and procedures distinguish three main cases in this respect. First, for project activities that are contingent on establishing legally recognized rights to lands or territories that indigenous peoples have traditionally owned, or customarily used or occupied, the borrower must indicate the steps and timetable for achieving legal recognition of such rights. Second, for project activities involving the commercial development of natural resources on such lands or of their cultural resources and knowledge, the borrower must include «arrangements to enable the Indigenous Peoples to share equitably in the benefits to be derived from such commercial development» and to receive these

[27] The World Bank, *Operations Manual, Policy & Procedure Framework, Operational Policy 4.10, Indigenous Peoples*, 2005 (revised in 2013 and 2024), para. 11.

benefits in a culturally appropriate way.[28] Third, for project activities involving the physical relocation of indigenous peoples, the borrower must thoroughly explore alternative solutions to avoid such relocation.[29] Notably, prior to project appraisal, the Bank needs to review the project design to ensure that it complies with the policy requirements and to incorporate the relevant plans prepared by the borrower into the loan agreement.[30] From this phase onward, the requirements set out in the policies become binding on the borrower as well, as they are covenanted in the loan agreement. Consequently, the enforcement of the corresponding obligations may be executed through various means, including suspension, withdrawal, or cancellation of funds by the Bank. Furthermore, the analysis will consider the recent changes introduced in this respect by the 2018 Environmental and Social Framework, which grants the borrower a more autonomous role in designing projects, while limiting that of the Bank to conducting due diligence on the borrower's capacity to develop the related activities in accordance with the prescribed requirements. Undoubtedly, these changes have generally raised important concerns about a potential reduction of the scope of the Bank's obligations under the Framework, as it no longer needs to 'ensure' that the borrower designs the project in a certain way but only to require the borrower to prepare and implement it so as to meet the prescribed requirements in a manner and within a timeframe acceptable to the Bank. At the same time, it is important to note that the new Framework has strengthened certain provisions related to indigenous peoples, stipulating that borrowers must obtain their FPIC under circumstances likely to affect them in a significant way, while also retaining the provision whereby the Bank cannot further process the aspects of the project for which such consent cannot be ascertained.

Against this backdrop, the research work will examine the findings of the Inspection Panel based on a selection of relevant cases, not only to determine the exact boundaries of the Bank's obligations *vis-à-vis* project-affected indigenous peoples, but also to assess whether and to what extent it interpreted the provisions of the operational policies and procedures dealing with indigenous peoples in a manner consistent with the existing hard and soft international legal instruments governing their rights. At the same time, it will examine the main consequences arising from such cases as, in various instances, its findings have led to significant developments within the Bank, such as the cancellation of investments or the formulation of enhanced environmental and social strategies at both the institutional and country levels.

As for IFC, compliance with policy provisions is covenanted in equity and loan agreements with business enterprises and financial intermediaries even more often than in the case of financing extended to public recipients. Specific provisions may require private entities seeking funding to fulfill special conditions for

[28] ibid., para. 18.

[29] ibid.

[30] The World Bank, *Operations Manual, Policy & Procedure Framework, Bank Procedure 4.10, Indigenous Peoples*, 2005 (revised in 2013 and 2024), para. 9.

environmental and social reporting. Bearing in mind that IFC has had a clear due diligence role in its projects since the development of the first modern version of its framework in 2006, the fourth chapter will investigate the way in which its policies progressively adapted to the evolving international legal regime concerning indigenous peoples. In particular, it will highlight their explicit adherence to hard and soft legal instruments. Furthermore, it will take into account the changes introduced in the latest version of its operational framework in 2012,[31] which pioneered the incorporation of the FPIC requirement under specific circumstances. The chapter will be enriched by an analysis of relevant cases addressed by the Compliance Advisor Ombudsman ('CAO'). Notably, in its compliance role, the CAO has dealt with a series of cases that highlight the relevance of the FPIC requirement in relation to projects, particularly pointing out that non-compliance in some cases may result in a broader negative impact on the cultural, economic, territorial rights, and interests of affected indigenous communities. The research work will assess these cases in order to determine whether and to what extent the CAO, in light of its peculiar institutional features, has contributed to making effective the requirements set out in the IFC's policies. Unlike the Panel, the CAO has in fact undertaken dispute resolution functions from its inception. In this context, the chapter will also analyze cases where the CAO has acted in this capacity to facilitate indigenous peoples' access to remedy, in line with international developments occurred in the business and human rights field. Furthermore, it will explore other institutional features of the CAO that can make its findings particularly effective, highlighting that it has been entrusted with the task of monitoring the progress of Management's actions over its recommendations from the outset.[32] Notably, this function, which was originally exclusive to the CAO, has recently been extended to the Panel, although on a case-by-case basis only.

Following a thorough analysis of the World Bank Group's practice, the fifth chapter will contribute to the debate on whether the organization should be regarded as a holder of international human rights obligations. Specifically, through a critical assessment of the limited existing literature, it will identify the theses that are theoretically tenable based on an approach that accords significance to empirical evidence, in alignment with the findings presented throughout the book.

Building on these considerations, the sixth chapter will further evaluate the World Bank Group's evolving engagement with the rights of indigenous peoples, with a focus on how its institutional practice—demonstrating a consistent and coherent voluntary commitment to financing projects in both the public and private sectors that uphold indigenous peoples' rights in alignment with international law—has progressively gained normative significance. Finally, the chapter will offer valuable insights into the legal implications of the reassessment of the World Bank Group's involvement in human rights discourse.

---

[31] International Finance Corporation, *IFC Sustainability Framework, Policy and Performance Standards on Environmental and Social Sustainability*, 2012.

[32] Bradlow and Fourie (2011, p. 24).

References

Boisson de Chazournes L (2011) Partnerships, emulation, and coordination. Toward the emergence of a *Droit Commun* in the field of development finance. In: Cissé H, Bradlow D, Kingsbury B (eds) The World Bank legal review, international financial institutions and global legal governance. World Bank, Washington, DC, pp 173–187

Bradlow D (2019) Multilateral development banks, their member states and public accountability: a proposal. IJIEL 11:1–17

Bradlow D, Fourie AN (2011) The evolution of operational policies and procedures at international financial institutions. Normative significance and enforcement potential. AUWCL 1–40

Bradlow D, Grossman C (1995) Limited mandates and intertwined problems: a new challenge for the World Bank and the IMF. HRQ 17(3):411–442

Hunter D (2020) Contextual accountability, the World Bank Inspection Panel, and the transformation of international law in Edith Brown Weiss's kaleidoscopic world. GELR 32(3):439–466

Neuman GL (2019) International organizations and human rights - the need for substance. In: Paper presented at YTL Law and Justice Centre Forum on Human Rights and Non-State Actors, King's College, London, 1 June 2018

Pauciulo D (2017) Remarks on the practice of regional development banks' (RDBs) accountability mechanisms and the safeguard of human rights. In: Adinolfi G et al (eds) International economic law: contemporary issues. Springer-Giappichelli, Cham-Turin, pp 23–39

Pauciulo D (2025) International financial law. In: Palombino FM (ed) Introduction to international economic law. Routledge, New York, p 195-249

Perinbam L (1966) The World Bank and the United Nations. https://www.elibrary.imf.org. Accessed 24 April 2025

Sarfaty GA (2012) Values in translation: human rights and the culture of the World Bank. Stanford University Press, Stanford

Suzuki E, Nanwani S (2005) Responsibility of international organizations: the accountability mechanisms of multilateral development banks. Mich J Int Law 27(1):177–225

The World Bank (2003) Reaching effective consensus: Monterrey and the development agenda. https://www.openknowledge.worldbank.org. Accessed 24 April 2025

UN (2002) Financing for development: building on Monterrey. https://www.un.org. Accessed 24 April 2025

UN Economic and Social Council (2024) Follow-up and review of the financing for development outcomes and the means of implementation of the 2030 Agenda for Sustainable Development, 19 April 2024. UN Doc. E/FFDF/2024/L.1. https://docs.un.org/. Accessed 24 April 2025

UN General Assembly (1997) Agenda for development, resolution 51/240 of 15 October 1997. UN Doc. A/RES/51/240. https://docs.un.org/. Accessed 24 April 2025

UN General Assembly (2000) United Nations Millennium Declaration, resolution 55/2 of 18 September 2000. UN Doc. A/RES/55/2. https://docs.un.org/. Accessed 24 April 2025

UN General Assembly (2015) Transforming our world: the 2030 agenda for sustainable development, resolution 70/1 of 21 October 2015. UN Doc A/RES/70/1. https://docs.un.org/. Accessed 24 April 2025

UN General Assembly (2016) Review of the United Nations peacebuilding architecture, resolution 70/262 of 12 May 2016. UN Doc. A/RES/70/262. https://docs.un.org/. Accessed 24 April 2025

Xanthaki A (2009) Indigenous rights and United Nations standards, self-determination, culture, and land. CUP, Cambridge

Chapter 2
The Challenged Relationship Between Development and Human Rights in the Context of World Bank Group's Operations

2.1 The World Bank Group's Multifaceted Engagement with Development Financing

Under international law, Multilateral Development Banks are international organizations established by sovereign states or regions, which are their shareholders, together with other international organizations in some cases. Currently, their main purpose is to raise the living standards in the developing countries they assist, ultimately achieving the goal of reducing global poverty.[1] These institutions, with the World Bank Group being the most prominent example given that it operates on a global scale, are financially independent.

This means that they do not solely rely on the paid-in subscriptions of their member countries. Their resources in fact also derive from the sale of bonds in the international capital markets and the servicing of their activities, which consist of providing financial support for public or private sector projects, typically in the form of loans, grants, equity or guarantees, in addition to policy advice and technical assistance. In any case, unlike commercial banks, they offer lower-cost financing, as they do not seek to gain substantial earnings from their shareholders in line with the development goals set in their mandate. Interestingly, they have features of commercial enterprises too, since the weighted voting powers of their Boards are approximately proportionate to the capital subscriptions of the country (or groups of countries) that they represent and do not follow the principle of 'one country one vote', which instead reflects the way the UN General Assembly operates.

[1] Notably, there is no strict definition of what constitutes a 'developing country'. Organizations like the IMF and the UN Development Programme ('UNDP') each have their own definitions and lists of developing countries. See Bunn (2000, p. 1449).

S. Solidoro, *Indigenous Peoples in the World Bank Group's Practice*, European Yearbook of International Economic Law,
https://doi.org/10.1007/978-3-032-05147-9_2

Notably, MDBs can be regarded as a special type of International Financial Institutions ('IFIs'), whose activities generally consist of disbursing funds for the achievement of various *ad hoc* public policy objectives. The broad category of IFIs includes specialized funds with a very restricted membership, such as the OPEC Fund, established in 1976 by the 12 States of the Organization of the Petroleum Exporting Countries, which exclusively finances development projects in non-member countries, and those which promote impact mitigation of climate change in developing countries, which is currently at the forefront of the UN agenda. Among them, the most prominent ones are the Adaptation Fund, established in 2001 to finance operations in developing countries that are parties to the 1997 Kyoto Protocol that are particularly vulnerable to the adverse effects of climate change; the Climate Investment Fund, launched in 2008 by nine countries and a group of Multilateral Development Banks including the World Bank Group, upon the initiative of the G8 and G20, to accelerate the low-carbon economy shift; and the Green Climate Fund, the world's largest dedicated fund helping respond to climate change with special regard to greenhouse gas concentrations in the atmosphere,[2] set up in 2010 by the countries that are parties to the UN Framework Convention on Climate Change.[3]

Undoubtedly, the best known IFI is the International Monetary Fund, which, unlike MDBs, does not lend for specific projects but provides support to countries hit by crises (and precautionary financing to help prevent them) to preserve financial stability and monetary cooperation.[4] Its foundation was central to the negotiations of the UN Monetary and Financial Conference, held in Bretton Woods, New Hampshire, just one year before the end of World War II, on 1 July 1944. At that landmark meeting, delegates from 44 countries discussed the future regulation of the international monetary system and the strategy to rebuild countries based on international cooperation. Together with the Fund, they decided to establish the International Bank for Reconstruction and Development.[5] The following decades witnessed the creation of smaller organizations with very similar functions at the

[2] For an overview of the entities currently making up the public international financial architecture, see the UN policy brief issued in May 2023 outlining the need for comprehensive reforms to address systemic inequities and to improve the effectiveness of international financial institutions, available at: https://www.un-ilibrary.org/content/papers/10.18356/27082245-29. Accessed 24 April 2025.

[3] The Convention has near-universal membership (198 Parties). Signed in 1992 and entered into force in 1994, it can be regarded as the parent treaty of the 2015 Paris Agreement (whose main aim is to limit the global average temperature rise this century to as close as possible to 1.5 degrees Celsius above pre-industrial levels), and the 1997 Kyoto Protocol as well. See UN, *United Nations Framework Convention on Climate Change*, 9 May 1992, Treaty Doc. 102-38, in *UNTS*, Volume 1771, p. 107 f.; UN, *Kyoto Protocol to the United Nations Framework Convention on Climate Change*, 10 December 1997, UN Doc. FCCC/CP/1997/L.7/Add.1, in *UNTS* Volume 2303, p. 162 f.; UN, *Paris Agreement to the United Nations Framework Convention on Climate Change*, 12 December 2015, UN Doc. FCCC/CP/2015/10/Add.1, in *UNTS* Volume 3156, p. 79 f.

[4] For a detailed analysis of the Bretton Woods international financial system's main features from the outset, see Lindbaek et al. (1998).

[5] For a comprehensive overview of the governance system of the Bretton Woods institutions, see Cafaro (2012).

regional level,[6] such as the European Investment Bank (1958), the Inter-American Development Bank (1959), the African Development Bank (1964), the Asian Development Bank (1966), and the European Bank for Reconstruction and Development (1991). All these institutions are empowered to implement a wide array of financial activities on the basis of their constituent instruments.

Since the present analysis primarily focuses on the World Bank Group's activities, the first MDB ever established, it is essential to understand how it operates in more detail. The organization presents a sophisticated institutional structure that has evolved over time. In addition to IBRD, entrusted with the task of lending to governments of middle-income and creditworthy low-income countries, it consists of IDA, created in 1960[7] to provide long-term credits and grants to governments of the poorest countries at little or no interest, for which there exist different sources of funds and eligibility schemes.[8] Together, they constitute the 'World Bank'. Although IBRD was initially reluctant to consider disbursing at concessional rates, the need to expand its lending activities to poor countries at affordable conditions led to the creation of this 'soft' loan arm, conceived as a trust fund to be replenished periodically by donor governments.

While the term 'World Bank' primarily refers to IBRD in this book and, in the context of financing extended to member countries, it also includes IDA, by contrast, the term 'World Bank Group' includes another entity that is part of the organization: the International Finance Corporation. Established in 1956 when its Articles of Agreement drafted by IBRD's Executive Directors came into effect, IFC represents the largest global financial institution dealing with the investments in the private sector exclusively: in 2022, it committed a record US$32.8 billion in 296 projects to private companies and financial institutions in developing countries.[9] IFC coordinates its activities with the World Bank, although remaining legally and financially independent of it, as established by its own Articles of Agreement.

In this context, it is important to note that, technically, the term 'World Bank Group' refers to two additional entities beyond IFC. The first one is the International Centre for Settlement of Investment Disputes ('ICSID'), established in 1966 with a multilateral treaty drafted by IBRD's Executive Directors,[10] which widely promotes international investments in the private sector, including through channels different from mere financing activities. In fact, ICSID provides international facilities for

[6] Crippa (2010, p. 533).

[7] IDA's Articles of Agreement, drawn up by IBRD's Executive Directors, came into effect on 24 September 1960.

[8] Payer (1982, p. 28).

[9] Information available on the IFC's website at: https://www.ifc.org/en/what-we-do/products-and-services. Accessed 24 April 2025.

[10] The treaty ('ICSID Convention') was drafted by IBRD Executive Directors and entered into force on 14 October 1966: see International Bank for Reconstruction and Development, *Convention on the Settlement of Investment Disputes between States and Nationals of Other States*, Washington, DC, 18 March 1965. For an extensive analysis of its practice, see Palombino (2018).

conciliation and arbitration of investment disputes between contracting states and nationals of other contracting states.[11] As an autonomous entity, it administers its cases in a different and separate way from the other entities of the organization. Each case is considered by an independent Conciliation Commission or Arbitral Tribunal, after hearing evidence and legal arguments from the parties. To date, ICSID has administered more than 900 cases.

The second one is the Multilateral Investment Guarantee Agency ('MIGA'), established in 1988, which offers political risk insurance and credit enhancement guarantees to help protect foreign direct investments against political and non-commercial risks.

All powers of the entities constituting the organization are vested in their Boards of Governors, the ultimate decision-making body in which all member countries (or shareholders) are represented. The Boards consist of a Governor and an Alternate per country serving for five years, generally chosen among ministers of finance or development. If a country is a member of IBRD, IDA, and IFC at the same time, the IBRD's Governors serve *ex officio* on the Board of the other two entities, and usually as country representatives in the ICSID Administrative Council. Therefore, while there are four separate boards, Executive Directors serving on these boards are usually the same. Notably, MIGA Governors and Alternates are appointed separately.

Regarding allocation of votes, in the case of IBRD and IFC, these are subject to a weighting system assigning each Governor a certain number of so-called *basic votes*, the same for each country.[12] Basic votes ensure that each member country has a voice in the entity's decisions, regardless of its financial contribution. In addition to that, a number of proportional *share votes* are assigned based on the country's quota power calculated by assigning one vote for each share of the capital stock that it holds. Votes are calculated in such a way that the sum of all basic votes represents 5.55% of the total of both basic and share votes for all members. Shares are allocated differently in the case of IDA, thus resulting in different voting powers. While the system of basic votes still applies, each member (and thus, each Governor) receives a number of votes based on the contributions pledged during each IDA replenishment cycle, where donor countries agree to contribute to IDA's funds through commitments (*subscription votes*). In the case of MIGA, in addition to share votes, each member receives a number of parity votes, which are calculated to ensure that the total number of votes held by the two groups of countries—developed and developing—is equal. By contrast, in the case of ICSID, each member country has one seat, and one vote, on the Administrative Council. Nevertheless, the Council, whose mandate is primarily intended to deal with the organizational matters related to ICSID's institutional framework, plays no role in the administration of individual cases that are decided by international jurists from all over the world.[13]

---

[11] The Convention has been signed and ratified by 156 States to date.

[12] This weighted voting system is similar to that of the IMF. See Gianaris (1990, p. 927).

[13] International Centre for Settlement of Investment Disputes (2021, p. 4).

The majority of the powers conferred on the Board of Governors are delegated to the Board of Executive Directors, except for those reserved to the former under the Articles of Agreement, such as the decision concerning the admission of new Member States or the approval of amendments to the Articles themselves.[14]

The Boards of Executive Directors are thus responsible for conducting the day-to-day business of the entities which are part of the World Bank Group. Executive Directors (and their Alternates) fulfill a dual function, as officials of the organization and as representatives of the member country that appointed or elected them. Under the IBRD's Articles of Agreement, each of the five member countries having the largest number of shares appoints an Executive Director; the remaining member countries, grouped in constituencies, elect the other Executive Directors. Presently, IBRD Board consists of 25 Executive Directors, appointed or elected every two years, representing 189 member countries. As in the case of the Board of Governors, IBRD Directors also serve *ex officio* on IDA and IFC Boards. In practice, the same people are also chosen for MIGA, which, however, formally appoints them autonomously. In terms of voting powers, they are subject to the same weighting system envisaged for the Governors; however, in this case, the countries' votes are grouped into constituencies and summed together. In the case of ICSID, its administrative responsibilities are handled by its Secretariat, which manages the day-to-day operations of the center.

Notably, the Boards of Executive Directors play a crucial role in carrying out most of the World Bank Group's activities, as they are in charge of managing and deciding on several different operations, including those regarding policy issues as well as the approval of loan and credit proposals. Their role needs to be read in conjunction with the functions exercised by the President, who serves as Chairman of the Boards and the Administrative Council of ICSID, although with no voting power, except in case of an equal division on a specific matter. The President, who is selected by the Boards, also operates as chief of the officers and the staff of each entity constituting the World Bank Group, supervising the ordinary business and general strategy of the organization[15] through the units responsible for regions and sectors, as well as general Management.

Out of the five entities constituting the World Bank Group, the present analysis will focus solely on those most similar in their functions of providing financing activities: IBRD, IDA, and IFC, all of which notably hold the status of UN Specialized Agencies. In the case of IBRD, this status is governed by the *ad hoc* Relationship Agreement entered into with ECOSOC in 1947.[16] Agreements

[14] International Bank for Reconstruction and Development, *Articles of Agreement*, Bretton Woods, 27 December 1945, in *UNTS*, Volume 2, p. 134 f., Sect. 2.

[15] ibid., Sect. 5.

[16] United Nations and International Bank for Reconstruction and Development, *Protocol concerning the entry into force of the Agreement between the United Nations and the International Bank for Reconstruction and Development,* New York, 15 April 1948, in Volume 16, p. 341 f. It is worth mentioning that, in order to join IBRD and its affiliates, a country must first become a member of IMF (Art. II, Section 1 of IBRD's Articles of Agreement). The Member State's

concluded with IFC in 1957[17] and IDA in 1961[18] stipulate that their relationships are governed by the agreement between IBRD and the United Nations.

In relation to their financing activities, it is important to highlight the clear distinction between those provided to public entities and those directed towards private entities. In the first case, this refers to public debt extended by IBRD and IDA to (or guaranteed by) member countries, which, in any case, can be beneficial to the private sector. The second category pertains to investment products with long tenor whose recipients are business enterprises or financial intermediaries, mainly including loans and minority equity stakes.

2.1.1 IBRD's and IDA's Financing Activities

In the case of IBRD and IDA, member countries can choose from among three different categories of financing, depending on their development needs, as identified in the so-called 'Country Partnership Framework', the national strategy prepared jointly with Bank staff. This important document outlines the Bank's engagement in line with its mission, identifying the most relevant medium-term development priorities at the national level, and serves as the main basis for member countries' loan proposals. Among them, the most traditional and largest employed instrument, the so-called Investment Project Financing ('IPF'), is the only one explicitly envisaged in the IBRD's Articles of Agreement. IPF plays a crucial role in achieving the Bank's goal of ending extreme poverty and improving people's living conditions by providing funding to governments in support of development objectives against specific public expenditures in a wide variety of sectors, including infrastructure, human development, agriculture, and public administration. IPF has a coverage that extends from the medium to the long-term (from five to ten years). Upon various conditions, IPFs can be disbursed to member countries in the form of loans (IBRD), credits (interest-free loan) or grants (IDA), or even as guarantees (IBRD and IDA).[19] Unlike commercial financing, this instrument may encompass knowledge-transfer from the Bank, meaning that,

---

quota in the IMF determines the amount of new members' capital subscription and, accordingly, its voting power, entailing that the IMF's governance principle whereby countries with the highest quotas have the greatest voting power and influence also applies to the World Bank Group.

[17] United Nations and International Bank for Reconstruction and Development, *Protocol concerning the entry into force of the Agreement between the United Nations and the International Bank for Reconstruction and Development (acting for and on behalf of the International Finance Corporation) on relationship between the United Nations and the International Finance Corporation*, New York, 1957, in UNTS, Volume 265, p. 312 f..

[18] United Nations and International Development Association, New York, 1961, in Volume 394, p. 221 f.

[19] IBRD's and IDA's guarantees can be either project- or policy-based. In the first case, they may be used to mitigate the risk of a potential payment (so-called payment guarantee) or performance default by a government (so-called loan guarantee). As for policy-based guarantees, they are

in some cases, the Bank can provide borrowers with support for project design in the conceptual stages of preparation as well as technical assistance during the implementation phase as a component of the project or even as a stand-alone project. IPFs may also be used as a crisis response tool to provide governments with immediate access to funds when certain triggers are met.[20]

The second category of financing instruments, the so-called Development Policy Financing ('DPF'), can also be extended to member countries as loans or guarantees. Created in 2004, DPF is the result of a merger of the features of 'Sectoral Adjustment Loans' and 'Structural Adjustment Loans'.[21] These operations faced sharp criticism for being considered quite 'intrusive' due to the imposition of austerity policies on extremely poor countries. Furthermore, they were seen as ineffective because of their potential to adversely affect the most vulnerable population groups.[22] Over time, the main features of the instrument have been revised to ensure that appropriate policy dialogue takes place, helping recipient countries develop their own solutions based on principles recognized as valid development approaches, rather than imposing standardized models.[23] Not earmarked for specific 'bricks and mortar' physical operations, such as those directed towards the construction of bridges or hydroelectric dams, Development Policy Financing differs in many other ways from Investment Project Financing. Envisaged to provide rapidly-disbursed financing in a more flexible manner directly to a country's general budget, usually in one *tranche*, this tool does not require a direct link to expenditures. It can be used both when countries are growing and stable ('programmatic' DPF, aimed at producing long-term structural effects) or adjusting to shocks ('standalone' or 'supplemental' DPF, typically employed for crises with sudden, transitory effects).[24] What makes DPF peculiar is the fact that it encompasses a mechanism formally known as 'conditionality'. The Bank's approval of a DPF is in fact conditioned upon the borrower government implementing a series of critical policy or institutional reforms anchored on a country's national or sectoral strategy, referred to as 'prior actions'.[25] Bank's approval is also conditioned on the satisfactory completion of the whole reform program, as originally agreed, and the maintenance of a sound macroeconomic policy framework, achievable through the government's demonstrated commitment towards consistent, sustainable, and credible fiscal and monetary policies,

---

applied in the context of development policy operations where the World Bank supports a member country with its program of policy and institutional actions.

[20] The World Bank (2024).

[21] Michalopoulos (1987, p. 32). See also Jayarajah and Branson (1995).

[22] Maasland and van der Gaag (1991, p. 52).

[23] The World Bank Operations Policy and Country Services (2005, p. 6).

[24] The World Bank (2022a, p. 23).

[25] The World Bank (2009, p. 4).

as determined by the Bank with inputs from IMF.[26] In addition to that, for multi-*tranche* Bank loans, there exist other conditions that the borrower will have to comply with—at various stages of the project cycle—in order to fully receive the disbursement (so-called *tranche*-release conditions).[27]

IPF and DPF also share some common features. They may include a regular deferred drawdown option ('DDO') or deferred drawdown option for catastrophe risks ('Cat DDO'), allowing the recipient country to postpone drawing down a loan for a defined period after the loan agreement has been declared effective. At the operational level, within the World Bank, they are both managed by the Operations Policy and Country Services ('OPCS') Vice Presidency and are implemented by the Bank's country teams in partnership with relevant units based in Washington, DC.

Finally, the third and most recent type of instrument, the so-called Program-for-Results Financing ('PforR'), grants disbursement of funds against measurable results, helping countries improve the design and implementation of their own development programs and achieve long-term results. Since its creation in 2012, there has been a steady increase in its use. As of 15 March 2023, there were 146 active operations totaling $47.8 billion in Bank's financing.[28] Currently, the majority of such instruments are being employed for countries to make them able to respond to contemporary crises, including those stemming from Covid-19, the war in Ukraine and climate emergency.[29]

Notably, IBRD raises all the funds that are lent in financial markets. Its yearly earnings, based on the margins it makes on lending, pay for World Bank's operating expenses, go into reserves to strengthen the balance sheet, and partly contribute to IDA's activities for low-income countries. From its side, IDA is also funded by contributions from governments of high- and middle-income countries, which are subject to periodic replenishments.[30]

Last but not least, it is worth mentioning that another vital part of the World Bank's services deals with knowledge support, as part of its non-lending activities portfolio. Through Advisory Services and Analytics ('ASA'), the Bank typically

[26] Given the high sensitivity of the matter, the Group of Twenty (G20) devised the 'Principles for Effective Coordination Between the International Monetary Fund and Multilateral Development Banks' in 2017, aimed at improving coordination among institutions in the decision-making process for countries facing macroeconomic vulnerabilities and requesting financing. The principles are available at: https://www.imf.org/external/np/g20/pdf/2018/082918.pdf. Accessed 28 April 2025.

[27] The World Bank (2007, p. 4).

[28] A detailed description of PforR's main features is available on the WB's website at: https://www.worldbank.org/en/programs/program-for-results-financing. Accessed 28 April 2025.

[29] The World Bank (2022b, p. 95).

[30] For an analysis of the reasons why Bank's lending activities (in addition to those based on research) are crucial to help capital flow from rich to poor countries (as this does not happen naturally), and to assist developing countries with dealing with global economic problems, see Subacchi and Vines (2023, p. 172). From the same economic policy perspective, but for an overview of the challenges currently influencing the World Bank's ability to strike an appropriate balance between public goods and countries' demand, see Morris (2023).

supports countries' knowledge with a wide range of analytical findings, policy notes and training programs. Although these activities fall outside the scope of the present analysis as not directly related to lending, it is worth mentioning that they are often incorporated into the Country Partnership Framework, serving as a potential basis for loan proposals. Furthermore, advisory support provided by the Bank may lay the foundation for an improved legal and institutional framework, enabling borrowers to rely on it when carrying out lending operations. Among the different ASA activities, national-level diagnostic reports play a special role, as they are often developed in collaboration with the public authorities of the concerned country, underpinning an early form of engagement with them.[31] These reports may focus on various themes, such as analyzing poverty or inequality issues, creating opportunities for increasing private investment, or developing mitigation strategies for climate change in relation to development outcomes.[32]

The World Bank is also increasingly relying on Reimbursable Advisory Services ('RAS'). While ASA are primarily financed through trust funds and other Bank's resources, RAS represent a distinct form of fee-for-service advisory support. Provided in response to specific member countries' requests, they are intended to help them design and implement better policies or strengthen their institutions for sustaining development over the long term, an activity that, in turn, may potentially lead to country-level projects supported by Bank's lending or guarantees.[33]

[31] Until 2017, advisory activities services were provided to external countries not involved in lending operations through Analytical and Advisory Activities ('AAA'). These included a series of activities that are similar in substance to those currently offered through ASA, but under a different name. The most prominent of these was Economic and Sector Work, providing country-level diagnostic research and analysis, such as economic memoranda, poverty assessments and public expenditure reviews, produced by the Bank in an effort to influence prospective national policies and stimulate the public debate. Other knowledge services offered to countries not involved in lending operations included impact evaluation, assessing the effects of development interventions relative to a specified counterfactual, as well as external training programs, focused on raising awareness or enhancing skills, particularly through the exchange of good practices. See Independent Evaluation Group (2006, p. 1); Independent Evaluation Group (2008, p. 1); Independent Evaluation Group (2022, p. 180). Other than external knowledge services, AAA included two additional products, not addressed to countries, such as: (i) public goods research, whose aim was to support the global debate on relevant issues, delivered in various forms, such as Open Data, Policy Research Working Papers, World Development Reports, books; and (ii) knowledge products addressed to internal Bank staff only. See The World Bank Operations Policy and Country Services (2011, p. 13); Doemeland and Trevino (2014, p. 5).

[32] This is the case of the Country Climate and Development Report, which is intended to implement its 2021–2025 Climate Change Action Plan and is carried out by IBRD and IDA jointly with IFC and MIGA. The report identifies the main pathways to reduce greenhouse gas emissions and climate vulnerabilities at the country level, while suggesting practical actions to support the low-carbon resilient transition, building on rigorous research and data. See The World Bank Group (2021).

[33] In addition to countries' national and subnational governments, clients can be State-owned enterprises, non-governmental and other not-for-profit organizations, as well as multilateral institutions (such as multilateral development banks).

2.1.2 IFC's Financing Activities

IFC's activities differ from the previous ones in that they focus on the private sector. As part of its financing efforts, IFC provides direct loans to private businesses with loan terms typically ranging from seven to 12 years. This only excludes micro, small, and medium enterprises and individual entrepreneurs. Furthermore, it extends direct lending to financial intermediaries and to various types of funds and facilities. Equity investments in businesses and financial institutions, generally between 5 and 20% of the asset value, represent another option. Through this activity, IFC provides recipients with long-term growth capital, while encouraging a broader share ownership through public listings.

While the present book primarily focuses on direct lending and equity investment activities with a long tenor that target private businesses or financial intermediaries, it is important to highlight that IFC also engages in a broader range of operations. Since 2009, it has begun raising financial resources through newly-established specialized funds that invest in high-potential, sustainable companies as well as financial institutions based in developing countries, with investments designed for long-term impact. These funds are not managed directly by IFC, but by its dedicated subsidiary, the IFC Asset Management Company. In addition, IFC undertakes short-tenor operations through trade finance, which offers guarantees, risk-sharing facilities, as well as loans and other structured products to support trade in emerging markets with maturities of up to three years.

Finally, it is worth noting that IFC also delivers technical, financial, and regulatory advisory services to both private entities and governments in connection with (but also independently of) lending operations and equity investments. When addressed to governments, these services aim to establish the conditions necessary to attract private capital or structure public-private partnerships to enhance access to high-quality infrastructure and basic services. However, since this study is exclusively concerned with IFC's financing operations involving private recipients, these activities are mentioned only to offer context for its broader institutional role.

2.2 The Contentious Political Prohibition Clauses Included in IBRD's Articles of Agreement

Since its inception, IBRD, the first entity ever established within the World Bank Group, has historically sought to avoid any association with human rights concerns, based on the mandate outlined in its constituent instrument, which forms the primary legal framework governing its operations. This instrument, concluded as an international treaty signed and ratified by sovereign governments, defines its purposes and legal capacity, thus serving as both the foundation and the limit for its actions. The analysis of this document, framed in pure economic and financial terms, is therefore crucial in order to determine whether the absence of any explicit reference to human rights may leave room for different considerations.[34]

Article I of IBRD's Articles of Agreement lists three different activities to define the boundaries of its mandate, which consists of: (i) supporting Member States in the reconstruction and development of their economies by facilitating the investment of capital for productive purposes and the reconversion of their facilities to peacetime needs, with special emphasis on developing countries; (ii) promoting private foreign investment by means of guarantees or participations in loans and other investments, and, when private capital is not available on reasonable terms, on financing provided on suitable conditions; as well as (iii) promoting both long-range balanced growth of international trade and equilibrium maintenance in balances of payments.[35] The purposes of IDA's activities, in furthering IBRD's objectives, are to «promote economic development, increase productivity and thus raise standards of living in the less-developed areas of the world».[36] IFC supplements IBRD's activities by «encouraging the growth of productive private enterprise in member countries».[37]

Notably, from the outset, IBRD's mission has been influenced by the political prohibitions set out in three interrelated clauses of its Articles of Agreement. The first, enshrined in Article IV, Section 10 ('Political Activity Prohibited'), bars any form of interference by the Bank in the political affairs of member countries. It also excludes any political influence from their side, emphasizing that the Bank's decisions should be guided solely by economic considerations:

> The Bank and its officers shall not interfere in the political affairs of any member; nor shall they be influenced in their decisions by the political character of the member or members concerned. Only economic considerations shall be relevant to their decisions, and these considerations shall be weighed impartially in order to achieve the purposes stated in Article I.[38]

The second clause, enshrined in Article III, Section 5(b), outlines similar restrictions regarding the use of funds derived from loans, stipulating that the Bank «shall make arrangements to ensure that the proceeds of any loan are used only for the purposes for which the loan was granted, with due attention to considerations of economy and efficiency and without regard to political or other non-economic influences or considerations». Last but not least, with special emphasis on the Bank's employee protection from political pressure potentially exerted by member

---

[34] Shihata (2000a, p. 158).

[35] International Bank for Reconstruction and Development, *Articles of Agreement*, Bretton Woods, 27 December 1945, in *UNTS*, Volume 2, p. 134 f., Article I. The Articles have been amended three times since they became effective (17 December 1965, 16 February 1989, and 27 June 2012).

[36] International Development Association, *Articles of Agreement*, Washington, DC, 24 September 1960, in *UNTS*, Volume 439, p. 249 f., Article I.

[37] International Finance Corporation, *Articles of Agreement*, Washington, DC, 20 July 1956, in *UNTS*, Volume 264, p. 115 f., Article I.

[38] See Article IV, Section 10 of the Articles of Agreement of the International Bank for Reconstruction and Development.

countries, Article V, Section 5(c) of the IBRD's Articles of Agreement provides that «[t]he President, officers and staff [...] owe their duty entirely to the Bank», and that each member country is obliged to respect that duty and «refrain from all attempts to influence any of them in the discharge of their duties».[39]

Plainly, all these provisions did not envisage a role for IBRD in the political reform of its borrowing countries. In addition to categorical prohibitions, the Articles of Agreement contain more nuanced provisions, nonetheless aimed at excluding non-neutral considerations from decisions or operations concerning lending activities. For instance, under Article III, Section 4(v), the conditions of making a loan or guarantee shall not be based on subjective considerations, but rather on the ability of the borrower to meet its obligations under the specific loan at stake. Furthermore, to ensure that financing decisions are not made on non-technical grounds, the Articles require the submission of a written report recommending a project, following a thorough evaluation of its merits by a competent committee.[40] Finally, with respect to the general provisions concerning loans and guarantees, «the Bank shall act prudently in the interests both of the particular member in whose territories the project is located and of the members as a whole».[41]

Political prohibitions can also be found in the Articles of Agreement of IDA—Article V, Section 1 (g); Article V, Section 6, and Article VI, Section 5(c)—and of IFC—Article III, Section 9; Article VI, Section 5(c).[42]

The same is true with reference to the majority of regional development banks,[43] with the only exception being the European Bank for Reconstruction and Development, whose charter explicitly authorizes the organization to support the economic transition process from a planned to a market-based economy as well as the political transformation into multiparty democracy of Central and Eastern European countries. This aspect can be easily understood by considering the unique circumstances that led to its establishment in 1990, following the

[39] See Article V (Organization and Management), Section 5 (c) (President and Staff) of the Articles of Agreement of the International Bank for Reconstruction and Development.

[40] See Article III (General Provisions Relating to Loans and Guarantees), Section 4 (iii) (Conditions on which the Bank may Guarantee or Make Loans), to be read in combination with Article V, Section 7 (Loan Committees).

[41] See Article III, Section 4 (v).

[42] It is noteworthy that the same provision is included in the MIGA Convention. Article 34 states that the Agency, its President and staff shall not interfere in the political affairs of any member. In any case, the Convention allows the staff to «take into account all circumstances surrounding an investment» rather than economic considerations only. International Bank for Reconstruction and Development, *Convention Establishing the Multilateral Investment Guarantee Agency*, Seoul, 11 October 1985, in *UNTS*, Volume 1508, p. 99 f.

[43] For instance, in the case of the Inter-American Development Bank, the restriction concerning political activities is stated by Article VIII, Section 5 (f) of the 1987 version of its Articles of Agreement.

collapse of communist regimes and the peak of the Washington consensus.[44] As a third-generation MDB,[45] its charter includes three broad components within its mandate: economic, political, and environmental considerations. Notably, its practice has influenced other organizations in a positive way, including the World Bank Group, contributing to the elaboration of a joint program of action to achieve measurable progress over the UN Sustainable Development Goals, with a particular focus on the recent challenges posed by climate change.[46]

Similarly, the reasons behind the inclusion of political prohibition provisions in IBRD's Articles of Agreement are rooted in historical context. Once this context is considered, it becomes clear that it was originally conceived solely as an organization designed to borrow funds from capital markets to finance its lending operations. When the delegates from Allied nations met in Bretton Woods, New Hampshire, in 1944, the prevailing assumption was that introducing political considerations could disrupt the business model of the newly established international cooperation system, which could only operate efficiently with a consistent degree of confidence in the neutrality of its actions. Furthermore, as a multilateral institution with a global membership encompassing a wide range of political beliefs, the acceptability of its mandate necessitated the depoliticization of its decisions.[47]

Finally, the limitations of its mandate can be seen as a practical application of the 'functionalist approach' to international organizations, which was widely accepted at the time of its establishment. This approach is also reflected in the technical mandate of all the organizations created before or shortly after World War II, such as the ILO, UNESCO, the FAO, the WHO, and the International Civil Aviation Organization. Notably, in the case of IBRD, this perspective framed development exclusively as an economic endeavor, primarily aimed at increasing growth as measured by gross domestic product, while relying on technical rather than political solutions.[48]

---

[44] Krever (2011, p. 297).

[45] MDBs can be categorized into three generations: (i) the first, marked by the creation of IBRD, primarily focused on reconstruction following World War II; (ii) the second, represented by IDA and other regional development banks established in the 1960s, with a focus on supporting developing countries; and (iii) the third, exemplified by the European Bank for Reconstruction and Development, which has gradually expanded its role in addressing development challenges over time. See Head (2008, p. 198).

[46] Collaboration among heads of MDBs recently culminated in the Marrakesh statement in 2023, a document summarizing the will to strengthen joint actions and build strong partnerships capable of tackling global emerging challenges in critical areas. A recent note entitled 'MDBs Working as a System for Impact and Scale', a document endorsed by the heads of several MDBs in Washington, DC, on 20 April 2024, and published on the website of the European Investment Bank, reports on the progress made on commitments under the Marrakesh statement. The document is available at: https://www.eib.org/en/press/all/2024-160-multilateral-development-banks-deepen-collaboration-to-deliver-as-a-system. Accessed 28 April 2025.

[47] Cissé (2011, p. 60).

[48] Lyons, Baldwin, and McNemar (1977), Ghebali (1985).

This approach led to a very well-known controversy with the UN in the 1960s. When IBRD was called for a suspension of its lending activities due to the human rights negative record of the governments of two member countries, the Legal Department, which had an opportunity to express its views on the interpretation of the Articles of Agreement, adopted a very strict stance. The controversy at stake stemmed from the Bank's lending operations in Portugal and South Africa, at a time when the UN's General Assembly was passing two resolutions in 1965, recommending the suspension of all assistance to these countries due to their *apartheid* policies.[49] Following a meeting between the UN Secretary General and the President of the Bank,[50] the two organizations agreed on a written exchange of views to resolve the matter. The IBRD's Legal Department prepared its statements in response to a Secretariat Memorandum from the UN dated 3 March 1967, which was followed by a letter from the Bank on 5 May 1967. Departing from the interpretation of the Relationship Agreement that governs the Bank's status as a UN specialized agency, the IBRD's General Counsel argued that, while the Bank is required to give «due regard for decisions of the Security Council under Articles 41 and 42 of the United Nations Charter» in the conduct of its activities, as stated in Article VI(2) of the Relationship Agreement ('Security Council'),[51] the situation is quite different as far as General Assembly resolutions were concerned. Bank's actions regarding loans are, in fact, matters to be determined by the independent exercise of its judgment in accordance with its own constituent instrument, as outlined in Article IV(3) of the Relationship Agreement ('Consultation and Recommendations'), which states:

> The United Nations recognizes […] that it would be sound policy to refrain from making recommendations to the Bank with respect to particular loans or with respect to terms or conditions of financing by the Bank. The Bank recognizes that the United Nations and its organs may appropriately make recommendations with respect to the technical aspects of reconstruction or development plans, programmes or projects.[52]

It was also noted that, according to the Relationship Agreement, aimed at preserving the respective independence of the two organizations, neither could make a formal recommendation to the other without reasonable prior consultation. In the Bank's view, such consultation had never taken place.[53]

---

[49] UN General Assembly (1965a), UN General Assembly (1965b).

[50] The exchange of opinions took place following a further Resolution issued in 1966, whereby the UN General Assembly requested the Secretary General to consult with IBRD to obtain its compliance with the provisions of Resolutions 2105 and 2107: see UN General Assembly (1966). For an extensive analysis of the dispute, see Bleicher (1970).

[51] United Nations and International Bank for Reconstruction and Development, *Protocol concerning the entry into force of the Agreement between the United Nations and the International Bank for Reconstruction and Development*, New York, 15 April 1948, in *UNTS*, Volume 16, p. 341 f., p. 350.

[52] ibid., p. 348.

[53] In this context, however, the UN argued that, considering the ongoing efforts made by its Secretariat since 15 March 1962, consultations (understood in a reasonable sense) had occurred

In a more general sense, the General Counsel argued that it would have been improper to accept the General Assembly's recommendations in the cases involved because of the prohibition contained in Article IV, Section 10 of the Bank's Articles of Agreement ('Political Activity Prohibited'). In doing so, the Counsel clarified that the adjective 'political' could refer not only to matters related to 'politics' in the narrow sense of the term, but also to those concerning the constitution of an organized society and the manner in which it manages its affairs, concluding that «the relevant resolutions of the General Assembly do indeed deal with the political affairs of the Governments of Portugal and South Africa». At the same time, while stating that the Bank was precluded from considering the political character of a member as a criterion for its lending decisions, the comments admitted that the organization «may and does take into consideration, and is influenced in its lending decisions by, the economic effects which stem from the political character of a member and from the censures and condemnations of that member by United Nations organs».[54]

The dispute was not settled in the end. Although the Bank ultimately suspended its lending activities, it invoked arguments different from political considerations in order to do so. Indeed, the Bank alleged that South Africa was no longer eligible to borrow under the Bank's 'graduation policy',[55] based on its technical inability to sustain a good level of institutional development and capital-market access in the long run. It took a similar stance in relation to Portugal, arguing that the country had high reserves, could otherwise borrow on reasonable terms, and, at that time, lacked sound development policies.[56]

Just a decade later, the newly enacted Section 701 (a) of U.S. Law 95-118 of 3 October 1977 raised another crucial dispute under the political prohibition clause enshrined in Article IV, Section 10 of the IBRD's Articles of Agreement, questioning whether the United States could use its voice and vote to raise issues that were then considered political in nature. The provision, which stipulated that the US government shall advance the cause of human rights in various Multilateral Development Banks, reads as follows:

> The United States Government, in connection with its voice and vote in the International Bank for Reconstruction and Development, the International Development Association, the International Finance Corporation, the Inter-American Development Bank, the African Development Fund, and the Asian Development Bank, shall advance the cause of human rights, including by seeking to channel assistance toward countries other than those whose governments engage in: (1) a consistent pattern of gross violations of internationally recognized human rights, such as torture or cruel, inhumane, or degrading treatment or punishment, prolonged detention without charges, or other flagrant denial to life, liberty, and the

prior to the adoption of the two resolutions by the UN General Assembly. See UN (1967, p. 114). See also Szasz (1979, p. 164).

[54] UN (1967, p. 124).

[55] On this point, see the working paper authored by Heckelman et al. (2011).

[56] Shihata (1988, p. 45).

security of person; or (2) provide refuge to individuals committing acts of international terrorism by hijacking aircraft.[57]

With respect to the practical consequences for US Executive Directors' voting modalities, the wording of letter (f) of the same section of the law made it possible for them to 'abstain' and not necessarily to 'vote against' loans with reference to countries engaged in violations of human rights.

The Bank's Legal Department was thus called to clarify whether the Articles of Agreement were applicable to the Executive Directors. Being appointed by member countries (or constituencies of member countries), and thus entrusted with the task of expressing their views, the position of Executive Directors as officials is indeed controversial and very different from that of the staff, who owe their duty entirely to the Bank and to no other authority. After determining that the prohibition in question applied to the Executive Directors, the Legal Department noted that, in any case, no legal sanction could be imposed to challenge their votes, even if they were driven by political considerations. This argument implicitly suggested that, under certain circumstances, the Bank could take human rights concerns into account, in line with U.S. Law 95-118 of 3 October 1977.[58]

Within the organization, the two instances mentioned above fueled the debate regarding the interpretation of the political prohibition clauses, a debate that continued to influence its activities for many years. It is only in recent decades that there has been a significant evolution in its practice, alongside the development of new legal interpretative trends related to the Articles of Agreement.

2.3 The Emergence of a New Mandate Through Practice

At this stage, it must be stressed that institutional practice carries significant legal weight and must be taken into consideration for the purposes of grasping the exact meaning to be attributed to the Articles of Agreement. As an international treaty, the Articles are subject to the application of the Vienna Convention, which, besides providing that the interpretation of its provisions needs to be made in good faith within the ordinary meaning to be given to its terms in their context, also stipulates that «any subsequent practice in the application of the treaty which establishes the

[57] US 95th Congress, *International Financial Institutions Act*, Public Law 95–118 of 3 October 1977, 91 Stat. 1067, Title VII (Human Rights), Section 701 (Assistant Policies).

[58] Shihata (1988, p. 46). In this regard, however, Shihata expressed a dissenting opinion, stating that, while human rights may generally become a relevant issue, at the same time, «the degree of respect paid by a government to human rights cannot by itself be considered an appropriate basis for the Bank's decision to make loans to that government or for the voting of its Executive Directors».

agreement of the parties regarding its interpretation» shall be taken into account, according to Article 31.3.b.[59]

IBRD's mission was originally designed to cover the cost of specific reconstruction or development projects by issuing guarantees to private lenders and providing direct loans only when its borrowers were unable to secure financing from the market on reasonable terms. Both IDA and IFC were established to play complementary roles, with IDA focusing on providing financial assistance to the world's poorest nations, while IFC was dedicated to supporting the private sector. Over time, the evolution of their operations has led to a substantial expansion of their mandates, extending far beyond the original scope outlined in their charters.

A formal revision of the concept of development began under McNamara's Presidency (1968–1981). The twin goals of poverty reduction and sustainable economic growth,[60] proclaimed as the new World Bank Group's mission during that phase,[61] transformed it into the organization as it is currently known and understood. IBRD began promoting the so-called 'Basic Needs Approach', recognizing that development should meet the essential social rights of the population.[62] During this phase, the total amount of lending activities to member countries increased 12-fold. Overall, it reached into new sectors for the first time, including the environment, rural development, water, sanitation, education, among others.[63] To enhance project quality, in 1970, McNamara created the operations evaluation unit, later renamed Operations Evaluation Department (now known as Independent Evaluation Group). Its primary task, which remains unchanged, is to provide independent evaluations of projects after completion. At the same time, IFC launched its advisory services, initially focused on the financial sector of lower-income countries, and later expanded to support reforms in the legal and institutional frameworks of countries around the world.[64]

In the subsequent years, after funding large infrastructure projects, which represented the main activity accomplished during the first 20 years of operations, IBRD, alongside IDA, shifted its focus to the implementation of public sector policies linked to legal and institutional reforms (1982–1994), an initiative often associated

[59] UN Conference on the Law of Treaties, *Vienna Convention on the Law of Treaties*, Vienna, 23 May 1969, in *UNTS*, Volume 1155, p. 331 f. The Conference was convened pursuant to General Assembly's resolutions 2166 (XXI) of 5 December 1966 and 2287 (XXII) of 6 December 1967.

[60] The term 'extreme poverty' was coined by the President McNamara during a famous speech to the Board of Governors at the 1973 Annual General Meeting held in Nairobi. The full text is available at: https://www.worldbank.org/en/archive/president-mcnamara-1973-nairobia-speech. Accessed 29 April 2025.

[61] International Bank for Reconstruction and Development (1978, pp. 26–37).

[62] Streeten (1979).

[63] The first loan for the environment was granted in 1971 for pollution control purposes in Brazil, which raised substantial concern over the way activities were carried out. The objective of the project was to provide 2 million people with piped water, improve service in the overloaded sections of the pipe networks, and enhance sewage collection and disposal. See The World Bank Group (2016).

[64] International Finance Corporation (2016, p. 50).

with the contentious term 'governance'. In particular, the activities supported by Structural Adjustment Programs, introduced in 1980, which were initially based on a specific form of conditionality tied to macroeconomic changes,[65] gradually emphasized the importance of ensuring a balanced income distribution.[66] In implementing all these innovations, the World Bank Group did not resort to an amendment to its Articles of Agreement.

In parallel with that, traditional investment projects came under attack for impacting the environment and vulnerable social groups, such as indigenous peoples, in a consistent way. In the 1980s, IBRD introduced the first generation of environmental and social safeguards into its work.[67] From the outset, IDA adopted a similar approach, customizing its policies to meet the specific needs of lower-income countries.

The promotion of a wide array of human rights belongs to the subsequent phase. In the 1990s, IBRD integrated the advancement of the role of women in its operations while trying to ensure fair conditions for involuntary resettlement and protection of indigenous peoples' distinctive culture. In 1991, it created the Global Environment Facility. Between 1990 and 1995, it lent $5.9 billion—about a third of its overall social sector lending for that period—for projects in health and education benefiting children.[68] In 1993, IBRD and IDA established the Inspection Panel, entrusted with the task of investigating complaints submitted by individuals allegedly harmed by Bank-funded operations non-compliant with environmental and social safeguards. Broad poverty reduction efforts were also supported in connection with debt relief and disbursement of loans with low-interest rates through the Heavily Indebted Poor Countries initiative launched by the World Bank jointly with the IMF in 1996 to reduce external debt repayments to sustainable levels.

Throughout the 1990s, the IFC also began reassessing its operations with a broader perspective, placing a greater emphasis on sustainability. The establishment of the CAO in 1999 was a significant step in promoting accountability and transparency of private sector operations, helping to build trust with communities and stakeholders affected by its projects.

65 On the revisited approach to conditionality and to understand how it evolved, see Koeberle et al. (2005).

66 Bank's adjustment lending has evolved progressively since then, expanding the range of activities now funded by the Bank to programs aimed at ensuring that vulnerable groups such as women, children, indigenous peoples, and other minorities obtain access to health, education, and other services. See Bradlow (1996, p. 57). On the criticism that such a type of lending raised, see Hunter (1996, p. 78), Adinolfi (2014). According to a prominent UN expert, years of structural adjustment programs eroded the welfare of millions of poor people across developing countries and denied their economic, social, and cultural rights: UN Commission on Human Rights (1999). On the specific negative effects of structural adjustment measures promoted by international financial institutions on the right to adequate housing, see UN Committee on Economic, Social and Cultural Rights (1991, para. 19).

67 Dann and Riegner (2019, p. 537).

68 Young (1996, p. vi).

At the same time, significant developments were occurring in the international landscape. The UN began to drive a process of gradual expansion concerning the interpretation of the concept of development through various initiatives. In 1986, the General Assembly adopted a Declaration proclaiming the right to development as an «inalienable human right by virtue of which every human person and all peoples are entitled to participate in, contribute to, and enjoy economic, social, cultural and political development, in which all human rights and fundamental freedoms can be fully realized».[69] In tune with this new approach, in 1990 the UN General Assembly convened the World Conference on Human Rights with resolution 45/155,[70] which took place in Vienna in June 1993, whose main outcome was the conclusion that «[d]emocracy, development and respect for human rights and fundamental freedoms are interdependent and mutually reinforcing».[71] A further advancement was recorded at the end of 1995 when, at the World Summit for Social Development held in Copenhagen gathered upon invitation of the UN, the heads of State of 186 countries adopted the 'Declaration on Social Development' and the related Programme of Action, an instrument reflecting the international community consensus on the need to put people at the center of equitable and sustainable development, to be conceived as a multifaceted process in which, *inter alia*, economic growth cannot be achieved without human rights protection. Among other members of the international community, UN specialized agencies were called upon to fulfill their responsibilities in the implementation of the outcomes of the World Summit.[72]

Just a few years later, prominent international legal scholars started undertaking other significant initiatives in the field. In the Netherlands, in October 2001, a group of experts drafted the 'Tilburg Principles on World Bank, International Monetary Fund and Human Rights', which delivered a detailed analysis of the twin Bretton Woods organizations' activities in the context of international human rights law and a discussion on how to redress the adverse human rights impact arising from their

[69] UN General Assembly (1986), Article 1. On the evolution of the concept of development in international economic law, see: Mauro (2015, p. 244), Malaguti (2017). From 2004 to 2010, the right to development was widely promoted by a dedicated UN Task Force, an independent expert body with semi-operational responsibilities established by the Commission on Human Rights (in its resolution 2004/7) and the Economic and Social Council (by its decision 2004/249), at the recommendation of the newly created intergovernmental Working Group on the Right to Development. The Task Force was in charge of issuing appropriate recommendations to the various actors involved in the implementation of the right to development. For an overview of its work, see Salomon (2006). Notably, its importance lay in its ability to bring together human rights experts and representatives from international development, finance and trade institutions, such as the World Bank Group, the International Monetary Fund, the World Trade Organization, and the United Nations Development Programme (UNDP), among others.

[70] UN General Assembly (1990).

[71] World Conference on Human Rights, *Vienna Declaration and Programme of Action*, 12 July 1993, Article 5, UN Doc. A/CONF/157/23, p. 5.

[72] UN (1995).

operations.[73] Notably, the Principles acknowledged the relevance of international human rights law to their mandate:

> International human rights law includes civil, cultural, economic, political and social rights, as well as the right to development. These rights are, each in their own way, relevant in the struggle against poverty as well as other activities performed by the World Bank and IMF, and, *mutatis mutandis*, other IFIs.[74]

Nevertheless, despite these trends signaling a significant shift in how international financial institutions were, and were expected to be, conducting their core operations, the interpretative dispute over the meaning of the IBRD's stated purposes in its charter remained particularly contentious.[75]

2.4 Recent Developments in the Interpretation of IBRD's Articles of Agreement

In a 1994 IBRD report, it was stated that, despite the indivisibility of human rights, the Bank was required to focus on aspects relevant to its mandate, in light of the prohibition clauses included in its Articles of Agreement. Therefore, despite increasing involvement in human rights-related operations and governance reforms, IBRD maintained that any interference with rights beyond those of an economic and social nature was outside the scope of its mandate:

> Although human rights are in a larger sense indivisible, the World Bank, as an international financial institution, deals with those aspects of human rights relevant to its mandate. Except in situations where the violation of human rights has created conditions hostile to effective implementation of projects or has other adverse economic consequences, or where there are international obligations relevant to the Bank, such as those mandated by binding decisions of the U.N. Security Council, the World Bank does not take into account the political dimensions of human rights in its lending decisions. The World Bank's Articles of Agreement prohibit the institution from taking political considerations into account, interfering in the political affairs of any country, or being affected by the political form or orientation of a country. Consistent with the Articles, the focus of the Bank's efforts in the area of human rights is on those rights that are economic and social in nature.[76]

Against this backdrop, Dr. Ibrahim F. Shihata shed light on some of the most controversial issues tied to human rights in connection with the IBRD's mandate. In 2000, he published a book collecting the legal opinions and memoranda submitted to the IBRD's Board of Executive Directors during his tenure as General Counsel of

---

[73] For an overview of the contents extensively discussed during the Conference, see Gille and Roos (2002).

[74] van Genugten (2003, p. 247).

[75] Clark (2002, p. 207).

[76] International Bank for Reconstruction and Development (1994, p. 53).

the World Bank (1983–1998).[77] In the book, he first clarified the exact scope of the political prohibition clauses, explaining that the term 'political' covered all those situations requiring IBRD to take a side in the internal affairs of the government of its borrowers. Second, he acknowledged the fact that, although the language of the political prohibition clauses was very strict, not allowing for any exception, IBRD had already admitted that it could take certain 'political' circumstances into account when relevant to its work, insofar as capable of generating clear economic effects:

> [T]he Bank cannot properly exceed its mandate and act as an agency in charge of political reform in its developing members. However, in pursuing its authorized purposes, the Bank may take economic considerations into account, even if they have political origins, or are associated with political factors as long as the economic effects are clearly established.[78]

With regard to economic effects, he clarified that IBRD was only required to consider those that were 'direct and obvious',[79] with the following characteristics: (i) clear and unequivocal; (ii) preponderant; and (iii) when associated with political actions or flowing from political events, of such magnitude and relevance as to raise concern for the Bank.[80]

Clearly, this argument widely justified the support for national legal and institutional reforms pursued through governance programs. Furthermore, in his book, Shihata specifically questioned whether IBRD was allowed to consider the promotion of civil and political rights in its lending decisions. After clarifying that this activity did not *per se* normally fall within its mandate, he argued that in two instances violations of such rights could become legitimate concerns for the Bank.

First, after clarifying that participation of affected people in the design and implementation of projects with an impact on the environment through consultations requires a reasonable measure of free expression and assembly, he held that IBRD's denial of lending for a project in the absence of this requirement could not be described as an illegitimate interference in the political affairs of the country concerned.

Second, he admitted that an extensive violation of such rights, when reaching pervasive proportions, could also become relevant to IBRD's decisions, when the violation had significant economic effects or led «to the breach of international obligations relevant to the Bank, such as those created under binding decisions of the UN Security Council».[81]

Notably, in a contemporaneous publication, he discussed whether loans should have been granted to countries with a record of human rights violations in an extensive way. In this regard, he contended that, on a general basis, Bank's lending for a

---

[77] Shihata (2000b).

[78] ibid., p. 247.

[79] ibid., pp. 245–282.

[80] ibid., p. 248 f. The three-tier test on which the identification of direct and obvious effects must be determined is based on Shihata's memorandum of 1990 on the issue of governance. On this aspect, see Bradlow (1996, p. 60), Darrow (2003).

[81] Shihata (2000b, p. 235).

specific productive purpose could not be considered in itself a violation of human rights law. On the contrary, it could ease the burden on the population rather than worsening their suffering. In these situations, withholding the Bank's lending could have amounted to depriving people of their 'right to development' as broadly intended and endorsed by the UN.[82]

All in all, these statements are of utmost importance. From a legal standpoint, one must observe that the Board of Executive Directors is the only organ entrusted with the task of legally interpreting the Articles, subject to the potential review of the Board of Governors at the request of any member country, by virtue of Article IX(a)(b) to be read in conjunction with Article V, Section 2(iv).[83] In practice, this activity has been carried out by the General Counsel, to whom the Board of Executive Directors has historically deferred responsibility. Indeed, starting from 1964, the Board has never issued any formal interpretation on its own initiative, the only exception being the decision on the standard value of the Bank's capital issued in 1986, which filled the gap created by the disappearance of the gold dollar.[84] Since then, whenever clarifications on the interpretation of the Articles were needed, the Board discussed them based on the legal opinions of the General Counsel, who provided the necessary input.[85]

Therefore, it should be acknowledged that Shihata's Board-endorsed legal opinions contributed to clarify the terms of the debate regarding the definition of the boundaries of the Bank's legal mandate.[86]

In 2003, the appointment of Robert Dañino as the new General Counsel marked a further evolutionary phase in the legal interpretation of the Articles of Agreement. Significantly, one of his first acts upon assuming the position was to establish a Working Group within the legal Vice-Presidency, which was entrusted with the task of analyzing the legal framework applicable to the Bank's development activities in connection with the human rights obligations attributable to member countries.

In a 2005 book summarizing his initial reflections on the legal aspects of the World Bank's work regarding human rights,[87] Dañino argued that, despite the constraints imposed by the financial nature of its activities, the purposes for which the Bank was originally created had gradually changed over time. As a result, its 'constitutional' objectives needed to be interpreted dynamically to align with the

[82] Shihata (2000a, pp. 180–182).

[83] In the case of IDA, reference is to Article X (a) to be read in conjunction with Article VI, Section 2 (c) (iv).

[84] IDA's practice followed the same course, with the sole exception of the formal interpretation of the 'gold dollar' matter issued in 1987.

[85] General Counsel's opinions do not represent an authoritative interpretation of the articles *per se*; the endorsement of the Board of Executive Directors confers them the necessary authority allowing for their incorporation into the Bank's practice. See Shihata (1997, p. 217), Shihata (1999, p. 1048).

[86] Shihata (1995), Ciorciari (2000, p. 349).

[87] Dañino (2005).

evolving concept of development. During Wolfensohn's Presidency (1995–2005),[88] which marked the beginning of the modern phase of the Bank's activities, these objectives were clearly shifting towards a new approach focused on poverty alleviation. Since this approach was based on social equity besides economic growth,[89] it began to embrace a stronger human rights dimension if compared to the past, as the allocation of a significant proportion of the Bank's lending to the attainment of the Millennium Development Goals could demonstrate.[90] All in all, in his view, human rights were no longer seen as merely a moral imperative, but had become an explicit and integral part of the Bank's work, similar to the way environmental concerns had been addressed in the previous two decades and anti-corruption efforts had been incorporated in the preceding five years.

In 2005, Dañino was further asked by the Bank's senior Management to explore the extent to which human rights considerations could be consistent with the Bank's mandate in light of the political prohibition clauses. In this regard, in his legal opinion, he first reiterated that the organization had to consider human rights issues only with reference to economic implications, provided this was done in a non-partisan, non-ideological and neutral manner.[91]

At the same time, Dañino held that the concept of political interference in the evolving international law on sovereignty could no longer be conceived in absolute terms. According to the most modern interpretation, human rights, rather than involving a 'loss' of sovereignty, could be regarded as directly flowing from the inherent dignity of every human being. In this regard, he referenced the interpretation of the United Nations Charter, including provisions that mandated non-interference in the domestic political affairs of Member States while also safeguarding human rights. He argued that, over time, the balance had clearly shifted in favor of the latter:

> At the time of the creation of the United Nations, the balance was interpreted in favor of sovereignty. Since then, the body of international human rights law has grown exponentially and now includes some twenty Conventions and Treaties, as well as a substantial body of general principles and customary international law related to human rights. The balance has therefore shifted in favor of protecting human rights, with the concept of sovereignty having itself been transformed by the evolution of human rights standards and the pursuit

[88] It is worth noting that, in 1999, the then-President of the World Bank Group circulated a proposal for a development framework with a new, long-term, integrated vision. This framework emphasized the need to address not only economic and financial issues, but also structural, social, and human dimensions in a balanced manner. It incorporated elements of good governance, democratic accountability, the protection of human rights, and the rule of law. The Board of Governors of both the World Bank Group and the International Monetary Fund endorsed the principles, which were taken as a basis for poverty reduction strategies for developing countries either seeking assistance or debt relief under the Highly Indebted Poor Country Initiative since then. As a consequence, this made the framework evolve from a proposal into a widely accepted tool in the Bank's practice. See Wolfensohn (2000).

[89] The World Bank (2005). On this aspect, see also McInerney-Lankford (2010, p. 279).

[90] The World Bank (2004, pp. 87–90).

[91] Dañino (2006, para. 14).

of human rights enforcement at all levels of international law in global, regional and domestic fora.[92]

Overall, the added value of his opinion lies in the emphasis placed on the international legal principles of indivisibility, interdependence, and interrelatedness of all human rights, as widely recognized by the international community.[93] Notably, he concluded that there was no stark distinction between civil and political rights, on the one hand, and economic, social, and cultural rights, on the other. Furthermore, he firmly held that in cases of violations of human rights of pervasive proportions, the Bank should have disengaged itself,[94] adding that the Articles of Agreement «permit and in some cases require the Bank to recognize the human rights dimensions of its development policies and activities, since it is now evident that human rights are an intrinsic part of the Bank's mission».[95]

The legal opinion was never openly discussed by the Board; nevertheless, it did not remain isolated. In the course of the same year, Ana Palacio, the newly elected General Counsel (2006–2008), authored a report acknowledging that the way the existing body of international human rights law with respect to civil and political rights could relate to the organization's activities was a matter ripe for analysis. Thus, bringing to the table the interconnection between human rights and development, the report recalled the abundant progress achieved at the UN level in this respect, and referenced several existing documents in this regard, such as the statement of Common Understanding on a Human Rights-Based Approach to Development Cooperation (2003),[96] jointly drafted by several UN bodies after convening a workshop on the matter; the report of the UN Millennium Project, commissioned by the Secretary-General to propose the best strategies for meeting the Millennium Development Goals (2005);[97] and Kofi Annan's report outlining the goals to be achieved in preparation for the Millennium+5 UN Summit (2005).[98]

In stating that the political dimension of human rights embodied values which were not interpreted in a uniform way at the time, Palacio admitted that «the

[92] ibid., para. 16.

[93] At para. 13, the opinion makes reference to two different conferences convened under the UN auspices. See UN, *Proclamation of Teheran*, 10 September 1968, UN Doc. A/CONF. 32/41; World Conference on Human Rights, *Vienna Declaration and Programme of Action*, 12 July 1993, Article 5, UN Doc. A/CONF/157/23.

[94] Dañino (2006, para. 22).

[95] ibid., para. 25. On the impact of economic, social, and cultural rights on the International Monetary Fund's activities, see Gianviti (2005, p. 114). According to Gianviti, General Counsel and former Director at the International Monetary Fund, the IMF - despite its status as a specialized agency of the United Nations - has limited objectives defined in its charter, which do not encompass human rights.

[96] The statement specifically referred to a human rights-based approach to development cooperation and programming by UN agencies, focusing on those who were most marginalized, excluded or discriminated against: UN (2003). For an overview of the strengths and weaknesses related to its application, see Uvin (2007), Broberg and Sano (2018).

[97] UN Millennium Project (2005).

[98] UN General Assembly (2005).

concept of universality underpinning the international human rights framework is a complex one, which must be assessed in progressive terms, and interpreted according to its current legal, political and historical context». With reference to the Bank's internal practice, the report acknowledged the evolution propelled by General Counsel Dañino with the proposition of a more permissive approach, framed in very different terms if compared to the pre-existing restrictive legal interpretation of the Bank's mandate. Indeed, once clarified that the Bank «can and sometimes should take human rights into consideration as part of its decision making process», Palacio further held that «[t]he challenge we now face is to clarify *how* these legal concepts should be specifically incorporated into the work of the Bank in order to further its mission of sustainable and equitable development».[99] Finally, based on the premise that the Bank could contribute to human rights in various areas, the report concluded that the legal principles enshrined in human rights norms could serve as a 'baseline' for assessing development policies and programs. It also suggested that these principles could create actionable legal obligations for Member States, arising directly from international treaties or national laws, the fulfillment of which had to be supported by the Bank when linked to its operations.[100]

In 2008, the World Bank Group launched the Nordic Trust Fund ('NTF'), the first initiative explicitly focused on integrating human rights into its work, despite the lack of a dedicated policy governing the matter. The NTF adopted a learning-by-doing approach focused on research and aimed at providing World Bank Group staff with guidance on relevant human rights aspects. Currently, the World Bank Group is also working on the creation of a new trust fund on human rights and development. A recent Working Paper summarizing the actions undertaken under this initiative admits that although the Articles of Agreement's interpretation seems to suggest that (civil and) political rights should fall outside the World Bank Group's mandate, they offer enough flexibility for incorporation of human rights into its work:

> [T]he Bank has historically avoided explicit use of human rights language. Its Articles of Agreement, which provide a legal framework for the organization's work, limit decision making to economic considerations and cautioned against interfering in the politics of member countries. Interpretations of these articles vary when it comes to the Bank's relationship with human rights. Some interpretations suggest political rights fall outside the Bank's mandate, compared with economic, social and cultural rights. The articles offer

[99] Palacio (2006, pp. 35–37).

[100] It is noteworthy that, in 2006, with two different Resolutions, the UN General Assembly, after recognizing the need to promote respect for human rights and fundamental freedoms for the purpose of addressing extreme poverty (including through the design of *ad hoc* mechanisms aimed at consolidating democratic institutions and governance), explicitly invited «the World Bank, the International Monetary Fund, the regional development banks and other relevant institutions to further integrate development dimensions into their strategies and policies, consistent with their respective mandates, and to fully implement the principles stated in those strategies and policies, in particular the objectives of pro-poor growth and poverty reduction». UN General Assembly (2006a, para. 5); the citation refers to UN General Assembly (2006b, para. 4).

> enough flexibility, though, to allow space for the incorporation of human rights into development work.[101]

Nowadays, political analysis is recognized as an essential part of preparing investment projects and development policy operations. The World Bank Group, and most other organizations performing similar functions, have acknowledged that certain political considerations are not permissible but actually necessary to fully understand countries' development challenges and their prospects for economic development. In a report dated 2014, the Head of the Governance and Public Sector Management Practice noted that, in the previous ten years, a process of significant exploration of a more politically informed approach to development had already occurred within the World Bank,[102] gaining significant momentum with the adoption of the Governance and Anticorruption Strategy in 2007. The report further emphasized that successful institutional reforms required addressing the political foundations and the factors that influence how institutions evolve.[103]

Broadly, the number of documents containing explicit references to human rights has steadily increased in the last few years. The Vision for Sustainable Development, a crucial statement accompanying the new environmental and social standards included in the Bank's new 2016 framework, solemnly holds that:

> [T]he World Bank's activities support the realization of human rights expressed in the Universal Declaration of Human Rights. Through the projects it finances, and in a manner consistent with its Articles of Agreement, the World Bank seeks to avoid adverse impacts and will continue to support its member countries as they strive to progressively achieve their human rights commitments.[104]

Although not legally binding, its added value lies in the emphasis it places on the Bank's activities that support the realization of human rights in their universality, thereby recalling the foundational UDHR in which these rights are articulated. Furthermore, it clarifies that the Bank's commitment to avoiding adverse impact in this respect should take place in accordance with the Articles of Agreement, and, in particular, with the provisions containing the long-debated 'prohibition' clauses, such as Article III, Section 5 (b) and Article IV, Section 10, as cited in a footnote.

At the global level, the World Bank Group's Strategy (2020–2025) for addressing challenges in settings dominated by fragility, conflict, and violence emphasizes the relevance of a people-centric approach with a strong commitment to 'leaving no one behind'. This principle is in fact at the heart of the World Bank's efforts to support the most vulnerable and excluded groups in such challenging contexts.[105]

Given all these considerations, it is evident that the former formalistic view, which holds that the World Bank Group cannot account for human rights in their

---

[101] See Kloeve (2019).

[102] Fritz, Levy, and Ort (2015, p. xi).

[103] ibid., p. 3.

[104] The World Bank, *The World Bank Environmental and Social Framework, A Vision for Sustainable Development*, 2017, pp. 1–2.

[105] The World Bank Group (2020, p. 18).

universality in its work, is now a perspective that can be regarded as overcome. Overall, the organization currently acknowledges the relevance of human rights to its activities,[106] although they are not explicitly incorporated into its mandate.

2.5 The Evolution of the Framework for Managing Environmental and Social Issues

As the recent trends concerning the activities of the World Bank Group demonstrate, an enlargement of the object of its mandate has progressively taken place through its practice. Without a doubt, a crucial shift occurred when IBRD and IDA formalized the procedures to be followed in their lending operations, on which IFC also largely relied for decades before adopting an autonomous set of operational instruments. These prescriptions began regulating several aspects of the financing activities to prevent and manage the impact produced upon vulnerable social groups of people and the environment in a very detailed way, setting out the requirements that borrowers must meet in order to obtain funds and also retain them under the organization's scrutiny.

In this regard, the Articles of Agreement of IBRD, IDA and IFC contain a provision stipulating that the Board of Governors, and the Executive Directors to the extent they are authorized, may adopt secondary rules, when necessary or appropriate (Article V, Section 2.f of the IBRD's Articles of Agreement; Article VI, Section 2.h of the IDA's Articles of Agreement; Article IV, section 2.h of the IFC's Articles of Agreement).[107] In spite of that, the procedures for the adoption of operational policies have spontaneously evolved within the organization in an informal way over time, reflecting the search for an appropriate balance between the institutional powers that historically saw opposition between the Management (and its staff) acting under the President's authority on the one hand, and the Board of Executive Directors representing member countries, on the other.

2.5.1 The Regime Applicable to IBRD's and IDA's Investment Project Financing

Originally conceived as a set of mere aspirational targets drawn from practice, the binding value of the Bank's procedural prescriptions governing IPF has been extremely controversial in the beginning. The prevailing view looked at them as internal quasi-administrative documents meant to assist individuals working for an international organization in the fulfillment of their tasks pursuant to the mandate of

---

[106] McInerney-Lankford (2023, p. 350).

[107] Klein (2019).

the organization itself. At the same time, there was already clear evidence that they could exert some sort of internal compliance 'pull' on the staff, who, when not acting in accordance with them, had to justify such derogations.[108] At a later stage, these statements underwent an evolutionary process that made them become binding on staff in a formal way.[109]

In a first phase, spanning from IBRD's early years of operations until the internal reorganization that also involved IDA in 1987, these prescriptions were mainly articulated in Operational Manual Statements ('OMSs') and Operations Policy Notes ('OPNs'), which were internally issued by Management. The then-existing office of the Senior Vice President of Operations under the authority of the President was in fact informally entrusted with the task of issuing them in the form of general instructions, occasionally supplemented by Operational Circulars or less formal notes. These documents, mostly applicable to both IBRD and IDA, contained basic provisions on how to manage the entire portfolio of the World Bank's lending and non-lending operations. The prescriptions regulating environmental and social aspects began to be adopted in the 1970s in the context of investment projects while Structural Adjustment Programs, introduced in 1980, followed their own autonomous system made up of less systematic rules.

After 1987, which marks the second stage of their refinement, all OMSs and OPNs have been gradually converted into Operational Directives ('ODs'). Starting from this phase, the Boards of Executive Directors of both IBRD and IDA have been increasingly involved in their issuance. A small number of these prescriptions, especially those raising more complex and sensitive issues, began to be discussed in draft form before the Boards, prior to being formally issued by Management. This conferred upon them an authoritative value, although their binding nature remained contentious.

The general rule was that staff were required to observe them, but only within the limits of their flexibility, as explicitly indicated by their text, and in accordance with the Articles of Agreement as interpreted by the Boards. Management, as the formal issuer of these instructions, could amend them or grant exceptions with its approval. After the abolition of the Bank's Senior Vice Presidencies in 1991,[110] approval was obtained from the Office of the President, typically following consultation with the Vice President and the General Counsel, though it usually stemmed from the relevant Managing Director.[111]

Meanwhile, ODs discussed in draft before the Boards of Executive Directors were acquiring a different status suggesting that their prior consultation was a

---

[108] Bradlow and Fourie (2020, p. 320).

[109] Dann (2019, pp. 554–555).

[110] Information available in the World Bank's Archives (Fonds, Records of the Senior Vice President of Operations), at: https://archivesholdings.worldbank.org/records-of-senior-vice-president-of-operations. Accessed 29 April 2025.

[111] Only in the case of statements reiterating Board-approved policies, exceptions were possible following the formal Board's approval of changes. See Shihata (2000c, pp. 41–46).

necessary procedural step at least for granting exceptions in order to avoid creating tensions in the relationship with Management.

At the same time, the World Bank was undergoing a legitimacy crisis. The strong criticism from Civil Society Organizations ('CSOs') accompanying investment projects, urged the Bank to pay renewed attention to the operational instruments governing environmental and social matters. In 1991, the harmful impact of the Sardar Sarovar irrigation project on the Narmada River in India and on displaced tribal peoples compelled the Bank to establish a panel to independently evaluate the project.[112] The resulting report, known as Morse Study, stressed the importance of adhering to the human rights standards concerning resettlement of tribal peoples as incorporated in Bank's operational instructions for the execution of investment projects and enshrined in the ILO Convention No. 107 of 26 June 1957,[113] which India had ratified. The report concluded that both the World Bank and the Indian government were responsible for the adverse impact generated by the project:

> Evolving respect for human rights has established new norms for resettlement and rehabilitation. The Bank's policies have been influential in establishing these norms, and India has adopted many of them. It ratified ILO 107 in 1958. [...] At the end of the day, however, the failure of India and the states to enforce the [...] Bank agreements, and the Bank's failure to enshrine its policies in the agreements, mean that involuntary resettlement resulting from the Sardar Sarovar Projects offends recognised norms of human rights—human rights that India and the Bank have been in the forefront to secure. [...] The Bank must ensure that in projects it decides to support the principles giving priority to resettlement and environmental protection are faithfully observed. This is the only basis for truly sustainable development.[114]

Shortly thereafter, in February 1992, the World Bank Group's President Lewis Preston announced the decision to set up an internal task force to assess the implementation status of other investment projects. After reviewing several documents, the task force headed by Vice-President Willi A. Wapenhans produced a report which shed light on the need to improve Bank's accountability in projects implementation. The report identified enhanced compliance with operational standards concerning social and environmental aspects as a key tool to achieve this objective,[115] along with other institutional reforms that the Bank actually implemented in subsequent years. These included the establishment of the Independent Inspection Panel in 1993, a permanent body reporting to the Board of Executive Directors to investigate complaints raised by people potentially or actually affected by project execution, and the creation of a Quality Assurance and Compliance Unit in 1999 to provide additional oversight of safeguards quality in Bank's projects.

---

[112] The panel was chaired by Bradford Morse, former head of the United Nations Development Programme. See Berger (1993), Kumar (2016, pp. 113–114).

[113] International Labour Organization, *Indigenous and Tribal Populations Convention*, C107, Geneva, 26 June 1957 (entered into effect on 2 June 1959).

[114] See Morse and Berger (1992, pp. 6, 14). It is worth noting that, at the request of the Indian government, the Bank canceled the remainder of the loan in 1993.

[115] Wapenhans (1992).

In parallel with that, the Bank resorted to a 'juridification' of its entire policy framework that gave it a more formal legal structure by totally overhauling it. In 1992, Management took the decision to gradually replace ODs with a reformed set of prescriptions. These included, on the one hand, the so-called Operational Policies ('OPs') and Bank Procedures ('BPs'), normally approved by the Boards before being issued, and pronounced to be binding on staff. On the other hand, Good Practices ('GPs'), aimed at disseminating knowledge based on previous World Bank's experience, as well as relevant international instruments and industry practices, were not considered binding.[116] Overall, this process, better known in the Bank's practice as *conversion*, was complemented by the Boards' approval of a general policy on disclosure of information in 1993,[117] which made the whole set of instruments publicly accessible. Since then, the procedures for the adoption and amendment of both OPs and BPs have been standardized over time in various ways, constantly striking the balance between the Boards and Management.[118]

In the wake of the conversion process, the Bank's prescriptions addressing environmental and social issues in investment project financing began to play a central role in its work.[119] The Bank adopted a total of 11 OPs and corresponding BPs

---

[116] For instance, among the most recent Good Practices, see those released in 2022 to address sexual exploitation, abuse, and sexual harassment in Investment Project Financing operations, which explicitly state that they are «advisory in nature and are not World Bank policy nor are they mandatory», and that they will be updated periodically to reflect emerging good practice. The World Bank (2022c).

[117] The World Bank issued its first Directive on Disclosure of Information in 1985. Nevertheless, the 1993 version was the first one approved by the Boards: The World Bank, *The World Bank Policy on Disclosure of Information*, 1994. Since then, the policy underwent further revisions (approved by the Board of Executive Directors) in 2001, 2005, and 2010. See The World Bank, *Bank Policy: Access to Information*, 1 July 2010 (revised in 2015), Catalogue No. EXC4.01-POL.01.

[118] In a recent document issued in 2014 to explain the various implications of the safeguard system applicable to IBRD and IDA, the Senior Vice President and WBG's General Counsel clarified that, in the hierarchy existing among the mandatory instruments, OPs are at the highest level for encompassing all the prescriptions requiring certain activities to be undertaken or restrained in order to achieve institutional goals, thus to be adopted (and amended) by the Board, whereas BPs, consisting of procedural steps to be followed by the staff to implement the policies, are a prerogative of the Management. The World Bank, *Guidance, Policy and Procedure Framework*, 8 January 2014, Catalogue No. LEG4.01GUID.01, p. 2.

[119] The most recent version of the general Bank's Operational Policy governing IPF operations in a general way (former Operational Policy 10.00, revised in 2012, 2013, and 2016) has been issued in December 2021 and revised in June 2024. The World Bank, *Bank Policy, Investment Project Financing*, 2024, Catalogue No. OPS5.03-POL.110. The Policy defines the obligations of the borrower *vis-à-vis* the Bank with respect to project elaboration, from its inception until approval, including under the implementation and monitoring phases. The framework governing the instrument also consists of the IPF Bank Directive (former Bank Procedure 10.00), whose latest version has been issued on 13 March 2023, that spells out the required Bank's actions to bring the funds disbursement to completion. The World Bank, *Bank Directive, Investment Project Financing*, 2023, Catalogue No. OPS5.03-DIR.116. Operational policies, directives, procedures and other instructions addressed to staff and applicable to Bank operations are all contained in the Operations Manual, available on the World Bank's website at: https://policies.worldbank.org/en/policies/operational-manual. Accessed 30 April 2025.

governing IPF operations, better known as 'safeguards'. For those dealing with the most sensitive issues, such as indigenous peoples and involuntary resettlement, the *ad hoc* procedure followed for their conversion envisaged public consultations with external stakeholders for the first time.[120] The safeguards formally introduced a clear distinction between Bank's and borrowers' obligations by listing their duties in a separate way. While OPs outlined provisions directed at borrowers, the procedural steps required internally within the Bank to provide adequate assistance were detailed in BPs.

Safeguards cover a wide variety of topics; among them, there are those providing directions on how to carry out an 'Environmental Assessment' (OP/BP 4.01),[121] and those concerning the elaboration of an 'Environmental Action Plan' by the borrower to address environmental and social issues, to be implemented and periodically revised with the Bank's support (OP/BP 4.02).[122] Furthermore, there exist other safeguards regulating specific aspects, such as 'Natural Habitats' (OP/BP 4.04),[123] 'Pest Management' (OP/BP 4.09),[124] 'Indigenous Peoples' (OP/BP 4.10),[125] 'Physical Cultural Resources' (OP/BP 4.11),[126] 'Involuntary Resettlement' (OP/BP 4.12),[127] 'Forests' (OP/BP 4.36),[128] and 'Dam Safety' (OP/BP 4.37).[129] This set of policies also includes OP/BP 4.00,[130] concerning the pilot use of national frameworks to address all these issues, provided their equivalence to the Bank's safeguard system, which has been rarely applied in practice.

Further revisions have taken place since then. Broadly, in 2010, a reorganization process aimed at streamlining the general policies governing IPF operations led to a consolidation of all instruments into a single document, OP/BP 10.00 (2013).[131]

---

[120] Green and Raphael (2000, pp. 139–148).

[121] The World Bank, *Operations Manual, Policy & Procedure Framework, Operational Policy and Bank Procedure 4.01, Environmental Assessment*, 1999 (revised in 2013 and 2024).

[122] ibid., *Operational Policy and Bank Procedure 4.02, Environmental Action Plan*, 2000 (revised in 2014, 2015, and 2024).

[123] ibid., *Operational Policy and Bank Procedure 4.04, Natural Habitats*, 2001 (revised in 2013 and 2024).

[124] ibid., *Operational Policy and Bank Procedure 4.09, Pest Management*, 1998 (revised in 2004 and 2024).

[125] ibid., *Operational Policy and Bank Procedure 4.10, Indigenous Peoples*, 2005 (revised in 2013 and 2024).

[126] ibid., *Operational Policy and Bank Procedure 4.11, Physical Cultural Resources*, 2006 (revised in 2013 and 2024).

[127] ibid., *Operational Policy and Bank Procedure 4.12, Involuntary Resettlement*, 2001 (revised in 2013 and 2024).

[128] ibid., *Operational Policy and Bank Procedure 4.36, Forests*, 2002 (revised in 2013 and 2024).

[129] ibid., *Operational Policy and Bank Procedure 4.37, Safety of Dams*, 2001 (revised in 2013 and 2024).

[130] ibid., *Operational Policy and Bank Procedure 4.00, Piloting the Use Borrower Systems to Address Environmental and Social Safeguard Issues in Bank-Supported Projects*, 2005 (revised in 2013 and 2024), p. 3.

[131] The World Bank Operations Policy and Country Services (2012).

The main change involved a shift in terminology for the supervisory tasks related to the post-appraisal phase, which have been renamed 'monitoring and implementation support functions', following the repeal of OP/BP 13.05 concerning Supervision.[132] Other provisions regarding Bank's remedies, such as OP/BP 13.40 ('Suspension of Disbursements'),[133] and OP/BP 13.50 ('Cancellations'),[134] converged into the new general policy instrument with no substantial change.

Meanwhile, safeguards began to follow an independent path of parallel revisions, with input provided by the Independent Evaluation Group ('IEG').[135] Recent Investment Project Financing activities, initiated on (or after) October 2018, are currently governed by a new Environmental and Social Framework ('ESF' or 'the Framework') approved by the IBRD's Board of Executive Directors on 4 August 2016 and applicable to IDA as well. The Framework, which marked the final stage in the evolution of the Bank's safeguards, primarily consists of two key documents. These are the Environmental and Social Policy,[136] addressed to the Bank only, listing its duties, depicted by using the broad expression 'due diligence', and the Environmental and Social Standards ('ESSs'),[137] prescribing the specific requirements applicable to borrowers, which together replaced most of the contents included in OPs/BPs. The Framework also includes the 'Vision for Sustainable Development', which, as already mentioned, represents an aspirational declaration stating that the World Bank's activities support the realization of human rights as expressed in the Universal Declaration of Human Rights.[138] Notably, the document states that Bank's vision goes beyond a 'do no harm' approach, as it seeks to maximize environmental and social outcomes of the projects it supports. Finally, the Framework is complemented by two Bank Directives: one addressing general environmental and social aspects,[139] and the other specifically detailing the Bank's approach to non-discrimination throughout the project cycle, with a focus on disadvantaged and vulnerable individuals and groups.[140] The adoption of the Framework encompassed the largest consultation ever conducted by the institution, reaching nearly 8000 stakeholders in 63 countries over three different phases. In terms of contents, while it mostly incorporates those included in the old safeguards, it gives them a new structure, also expanding the thematic coverage to cope with sensitive and recent challenges emerged in the context of projects execution, having intro-

[132] The World Bank, *Operations Manual, Policy & Procedure Framework, Operational Policy and Bank Procedure 13.05, Project Supervision*, 2001.

[133] ibid., *Operational Policy and Bank Procedure 13.40, Suspension of Disbursements*, 1996.

[134] ibid., *Operational Policy and Bank Procedure 13.50, Cancellations*, 2002.

[135] Independent Evaluation Group (2010).

[136] The World Bank, *The World Bank Environmental and Social Framework*, 2017, pp. 3–11.

[137] ibid., pp. 13–101.

[138] ibid., pp. 1–2.

[139] The World Bank, *Environmental and Social Bank Directive/Procedure for Investment Project Financing*, 2017 (last revised in 2023), Catalogue No. OPS5.03-DIR.118.

[140] The World Bank, *Bank Directive, Addressing Risks and Impacts on Disadvantaged or Vulnerable Individuals or Groups*, 2021, Catalogue No. EXC5.07-DIR.117.

duced brand-new prescriptions for labor, working conditions as well as biodiversity conservation and climate change. Notably, the transition from the old safeguards to the Framework will take several years, as projects approved under the former will continue applying them through the end of their cycle.

It must be stressed that the Framework has introduced two innovative procedural guarantees upon the implementation phase, which have strengthened the borrower's commitment to the protection of the rights of the actors involved in the project, giving them an opportunity for making their concern heard during project execution already. First of all, by virtue of ESS-10 ('Stakeholder Engagement and Information Disclosure'), borrowers are required to engage with concerned stakeholders, including individuals or groups who may have a mere interest in the project. On a more general basis, borrowers must also institute project-based grievance mechanisms to allow affected people to bring complaints on the ground, thus facilitating early resolution of their concerns.

Last but not least, it is worth remarking that, by being emulated by other Multilateral Development Banks over the past few decades, the World Bank's prescriptions governing environmental and social risks management have played a key role in establishing harmonized normative standards that may eventually evolve into a form of *droit commun* governing such operations in the field of development finance.[141]

2.5.2 *Other Lending Instruments: Delimiting the Scope of Inquiry*

For IBRD's and IDA's lending activities different from Investment Project Financing, environmental and social aspects are regulated in a less systematic way. Their evolution has, in fact, followed a different path. In the case of Development Policy Financing (former Sectoral and Structural Adjustment Lending), the operational instrument setting out its general features is the 'Bank Policy on Development

[141] Among the most recent trends emerging in international legal discourse, it is worth mentioning those that focus on the harmonization of standards among different international organizations. These trends compare such processes to the administrative rules and procedures found in domestic law. From this perspective, operational policies and procedures could potentially evolve into 'global administrative law', an emerging body of norms that apply to administrative processes involving more than just intra-State structures of legal and political authority. Such norms, based on transparency, accountability, and participation, would emanate from a wide variety of regulatory institutions of global governance, such as intergovernmental bodies, as well as from entities that are not traditionally considered subjects of international law, including private transnational bodies. See Kingsbury et al. (2005, p. 17), David Hunter (2010, p. 206), Bradlow and Fourie (2013, p. 10). According to this line of thought, global administrative law should be distinguished from traditional international law, which is non-hierarchical by definition and largely arises on a voluntary basis. See also Cassese et al. (2012, p. 7).

Policy Financing', whose latest version has been revised in June 2024,[142] following the 2015 Retrospective Report (2015).[143]

The reasons behind this approach can be easily explained by the fact that this type of lending is aimed at promoting programmatic macroeconomic or sectoral reforms that are typically conceived to produce positive effects. In light of its characteristics, Development Policy Financing is based on very well-developed rules governing conditionality but on a rather fragmented approach with reference to environmental and social risks management. Nevertheless, there is also the possibility of unintended negative effects in the short or long term. For instance, a project aimed at increasing investments in mining by adjusting royalty rates may lead to significant damages to the environment.[144] Notably, the Bank must currently assess prior actions to determine whether they are likely to generate significant impacts, particularly on poor and vulnerable groups, or on the environment, forests, and other natural resources. However, no specific assessment of the consequences resulting from the disbursement is foreseen. The Bank is, in fact, only required to perform *ex-ante* identification of the potential adverse effects arising from the supported program, without considering those that may occur at a later stage. Nevertheless, starting from 1 July 2023, these operations need to be aligned with the goals of the Paris Agreement on climate change, as determined by the Bank.

As for Program-for-Results Financing, regulated by its own operational instruments, updated in 2024,[145] environmental and social risks are managed in a way that seems a compromise between the two above-mentioned approaches. The Bank conducts a social and environmental assessment prior to determining whether to proceed with the operation. Although there exist no specific policies on environmental and social issues, activities that are deemed likely to have significant adverse impact are not eligible for PforR Financing. As for the implementation phase, the Bank may agree with the borrower on specific actions to be taken, including measures to address identified weaknesses and strengthen institutional capacity.

Although it is possible that the policy provisions regulating DPF and PforR may evolve to address environmental and social aspects more comprehensively in the

---

[142] The World Bank, *Bank Policy, Development Policy Financing*, 2017 (last revised in 2024), Catalogue No. OPS5.02-POL.120, para. 16. The policy replaced former OP 8.60, introduced in August 2004. Supplementary provisions can be found in the Bank Procedure 8.60, last revised in 2014. Notably, DPF instruments have evolved considerably over the last 20 years in many respects. For example, budget support operations, once primarily used in countries with well-developed institutional structures and governance, are now increasingly employed in lower-capacity countries, including fragile states. More information is available on the Independent Evaluation Group's website at: https://ieg.worldbankgroup.org/podcast/learning-development-policy-financing. Accessed 30 April 2025.

[143] The World Bank Group (2015, p. 55).

[144] Independent Evaluation Group (2015, p. ix).

[145] The World Bank, *Bank Policy, Program-for-Results Financing* (effective since 11 November 2017, revised on 25 March 2022), 2024, Catalogue No. OPS5.04-POL.123; The World Bank, *Bank Directive, Program-for-Results Financing* (effective since 17 September 2020, revised on 8 March 2022), 2024, Catalogue No. OPS5.04-DIR.109.

future, the current framework does not support in-depth research in this context. Accordingly, the analysis will focus exclusively on Investment Project Financing.

2.5.3 The Framework Governing IFC's Operations

The evolution of the instruments governing IFC's financing activities has marked an initial overlap with IBRD's and IDA's framework concerning environmental and social risks management. IFC's early engagement with such matters dates back to 1988, when the first environmental specialist was hired.[146] Shortly thereafter, in 1990, IFC introduced a first set of internal procedures, requiring its investment projects to undergo an environmental review to ensure alignment with the «spirit and the intent of the appropriate Bank guidelines and policies».[147] Nevertheless, since the World Bank's framework was designed to regulate lending to governments rather than private companies or financial intermediaries, these requirements left significant room for interpretation and had a limited impact on improving the environmental performance of IFC-funded activities for some time.[148] In 1993, although IFC redefined its position by reaffirming its commitment to comply with the relevant World Bank's policies and guidelines,[149] it did not specify which instruments were deemed appropriate within its scope of action. A few years later, the Pangue hydroelectric project, the first IFC's big private infrastructure investment in Chile, which was approved in 1992, made local advocacy groups and non-governmental organizations ('NGOs') question its effective ability to foster private sector development for the adverse impacts produced upon the environment and the indigenous peoples living in the project area.[150] Similar to the case of the Bank, in 1996, following widespread criticism of the project, President Wolfensohn commissioned an independent review that identified several shortcomings in IFC's project management in this regard. As a result, the IFC was compelled to adapt the newly introduced Bank's safeguard policies for its own use.[151] In the same year, IFC hired its first social specialist. In September 1998, with a formal decision adopted by its Board of Executive Directors,[152] it started relying on the contents of OP 4.01 ('Environmental Assessment'), OP 4.04 ('Natural Habitats'), OP 4.09 ('Pest Management'), OP 4.36 ('Forestry'), OP 4.37 ('Safety of Dams'), OP 7.50 ('International Waterways'), in addition to the Operational Policy Note on manage-

[146] Independent Evaluation Group (2009, p. 2).

[147] International Finance Corporation, *Procedure for Environmental Review of IFC Projects*, March 1990 (in effect until December 1992), para. 1.

[148] Lee (2001, p. 477).

[149] International Finance Corporation (1993).

[150] For an analysis of the main issues posed by the controversial Pangue Dam infrastructure project in Chile, see Park (2010).

[151] International Finance Corporation (2016, p. 92).

[152] Compliance Advisor Ombudsman (2003, p. 20).

ment of cultural property (OPN 11.03). As the two instruments addressing social issues were still undergoing the complex review process that would eventually transform them into the modern safeguard version, at the time, IFC could rely on OD 4.20 ('Indigenous Peoples') of 1991, and OD 4.30 ('Involuntary Resettlement') of 1990. Within this context, the IFC independently adopted only a policy statement emphasizing its commitment to avoid financing activities involving forced labor,[153] directly or through financial intermediaries, as defined on the basis of Article 2 of ILO Convention No. 29 of 1930,[154] and Article 32.1 of the UN Convention on the Rights of the Child.[155] The statement was approved by its Board of Executive Directors in March 1998.

During the same year, the framework was supplemented by the Environmental Health and Safety ('EHS') Guidelines, included in the WBG's Pollution Prevention and Abatement Handbook,[156] which described good industry practices for environmental assessments of pollution-sensitive projects. Furthermore, the IFC's Management approved a new version of the requirements to be followed in the review of all the issues posed by investments related to private sector projects, including subprojects managed by financial intermediaries, before and after appraisal, renamed Environmental and Social Review Procedures ('ESRPs').[157]

The new internal instruments adopted by IFC gained widespread acceptance to the point that, in June 2003, IFC advised ten leading banks from seven countries on the adoption of a voluntary set of environmental and social guidelines for project financing based on its policies and the EHS Guidelines as well.[158] Over time, the so-called Equator Principles have been adopted by over a hundred financial institutions worldwide, becoming recognized as the most authoritative benchmarks in the field of social and environmental risk management arising from financial activities across a wide range of sectors, including oil, mining, and gas.

In the meantime, within IFC, the idea that an autonomous version of the safeguard policy framework was necessary began to gain momentum, following an initiative by the Compliance Advisor Ombudsman. In 2003, the CAO published an advisory report containing a set of recommendations aimed at revisiting some of the framework's key elements to better address the specific needs of the private sector. After comprehensive external and internal consultations, on 21 April 2006, the IFC's Board of Executive Directors approved the first version of its Sustainability

---

[153] International Finance Corporation, *IFC's Policy Statement on Forced Labor and Harmful Child Labor*, 1998.

[154] International Labour Organization, *Forced Labour Convention*, C029, Geneva, 28 June 1930. The Convention came into force on 1 May 1932.

[155] UN General Assembly, *Convention on the Rights of the Child*, Resolution 44/25 of 20 November 1989 (entered into force on 2 September 1990), in *UNTS*, Volume 1577, p. 3 f.

[156] The World Bank Group, *Pollution Prevention and Abatement Handbook, Toward Cleaner Production*, 1998.

[157] International Finance Corporation, *Procedure for Environmental and Social Review of Projects*, 1998.

[158] International Finance Corporation (2005, p. 22).

Framework, consisting of a 'Policy on Social and Environmental Sustainability',[159] which emphasized that efforts to conduct its operations in a manner that does 'no harm' to people or the environment are central to its development mission. It also included a set of eight 'Performance Standards'[160] ('PSs'), and a 'Disclosure Policy',[161] containing a list of the documents that the institutions committed to making available to the public. The new framework applied to investments undergoing IFC's initial credit review process starting from the date of its effective introduction on 30 April 2006. This marked the beginning of key autonomous developments within IFC. Its framework introduced a two-tier structure, clearly distinguishing the commitments of the institution from those of the financing recipients, a model that would later influence the development of the World Bank's ESF in 2016. In addition to that, the institution completed a massive update process of other documents, with the adoption of a revised version of both ESRPs[162] and their accompanying Guidance Notes. Furthermore, in 2008, in cooperation with the World Bank, IFC revised the EHS Guidelines.[163] One final important development during this phase occurred with the 2007 revision of the IFC's exclusion list, which was first published in 1998, and included, among other things, the production or trade in any product or activity considered illegal under the laws or regulations of the host country or international conventions and agreements.[164]

In 2009, upon the request of the Committee on Development Effectiveness ('CODE'), IFC started reporting on the implementation progress of its Sustainability Framework.[165] Based on the report, the IFC's Management and the Board of Executive Directors agreed to review and update the 2006 Sustainability Framework. Following an 18-month process of public consultations, the latest version has been released in August 2011, becoming effective on 1 January 2012.[166]

---

[159] International Finance Corporation, *Policy on Social and Environmental Sustainability*, 30 April 2006.

[160] International Finance Corporation, *International Finance Corporation's Performance Standards on Social & Environmental Sustainability*, 30 April 2006.

[161] International Finance Corporation, *IFC Disclosure Policy*, 30 April 2006.

[162] International Finance Corporation, *Environmental and Social Review Procedure*s *Manual*, 2006. Such version underwent further revisions in 2007, 2009, 2013, 2016, and 2025. The latest version is available at: https://www.ifc.org/en/insights-reports/2016/publications-policy-esrp. Accessed 30 April 2025.

[163] International Finance Corporation, *Environmental, Health and Safety General Guidelines*, 30 April 2007.

[164] International Finance Corporation, *Exclusion List*, 30 July 2007.

[165] International Finance Corporation (2009, p. 31).

[166] International Finance Corporation, *IFC Sustainability Framework, Policy and Performance Standards on Environmental and Social Sustainability*, 2012. Meanwhile, MIGA, which had previously relied on World Bank's safeguard policies to assess its projects (and on IFC staff for their review), adopted an *interim* version of its policies in 2002. A few years later, in 2007, it introduced a framework nearly identical to that of the IFC, which was updated in 2013. See Multilateral Investment Guarantee Agency, *Policy on Environmental and Social Sustainability*, 2013; Multilateral Investment Guarantee Agency, *Performance Standards on Environmental and Social Sustainability*, 2013.

2.6 Role of the World Bank Group vs the Borrower During the Project Cycle

World Bank Group's involvement in the project cycle can vary significantly depending on the specific operations involved. On a general basis, it is noteworthy that the provisions outlined in the operational policies are formally binding on IBRD, IDA, and IFC, which, in turn, aim at ensuring borrower's compliance by exerting a peculiar form of environmental and social conditionality prior to project approval, which consists of denying disbursement when the required provisions are not incorporated into the project design. Once integrated into the legal agreement in the form of covenants, these provisions become formally binding on borrowers as well.[167]

Given the significant differences in the project cycle characteristics between the public and private sectors, it is deemed appropriate to address their analysis separately.

2.6.1 *Public Sector Projects*

Defining the general boundaries of the role played by the borrower and the World Bank at the different stages of the project cycle is a complex task, given the diverse functions performed by the latter.[168] As a lending institution, indeed, the Bank needs to ensure that disbursed funds are solely used for the purpose for which the loan was extended. Additionally, in its capacity as a development institution, the Bank has a continuous responsibility to support member countries in achieving development objectives on a sustainable basis.[169] When not linked to a specific project, this activity is carried out through the delivery of non-lending Advisory Services and Analytics. Notably, with reference to environmental and social matters arising from investment project financing operations, the new Framework, applicable to projects initiated on or after October 2018, has recently clarified that technical assistance supported by IPF, as a component of a project or as a stand-alone project, is subject to the application of the general provisions outlined in ESS-1.[170]

[167] In the case of public sector projects, influential World Bank's legal doctrine conceives such agreements as bilateral treaties governed by international law, creating an international legal obligation for the borrower to comply with the specific environmental and social measures agreed upon during project preparation. See Shihata (2000a, p. 515).

[168] Over time, necessary changes to the project cycle approach have been driven by the need to more extensively involve borrowers and to improve risk management. In this respect, see Picciotto and Weaving (1994).

[169] Bradlow and Fourie (2020, p. 323).

[170] The World Bank Group, *The World Bank Environmental and Social Framework*, 2017, p. 5.

Overall, the basic approach stipulated in the policies is that, following an initial phase focused on project conception, during which the borrower and the Bank both play a prominent role, in the subsequent ones there is a more distinct allocation of responsibilities. Specifically, after the disclosure of the basic project ideas and the identification of risks, the borrower assumes full responsibility for conducting the preparatory work necessary to launch the project, with particular focus on assessing potential adverse environmental or social impacts. Meanwhile, the Bank's role is to appraise compliance with internal policies and review all aspects of the project, which serves as a basis for negotiations, while offering guidance as needed. Finally, following formal Board of Executive Directors' approval, the borrower is responsible for project implementation as agreed with the Bank, while the Bank oversees the implementation process through progress reports based on the data provided by the borrower.[171]

Against this backdrop, the new Framework has introduced two novelties, the practical effects of which will be assessed in the near future. First, its enactment has marked a more pronounced shift towards the concept of full borrower's 'ownership' of the project regarding environmental and social matters, by providing a general 'due diligence' obligation of the Bank, rather than specifying its contents with respect to each safeguard.[172] By virtue of this general obligation, in the phase preceding the formal loan approval, the Bank needs to 'require' that borrowers prepare projects so that they meet the ESSs in a manner and a timeframe acceptable to the Bank, instead of 'ensuring' the consistency of borrower's actions with applicable policies, with more emphasis on the procedure rather than on the results. Second, with reference to supervision in the implementation phase, the Framework has adopted more nuanced language, aligning with the general policy governing IPF operations, by opting for terms such as 'monitoring' and 'implementation support' in describing the Bank's obligations during this phase.[173]

Turning to a more in-depth examination of the project cycle, it is important to note that it comprises six different stages. During the first one ('Identification'), the project proposal is formally presented by the borrowing country based on the Country Partnership Framework, the general strategy prepared jointly with the World Bank Group that defines the country's main priorities for ending extreme

[171] Baum (1978, p. 11).

[172] This shift in paradigm is part of a broader change within the development finance sector, exemplified by the Paris Declaration on Aid Effectiveness adopted in 2005 and reaffirmed in Accra in 2008 at ministerial-level forums convened by the Organisation for Economic Co-operation and Development.

[173] Following the consolidation of the general policies concerning IPF operations into OP/BP 10.00, the safeguards, instead, continued employing the term 'supervision' to describe the Bank's obligations during project implementation.

poverty[174] over a four- to six-year period.[175] Once the Bank and the borrower have agreed on an initial project concept and its beneficiaries, the Bank's country team elaborates the basic ideas, all summarized in the 'Project Concept Note', which broadly describes the outline of the project, its risks, alternative scenarios for implementation and prospective timetable. Furthermore, it delivers two documents which are disclosed to the public, the 'Project Information Document', providing general data on the type of Bank's financial assistance envisaged for the project as well as its development objectives, and the Integrated Safeguards Sheet ('ISS'), through which the Bank identifies the risks triggering the application of its environmental and social policies. The Bank thus assesses the profile of the prospective project, assigning the operations to a specific category, among which 'A' is used for projects involving the maximum risk of impact, 'B' is the intermediate category, and 'C' is associated with very low risks. At this stage, the main environmental and social issues, along with the prospective borrower's preliminary actions to mitigate the impacts of implementation, have been identified. Notably, the new Framework has replaced the ISS with the Environmental and Social Review Summary ('ESRS'), which also includes information on the Bank's ranking of the potential risks associated with the project, which is now assigned to four new broader categories (High, Substantial, Moderate or Low). As in the safeguards regime, it is the Bank that establishes the project classification, which is continuously reviewed in line with its due diligence obligations and can be modified, if necessary, at later stages.[176] In any case, the borrower's capacity to deal with the issues posed by the project and to act in a manner consistent with the Framework is always taken into account.[177]

The second phase ('Preparation') is country-driven and deals with the analytical study of all relevant aspects, including financial and economic ones. At this stage, while the borrower remains primarily responsible, the Bank may serve as a vehicle for global knowledge transfer by providing technical assistance, if needed. For

---

[174] In 2014, the Country Partnership Framework replaced both the 'Country Assistance Strategy' and the 'Poverty Reduction Strategy Paper' previously produced by low-income countries assisted by IDA. The draft text of the Directive describing the new approach to country engagement was distributed to the WBG's Boards to obtain their approval on 27 May 2014: see The World Bank Group (2014). The final text of the Directive has been issued on 1 July 2014 (and is applicable to the whole WBG starting from the same date): The World Bank Group, *World Bank Group Directive, Country Engagement*, 2014, Catalogue No. OPCS 5.01-DIR.01.

[175] In drafting the Country Partnership Framework, the WBG begins with the member country's own vision for its development goals, which may be laid out in a poverty-focused national development strategy. Following a cycle of reforms implemented in 2015, the process builds on the findings of a specific analytical tool used by WBG staff in close consultation with the country's national authorities and other stakeholders, known as 'Systematic Country Diagnostics'. Notably, this tool is designed to address five main sets of questions, one of which is: 'How sustainable (environmentally, socially, and fiscally) is the current pattern of growth, distribution, and poverty reduction?'. Detailed information is available at: https://openknowledge.worldbank.org/collections/51faed2a-0a03-5122-8e91-7d9e28a0a3f6. Accessed 2 May 2025.

[176] The World Bank, *Environmental and Social Bank Directive/Procedure for Investment Project Financing*, 2017 (last revised in 2023), Catalogue No. OPS5.03-DIR.118, 2017, p. 10.

[177] The World Bank, *Environmental and Social Framework*, 2017, p. 6.

instance, it may support the country in identifying ways to implement arrangements with relevant agencies, such as those designated for environmental and social risks management, and in conducting relevant reviews and studies. In this respect, two different types of provisions apply depending on when the project was approved.

Projects approved before October 2018 that, based on the preliminary screening conducted by the Bank, are assigned to Category A or B, require the borrower to prepare an Environmental Impact Assessment, which considers natural and social aspects in an integrated way, and, as part of the assessment, other instruments or a combination of them, as appropriate. Based on OP 4.01,[178] these may include regional, sectoral, strategic, audit, hazard or risk assessments, environmental management plans or environmental and social management frameworks. These instruments include a wide variety of mitigation measures, as well as monitoring and institutional strengthening arrangements with the Bank, framed in the specific context in which the operations will take place and depending on the specific needs of the involved area. A Resettlement Action Plan or an Indigenous Peoples Development Plan may also be required, as appropriate. The preparation of these plans, which are meant to be incorporated into the legal agreement as attachments, is particularly relevant as the Bank may grant or deny its appraisal based on them.

For more recent projects, the Framework has provided a regime mirroring these provisions insofar as it requires the borrower to carry out a comprehensive Environmental and Social Assessment and to decide on the additional tools to be prepared in consultation with the Bank (ESS1-Annex 1). Apart from the terminology change in the definition of the assessment, which emphasizes the relevance of social aspects, the provision substantially encompasses a choice among instruments that are almost identical compared to those listed under the previous version of the policy. On the other hand, the Framework has introduced some novelties. The assessment is extended to all proposed projects, regardless of the risks they pose, an aspect that substantially enhances the effectiveness of prescribed requirements. Furthermore, for projects having high or substantial risks (or encompassing a general borrower's limited capacity), the borrower needs to recruit independent specialists to carry out the assessment. Finally, all the actions that the borrower needs to undertake in order to comply with the Standards within a specified timeframe need to be summarized into a single sole document, the Environmental and Social Commitment Plan ('ESCP'), to be forming part of the legal agreement concluded with the Bank.[179] The ESCP represents a lively document, that is constantly updated, and includes the Bank's due diligence assessment as well as the outcome of the consultations carried out with the relevant stakeholders.

During the third phase ('Appraisal'), the borrower and the Bank jointly review the work already done: documents already released to the public are updated and disclosed once more when agreement is reached on the viability of all aspects. The

---

[178] The World Bank, *Operations Manual, Policy & Procedure Framework, Operational Policy and Bank Procedure 4.01*, 1999 (revised in 2013 and 2024), para. 7.

[179] The World Bank, *Environmental and Social Framework*, 2017, p. 9.

project thus enters the fourth stage ('Negotiation and Approval'). The Bank finalizes the so-called 'Project Appraisal Document', setting out all loan conditions, which is submitted to the Board of Executive Directors for approval, along with other financial and legal documents. Then, during the fifth phase ('Implementation'), the concerned government prepares the specifications for the project and the environmental and social impact mitigation measures already set out in the agreed plans. Since the project is considered finalized in this phase, unexpected events, circumstances or delays may lead to a review of the original loan conditions.

The Bank constantly verifies progress over implementation. Twice a year, it produces a detailed update jointly with the borrower that serves as a basis for drafting the 'Implementation Status and Results Report', a self-evaluation exercise. Similarly, at the end of the loan disbursement period ('Completion' phase), with input from the borrower (and involved stakeholders, if appropriate), the Bank compiles the 'Implementation Completion and Results Report', describing the project outcomes and assessing how the entire operation complied with the Bank's operations policies. After completion, an independent form of assessment ('Validation and Evaluation' phase) is carried out by the Independent Evaluation Group in order to measure the project results against its original objectives. Although physically forming part of the World Bank Group, the IEG is independent from Management as it reports directly to the Boards of Executive Directors. IEG's role in post-project evaluation is very relevant, as it examines the environmental and social aspects of completed operations and draws lessons from past practice.[180] Its approach is harmonized with internationally accepted evaluation principles, including those reflected in the (i) Quality Standards for Development Evaluation used by the Development Assistance Committee of the Organisation for Economic Co-operation and Development ('OECD');[181] the (ii) Good Practice Standards of the Evaluation Cooperation Group, established in 1996 by the heads of evaluation of Multilateral Development Banks to promote harmonization of evaluation standards among such institutions; and the (iii) Norms and Standards of the UN Evaluation Group.

Among its activities, one of the most relevant is the 'Implementation Completion and Results Report Review', conducted to validate 100% of World Bank's projects within 180 days from the submission date of the self-evaluation conducted by the Bank's project teams. While such reviews are based on the same criteria, the preparation of strategically selected evaluations through 'Project Performance Assessment Reports', carried out for approximately 20% of the Bank's project portfolio only, represents a peculiar type of assessment that relies on a much wider range of evidence, usually including, but not limited to, that stemming from literature review, portfolio analysis and country missions, involving site visits and interviews with different stakeholders. Last but not least, all evaluations produced by the Bank internally and at the IEG's level, are subject to the assessment of the CODE, which supports the Boards of Executive Directors of the World Bank Group by providing

---

[180] The World Bank, *IBRD/IDA/IFC/MIGA Policy, Independent Evaluation Group Mandate*, 2018.

[181] Organisation for Economic Co-operation and Development (2010).

guidance on strategies, monitoring the quality and results of operations, and overseeing, or liaising on, the work of the entities that are part of the accountability framework, including, besides the IEG, the IBRD/IDA Inspection Panel and the IFC/MIGA Compliance Advisor Ombudsman.[182]

2.6.2 *Private Sector Projects*

Unlike the case of projects financed by IBRD and IDA, there is no standard application form for IFC's activities: businesses or financial intermediaries ('the client') seeking financing through a loan or equity investment[183] can approach the institution directly by submitting a proposal, which goes through different phases of a specific cycle before being approved. After the identification of suitable projects ('Business Development' phase) based on conversations with the client, IFC's investment officers prepare a description of the project ('Early Review' phase), which may also lead to a pre-appraisal visit to identify potential issues. A provisional categorization of the project, depending on the potential environmental or social risks or impacts it entails (A for significant impacts, B for limited impacts, and C for minimal impacts) is provided at this stage. Notably, for operations with an indeterminate impact at the time of the IFC's decision to invest, as in the case of equity investments, the category determination is based on the risks inherent to the particular sector and the context of the business activity's setting.[184] The categorization follows the same criteria for activities involving investments in financial intermediaries (FI-1, FI-2, FI-3). In this case, unless funds are intended for a specific end use, IFC considers the entire portfolio of the intermediary in its evaluation.

Thus, the client, in coordination with other responsible government agencies and third parties, where required, identifies and assesses relevant adverse risks or impacts that are already known through an appropriate Environmental and Social Management System ('ESMS'), to be maintained and used throughout the project cycle. As a result of this process, the client identifies the necessary mitigation measures, when avoidance is not feasible, through an Environmental and Social Action Plan ('ESAP') that may incorporate sub-plans to deal with specific matters that require special consideration, such as those related to indigenous peoples, resettlement or biodiversity.[185] Financial intermediary clients are also required to develop an ESMS to identify and assess the risks and impacts associated with either the

[182] The World Bank Group, *Terms of Reference of the Committee on Development Effectiveness*, Annex C, 2009.

[183] It is worth noting that IFC financing also includes quasi-equity and hybrid products that combine elements of both loans and equity investments.

[184] International Finance Corporation, *IFC Sustainability Framework, Policy and Performance Standards on Environmental and Social Sustainability*, 2012, p. 9.

[185] ibid., p. 19. In particular, see PS-1 on the assessment and management of environmental and social risks and impacts.

business operation being considered for financing or their entire portfolio of operations.

During the 'Appraisal' or 'Due Diligence' phase, the IFC's investment team assesses whether the proposal is financially sound and analyzes all its other aspects in order to verify whether the client is able to meet the Performance Standards through its ESMS. For category A and B projects, where appropriate, the Lead Environmental or Social Specialist prepares the Environmental and Social Review Summary document, which outlines the risks and impacts of the project, based on the information elaborated by the client in its various assessments.[186] The ESAP is also reviewed. For FI-1 and FI-2 operations, unless funds are intended for a specific end use, the assessment is focused on the prospective ability of financial intermediaries to require that their borrowers or investees comply with the Performance Standards. Therefore, the ESAP typically includes all the measures that IFC deems necessary to strengthen the Environmental and Social Management System.[187]

Based on recommendations of the investment team, the IFC's managerial department decides whether or not to approve the project ('Investment Review' phase).

In the following phase, the IFC's project team starts negotiating the terms and conditions of its participation in the project ('Negotiations' phase), after which the information regarding the proposal contained in the 'Summary of Investment Information', and, where applicable, the ESRS and ESAP, is posted on the IFC's Project Information and Data Portal ('Public Disclosure' phase). The following step is the submission of the project to the IFC's Board of Executive Directors ('Review and Approval' phase). IFC and the client thus sign the legal agreement ('Commitment' phase), in which the client agrees to comply with all applicable Performance Standards and to submit regular monitoring reports to facilitate IFC's supervision. The final legal agreement also includes the terms of the ESAP, along with any other environmental and social commitments in the form of covenants. In accordance with the provisions of the agreement, IFC disburses the funds, which are often released in stages or contingent upon the completion of specific steps ('Disbursement of Funds' phase). As IFC needs to ensure compliance with the conditions set out in the agreement, it monitors the information transmitted by the client on its financial, environmental, and social performance. At this stage, it may also identify opportunities with the client for project enhancement through advisory services.

It is noteworthy that the delivery of advisory services in connection with an investment or even as standalone projects,[188] is subject to a similar, although smoother, cycle. If the IFC's review of the proposed activity reveals environmental

---

[186] International Finance Corporation, *Environmental and Social Review Procedures Manual*, 2025, p. 18, para. 4.30.

[187] International Finance Corporation, *Guidance Note on Financial Intermediaries*, 2023, p. 9.

[188] This applies to advisory services provided to both private entities and governments. See International Finance Corporation, *Environmental and Social Review Procedures Manual*, 2025, p. 38, para. 6.2.

or social risks during appraisal, the advice provided to the client must align with the Performance Standards and be monitored during the implementation phase.

In the case of both investments and advisory services, at the end of the cycle, IFC tracks the project's contribution to development against key indicators that are set out at the beginning ('Project Supervision and Development Outcome Tracking' phase). Evaluations are carried out on an annual basis ('Evaluation' phase), and are complemented by those carried out by the IEG, as in the case of the Bank. Nevertheless, none of these evaluation documents are publicly available. The project is considered closed when the investment is repaid in full, when IFC divests its equity stake by selling it, or the advisory services are delivered ('Closing' phase).[189]

2.7 The Establishment of Independent Accountability Mechanisms: Preliminary Remarks

While the World Bank Group's engagement with environmental and social matters in financing activities dates back to the adoption of the safeguards, it was only with the establishment of its International Accountability Mechanisms that compliance with these policies began to be enforced.

The Inspection Panel, an independent body established in 1993 through two identical resolutions adopted by the Boards of Executive Directors of IBRD and IDA,[190] was tasked with hearing complaints from individuals affected by the implementation of projects funded by both entities.

Its main function is to assess the proper implementation of all policies related to the Bank's operations, with those addressing environmental and social concerns being the most frequently raised in the complaints brought to its attention.[191] Shortly thereafter, in 1999, IFC (jointly with MIGA) followed the same pattern with the establishment of the Compliance Advisor Ombudsman. Since then, IAMs have continued to proliferate at a rapid pace, with the creation of the Independent Project Accountability Mechanism at the European Bank for Reconstruction and Development in 1991, the Accountability Mechanism at the Asian Development Bank in 1995, the Independent Recourse Mechanism at the African Development Bank in 2004, the Complaints Mechanism at the European Investment Bank in 2008, and the Independent Consultation and Investigation Mechanism at the Inter-American Development Bank in 2010, to name the major ones.

IAMs share common features regarding the admissibility criteria for complaints, which can be submitted directly or through local representatives by any individual

[189] General information on IFC's project cycle is available at: https://www.ifc.org/en/what-we-do/products-and-services/ifc-project-cycle. Accessed 2 May 2025.

[190] The reference is to IBRD's Resolution No. 93-10 and IDA's Resolution No. 93–6, both adopted on 22 September 1993.

[191] For a comprehensive review of its mandate and functions, see Seatzu (2008).

or group whose rights or interests have been, or are likely to be, harmed by an alleged action or omission of the involved institution. Their role centers on evaluating the organization's adherence to its own operational policies, which forms the core of their investigative work. Throughout this process, IAMs collect the necessary facts to determine how the organization interpreted and applied the policies, assessing both whether it met relevant requirements and whether its actions led to the harm experienced by the requesters.

However, as IAMs are not adjudicatory bodies, their decisions are not legally binding in the way a court's judgment would be.[192] Furthermore, they are unable to apply international agreements to which borrowing member countries are parties, entailing that they cannot formally act as enforcers of their human rights obligations. Finally, they are not vested with the general law-making authority to amend existing operational policies or enact new ones, as they can only adopt internal rules for procedural matters related to their work.[193]

Nevertheless, if an infringement is identified during the investigation, they can make recommendations regarding how future project operations should be conducted and propose the adoption of corrective measures to bring the project into compliance. As their findings encourage greater diligence in the preparation of future projects also due to their exposure to public attention—thus having a broader impact beyond the specific complaint at hand—they may trigger internal processes potentially leading to the amendment of the policies, with the ultimate effect of refining their contents to better address specific needs, whether related to a particular sector, vulnerable group, or region.[194] As stated in 2020 by the UN Independent Expert on the Promotion of a Democratic and Equitable International Order, «independent accountability mechanisms foster a culture of accountability towards the proper implementation of such policies and standards, and can suggest areas for improvement at the provision and implementation levels».[195] This function is particularly relevant for the purposes of the present analysis, as it empowers IAMs to develop relevant trends concerning the interpretation of the policies.

Broadly speaking, it is also important to acknowledge that, within the limits of their mandate, IAMs provide project-affected people with access to an independent

---

[192] Shihata (2000c), p. 234. It is noteworthy that the institutions whose conduct IAMs investigate enjoy immunity from legal action before national courts. Nevertheless, a fishing community affected by the execution of a project has recently sued IFC before US courts after Management failed to implement the findings contained in a CAO's report. In February 2019, the US Supreme Court ruled that, under national statutory law, international organizations performing functions that can be qualified as 'commercial', having an adequate nexus with the United States, do not enjoy absolute immunity from lawsuits in the national territory, overturning longstanding precedents of the US Court of Appeals in the District of Columbia Circuit. *Budha Ismail Jam et al v International Finance Corp*, No. 17-1011, 586 U.S. (2019) 139 S. Ct. 759; 203 L. Ed. 2d 53. This innovative trend has not been echoed by other rulings so far; for instance, in August 2020, a US federal court held that the World Bank Group cannot be sued for any damage caused by its lending.

[193] Boisson de Chazournes (2000, p. 294).

[194] Tignino (2020).

[195] UN General Assembly (2020, p. 10).

body before which they can express their concerns and seek recourse. In this regard, the case of the Compliance Advisor Ombudsman is particularly interesting, as it is explicitly mandated to facilitate access to remedy for victims of business-related human rights abuses, therefore playing a vital role in translating a fundamental tenet of international human rights law into practice.[196] This is especially evident when it exercises its dispute resolution functions, which foster the achievement of agreements leading to the adoption of remedial measures by businesses, such as apologies, financial or non-financial compensation and guarantees of non-repetition.[197]

References

Adinolfi G (2014) Aggiustamento economico e tutela dei diritti umani: un conflitto inesistente per le istituzioni finanziarie internazionali. Diritti umani e diritto internazionale 8:319–350

Baum WC (1978) The World Bank project cycle. Finance & Development. International Monetary Fund, Washington, DC

Berger TR (1993) The World Bank independent review of India's Sardor Sarovar projects. Am Univ Int Law Rev 9(1):33–48

Bleicher SA (1970) UN v. IBRD: a dilemma of functionalism. Int Org 24(1):31–47

Boisson de Chazournes L (2000) Policy guidance and compliance: the World Bank operational standards. In: Shelton D (ed) Commitment and compliance: the role of non-binding norms in the international legal system. OUP, Oxford-New York, pp 281–303

Bradlow D (1996) The World Bank, the IMF, and human rights. J Transnatl Law Contemp Probs 6:47–90

Bradlow D, Fourie AN (2013) The operational policies of the World Bank and the International Finance Corporation, creating law-making and law-governed institutions? Int Organ Law Rev 10:3–80

Bradlow D, Fourie AN (2020) The multilateral development banks and the management of the human rights impacts of their operations. In: Deva S, Birchall D (eds) Research handbook on human rights and business. Edward Elgar, Cheltenham-Northampton, pp 315–333

Broberg M, Sano HS (2018) Strengths and weaknesses in a human rights-based approach to international development - an analysis of a rights-based approach to development assistance based on practical experiences. Int J Hum Rights 22(5):664–680

Bunn ID (2000) The right to development: implications for international economic law. Am Univ Int Law Rev 15(6):1425–1467

Cafaro (2012) Il governo delle organizzazioni di Bretton Woods. Analisi critica, processi di revisione in atto e proposte di riforma. Giappichelli, Torino

Cassese S et al (2012) Global administrative law: an Italian perspective. European University Institute, Florence

Ciorciari JD (2000) The lawful scope of human rights criteria in World Bank credit decisions: an interpretive analysis of the IBRD and IDA Articles of Agreement. Cornell Int Law J 33(2):331–371

Cissé (2011) Should the political prohibition in charters of international financial institutions be revisited? The case of the World Bank. In: Cissé H, Bradlow D, Kingsbury B (eds) The World Bank legal review, international financial institutions and global legal governance. World Bank, Washington, DC, pp 59–92

[196] UN Human Rights Council (2018).

[197] UN Office of the High Commissioner for Human Rights (2022, p. 59).

Clark DL (2002) The World Bank and human rights: the need for greater accountability. Harv Hum Rights J 15:205–226

Compliance Advisor Ombudsman (2003) A review of IFC's safeguard policies. Core business: achieving consistent and excellent environmental and social outcomes. January 2003. https://www.cao-ombudsman.org/. Accessed 2 May 2025

Crippa AL (2010) Multilateral development banks and the human rights responsibility. Am Univ Int Law Rev 25(3):531–577

Dañino R (2005) The legal aspects of the World Bank's work on human rights: some preliminary thoughts. In: Alston P, Robinson M (eds) Human rights and development: towards mutual reinforcement. OUP, Oxford, pp 509–524

Dañino R (2006) Legal opinion on human rights and the work of the World Bank. https://opil.ouplaw.com/. Accessed 28 April 2025

Dann P (2019) Institutional law and development governance: an introduction. LDR 12:537–560

Dann P, Riegner M (2019) The World Bank's environmental and social safeguards and the evolution of global order. LJIL 32(3):537–559. https://doi.org/10.1017/S0922156519000293

Darrow M (2003) Between light and shadow: the World Bank, the International Monetary Fund and international human rights law. Hart Publishing, Oxford

Doemeland D, Trevino J (2014) Which World Bank reports are widely read? https://documents1.worldbank.org/. Accessed 24 April 2025

Fritz V, Levy B, Ort R (2015) Problem-driven political economy analysis: the World Bank's experience. World Bank, Washington, DC

Ghebali VY (1985) The politicisation of UN specialised agencies: a preliminary analysis. Millenn J Int Stud 14(3):317–334. https://doi.org/10.1177/03058298850140030501

Gianaris WN (1990) Weighted voting in the International Monetary Fund and the World Bank. Fordham Int Law J 14(4):910–945

Gianviti F (2005) Economic, social and cultural human rights and the International Monetary Fund. In: Alston P (ed) Non-state actors and human rights. OUP, Oxford, pp 113–139

Gille C, Roos SR (2002) World Bank, IMF and human rights: conference held at Tilburg University, 11-13 October, 2001. GLJ 3(2):E8

Green KM, Raphael A (2000) Third environmental assessment review (FY 96-00). World Bank, Washington, DC

Head JW (2008) Law and policy in international financial institutions: the changing role of law in the IMF and the multilateral development banks. Kan J Law Pub Policy 17:194–229

Heckelman JC, Knack S, Rogers FH (2011) Crossing the thresholds: an analysis of the IBRD graduation policy. World Bank, Washington, DC

Hunter D (1996) The role of the World Bank in strengthening governance, civil society, human rights. In: Lending credibility: new mandates and partnerships for the World Bank. Available via World Bank. https://documents1.worldbank.org/curated/en/248181468139494966/pdf/455400WP00BOX334106B01PUBLIC1.pdf. Accessed 24 April 2025

Hunter D (2010) Internal law and public participation in policy-making at the international financial institutions. In: Bradlow D, Hunter D (eds) International financial institutions and international law. Wolters Kluwer, Alphen aan den Rijn, pp 199–238

Independent Evaluation Group (2006) The World Bank's economic and sector work and technical assistance, an Independent Evaluation Group (IEG) review. https://documents1.worldbank.org/. Accessed 24 April 2025

Independent Evaluation Group (2008) The World Bank's economic and sector work and technical assistance, FY00-06. https://documents1.worldbank.org/. Accessed 24 April 2025

Independent Evaluation Group (2009) Evaluation of the World Bank Group's experience with safeguard and sustainability policies (1999-2008). https://documents1.worldbank.org/. Accessed 28 April 2025

Independent Evaluation Group (2010) Safeguards and sustainability policies in a changing world. An independent evaluation of World Bank Group experience. https://documents1.worldbank.org/. Accessed 29 April 2025

Independent Evaluation Group (2015) Managing environmental and social risks in development policy financing. https://documents1.worldbank.org/. Accessed 29 April 2025

Independent Evaluation Group (2022) Results and performance of the World Bank Group. https://ieg.worldbankgroup.org/. Accessed 24 April 2025

International Bank for Reconstruction and Development (1978) World development report. https://documents1.worldbank.org/. Accessed 28 April 2025

International Bank for Reconstruction and Development (1994) Governance: the World Bank's experience. World Bank, Washington, DC

International Centre for Settlement of Investment Disputes (2021) Introducing ICSID: the global leader in international investment dispute settlement. https://icsid.worldbank.org/. Accessed 24 April 2025

International Finance Corporation (1993) Environmental analysis and review of international finance corporation projects. International Finance Corporation, Washington, DC

International Finance Corporation (2005) Investing in progress with experience, innovation, and partnership, annual report, vol I. https://openknowledge.worldbank.org/. Accessed 2 May 2025

International Finance Corporation (2009) IFC's Policy and Performance Standards on social and environmental sustainability and Policy on disclosure of information: report on the first three years of application. https://documents.worldbank.org/. Accessed 2 May 2025

International Finance Corporation (2016) IFC: the first six decades, leading the way in private sector development, a history. https://documents1.worldbank.org/. Accessed 24 April 2025

Jayarajah C, Branson W (1995) Structural and sectoral adjustment, World Bank experience, 1980-92. World Bank, Washington, DC

Kingsbury B, Krisch N, Stewart RB (2005) The emergence of global administrative law. Law & CP 68:15–62

Klein (2019) International organizations or institutions, internal law and rules. MPEPIL. OUP, Oxford. https://opil.ouplaw.com. Accessed 24 April 2025

Kloeve E (2019) Nordic Trust Fund completion report 2009-2018: ten years of building knowledge on human rights in the World Bank Group. World Bank, Washington, DC

Koeberle S et al (2005) Conditionality revisited, concepts, experiences and lessons. World Bank, Washington, DC

Krever T (2011) The legal turn in late development theory: the rule of law and the World Bank's development model. Harv Int Law J 52(1):287–319

Kumar M (2016) The World Bank and human rights. World Affairs J Int Iss 20(1):110–125

Lee C (2001) International Finance Corporation: financing environmentally and socially sustainable private investment. In: Schlemmer-Schulte S, Tung KY (eds) Liber Amicorum Ibrahim F.I. Shihata. International finance and development law. Kluwer Law International, The Hague, pp 469–481

Lindbaek J, Pfeffermann G, Gregory N (1998) The evolving role of multilateral development banks: history and prospects. In: International financial institutions in the 21st century. European Investment Bank papers. Available via EIB. https://www.eib.org/files/efs/eibpapers/eibpapers_1998_v03_n02_en.pdf. Accessed 24 April 2025

Lyons GM, Baldwin DA, McNemar DW (1977) The 'politicization' issue in the UN specialized agencies. In: Kay DA (ed) The changing United Nations: options for the United States, vol 32. Praeger Publishers, New York-London, pp 81–92

Maasland A, van der Gaag J (1991) World Bank-supported adjustment programs and living conditions. In: Corbo V, Fischer S, Webb SB (eds) Adjustment lending revisited, policies to restore growth, a World Bank symposium. World Bank, Washington, DC, pp 40–63

Malaguti MC (2017) Sviluppo e diritto internazionale dell'economia. In: Triggiani E et al (eds) Dialoghi con Ugo Villani. Cacucci, Bari, pp 560–578

Mauro MR (2015) The protection of non-economic values and the evolution of international economic organizations: the case of the World Bank. In: Virzo R, Ingravallo I (eds) Evolutions in the law of international organizations. Brill Nijhoff, Leiden-Boston, pp 244–274

McInerney-Lankford S (2010) International financial institutions and human rights: select perspectives on legal obligations. In: Bradlow D, Hunter D (eds) International financial institutions and international law. Wolters Kluwer, Alphen aan den Rijn, pp 239–285

McInerney-Lankford S (2023) International human rights law, politics and international financial institutions: the case of the World Bank. In: Andreassen B (ed) Research handbook on the politics of human rights law. Edward Elgar, Cheltenham-Northampton, pp 339–364

Michalopoulos C (1987) World Bank programs for adjustment and growth. In: Khan MS, Goldstein M, Corbo V (eds) Growth-oriented adjustment programs. Proceedings of a symposium held in Washington, DC, February 1987. International Monetary Fund, Washington, DC, pp 15–62

Morris S (2023) Development finance cooperation amidst great power competition: what role for the World Bank. Oxf Rev Econ Policy 39(2):379–388

Morse B, Berger TR (1992) Sardor Sarovar: report of the independent review. Resource Futures International, Ottawa

Organisation for Economic Co-operation and Development (2010) Quality standards for development evaluation, DAC guidelines and reference series. https://www.oecd.org/. Accessed 2 May 2025

Palacio A (2006) The way forward, human rights and the World Bank: special report. In: Development outreach, human rights and development, vol 8. World Bank, Washington, DC, pp 35–37

Palombino FM (2018) Fair and equitable treatment and the fabric of general principles. TMC Asser Press: The Hague; Springer: Berlin

Park (2010) World Bank Group interactions with environmentalists: changing international organisation identities. Manchester University Press, Manchester

Payer C (1982) World Bank: a critical analysis. NYU Press, New York

Picciotto R, Weaving R (1994) A new project cycle for the World Bank? In: Finance & development. International Monetary Fund, Washington, DC

Salomon ME (2006) The significance of the UN task force on the right to development. In: Development outreach, human rights and development, vol 8. World Bank, Washington, DC, pp 27–29

Seatzu F (2008) Il Panel di ispezione della banca mondiale. Contributo allo studio della funzione di controllo nelle banche internazionali di sviluppo. Giappichelli, Torino

Shihata IFI (1988) The World Bank and human rights: an analysis of the legal issues and the record of achievements. Denv J Int Law Policy 17(1):39–66

Shihata IFI (1995) Prohibition of political activities in the Bank's work legal opinion by the Senior Vice President & General Counsel. World Bank, Washington, DC

Shihata IFI (1997) Role of the World Bank's General Counsel. In: Hargrove JL (ed) Implementation, compliance and effectiveness. Proceedings of the 91st Annual Meeting of the American Society of International Law, 9–12 April 1997, Washington, DC, vol 91. CUP, Cambridge, pp 214–222

Shihata IFI (1999) The creative role of the lawyer - example: the office of the World Bank's General Counsel. Cath Univ Law Rev 48(4):1041–1053

Shihata IFI (2000a) The World Bank in a changing world, vol III. Brill, The Hague-London-Boston

Shihata IFI (2000b) The World Bank legal papers. Martinus Nijhoff Publishers, The Hague-Boston-London

Shihata IFI (2000c) The World Bank Inspection Panel: in practice, 2nd edn. OUP, Oxford-New York

Streeten PP (1979) Basic needs: premises and promises. World Bank, Washington, DC

Subacchi P, Vines D (2023) Fifty years on: what the Bretton woods system can teach us about global macroeconomic policy-making. Oxf Rev Econ Policy 39(2):164–182

Szasz PC (1979) The international legal aspects of the human rights program of the United States. Cornell Int Law J 12(2):161–174

The World Bank (2004) The World Bank annual report 2004, vol 1. https://documents1.worldbank.org/. Accessed 28 April 2025

The World Bank (2005) Equity and development, world development report 2006. World Bank, Washington, DC

The World Bank (2007) Conditionality in development policy lending. Report 41581. 15 November 2007. https://documents1.worldbank.org/. Accessed 24 April 2025

The World Bank (2009) 2009 Development policy retrospective: flexibility, customization and results. Report 52207. 25 November 2009. https://documents1.worldbank.org/. Accessed 24 April 2025

The World Bank (2022a) 2021 Development policy restrospective: facing crisis, fostering recovery. https://documents1.worldbank.org/. Accessed 24 April 2025

The World Bank (2022b) Helping countries adapt to a changing world. Annual report. https://documents1.worldbank.org/. Accessed 24 April 2025

The World Bank (2022c) Environmental & social framework for IPF operations, addressing sexual exploitation and abuse and sexual harassment (SEA/SH) in human development operations, Good Practice Note. https://thedocs.worldbank.org/. Accessed 30 April 2025

The World Bank (2024) Investment Project Financing (IPF) with a Deferred Drawdown Option (DDO). https://thedocs.worldbank.org/. Accessed 24 April 2025

The World Bank Group (2014) World Bank Group: a new approach to country engagement. https://documents1.worldbank.org/. Accessed 2 May 2025

The World Bank Group (2015) 2015 Development policy financing retrospective, results and sustainability. https://thedocs.worldbank.org/. Accessed 30 April 2025

The World Bank Group (2016) First loan for pollution control, Brazil. https://documents1.worldbank.org/. Accessed 24 April 2025

The World Bank Group (2020) World Bank Group strategy for fragility, conflict, and violence 2020-2025. https://documents1.worldbank.org/. Accessed 29 April 2025

The World Bank Group (2021) Climate change action plan 2021–2025: supporting green, resilient, and inclusive development. https://openknowledge.worldbank.org/. Accessed 28 April 2025

The World Bank Operations Policy and Country Services (2005) Review of World Bank conditionality. https://documents1.worldbank.org/. Accessed 24 April 2025

The World Bank Operations Policy and Country Services (2011) Towards open knowledge: the state of World Bank knowledge services. https://documents1.worldbank.org/. Accessed 24 April 2025

The World Bank Operations Policy and Country Services (2012) Investment lending reforms: modernizing and consolidating operational policies and procedures. https://documents1.worldbank.org/. Accessed 29 April 2025

Tignino M (2020) Human rights standards in international finance and development: the challenges ahead. In: McIntyre O, Nanwani S (eds) The practice of Independent Accountability Mechanisms (IAMs): towards good governance in development finance. Brill Nijhoff, Leiden-Boston, pp 105–133

UN (1967) Consultation with the International Bank for Reconstruction and Development: report of the Secretary-General of 15 September 1967. https://legal.un.org/. Accessed 24 April 2025

UN (1995) Report of the UN World Summit for social development, Copenhagen, 6–12 March 1995. UN Doc. A/CONF.166/9. https://docs.un.org/. Accessed 28 April 2025

UN (2003) The human rights based approach to development cooperation. Towards a common understanding among UN agencies. UN, New York

UN Commission on Human Rights (1999) Report of the Independent Expert on the effects of structural adjustment policies on the full enjoyment of human rights, 55th Session, 1999. UN Doc. E/CN.4/1999/50. https://docs.un.org/E/CN.4/1999/50. Accessed 24 April 2025

UN Committee on Economic, Social and Cultural Rights (1991) General Comment No. 4: the right to adequate housing, Article 11(1) of the Covenant, 6th Session. UN Doc. HRI/GEN/1/Rev.8. https://docs.un.org/. Accessed 24 April 2025

UN General Assembly (1965a) Implementation of the Declaration on the Granting of Independence to Colonial Countries and Peoples. Resolution 2105 (XX) of 20 December 1965. UN Doc. A/RES/2105. https://docs.un.org/. Accessed 24 April 2025

UN General Assembly (1965b) Question of Territories Under Portuguese Administration. Resolution 2107 (XX) of 21 December 1965. UN Doc. A/RES/2107. https://docs.un.org/. Accessed 24 April 2025

UN General Assembly (1966) The policies of apartheid of the Government of the Republic of South Africa. Resolution 2202 (XXI) of 16 December 1966. UN Doc. A/RES/2307. https://docs.un.org/. Accessed 24 April 2025

UN General Assembly (1986) Declaration on the Right to Development. Resolution 41/128 of 4 December 1986. UN Doc. A/Res/41/128. https://docs.un.org/. Accessed 28 April 2025

UN General Assembly (1990) World Conference on Human Rights. Resolution 45/155 of 18 December 1990. UN Doc. A/RES/45/155. https://docs.un.org/. Accessed 28 April 2025

UN General Assembly (2005) In larger freedom: towards development, security and human rights for all: report of the Secretary-General. 26 May 2005. UN Doc. A/59/2005/Add.3. https://docs.un.org/. Accessed 29 April 2025

UN General Assembly (2006a) Human rights and extreme poverty. Resolution 61/157 of 19 December 2006. UN Doc. A/RES/61/157. https://docs.un.org/. Accessed 29 April 2025

UN General Assembly (2006b) International financial systems and development. Resolution 61/187 of 20 December 2006. UN Doc. A/RES/61/187. https://documents.un.org/. Accessed 29 April 2025

UN General Assembly (2020) The interplay between the economic policies and safeguards of international financial institutions and good governance at the local level. Report of the Independent Expert on the Promotion of a Democratic and Equitable International Order. 10 August 2020. UN Doc. A/HRC/45/28. https://documents.un.org/. Accessed 30 April 2025

UN Human Rights Council (2018) Improving accountability and access to remedy for victims of business-related human rights abuse: the relevance of human rights due diligence to determinations of corporate liability. Report of the United Nations High Commissioner for Human Rights. 1 June 2018. UN Doc. A/HRC/38/20/Add.2. https://docs.un.org/. Accessed 30 April 2025

UN Millennium Project (2005) Investing in development: a practical plan to achieve the Millennium Development Goals. James & James (Science Publishers), London-Sterling

UN Office of the High Commissioner for Human Rights (2022) Remedy in development finance: guidance and practice. UN, New York-Geneva

Uvin P (2007) From the right to development to the rights-based approach: how 'human rights' entered development. Dev Pract 17(4–5):597–606

van Genugten W (2003) Tilburg Guiding Principles on World Bank, IMF and human rights. In: van Genugten W, Hunt P, Mathews SM (eds) World Bank, IMF and human rights. Wolf Legal Publishers, Nijmegen, pp 247–255

Wapenhans WA (1992) Effective implementation: key to development impact. World Bank, Washington, DC

Wolfensohn JD (2000) The comprehensive development framework. World Bank, Washington, DC

Young ME (1996) Early child development: investing in the future. World Bank, Washington, DC

Chapter 3
Relevant Practice Concerning Indigenous Peoples in Public Sector Projects

3.1 The Interface of World Bank's Indigenous Peoples Policies with International Law

Among Multilateral Development Banks, the World Bank has been a pioneer in establishing a comprehensive set of internal rules that set specific standards for investment project financing operations involving indigenous peoples, who are among the vulnerable groups most significantly impacted by this type of operations. As reported by the Bank, indigenous peoples retain 80% of the world's remaining biodiversity and 36% of the remaining intact forests. Besides directly preserving these areas, they hold vital ancestral knowledge and expertise on how to adapt, mitigate, and reduce climate and disaster risks.[1] The Bank's evolving operational framework for projects involving indigenous peoples is of particular importance, given its strong interconnections with the broader set of environmental and social safeguard policies. Indigenous peoples frequently inhabit critical ecosystems that need to be preserved *per se* (OP/BP 4.04 on Natural Habitats and 4.36 on Forests; new ESS-6 on Biodiversity Conservation).[2] They also bear a strong cultural heritage component, closely linked to their sacred sites (OP/BP 4.11 on Physical Cultural Resources, new ESS-8 on Cultural Heritage).[3] Last but not least, displacement of populations from their territories as a consequence of project operations is a highly sensitive issue due to the profound and often devastating effects on their cultural identity,

[1] Information available on the World Bank's website, at: https://www.worldbank.org/en/topic/indigenouspeoples. Accessed 2 May 2025.

[2] The World Bank, *Environmental and Social Framework*, 2017, pp. 67–72.

[3] ibid., pp. 85–88.

S. Solidoro, *Indigenous Peoples in the World Bank Group's Practice*, European Yearbook of International Economic Law,
https://doi.org/10.1007/978-3-032-05147-9_3

livelihoods, and connection to ancestral lands (OP/BP 4.12 on Involuntary Resettlement, new ESS-5 on Land Acquisition).[4]

In the last few years, the World Bank's attention towards the matter has followed innovative paths. Inclusion of indigenous peoples currently represents one of the topics at the forefront of its development agenda. Recently, the Bank has acknowledged the critical importance of increasing its staff's awareness of the human rights of indigenous peoples in order to enhance the quality of its engagement in this area, both through advisory services and operational work.[5]

Historically, the World Bank began playing a key role in supporting the promotion of indigenous peoples' rights in connection with its financing activities in the 1980s. In a study initiated in 1982, just before the issuance of the first policy on the matter, the Bank's Office of Environmental Affairs highlighted that an increasing number of international instruments were being adopted to recognize traditional tribal land tenure, protect social and cultural rights, and preserve the identity of indigenous communities.

A basic list of such instruments was contained in an annex to the main document,[6] including hard and soft legal sources, such as the International Bill of Human Rights, the ILO Discrimination (Employment and Occupation) Convention (1960),[7] the UN Declaration on the Elimination of All Forms of Racial Discrimination (1963) and the related Convention,[8] in addition to the ILO Convention No. 107 of 26 June 1957,[9] the first international treaty ever addressing indigenous peoples' rights, among others. In a section devoted to 'International Legislation', the study emphasized that, as a specialized agency of the UN, the Bank could not support projects posing a serious risk of harm to 'tribal groups', while also underscoring the importance of ensuring that member countries, as signatories to the UN Charter, complied with these international legal instruments in lending operations:

> The Bank, as an affiliate of the United Nations, should prudently be assured that those borrowers who are signatory to the UN charter are complying with the spirit of the United Nations charter, international covenants, treaties, and agreements, when it lends for projects

---

[4] ibid., pp. 53–64.

[5] In pursuit of this critical objective, the Bank has provided grants for a series of workshops to be held at both the global and regional levels, focusing on international standards related to indigenous peoples. The workshops are directed at encouraging the adoption of a human rights-based approach to development in Bank's operations. See The World Bank (2019a, p. 11).

[6] Goodland (1984, pp. 38–39).

[7] International Labour Organization, *Discrimination (Employment and Occupation) Convention*, C111, Geneva, 4 June 1958 (entered into effect on 16 June 1960).

[8] UN General Assembly, *Declaration on the Elimination of All Forms of Racial Discrimination*, Resolution 1904 (XVIII) of 20 November 1963, UN Doc. A/RES/18/1904; UN General Assembly, *International Convention on the Elimination of All Forms of Racial Discrimination*, Resolution 2106 (XX) of 21 December 1965 (entered into effect on 4 January 1969), UN Doc. A/RES/2106 (XX), in *UNTS*, Volume 660, p. 195 f.

[9] International Labour Organization, *Indigenous and Tribal Populations Convention*, C107, Geneva, 26 June 1957 (entered into effect on 2 June 1959).

> affecting tribal people. Clearly, the Bank cannot assist borrowers with projects if tribal groups may be seriously harmed thereby.

Against this backdrop, the study shed light on the main features of the emerging internal Bank's framework applicable to investment projects, clarifying that principles widely recognized in international law, such as equality and non-discrimination, were commonly applied. The study also emphasized the significance of the Bank's role in advancing indigenous peoples' rights at the national level, particularly through supporting borrowers in implementing legislation aligning with international conventions or the UN Charter. In the absence of such legislation, the Bank could encourage dialogue aimed at introducing new legal measures. Additionally, the Bank could seek to include appropriate covenants in project agreements to mitigate potential risks:

> Where legislation that is consistent with international conventions or the UN charter exists, project design will assist in implementing such legislation to the extent that Bank projects may affect tribal areas. Where no legislation exists, the Bank will discuss with the borrower how the risks of the investment may be decreased and the design improved by, for example, the enactment of legislation before the project becomes effective. Or the Bank may include project covenants that would accord affected tribal groups an appropriate status with non-tribals, as well as any necessary measures to protect tribal culture and resource bases.[10]

Shortly thereafter, in February 1982, the Bank adopted its first formal policy on 'Tribal People in Bank-financed Projects', also known as Operational Manual Statement 2.34 (OMS 2.34). The statement included several provisions reflecting the spirit of the ILO Convention of 1957. For instance, its definition of tribal peoples referring to ethnic groups exhibiting characteristics such as limited or partial integration into the dominant society's social norms ('Characteristics' section, paragraph 2) closely mirrors the terminology used in the initial part of the Convention to define its subjective scope of application. Furthermore, the primary objective of the statement—that development projects involving tribal peoples should allow time and conditions for acculturation within the borrower countries' territories—aligns with the actions that State parties to the ILO Convention were obligated to undertake.[11] At the same time, OMS 2.34 explicitly integrated the principles of equality and non-discrimination into the Bank's framework, asserting that, as most tribal peoples did not receive the same national or local social services typically available to other citizens due to their unique characteristics, the inclusion of specific project components to safeguard their interests and, whenever feasible, to enhance their well-being, was necessary. This aligns with Article 2.2.a of the ILO Convention, which stipulates that governments' actions should include measures ensuring that tribal peoples can benefit on an equal footing from the rights and opportunities granted to citizens by national laws or regulations.

---

[10] Goodland (1984, p. 12).

[11] According to Article 2.1 of the ILO Convention of 1957, «Governments shall have the primary responsibility for developing co-ordinated and systematic action for the protection of the populations concerned and their progressive integration into the life of their respective countries».

Delving deeper into the implications of OMS 2.34 within the project context, the statement outlined the respective tasks assigned to both the Bank and the borrower throughout the project cycle, drawing a general system of responsibility distribution that reflects its modern guise. Specifically, it envisaged: (i) the Bank's preliminary *identification* of the location and 'degree of acculturation' of tribal peoples; (ii) the borrower's design of a 'tribal component' at an early stage of the project (noting that it was most effectively designed before or during project *preparation*); (iii) the Bank's assessment of the tribal component, alongside an evaluation of the borrower's national legal framework, during *appraisal* (prior to loan approval); (iv) the Bank's *supervision* during project *implementation*, potentially encompassing the tribal component update and its reassessment.[12]

A very relevant clause encompassing the Bank's commitment to the preservation of their land rights held that «[a]s a general policy, the Bank will not assist development projects that knowingly involve encroachment on traditional territories being used or occupied by tribal people unless adequate safeguards are provided». With increasing momentum, the operational statement continued by indicating that when producing undesired effects, projects were supposed to be designed so as to prevent or mitigate them, concluding that: «[t]he Bank will assist projects *only* when satisfied that the Borrower or relevant government agency supports and can implement measures that will effectively safeguard the integrity and well-being of the tribal people». ('General Policies' section, paragraph 5).

Thus, the tribal component developed by borrowers played a pivotal role, encompassing a range of substantial measures to adjust the project in accordance with indigenous peoples' rights protection. These measures included the recognition and demarcation of areas containing resources essential for sustaining their traditional livelihoods, the maintenance of their health and cultural integrity, and the establishment of a forum to ensure their participation in relevant decisions, in addition to adjudication and redress of grievances.[13]

Following the adoption of OMS 2.34, several developments took place within the Bank. In 1987, in the aftermath of its institutional reorganization, the Bank started paying more attention to the performance of projects affecting tribal peoples. The process aimed at recasting OMS 2.34 was thus set in motion. In this regard, it is important to highlight that the reviews systematically carried out by the Bank since then, aimed at facilitating policy revisions, are of crucial relevance as they provide insight into the reasoning behind the choices that led to the development of the various versions of the instruments over time. Since these reviews often considered the evolution of relevant international law, which led to the substantial incorporation of its principles into investment project frameworks, their analytical approach will be given the utmost consideration in this context.

In the absence of written procedural guidelines establishing the procedure to be followed in the (development or) modification of its policies and procedures, the

[12] The World Bank Operations Policy and Country Services (2011), Annex 1, pp. 44–46.

[13] ibid., paras. 7–8, 'Tribal Component in Development Projects' section.

Bank initially carried out this process at the internal level exclusively. It began to envision the involvement of civil society stakeholders, which led to the development of a more democratic-oriented procedure only at a later stage, with the adoption of safeguards.

The review related to OMS 2.34, the first ever conducted, was entirely internal. Launched in 1989 and managed by the Office of Environmental and Scientific Affairs, it was developed in close collaboration with specialists from the International Labour Organization, who used the newly adopted ILO Convention No. 169 of 1989,[14] updating and replacing the 1957 version, as a guiding framework.[15] Specifically, it analyzed 33 projects implemented between 1982 and 1986, known to have had demonstrable effects on indigenous peoples' lands, resources, and culture. The results were shared with each of the five regional offices of the Bank. One of the main conclusions was that the Bank had made significant progress in identifying tribal peoples potentially affected by projects, while admitting that the design of tribal components remained unsystematic. Overall, the review emphasized the need to broaden the scope of the policy, which, according to Bank staff, had primarily been interpreted as applying to relatively small and isolated groups, such as the Rainforest Indians of South America or the *Pygmies* or *Bushmen* of Central and Southern Africa. This interpretation, however, although justified by the wording of OMS 2.34, excluded larger and more heterogeneous tribal populations, which, though integrated into national and regional political economies, still maintained a strong sense of ethnic identity and cultural distinctiveness.[16] Clearly, a new definition, more focused on the recognition, and appreciation, of diverse socio-cultural systems as such, was needed. By that time, the promotion of inclusion for poor and marginalized people worldwide had already become part of the Bank's agenda, driven by the growing emphasis on participatory forms of development and the integration of social and cultural analysis into its investment programs. In 1991, after two years of internal discussion, the Bank approved the new version of the policy (OD 4.20 or 'the Directive').[17]

As pointed out by Shelton Davis, a World Bank sociologist whose work primarily focused on developing policies to safeguard the rights of indigenous communities, the result was a more pronounced alignment of the Bank's approach with contemporary international legal thinking on the matter.[18]

---

[14] International Labour Organization, *Convention concerning Indigenous and Tribal Peoples in Independent Countries*, C169, Geneva, 27 June 1989 (entered into effect on 5 September 1991).

[15] The World Bank Operations Policy and Country Services (2011, p. 1).

[16] Davis (2021, pp. 197–198). The original version of this article was prepared for a panel discussion on 'Indigenous Peoples and Ethnic Minorities' at the Denver Initiative Conference on Human Rights, University of Denver Law School, Colorado, April 1993. Notably, the author formally contributed to the independent desk review of OD 4.20 conducted by the Operations Evaluation Department in 2003.

[17] The World Bank Operations Policy and Country Services (2011), Annex 2, pp. 0–6.

[18] Davis (2021, p. 204).

OD 4.20 represents the earliest modern version of the Bank's policy on indigenous peoples for several reasons. First of all, the definitional criteria used to identify them are much more comprehensive than those contained in OMS 2.34. The Directive introduced the term 'indigenous peoples' and equated it to other expressions, such as 'indigenous ethnic minorities', 'tribal groups', and 'scheduled tribes'. Its subjective scope of application was thus particularly wide in principle. This was certainly a major innovation compared to OMS 2.34, most likely brought by the influence exerted by the language employed by the second version of the ILO Convention adopted in 1989, two years prior to the introduction of the new policy. Notably, in defining its boundaries, the policy instrument employed for the first time the concept of 'vulnerability', holding that all the above-mentioned expressions had to be referred to «groups with a social and cultural identity distinct from the dominant society that makes them vulnerable to being disadvantaged in the development process» (paragraph 3). Furthermore, all these different social groups were drawn together by a very concise list of characteristics that, when present, could help identify them, such as: (i) a close attachment to ancestral territories and natural resources; (ii) self-identification (and identification by others) as a distinct cultural group; (iii) an indigenous language, often different from the national one; (iv) presence of customary social and political institutions; and (v) subsistence-oriented production (paragraph 5). The policy also explicitly held that, given the existence of various contexts in which indigenous peoples were found, no single definition could capture their diversity. In this regard, national legislation could provide a preliminary basis only for their identification. It is interesting to note that, besides being consistent with the ILO Convention of 1989, which mainly relies on the self-identification criterion to identify indigenous and tribal peoples (Article 1.2), the policy provisions also adhered to the findings of a seminal study on discrimination against indigenous populations carried out by the UN Special Rapporteur Martínez Cobo in 1982.[19] This piece of work laid the foundations for modern international human rights legal thinking in this field and led to the establishment, during the same year, of the first UN mechanism with a mandate to exclusively address issues related to indigenous peoples, the Working Group on Indigenous Populations, replaced by the Expert Mechanism in 2007. The study, based on a survey of the definition of indigenous peoples used at that time across a wide sample of countries, concluded that the elements typically considered were twofold. On one hand, substantial importance was placed on objective criteria such as ancestry, culture, and language. On the other hand, it noted that self-identification, as a subjective criterion, was gaining increasing significance. Lastly, it remarked that differentiating between purely subjective and objective elements remained a challenging task.[20]

That said, several other key features of OD 4.20 warrant special attention due to their innovative nature for the following reasons:

---

[19] Martínez Cobo was appointed Special Rapporteur in 1971 by the Sub-Commission on the Prevention of Discrimination and the Protection of Minorities, a subsidiary body of the UN Commission on Human Rights.

[20] UN Commission on Human Rights (1983, para. 21).

(a) The Directive explicitly introduced the concept of full respect of indigenous peoples' 'human rights', in addition to their dignity and cultural uniqueness as an overall objective of the policy (paragraph 6), a statement that has been reiterated in all the subsequent versions, albeit with some modifications. Furthermore, in the section dedicated to the general description of the policy objectives, a provision regarding the direct involvement of indigenous peoples in issues affecting them introduced the term *informed participation* for the first time, emphasizing the crucial importance of providing adequate guarantees for their full and effective engagement (paragraph 8). This provision reflected the then-current status of international indigenous human rights discourse, not mature to the point of considering informed consent as a consolidated tenet instrumental to the fulfillment of the self-determination right in the context of development projects, yet making its way towards it. In this regard, Article 6.1.a of the 1989 ILO Convention prescribes that governments consult indigenous peoples through appropriate procedures, particularly through their representative institutions, and carry out this consultation in good faith, although in the different context of legislative or administrative measures that may affect them directly. It also mandates that governments «establish means by which these peoples can freely participate, to at least the same extent as other sectors of the population, at all levels of decision-making»,[21] for the purpose of achieving agreement or consent to the proposed measures as a general norm.[22] Consistent with OD 4.20, in the specific context of development projects, the Convention indicates that indigenous peoples «shall *participate* in the formulation, implementation and evaluation of plans and programmes for national and regional development which may affect them directly» [*italics added*].[23]

(b) Another provision in the same section provided the Bank with a means of rejecting the borrower's proposal for obtaining the financing before entering into a contractual relationship with it: «[c]ases will occur, especially when dealing with the most isolated groups, where adverse impacts are unavoidable and adequate mitigation plans have not been developed. In such situations, the Bank will not appraise projects until suitable plans are developed by the borrower and reviewed by the Bank» (paragraph 9). Compared to the previous version enshrined in OMS 2.34, this clause seems more focused on the importance of developing suitable plans to be approved by the Bank than on the substantial result of 'effectively safeguarding' indigenous peoples' well-being. However, a closer examination reveals that it merely clarifies the procedural approach the Bank should follow when deciding whether or not to assist a project, placing this decision within the broader context of the project cycle. The additional statement in the same paragraph, which asserts that «[i]n sum, a full range of

[21] International Labour Organization, *Convention concerning Indigenous and Tribal Peoples in Independent Countries*, C169, Geneva, 27 June 1989 (entered into effect on 5 September 1991), Article 6.1.b.

[22] ibid., Article 6.2.

[23] ibid., Article 7.1.

positive actions by the borrower must *ensure that indigenous people benefit from development investments*», [*italics added*] supports this interpretation.

(c) In clarifying the Bank's role in addressing issues related to indigenous peoples, OD 4.20 explicitly listed the three different activities through which the institution committed to protecting their rights, with a significant impact on countries planning on requesting funds or actual borrowers using such funds during the project implementation. These were (and still are), namely: (i) the preparation of country Economic and Sector Work, currently falling under the category of Advisory Services and Analytics, aimed at building a record of information on national trends, forming the basis of the Bank-country dialogue and potentially leading to the enhancement of the national policy framework or the institutional capacity of prospective borrowers. Clearly, as specified by the Directive, this represented a pre-condition for designing and implementing stronger project components dealing with indigenous peoples and it was thus instrumental for providing funds to the involved country (paragraph 11); (ii) the delivery of technical assistance throughout the project cycle, and especially during its preparation, to reinforce the relevant government institutions or even to support development initiatives taken by indigenous peoples themselves (paragraph 12); (iii) the actual funding of investment projects, an activity expected to include a development plan consistent with the Bank's policy when affecting indigenous peoples (paragraph 13).

(d) On the last point, it is worth stressing that, as in the previous version reflected in OMS 2.34, the Directive required the borrower to prepare a specific component, renamed Indigenous Peoples Development Plan ('IPDP'), to be either included within broad Bank-funded development projects, or, when indigenous peoples were the main beneficiaries, identified with the project itself. The Directive included several provisions detailing its prerequisites, both in terms of contents and technical, institutional, and financial arrangements (paragraphs 14–15). Using more rigorous language than OMS 2.34, it clarified that the IPDP was solely the borrower's responsibility; at the same time, it was expected to be available for the Bank's review before project appraisal (paragraph 18). Notably, among the elements to be included in the plan by the borrower, in addition to a comprehensive diagnosis of the socioeconomic context, one of the most relevant was the strengthening of national or local legislation regulating land tenure issues, when necessary, with the Bank's assistance, for the purpose of «establishing legal recognition of the customary or traditional land tenure systems of indigenous peoples». The Directive also stipulated that, for traditional lands brought into State domain, alternative arrangements should be implemented «to grant long-term, renewable rights of custodianship and use to indigenous peoples» over such lands (paragraph 15.c).

(e) Another key provision is the one detailing the procedural guarantees ensuring indigenous peoples' participation in decision-making processes throughout all phases of the project cycle, to be incorporated into the IPDP by the borrower. Besides stating that proper mechanisms should be devised and maintained to this end in quite a formal manner, the Directive included some observations of crucial relevance. Notably, when emphasizing the importance of indigenous representative organizations, especially in large groups, OD 4.20 stated that these organizations were best suited to provide «effective channels for communicating local preferences», while also recognizing the pivotal role played by traditional leaders in ensuring genuine representation (paragraph 15.d).[24] In this regard, OD 4.20 fully aligns with the provisions of the 1989 ILO Convention, according to which governments shall «consult the peoples concerned, through appropriate procedures and in particular through their representative institutions».[25]

(f) OD 4.20 introduced another significant innovation by formalizing the borrower's commitment to implementing the IPDP, prescribing the incorporation of the plan into the loan documents. This aspect is of utmost relevance, as it conferred binding value to the IPDP. Furthermore, the same provision stipulated that Bank staff should be provided with clear benchmarks to facilitate supervisory functions through *ad hoc* legal provisions (paragraph 20), thus formalizing the role to be played by the borrower *vis-à-vis* the Bank in the phase following implementation.

Just a year after the introduction of OD 4.20, in 1992, following the general Management's decision to carry out its policy conversion process, Directives—overtly containing a mix of policies, procedures and guidance notes reflecting what should have been sought rather than what could have been done in practice—started being replaced by safeguard policies. The draft text of the new Operational Policy and Bank Procedure concerning indigenous peoples was discussed in 2001 for the first time. As the review process envisaged disclosure for public discussion, a long phase of consultations was carried out between July 2001 and February 2002 with various external stakeholders, including national development institutions, representatives of borrower governments, NGOs, and indigenous organizations.

In 2003, the World Bank Group former Operations Evaluation Department ('OED'), now known as the Independent Evaluation Group, established a panel of experts composed of three professors with backgrounds in anthropology and sociology. One of them, Rodolfo Stavenhagen, who was then serving as the UN Special Rapporteur on Indigenous Peoples, was appointed to head the panel.

The panel carried out a two-phase review of how the Bank had implemented OD 4.20, with the goal of recasting it. This process marked the beginning of a technique designed to update operational instruments based not only on public consultations but also on internal reviews conducted in a more independent manner. In more detail, the first phase focused on analyzing a significant number of investment projects appraised after January 1992 and closed before 31 May 2001. In its report dated 10 January 2003, out of 126 projects with potential negative effects on indigenous peoples, the panel identified several shortcomings in 16 of them. These issues were

[24] On this point, OD 4.20 added that, in the absence of a reliable method to guarantee full local-level participation, the Bank's sociological and technical advice was likely to be needed.

[25] ibid., Article 6.1.a.

mainly due to a lack of indigenous people's participation, and the frequent absence of proper monitoring indicators, despite specific provisions in OD 4.20 addressing these aspects. At the same time, according to the panel, the application of OD 4.20 had positively influenced the design of Bank-financed projects, particularly in terms of their overall objective of poverty reduction, creating substantial benefits for indigenous peoples, especially in India, Indonesia, and the Latin America and Caribbean region.[26] The OED report also held that insufficient ownership of the OD 4.20 in several countries had led to major problems, such as China, India, and Indonesia, given the absence of proper national domestic legislation aimed at dealing with such vulnerable groups. In any case, it recommended a more general proactive Bank's attitude in order to better adhere to the spirit, as well as the letter, of OD 4.20.[27]

Regarding the identification of indigenous peoples, one of the most sensitive issues in the interplay between the Bank's standards and national legal regimes, the OED report recommended a careful review of the division of responsibilities between the Bank and the borrower «to ensure clarity of roles, thus avoiding the dilution of accountability» in policy formulation.[28] In outlining the approach that the Bank should have adopted, the review proposed a mixed solution. It suggested that the identification process should normally rely on the country's legal framework as a preliminary basis to avoid differential treatment of citizens within the same country, as stated in OD 4.20. However, for particularly weak frameworks that fell short of the Bank's standards, the review acknowledged that vulnerable groups could be treated by the Bank in alignment with its broader poverty reduction mandate.[29]

After being shared with the Bank's Management to obtain its response, the report was presented to the CODE, the body supporting the Board of Executive Directors in monitoring the quality and results of the World Bank Group's operations, which further discussed the matter in a meeting held on 18 September 2002. Focusing on the most relevant issues, the Committee's main findings supported granting a stronger degree of protection to indigenous peoples, based on a thorough revision of OD 4.20. It fully endorsed the OED's recommendation to rely on national approaches for the identification process in principle, while also noting that following such legal frameworks—where they existed—could have led to the exclusion of a large number of indigenous groups from benefiting from the policy provisions. It concluded that, regardless of the use of a country's legal framework, «it was still necessary for the Bank to have its own policy to address […] issues at the project-level and to maintain mechanisms for the exercise of the judgment of social scientists to determine whether the groups affected in a particular project are the ones intended to be covered by the policy». In doing so, it acknowledged that «in formulating policies,

[26] Operations Evaluation Department (2003a, p. 23).

[27] ibid., p. 1.

[28] ibid., p. 11.

[29] ibid., p. 25.

the Bank takes into account national as well as *international law*, and decides what policies are best to assist in achieving the objectives of the Bank. In addition, *the Bank's agreements with Borrowers are binding* notwithstanding the provisions of any national law to the contrary». [*italics added*].[30] Two different observations can be drawn from such statements. On the one hand, the Committee emphasized the autonomous approach that the Bank should have followed in the identification phase—a crucial process that determines whether policies are triggered for specific projects—while also noting that these policies often incorporate international legal norms. On the other hand, it clarified and expanded the meaning of the vague provision included in paragraph 20 of OD 4.20, which states that the borrower's commitment to implementing the plan should be reflected in the loan documents.

During the second phase of the review, the Operations Evaluation Department formulated other relevant observations. In particular, its second report noted that in countries located in the Middle East and North Africa, the lack of consistency with the Bank's approach was high, due to the absence of a clear legal differentiation between the terms 'indigenous' and 'ethnic minority', which, at that time, created a gray area in the regional debate. In this regard, the report recommended that the Bank adopt a more strategic approach, tailored to the specific country involved in the lending process.[31]

At that stage, the path leading to the adoption of the new operational instrument, OP/BP 4.10, which took into due account all OED's findings, once again involved external actors. Although the process became more transparent and increasingly based on public participation, building consensus on the new text proved difficult. Ultimately, it was rejected by indigenous organizations in December 2004 during the final round of consultations.[32] A revised version was subsequently released and finally approved. The policy instrument was formally issued by the IBRD's Board of Executive Directors on 20 May 2005;[33] it is still in force for projects approved before 1 October 2018.

As in its previous version, the new operational policy specifies that Bank-financed projects must include measures to avoid potential adverse impacts, adding that, when not feasible, measures to minimize (in addition to mitigate) or compensate for such negative effects should also be incorporated. Additionally, with more detailed wording, the policy states that projects must be designed to ensure that indigenous peoples receive culturally appropriate as well as gender- and intergenerationally inclusive benefits, which should be outlined in a plan. This plan is now referred to as the 'Indigenous Peoples Plan' ('IPP') or 'Indigenous Peoples Planning Framework' ('IPPF'), and its requirements are detailed in paragraphs 12–15.

---

[30] ibid., Attachment VI, p. 49.

[31] Operations Evaluation Department (2003b, p. 41).

[32] On this aspect, see Errico (2006, p. 372).

[33] The World Bank, *Operations Manual, Policy & Procedure Framework, Operational Policy 4.10, Indigenous Peoples*, 2005 (revised in 2013 and 2024); ibid., *Bank Procedure 4.10, Indigenous Peoples*, 2005 (revised in 2013 and 2024).

Contrary to its predecessor, OP 4.10 clarifies that terms such as 'indigenous ethnic minorities', 'aboriginals', 'hill tribes', 'minority nationalities', 'scheduled tribes' or 'tribal groups' can be used interchangeably in different countries to refer to 'indigenous peoples'. Notably, in relation to attachment to ancestral territories, it replaces the term 'close' with 'collective', thus aligning with modern international legal thinking that recognizes the collective nature of indigenous peoples' rights to lands, territories, and resources.

Overall, the policy presents other innovative aspects.

First, it settles the contested use of country systems in the identification of indigenous peoples' presence (or collective attachment to the project area, as rephrased in the new formulation) by granting the Bank the authority to decide whether to utilize them.[34] This decision is made in accordance with the provisions of OP/BP 4.00, which encourages the use of country systems, provided they are sufficiently aligned with the Bank's framework. In cases where national systems have gaps, the borrower must commit to addressing them to strengthen the system beyond individual project contexts.[35]

Second, responsibilities between the Bank and the borrower are distributed in a very clear way, following a substantial refinement of the wording of OD 4.20. Reference is made to an initial 'screening' phase during project preparation, to be carried out by the Bank,[36] and to the preparation of a 'social assessment' tailored to indigenous peoples, which needs to be developed by the borrower in the subsequent phase. The assessment is aimed at evaluating the legal and institutional framework applicable to indigenous peoples, collecting baseline information on their characteristics, including lands and the natural resources on which they depend,[37] as well as assessing positive and negative effects associated with the project and alternatives scenarios.[38] As part of the determination of potential negative effects, the borrower needs to conduct an analysis based on 'free, prior, and informed consultation' with affected indigenous peoples, which replaces the 'informed participation' requirement. In doing so, the borrower needs to pay special attention to their vulnerability, close ties to lands and natural resources and lack of access to opportunities relative to other social groups within the same geographic context in which they live.[39] In case such negative effects exist, the borrower needs to engage in consultation with indigenous peoples in order to ascertain 'broad community support'.[40] Provided that

[34] The World Bank, *Operations Manual, Policy & Procedure Framework, Operational Policy 4.10, Indigenous Peoples*, 2005 (revised in 2013 and 2024), para. 5.

[35] The World Bank, *Operations Manual, Policy & Procedure Framework, Operational Policy and Bank Procedure 4.00, Piloting the Use of Borrower Systems to Address Environmental and Social Safeguard Issues in Bank-Supported Projects*, 2005 (revised in 2013 and 2024), p. 3.

[36] The World Bank, *Operations Manual, Policy & Procedure Framework, Operational Policy 4.10, Indigenous Peoples*, 2005 (revised in 2013 and 2024), paras. 6(a); 8.

[37] ibid., Annex A.

[38] ibid., paras. 6.b and 9.

[39] ibid., Annex A, para. 2.d.

[40] ibid., paras. 6c and 10.

such support exists, the borrower prepares a detailed report documenting any formal agreement reached with them.

Third, the policy instrument incorporates a provision stating that, at this pre-appraisal stage, the Bank, upon reviewing the report, «does not proceed further with project processing if it is unable to ascertain that such support exists» (paragraph 11, reiterated in paragraph 1). This provision can be seen as a more refined version of the clause in OD 4.20, which stated that the Bank «will not appraise projects until suitable plans are developed by the borrower and reviewed by the Bank».

Fourth, BP 4.10, which is addressed mainly to the Bank, specifies that the Indigenous Peoples Plan is attached to the Project Appraisal Document as an annex (paragraph 10), which the borrower has to implement based on the loan agreement that incorporates it (paragraph 11).

A few years after the enactment of the Policy, in 2011, a new learning review was launched to assess the implementation of OP/BP 4.10 during the period 2006–2008.[41] The review acknowledged that it was difficult to determine whether and to what extent 'broad community support' could be granted in practice. It also noted that an increasing number of international legal instruments were incorporating the 'Free, Prior, and Informed Consent' requirement, including the 2007 United Nations Declaration on the Rights of Indigenous Peoples (UNDRIP). This reference is of utmost importance as Article 32 of the Declaration frames FPIC in the specific context of projects, stating that States should obtain indigenous peoples' consent prior to the approval of «any project affecting their lands or territories and other resources, particularly in connection with the development, utilization or exploitation of mineral, water or other resources».

The review also took into consideration the policy provisions enacted by other international financial institutions, such as the Inter-American Development Bank in 2006, the Asian Development Bank in 2008, the International Fund for Agricultural Development in 2009, and IFC in 2011, among others.[42] Finally, the approval of the new Environmental and Social Framework in 2016 resulted in the adoption of ESS-7 on 'Indigenous Peoples and Sub-Saharan African Historically Underserved Traditional Local Communities',[43] which properly incorporated FPIC, thus aligning its contents with the most modern developments occurred at the international legal level. In this regard, in 2018, the Expert Mechanism on the Rights of Indigenous Peoples, in a study carried out to analyze the progress made on the implementation of FPIC as a human rights norm embodied in the UNDRIP, held that the new World Bank Standards improved its adherence to the human rights-based approach much more than its predecessor.[44]

---

[41] The Review was prepared by the World Bank Quality Assurance and Compliance Unit of the Operations Policy and Country Services (OPCS) Vice Presidency (in collaboration with the Social Development Department of the Sustainable Development Vice Presidency). See The World Bank Operations Policy and Country Services (2011).

[42] ibid., Annex 9, p. 19.

[43] The World Bank, *Environmental and Social Framework*, 2017, pp. 75–83.

[44] UN Human Rights Council (2018, p. 15).

In this regard, the framework adopts a twofold approach, strengthening existing provisions on consultations and, in particular cases, requiring the acquisition of FPIC. ESS-7 in fact requires borrowers to generally carry out meaningful consultations with indigenous peoples' representative bodies and organizations, such as councils of elders, village councils, chieftains or other community members (paragraph 23) at multiple stages of the project. This currently ensures that consultations are linked to the grass roots indigenous organizations whose lands and resources might be adversely affected by a Bank-funded project. In this regard, the new Framework has also broadened its subjective scope of application to include pastoralists and peoples in voluntary isolation.

Furthermore, ESS-7 stipulates that under three special circumstances, borrowers will also need to obtain their FPIC. The circumstances listed under ESS-7 are those in which the project (i) has adverse impacts on land and natural resources subject to indigenous peoples' traditional ownership or under their customary use or occupation; (ii) causes their relocation from such lands or natural resources; or (iii) has significant impact on their cultural heritage, that is material to their identity, cultural, ceremonial, or spiritual values (paragraph 27). Furthermore, it reiterates the Bank's commitment to not financing projects for which the FPIC cannot be ascertained. It also specifies that, when FPIC concerns only specific aspects of the project, the borrower must ensure that no adverse impacts arise regarding the remaining aspects, if the Bank decides to continue processing the project.[45]

Undoubtedly, the introduction of FPIC into the World Bank's operational framework marks a significant step in its normative evolution. Conceived as a consultation process that does not necessarily require unanimity, its current formulation broadly aligns with the interpretation provided by former UN Special Rapporteur on the Rights of Indigenous Peoples, James Anaya (2008–2014).[46] At the same time, the Bank itself has recently acknowledged that this remains a topic of ongoing debate at both the national and international levels.[47] Against this backdrop, a crucial element to consider is the need to ensure that FPIC does not become a mere goodwill practice—a risk that can be mitigated if it is interpreted in line with the emerging consensus among human rights bodies, which view it as a norm imposing both procedural and substantive requirements. This is especially important in the context of large-scale development projects, which frequently impact indigenous peoples' rights.[48]

---

[45] ibid., para. 27.

[46] The 2009 Annual Report of the UN Special Rapporteur on the Situation of Human Rights and Fundamental Freedoms of Indigenous People generally suggested that the concept of FPIC in UNDRIP should not be interpreted in the sense of creating a *veto* power, as it rather refers to an obligation to consult in good faith. See UN Human Rights Council (2009, p. 16). For an analysis of FPIC in light of general international law, see Barrie (2024, p. 195 f). It is interesting to note that other IFIs have adopted an Indigenous Peoples policy that incorporates FPIC in exactly the same manner: see Green Climate Fund, *Indigenous Peoples Policy*, 1 March 2018, p. 14. Notably, the Fund is guided by the provisions of the UN Framework Convention on Climate Change in its actions and is accountable for them to the United Nations.

[47] The World Bank Group (2015, p. 53).

[48] UN Human Rights Council (2018, p. 13).

3.2 Policy Instruments Encompassing an 'Escape' Clause

Beyond the policy specifically dedicated to indigenous peoples, there are other operational instruments that play a crucial role in shaping how the World Bank effectively imposes its *de facto* environmental and social conditionality on the borrower prior to entering into a loan agreement, which are relevant for the purposes of the present analysis.

With reference to the general policies regulating investment project financing, OMS 2.20 ('Project Appraisal'), introduced in January 1984, marked a watershed in the aspects to be taken into consideration in the Bank's appraisal from an international legal standpoint. The provision in fact prescribed that the Bank should ensure the consistency of the project loan with the terms of any existing international agreement ratified by the borrower, including those of an environmental nature:

> The project's possible effects on the country's environment and on the health and well-being of its people must be considered at an early stage. The project should adapt the standards of protection to the circumstances of the project and country, and incorporate those environmental measures that are considered essential and appropriate. Should international agreements exist that are applicable to the project and area, such as those involving the use of international waters, the Bank should be satisfied that the project loan is consistent with the terms of the agreement. In countries where the laws, rules or regulations governing environmental matters may be inadequate, the staff should consider the merits of encouraging appropriate legislation, if necessary, to mitigate serious adverse environmental consequences of a project.[49]

Over time, while the Bank has fragmented the contents of OMS 2.20 related to 'Sociological Aspects'—encompassing the Bank's review of the projects with an impact on ethnic minorities, resettled populations and women—into a number of instruments addressing specific issues, including safeguards,[50] it partly replaced the general project appraisal provisions with OP/BP 6.00 on 'Bank Financing' after 2004. At a later stage, it decided to phase out OMS 2.20 as a general instrument governing IPF operations, as part of the modernization effort that resulted in the consolidation of the Bank's operational framework.

---

[49] The World Bank, *Operational Manual Statement 2.20, Project Appraisal*, January 1984, para. 24. For an overview of OMS 2.20 with particular reference to the consideration of sociological aspects in project appraisal, see Salman (2009, p. 169).

[50] Starting from 1991, some of its contents have been partly transposed into OD 4.15 on Poverty Reduction (later superseded by OP/BP 1.00 in July 2014), and, at a later stage, in 1994, into OP 4.20, entitled 'The Gender Dimensions of Development', as part of the Bank's overall poverty reduction initiative. Since 1985, projects concerning international waterways have been regulated by *ad hoc* instruments, such as OMS 2.32, which, after undergoing some minor modifications, have been reflected in OD 7.50 of 1990, and then in OP/BP 7.50 of June 2001. Such instruments have always attached great relevance to cooperation with riparian states, encouraging borrowing states to conclude agreements with them in order to guarantee the efficient use of waterways. By contrast, provisions concerning ethnic minorities (and indigenous peoples), jointly with resettlement matters, have been transposed into other safeguard policies. See Operations Evaluation Department (2001a, p. 2).

Therefore, the rules concerning appraisal are outlined in OP/BP 10.00 of April 2013,[51] which no longer refers to compliance with international agreements. The reclassification of the instrument as 'Bank Policy' in 2018 (with the most recent revision in 2024), intended to incorporate the purely formal modifications introduced by the Environmental and Social Framework,[52] did not result in any substantive changes. Notably, Table 3.1 provides an overview of the transition from OMS 2.20 and other relevant policy instruments to the current framework.

By contrast, considerations regarding environmental impacts, often intertwined with those affecting indigenous peoples as inhabitants of forests and other biodiversity-rich ecosystems, have driven independent developments in the evolution of safeguards. With the adoption of OMS 2.36 ('Environmental Aspects of the Bank's Work') in May 1984, the Bank actually committed not to finance projects that contravene «any international environmental agreement to which the country on whose territory the project is located is a party», or that significantly alter «natural areas designated by international conventions as World Heritage sites or Biosphere Reserves».[53] Following the enactment of its revised version in 1989, renamed Operational Directive 4.01, which started making systematic use of Environmental Assessment ('EA') as a standard procedure for Bank-financed projects, the provision mentioning compliance with international treaties disappeared from the text.

In 1999, Operational Policy 4.01, which for the first time integrated social aspects—such as involuntary resettlement, indigenous peoples, and physical cultural resources—into the EA, took again stock of the country's national legal framework and its relevant international environmental obligations. The policy provides that the Bank cannot finance projects contravening them:

> EA [...] also takes into account the variations in project and country conditions; the findings of country environmental studies; national environmental action plans; the country's overall policy framework, national legislation, and institutional capabilities related to the environment and social aspects; and obligations of the country, pertaining to project activities, under relevant international environmental treaties and agreements. The Bank does not finance project activities that would contravene such country obligations, as identified during the EA.[54]

Currently, other specific policies related to the environment take this aspect into consideration. This is the case of OP 4.36 concerning Forests (2002), whereby the «Bank does not finance projects that contravene applicable international

[51] The World Bank Operations Policy and Country Services (2012, p. 6).

[52] The World Bank, *Bank Policy, Investment Project Financing*, 2024, Catalogue No. OPS5.03-POL.110, p. 8.

[53] The World Bank, *Operational Manual Statement 2.36, Environmental Aspects of the Bank's Work*, 1984, paras. 9.e and 9.g. See also Shihata (1992, p. 6).

[54] The World Bank, *Operations Manual, Policy & Procedure Framework, Operational Policy 4.01, Environmental Assessment*, 1999 (revised in 2013 and 2024), para. 3.

Table 3.1 Historical evolution of World Bank's policy instruments relevant to investment projects involving indigenous peoples

First generation, Operational Manual Statements (before 1987)	Second generation, Operational Directives (after 1987)	Third generation, Operational Policies and Bank Procedures (1992–2013)	Changes following the modernization of IPF policies with the introduction of OP/BP 10.00 'IPF' (investment lending reform) (2013)	Changes following the adoption of the Environmental and Social Framework (2016, came into effect on 1 October 2018)	Changes following the conversion of OP/BP 10.00 into Bank Policy 'IPF' and Bank Directive 'IPF' to reflect the new E&S framework (1 October 2018)
OMS 2.20, 'Project Appraisal' (January 1984)	Partly transposed into OD 4.15, 'Poverty Reduction' (1991) and other instruments	Partly transposed into OP/BP 6.00, 'Project Financing' (2004)	Phased out; absorbed by OP/BP 10.00 (formal and substantial changes)	Safeguards follow their own regime with regards to appraisal (no change)	Not applicable (no change)
OMS 3.50, 'Project Supervision' (1979)	OD 13.05, 'Project Supervision' (1989)	OP/BP 13.05, 'Project Supervision' (2001)	Supervision functions are converted into monitoring and implementation support (OP 13.05 is transposed into para. 19 of OP 10.00; BP 13.05 into para. 37 of BP 10.00) (formal and substantial changes)	No change (brand-new provisions concerning E&S due diligence are introduced, in addition to others on monitoring and implementation support with a focus on E&S project performance: Sections C and H of E&S Policy for IPF; sub-sections III.2 and III.6 of E&S Directive/Procedure for IPF) (no change)	Former para. 19 of OP 10.00 is converted with marginal adjustment into para. 20 of Bank Policy, 'IPF', revised in 2024; former para. 37 of BP 10.00 into para. 44 of Bank Directive 'IPF', revised in 2023) (marginal adjustments)
	OD 13.40, 'Suspension of Disbursements' (1989)	OP/BP 13.40, 'Suspension of Disbursements' (1996)	OP 13.40 is transposed into para. 25 of OP 10.00; BP 13.40 into para. 37 of BP 10.00 (formal changes)	No change (for E&S aspects, the new WB E&S Policy refers back to OP 10.00) (no change)	Former para. 25 of OP 10.00 is converted into para. 27 of Bank Policy; former para. 37 of BP 10.00 into para. 45 of Bank Directive (marginal adjustments)

(continued)

Table 3.1 (continued)

First generation, Operational Manual Statements (before 1987)	Second generation, Operational Directives (after 1987)	Third generation, Operational Policies and Bank Procedures (1992–2013)	Changes following the modernization of IPF policies with the introduction of OP/BP 10.00 'IPF' (investment lending reform) (2013)	Changes following the adoption of the Environmental and Social Framework (2016, came into effect on 1 October 2018)	Changes following the conversion of OP/BP 10.00 into Bank Policy 'IPF' and Bank Directive 'IPF' to reflect the new E&S framework (1 October 2018)
	OD 13.50, 'Cancellations' (1989)	OP/BP 13.50, 'Cancellations' (2002)	OP 13.50 is transposed into para. 25 of OP 10.00; BP 13.40 into para. 38 of BP 10.00 (formal changes)	As above (no change)	Former para. 25 of OP 10.00 is converted into para. 27 of Bank Policy; former para. 38 of BP 10.00 into para. 46 of Bank Directive (marginal adjustments)
OMS 2.34, 'Tribal People in Bank-Financed Projects' (1982)	OD 4.20, 'Indigenous Peoples' (1991)	OP/BP 4.10, 'Indigenous Peoples' (2005)	Not applicable (no change)	Converted into ESS-7, 'Indigenous Peoples/ Sub-Saharan African Historically Underserved Traditional Local Communities' (with changes in terminology regarding free, prior, and informed consultations, converted into FPIC); former BP 4.10 is converted into E&S Policy (formal and substantial changes)	Not applicable (no change)

First generation, Operational Manual Statements (before 1987)	Second generation, Operational Directives (after 1987)	Third generation, Operational Policies and Bank Procedures (1992–2013)	Changes following the modernization of IPF policies with the introduction of OP/BP 10.00 'IPF' (investment lending reform) (2013)	Changes following the adoption of the Environmental and Social Framework (2016, came into effect on 1 October 2018)	Changes following the conversion of OP/BP 10.00 into Bank Policy 'IPF' and Bank Directive 'IPF' to reflect the new E&S framework (1 October 2018)
OMS 2.33, 'Social Issues of Involuntary Resettlement in Bank-Financed Projects' (1980)	OD 4.30, 'Involuntary Resettlement' (1990)	OP/BP 4.12, 'Involuntary Resettlement' (2001)	Not applicable (no change)	Converted into ESS-5, 'Land Acquisition, Restrictions on Land Use and Involuntary Resettlement' (formal changes)	Not applicable (no change)
OMS 2.36, 'Environmental Aspects of the Bank's Work' (1984)	OD 4.01, 'Environmental Assessment' (1991)	OP/BP 4.01, 'Environmental Assessment' (1999)	Not applicable (no change)	Converted into ESS-1, 'Assessment and Management of Environmental and Social Risks and Impacts'; former BP 4.01 is converted into E&S Policy (formal changes)	Not applicable (no change)
OPN 11.02, 'Wildlands' (1986)	Not applicable	OP/BP 4.04, 'Natural Habitats' (1995)	Not applicable (no change)	Converted into ESS-6, 'Biodiversity Conservation and Sustainable Management of Living Natural Resources'; former BP 4.04 is converted into E&S Policy (formal changes)	Not applicable (no change)
	OD 4.36, 'Forestry' (1993)	OP/BP 4.36, 'Forests' (2002)	Not applicable (no change)	As above (merged into ESS-6) (formal changes)	Not applicable (no change)

Source: Author's own elaboration

environmental agreements».[55] Similar considerations apply to another provision, contained in OP 4.04 concerning Natural Habitats (2001), holding that «[t]he Bank does not support projects that, in the Bank's opinion, involve the significant conversion or degradation of critical natural habitats».[56] According to Annex A to the policy instrument, critical natural habitats include «areas officially proposed by governments as protected areas», such as the «reserves that meet the criteria of the World Conservation Union (IUCN) classifications», and the «areas initially recognized as protected by traditional local communities (e.g., sacred groves)».[57]

While all the aforementioned instruments remain applicable to projects approved before 1 October 2018, the more recent Environmental and Social Framework has partially amended these provisions by placing primary emphasis on the role of the prospective borrower in ensuring that its international obligations are considered in the environmental and social assessment,[58] omitting any reference to the former Bank's commitment not to finance projects contravening such obligations. Against this backdrop, the only exception is the case of 'Critical Habitats', defined as areas with high biodiversity value, for which ESS-6 explicitly states that the borrower cannot implement any project activity unless «[a]ll due process required under international obligations or national law that is a prerequisite to a country granting approval for project activities in or adjacent to a critical habitat has been complied with».[59] For all the other cases not covered by the biodiversity conservation standard, one may argue that this will weaken the Bank's role in ensuring that countries' relevant international obligations are met. Nevertheless, in spite of the enhanced borrower's ownership of the project that broadly inspired the whole safeguards' review, there exist strong requirements concerning the Bank's due diligence activities, whose main purpose is to «assist the Bank in deciding whether to provide support for the proposed project and, if so, the way in which environmental and social risks and impacts will be addressed in the assessment, development and implementation of the project».[60] This entails that, as in the past, the Bank will certainly have to review the assessment carried out by the borrower, in order to ensure that the standards prescriptions are met. Such an assessment currently includes the verification of the existence of its international obligations, which are no longer limited to those stemming from treaties of an environmental nature. Consequently, one could argue that the Bank is still fully entitled to refuse financing for projects that contravene these provisions. However, the impact of these changes will ultimately need to

[55] The World Bank, *Operations Manual, Policy & Procedure Framework, Operational Policy 4.36, Forests*, 2002 (revised in 2013 and 2024), para. 6. On the role played by the Bank's investment project financing activities and the Panel's practice in implementing the obligations arising from multilateral environmental agreements, see Lin (2016, p. 246).

[56] The World Bank, *Operations Manual, Policy & Procedure Framework, Operational Policy 4.04, Natural Habitats*, 2001 (revised in 2013 and 2024), para. 4.

[57] ibid., Annex A, Definitions, para. 1(b)(i).

[58] The World Bank, *Environmental and Social Framework*, 2017, pp. 15–29, para. 26.

[59] ibid., p. 70.

[60] ibid., p. 7.

be assessed in light of the future Panel's practice, which may offer valuable insights into the best way to interpret the new provisions.

3.3 The Inspection Panel's Mandate

The World Bank Inspection Panel has been the first Independent Accountability Mechanism ever created within a Multilateral Development Bank. As prominent international legal scholars have argued, in its capacity as a citizen-driven accountability mechanism able to respond to grievances stemming from activities funded by international organizations, it empowered groups of individuals to bypass governments, thus seeking the independent review of their rights in a way that had no precedent in international law.[61] Indeed, in spite of its *sui generis* institutional features, which make it a fact-finding body rather than an adjudicatory one,[62] the Inspection Panel has opened up a significant direct channel of communication between individuals and the ultimate organ responsible for conducting the day-to-day business of the World Bank, the Board of Executive Directors, through the creation of a forum where private actors may hold an international organization «directly accountable for the consequences of its failure to follow its own rules and procedures».[63]

Established with a Resolution approved by the IBRD's and IDA's Boards of Executive Directors in 1993, it underwent two important reviews in 1996 and 1999 (with the so-called *Clarifications*).[64] Notably, in 2020, a further Resolution has set

[61] Hunter (2003, p. 206). As noted by Francioni, «[i]ndividuals access to international remedies has gained much recognition in the practice of the last quarter of a century. Leaving aside the human rights aspect of this phenomenon [...] this is especially true in the field of international economic law. Here we can witness [...] the establishment in the early 1990s of the World Bank Inspection Panel, which, although it is not an adjudicatory organ, is capable of providing a flexible sui generis mechanism to take into account private interests and the social impact of the Bank's financing projects». See Francioni (2007, p. xxvii).

[62] As there is no generally accepted definition of 'fact-finding body', the concept can have different meanings depending on the context in which it is used. Shihata has referred to this term to describe the Panel as a body whose findings are not legally binding on the Bank's decision-making organs, although with an overwhelming impact: Shihata (2000a, p. 214). Notably, the International Law Association has qualified it as a mechanism through which individuals can seek non-judicial remedial action against international organisations, observing that «[t]he investigatory powers of an Inspection Panel comprise political, administrative and legal forms of accountability. Its findings cannot be reconsidered or changed through a political process». International Law Association (2004, p. 46).

[63] Bradlow (1994, p. 554).

[64] The first review, mandated in the Resolution establishing the Panel, was completed in October 1996. Once again, in September 1997, the Executive Directors agreed on the need to review the Panel's functioning by setting up a Working Group, which summarized its findings in a proposal. On 20 April 1999, the Board approved the 'Conclusions of the Board's Second Review of

forth the role of a new Accountability Mechanism ('AM'),[65] operational since July 2021, which established a dispute resolution function, managed independently by an *ad hoc* service ('Dispute Resolution Service'). Since then, the AM has started housing the Panel as well, without altering its mandate, which still involves receiving requests for inspection by any group of two or more individuals (or their representatives) in the borrower's territory, whose rights or interests have been, or are likely to be, directly affected by a Bank's action or omission as a result of the failure to follow its operational policies and procedures.[66]

Nowadays, the Panel can resort to the advisory function through the AM before investigating the case. In particular, if a request for inspection is deemed eligible by the Inspection Panel, the Accountability Mechanism Secretary offers both the requesters and the borrower the option of voluntary, independent dispute resolution. When the parties do not agree on choosing this option or when an agreement is not reached, the Panel can initiate the compliance function. Furthermore, the Panel may provide advisory services in the form of lessons learned from its cases through publications. In this regard, the recent Resolution, which redefined the scope of its mandate in 2020, has specifically excluded the extension of these services to the merits of specific Bank policies, procedures, directives, or similar policies.[67] Nevertheless, it cannot be disputed that the Panel has played a crucial role in clarifying the contents of these operational instruments from its early years of operations, as its extensive practice demonstrates.

In this context, it is also worth noting that, over time, the Panel has attracted significant criticism, particularly from NGOs and human rights activists, due to structural limitations inherent in its institutional design. Formally established by a Resolution of the Boards of Executive Directors, to be regarded as an internal act of the organization, the Panel could have benefited from a greater degree of independence had it been created through an amendment to the Articles of Agreement, with the required *quorum* within the Board of Governors.[68] Nevertheless, the intention to create a subsidiary body of the Board of Executive Directors was already evident during the process leading to its establishment. On 10 September 1993, the then

Inspection Panel', which amended the 1993 Resolution that established the Panel and the 1996 Clarifications. For an overview of the whole review process, see Inspection Panel (2000a, p. 40).

[65] International Bank for Reconstruction and Development and International Development Association, *The World Bank Accountability Mechanism*, Resolution No. IBRD 2020-0005 and Resolution No. IDA 2020-0004, 8 September 2020.

[66] International Bank for Reconstruction and Development and International Development Association, *The World Bank Inspection Panel*, Resolution No. IBRD 2020-0004 and Resolution No. IDA 2020-0003, 8 September 2020, para. 13. It is noteworthy that the assessment concerning compliance with guidance notes, good practice notes, and similar documents or statements is excluded from the purview of the Inspection Panel's mandate.

[67] ibid., para. 59.

[68] According to Article VIII of IBRD's Articles of Agreement, proposals for amendments, whether emanating from a member country, a governor or the Executive Directors, shall be communicated to the Chairman of the Board of Governors and accepted by three-fifths of the members, having 85% of the total voting power.

World Bank President, Lewis Thompson Preston, submitted a Memorandum to the Board of Executive Directors, clarifying that the main objective of the Panel's inspection function was to provide 'independent judgment' to help solve cases where it was asserted that people's rights and interests had been adversely affected while also improving the whole system for quality control in project preparation and supervision. According to the document, this new function was in no way supposed to diminish the role of the Board in the governance of the Bank.[69] Notably, at that time, although the Executive Directors did not grant formal status to the Memorandum—since it was neither adopted nor approved during their discussions, which focused exclusively on the draft Resolution—several of its key elements were nonetheless accepted in substance, including those concerning the fact-finding powers of the Panel. Indeed, it was agreed that the Panel could well investigate the complaints found to be eligible and make its independent findings accordingly, but only with the approval of the Executive Directors.[70] At the operational level, this meant that the Panel lacked proper decisional power on whether an investigation was warranted: the Bank Executive Directors were in fact in charge of authorizing the prosecution of investigations,[71] an aspect leading to significant politicization of the Panel's functioning in the first few years of its operations. Notably, since the issuance of the 1999 Clarifications, the Board, while formally retaining ultimate authority for deciding, began supporting every recommendation for investigations,[72] thereby allowing for a more progressive interpretation of the Panel's mandate.

Broadly, the procedure outlined for the Panel to address claims involves continuous dialogue among all the parties concerned: after receiving a request for inspection, Management shall provide evidence that it has complied, or intends to comply, with the relevant Bank's policies and procedures allegedly violated within 21 business days. The Panel, which is typically composed of three members, may agree or disagree on such observations. In any case, it has to formally submit a recommendation to the Executive Directors concerning the need to investigate the matter within the subsequent 21 business days, provided the case meets the eligibility criteria.[73] In

[69] The Memorandum submitted by the President, titled 'Operations Inspection Function: Objectives, Mandate and Operating Procedures for an Independent Inspection Panel' was circulated to a limited audience. A comprehensive analysis of the drafting history of the Resolution and its interpretation can be found in Shihata (2000a, p. 30).

[70] Ragazzi (1995, p. 533).

[71] Sciso (2017, p. 125).

[72] According to para. 9 of the 1999 Clarifications: «if the Panel so recommends, the Board will authorize an investigation without making a judgment on the merits of the claimants' request, and without discussion», with the sole exception of technical eligibility criteria.

[73] According to para. 30 of the Executive Directors 2020 Resolution, in case of authorization of an investigation, the newly established Accountability Mechanism Secretary should offer an opportunity for dispute resolution to the affected parties and the borrower; the outcome of this phase is notified to the Panel, the Directors, and Management within 30 business days after the authorization. In case the parties do not accept to pursue dispute resolution or when they do not reach an agreement, the Panel finally initiates the investigation, otherwise the case can be considered closed upon this stage with the signature of the Dispute Resolution Agreement.

particular, the Panel must verify whether the request meets specific technical criteria. In accordance with criterion 'b" of the most recent version of its Operating Procedures (2022),[74] the request should include «a description of the harm or potential harm (material adverse effects) that, according to Requesters, is the result of a serious violation by the Bank of its policies and procedures». In any case, the assessment concerning the standard of causal connection between the Bank's conduct and the alleged harm is not performed in a very analytical way at this stage.

For inspections that go forward, the Panel enjoys broad investigatory powers including access to all records of the Bank's Management and its staff, field visits and interviews with affected people. In the investigation phase, the Panel is called upon to determine whether the causal link between the Bank's conduct and the alleged harm exists in a 'plausible way', for the purpose of issuing the recommendation establishing whether the matters as presented in the request warrant an investigation. Against this backdrop, another element that the Panel needs to take into careful consideration is the serious character of the alleged harm, or the serious character of the possible non-compliance by the Bank with its operational policies and procedures.[75]

The final report concluding the investigation phase—one of the most significant elements of the whole process—finally evaluates the Bank's conduct and assesses the material adverse effects stemming from the failure to observe its policy and procedures. Within six weeks from receiving the final report, and after having consulted with the affected parties, Management addresses the non-compliance findings with a series of proposed actions ('Management Action Plan'), together with its observations and recommendations ('Management Report and Recommendation'), which are approved by the Executive Directors. Interesting institutional developments introduced with the latest review pertain to the post-investigation phase. Significantly, until a few years ago, this phase was the responsibility of Management only, which had to independently report on the progress of the Management Action Plan ('MAP') to the Board of Executive Directors periodically. In turn, the Board had to decide about the verification of adequateness of the plan and the completion of the proposed actions. More recently, the Board of Executive Directors has authorized the Panel, jointly with the Bank's Group Internal Audit, to carry out an independent verification of the implementation of those MAPs approved after 8 September 2020 in some specific cases.[76] Although subject to the Board's approval,

[74] On this point, the text of the Operating Procedures mirrors the contents of the previous ones issued in 2014, as well as the 1999 Clarifications. Inspection Panel, *Operating Procedures*, December 2022, p. 16.

[75] ibid., p. 20. An interesting aspect of the investigation methodology, as outlined in the Operating Procedures, is its emphasis on active engagement with the public, including not only the requesters but also the UN and other organizations, civil society representatives, and independent experts. The Panel may request or receive information from all of these parties when appropriate.

[76] In doing so, the Panel will be able to rely on a proper framework containing the proportionality criteria and modalities for verification, prepared jointly with the Group Internal Audit and the Bank Management.

the attribution of the verification function to the Panel gives it a greater role in the follow-up phase for the purpose of ensuring that actions are effective and properly implemented. Such functions now closely resemble those performed by the most recently established IAMs at other Multilateral Development Banks, including the Compliance Advisor Ombudsman at IFC, as well as those granted to UN treaty bodies when deciding on individual complaints within their mandate, which involves overseeing States' implementation of their human rights obligations under the treaties they have ratified.[77] It is worth noting that the Board has already adopted this approach in its previous practice, albeit in an informal capacity. For instance, in the *India: Mumbai Urban Transport Project (First Request)* (2004) case dealing with involuntary resettlement, the Bank suspended disbursements on the road and on the resettlement components until the MAP satisfactory completion, conferring the task of monitoring its implementation to the Panel. After finding a significant lack of consultations of the residents involved in the project, the Panel provided several different inputs aimed at improving the outcome of the actions proposed by Management. Notably, the latter, who continued reporting on the MAP progress on a constant basis, addressed the majority of the issues raised by the Panel over the subsequent years,[78] with a final significant positive impact on the overall performance of the project.

3.4 Protection of Indigenous Peoples' Rights in the Inspection Panel's Practice

Complaints regarding indigenous peoples' rights are among those most frequently framed on human rights grounds by requesters. From its establishment in 1994 to July 2025, the Inspection Panel has handled a total of 177 cases, 50 of which have raised issues related to the Bank's failure to comply with policies concerning indigenous peoples in the request for inspection. Among them, 15 cases have shown specific relevance for the present analysis. Notably, while in the early cases (1994–2005), the Panel's findings addressed a wide range of human rights considerations in interpreting the Bank's policies, even leading to the dismissal of certain projects, it later explicitly referenced key provisions of international legal instruments and made extensive use of the case law of the Inter-American Court of Human Rights ('IACtHR') (2006–2009). Finally, its subsequent practice (2012-present) demonstrates significant attention to human rights issues, particularly through the development of relevant considerations regarding indigenous peoples' land and natural resource rights, leading to a notable consolidation of its approach to various

[77] For an overview of the challenges faced by the UN Treaty bodies in the implementation of their recommendations, see Fox Principi (2017).

[78] Inspection Panel (2013, p. 1). For a comprehensive analysis of the case, see Oleschak-Pillai (2010, pp. 425–427).

matters. In this regard, Table 3.2 illustrates how all these cases contributed to the evolution of the Panel's reasoning on indigenous peoples' rights, summarizing both the key findings and the resulting outcomes in relation to projects.

3.4.1 *Early Cases (1994–2005)*

3.4.1.1 Nepal: Arun III Proposed Hydroelectric Project and Restructuring of IDA Credit (1994)

The case, the first one leading to an extensive analysis of the harm produced as a result of Bank's policy violations in the history of the Panel's practice, related to a new IDA project (Arun III Hydroelectric Project) jointly with the restructuring of an existing IDA credit aimed at financing the former (Arun III Access Road Project, Credit 2029-NWP), collectively referred to as 'Arun III'. The operation was aimed at meeting Nepal's electrical needs through the construction of a 201 kW run-of river hydroelectric power scheme in the Sankhuwa-Sava District of Nepal (including a 68-meter dam), a series of transmission lines from there to the Duhabi municipality, as well as a 122-km access road running to the dam site. At first, the project, to be partially funded by the Bank at an estimated cost of US$800 million, raised serious concern about the capacity of Nepal's economy to sustain it.[79] During the implementation phase, in 1992, to reduce the total expenditure, the borrower decided to revise the project design by a change in access road alignment (from the hill to the valley), which resulted in various environmental and social issues. The proceeding before the Panel started in October 1994, following the receipt of a request for inspection that included several claims, one of which raised concerns about local and indigenous people displaced from the original hill route not being adequately compensated for not having been offered the option of receiving land instead of money. The requesters asked the Panel to keep their identities confidential.

The Panel's Recommendation and Report, published on 16 December 1994, generally emphasized the need for further investigation into certain IDA's omissions during the preparation and appraisal phases. Furthermore, it highlighted that, among the displaced people, vulnerable groups such as ethnic minorities were unfamiliar with a cash-based economy. This introduced indirect human rights considerations into its analysis, as reflected in remarks emphasizing that this issue required special attention due to the potential risks it posed to the welfare of these groups.[80] The

[79] The overall value of the project was estimated at $1.1 billion; however, the annual per capita income in Nepal was $170, and the annual Nepalese budget amounted to $500 million (approximately). The project was supposed to generate about 200 megawatts of electricity for consumption (mainly in the capital and urban areas). In order to repay the loan, the World Bank had required a 100% increase in the electricity tariff in the whole country: Escher (1995, p. 5).

[80] Inspection Panel (1994, p. 19, para. 89).

Panel also acknowledged that the Regional Action Plan prepared by the Nepalese implementing agency to comply with the actions required by OD 4.01 ('Environmental Assessment') and OD 4.20 ('Indigenous Peoples') regarding risk detection and mitigation measures in relation to the induced effects of the project,[81] had not been properly reviewed by the Bank following the proposed change in the access road alignment, which occurred after the formal approval of the project.

After the Board of Executive Directors approved the recommendation to further investigate the case, the Panel published its findings a few months later, in June 1995. The findings confirmed that IDA had violated the policy concerning resettlement program supervision and «consequently failed to enforce covenants in the Credit Agreement» with regard to all the people already displaced from the hill route. The Panel also held that the initial version of the Regional Action Plan, largely based on a study conducted by a Nepalese NGO specializing in nature conservation, had appropriately assessed the likely induced effects of the project, including migration, deforestation, changes in the biomass balance of the Arun Valley, and shifts in occupation and economic opportunities, all of which could place specific groups of people at risk. However, the Panel found that the Regional Action Plan was not yet complete, mainly due to the lack of experience on the part of IDA to oversee its design.

Notably, in developing its reasoning, the Panel had a chance to express its view on the matter concerning identification of ethnic groups as indigenous peoples under OD 4.20 in the project-affected area. More precisely, it held that the presence of individuals scattered throughout the territory who were living in conditions not far from modernity, similar to those of non-indigenous peoples, imposed a flexible interpretation of the provision enshrined in paragraph 3 of OD 4.20,[82] so as to require the Bank to monitor the condition of those social groups chronically vulnerable to potential damages resulting from development projects in a special way. This perspective, which in weighing the various aspects used to identify indigenous peoples under OD 4.20 prioritized vulnerability over distinctiveness,[83] underscores the creative role played by the Panel's practice in advancing the goal of preventing adverse impacts on indigenous peoples from Bank-funded projects on a case-by-case basis.[84] The Panel also clarified that, following the recent enactment of the policy instrument, it should have been interpreted differently from its predecessor,

---

[81] The Arun III project was based on an innovative approach to coping with adverse environmental and socio-economic impact. In addition to the above-mentioned (i) Regional Action Program aimed at assessing risks and identifying corresponding mitigation measures for the induced effects of the project, the borrower was supposed to develop: (ii) an Environmental Mitigation Plan, dealing with the direct effects stemming from the road construction activities; and (iii) a Land Acquisition, Resettlement, and Compensation Plan. The three components jointly constituted the 'Environmental Action Plan', required to cover the full range of risks related to the project according to World Bank OD 4.01. See The World Bank (1994, p. 3).

[82] Inspection Panel (1995a, p. 31, para. 110).

[83] ibid., p. 31, para. 113.

[84] Bradlow (1996, p. 279).

former OMS 2.34, particularly in terms of its scope of application, which was no longer limited to isolated tribal groups. Upon closer examination, the Panel's findings effectively anticipated the more precise language later incorporated into OP 4.10, paragraph 2, which describes indigenous peoples as those «social groups with identities that are *often* distinct from dominant groups in their national societies» [*italics added*].[85] At large, this approach also aligns with modern international legal thinking that recognizes the right of indigenous peoples to internal self-determination in all its forms, regardless of their purported level of integration into the mainstream society. According to the UNDRIP, indigenous peoples should in fact have autonomy in promoting, developing, and maintaining their institutional structures and distinctive spirituality, traditions, procedures and practices, including judicial systems or customs, by virtue of their unique and diverse characteristics. This right to self-government is enshrined in Article 4 of the UNDRIP and reflected in the constitutions of several countries, such as Bolivia, Ecuador, Mexico and South Africa.[86] At the same time, pursuant to Article 5 of the UNDRIP, indigenous peoples retain the right to make choices about how to balance their cultures and traditions with economic development by remaining free to decide whether or not to participate in the political, economic, social, and cultural life of the State.[87]

It is also noteworthy that this approach corresponds with the position adopted in 2010 by the African Commission on Human and Peoples' Rights ('AfrCommHPR') in a well-known communication regarding the displacement of a community from its traditional lands in Kenya. In that case, the AfrCommHPR recognized the *Endorois* as indigenous peoples in light of the existence of a sacred relationship with their ancestral lands and of the element of self-identification. The Commission reached this conclusion based on the premise that 'indigenous peoples' is a contested term, and that «there is no universal and unambiguous definition of the concept, since no single accepted definition captures the diversity of indigenous cultures, histories and current circumstances. The relationships between indigenous

[85] The corresponding provision in the Environmental and Social Framework (ESS-7, para. 3) represents a compromise between the two earlier versions, as it adopts phrasing closer to OD 4.20 while also incorporating terms that can be interpreted in flexible ways. It recognizes that indigenous peoples have 'identities', but for the first time, it also acknowledges their 'aspirations', which differ from those of mainstream groups in national societies and are often disadvantaged by traditional models of development. See The World Bank, *Environmental and Social Framework*, 2017, p. 75, para. 3.

[86] Cats-Baril (2020, pp. 63–66).

[87] It remains clear that indigenous peoples, should they so wish, have the right to political participation and representation, as affirmed in the constitutions of numerous countries, including Bolivia, Burundi, Colombia, Denmark, Nepal, New Zealand, the Philippines, Uganda, USA, Venezuela, and Zimbabwe, and as recognized in 2005 by the Inter-American Court of Human Rights in *Yatama v Nicaragua.* See Tomaselli (2017, p. 412), Cats-Baril (2020, pp. 99–103). See also Inter American Court of Human Rights, *Case of Yatama v Nicaragua*, Judgment of 23 June 2005 (Preliminary Objections, Merits, Reparations and Costs), Series C, No. 127.

peoples and dominant or mainstream groups in society vary from country to country».[88]

Interestingly, the case led to significant developments. Concerns about the project's economic justification in the context of Nepal's overall economy prompted the Bank to ask external expert Maurice Strong, former Secretary General of the UN Conference on Environment and Development, to conduct an independent project review. The review assessed alternative approaches for supporting Nepal in meeting its energy needs, as outlined in a President's memorandum to the Board of Executive Directors dated 2 August 1995.[89] Notably, the results of the review, along with the findings of the Panels' Investigation Report, determined the decision of the then-incoming World Bank Group President, James Wolfensohn, to withdraw financial support for the project.

All in all, the case epitomizes the positive influence that the Panel may exert on the Bank when major issues related to funded projects arise. Suffice it to add that, throughout the following decade, the Bank did not grant any financing to the Nepalese government in the hydropower sector. Notably, the 1996 Country Assistance Strategy for Nepal, which outlined the World Bank's lending priorities following the Arun III inspection case, focused on the promotion of «private investment in technically, economically, environmentally, and socially sound [hydropower] projects».[90]

3.4.1.2 Brazil: Rondônia Natural Resources Management Project (1995)

On 16 June 1995, the Panel was confronted with another claim, leading to an investigation on similar matters, which was submitted by 24 NGOs representing groups of small farmers, rubber-tappers, and indigenous communities. These groups were all residents of a Brazilian federative unit, particularly rich in biodiversity, encompassing over 20 million hectares of the Amazon forest. Their main allegation was that the *Brazil: Rondônia Natural Resources Management Project* (1995), initially conceived to benefit local indigenous people exclusively, was instead having the opposite effect. Specifically, the requesters argued that a particular project component, which focused on investments in socio-economic infrastructure, had led to road rehabilitation and construction works that facilitated environmental degradation.

The project, locally known as 'PLANAFLORO',[91] was primarily based on large-scale social and economic 'agro-ecological' zoning. It aimed both to develop inte-

[88] See the Communication No. 276/2003 of 4 February 2010, para. 147, of the African Commission on Human and Peoples' Rights, available at: https://www.refworld.org/jurisprudence/caselaw/achpr/2010/en/71724. Accessed 2 May 2025.

[89] Inspection Panel (2003a, p. 57).

[90] Buntaine (2015, p. 103).

[91] The project involved a Bank loan of US$167 million; it was approved in March 1992. Starting from June 1992, a parallel natural resource management project was carried out in Mato Grosso,

grated farming systems in areas suitable for permanent agriculture and to demarcate and protect other specific areas, including local indigenous Amerindian territories and ecological reserves, while also combating illegal deforestation, wood transport and forest fires. Since the project sought to address the issues that arose from a previous Bank-funded project in the same area during the 1980s, known as 'POLONORESTE,' the case sparked a lively debate both within the Bank and externally. Notably, prominent international legal scholars pointed out that the core issue in implementing the project was the lack of political commitment from federal and national authorities to make the necessary changes to establish and protect the zoning plans.[92]

Unlike the *Nepal: Arun III* case, the Panel's Report and Recommendation was very concise, stating that it had found sufficient evidence of material adverse effects resulting from the Bank's conduct, and, as a result, recommended further investigation of the case.[93] It also noted that national and federal authorities had begun taking a number of positive actions, and thus made comments regarding their conduct in a manner unrelated to the Bank's actions and omissions. This led the Panel to venture beyond the scope of its mandate, which, according to the Resolution establishing it,[94] is limited to determining whether the Bank has failed in «its follow-up on the borrower's obligations under loan agreements with respect to [...] policies and procedures», provided that such failure has resulted in, or threatens to result in, a material adverse effect:

> Since the Panel's function is limited to investigating the alleged failure of the *Bank* to follow its own policies and procedures, it cannot comment on actions which are the responsibility of other parties, such as the borrower or project executing entities. In this instance however, the Panel would like to record the fact that it is impressed with the Federal and State authorities' and agencies' renewed commitment to the objectives and execution of PLANAFLORO. This commitment was conveyed to the Inspector during his visit to Brazil and has been demonstrated through a number of recent actions aimed at removing some of the obstacles to the timely execution of PLANAFLORO and the achievement of its objectives.[95]

After reviewing the Panel's report, the Board expressed the view that insufficient factual information had been provided. On 12 September 1995, the Panel was therefore tasked with conducting a special review to further substantiate the materiality of the damages and to determine whether these damages had resulted from a

---

locally known as PRODEAGRO. Both projects were based on the Bank's previous experience in the Amazon region during the 1970s and 1980s. See Redwood III (2002).

[92] Hunter (1996, p. 2).

[93] Inspection Panel (1995b, p. 3).

[94] The latest version of the resolution, adopted by IBRD and IDA in 2020, did not alter the Inspection Panel's functions in this regard. See specifically paragraph 13 (formerly paragraph 12 in the 1993 version) and paragraph 15.a (formerly paragraph 14.a in the 1993 version) of the section titled 'Powers of the Panel'. International Bank for Reconstruction and Development and International Development Association, *The World Bank Inspection Panel*, Resolution No. IBRD 2020-0005 and Resolution No. IDA 2020-0004, 8 September 2020.

[95] Inspection Panel (1995b, p. 3).

deviation from the Bank's policies and procedures. The additional review confirmed the presence of significant environmental damage in the project area, including deforestation and loss of income for indigenous people and rubber tappers, and established a causal link with the Bank's inadequate supervision. One of the Panel's main conclusions was that there was no evidence that the Bank had adequately considered enforcing the obligations of the borrower (Brazil) and its implementing agency (Rondônia State Secretariat of Planning) as stipulated in the loan documents. In particular, compliance with OD 13.05 ('Supervision') should have prompted Management to act promptly to identify and address implementation issues. Furthermore, Management did not consider the remedy outlined in OD 13.40 ('Suspension of Disbursement') until after the request for inspection was filed. Notably, this option had proven effective in securing tangible results for the protection of Amerindian peoples during the previous POLONORESTE project in 1985. At the time, the Bank's decision to suspend disbursements, made on environmental and social grounds for the first time, was ultimately reversed when federal authorities began taking actions aligned with the protection of vulnerable Amerindian territories.

The additional review also included general statements addressing indigenous peoples' human rights, highlighting a significant concern for their intergenerational welfare. This was particularly evident in the Panel's focus on the future of health services in indigenous areas within the *Rondônia* territory after project completion. However, this concern was unrelated to the Bank's funding activities, leading the Panel, once again, to exceed the boundaries of its mandate. Specifically, the Panel argued that the positive outcomes of the Amerindian project component—particularly the provision of health services—would not be sustainable in the future without continued Bank's financing:

> Part A.6 of the Project Agreement lists five major requirements for assistance to the Amerindians. Section 3.06 places particular emphasis on registration of the reserves, and provision of health care to all indigenous areas. In internal reports it is acknowledged that illegal logging in their reserves is still not under control. Furthermore, the Uru-eu-wau-wau reserve is still not fully registered. There is wide-spread recognition that this component is poorly managed, and has so far failed to attain its objectives. Provisional health measures, for example, are not sustainable without Bank financing of recurrent expenditures.[96]

In response to the Panel's additional review, Management, jointly with the borrower, prepared a remedial action plan. After reviewing both documents, on 25 January 1996, the Board decided that there was no need for an investigation; nevertheless, for the first time, it asked the Panel to play a role in the implementation phase by following up on the execution of the remedial action plan.

In its Progress Report, the Panel made several observations aimed at enhancing the borrower's limited institutional capacity, particularly in light of Management's proposal to restructure the project in response to a mid-term review. This review, a critical mechanism typically conducted halfway through the implementation phase,

[96] ibid., p. 25.

is intended to ensure that Bank-funded projects remain on track and effectively contribute to their intended development objectives.[97]

Indeed, in February 1998, amendments to the legal agreement with the Brazilian government were signed.

The project ultimately yielded mixed results, as documented by multiple audit outcomes. In 2003, the final Bank's Implementation Completion and Results Report ('ICR') indicated that the performance of both the Bank and the borrower was unsatisfactory. At the same time, support for the indigenous component was deemed partially achieved. Nevertheless, during the implementation period, the indigenous population in Rondônia grew by 10%. Furthermore, at that time, around 99% of them were residing in areas with demarcated boundaries as a result of the process of land regularization promoted by FUNAI, the Brazilian implementing agency. However, the institutional framework remained weak.[98] The report also noted that, among the activities outlined in the revised loan agreement, the improvement of Rondônia's environmental policy and legal framework for natural resource conservation had been partially achieved through the approval of new legislation, although not all of the proposed bills had yet been approved by the Legislative Assembly.[99] The independent Implementation Completion Report Review ('ICRR') provided by the Operations Evaluation Department in September 2007 confirmed these results. It highlighted that land tenure regularization had led to the creation of conservation units covering 20% of Brazil's national territory. However, it also noted that the protection of indigenous lands was being hindered by weak or nonexistent management and enforcement procedures.[100]

3.4.1.3 Argentina, Paraguay: Yacyretá Hydroelectric Project II (1996)

In the *Argentina, Paraguay: Yacyretá Hydroelectric Project II* case (1996), associated with the largest project dam ever undertaken in Latin America on the border between Paraguay and Argentina, the claim submitted by the NGO Sobrevivencia on 12 September 1996 alleged that the environment, as well as the standards of living, health, and economic well-being of the local indigenous people, had been, and could potentially continue to be, adversely affected. This was due to the Bank's failure to ensure, through supervision and enforcement of legal covenants, the adequate execution of the environmental mitigation and resettlement activities included in the project, following the filling of the Yacyretá reservoir to 67 meters above sea level.[101]

---

[97] Inspection Panel (1997a, p. 5).

[98] The World Bank (2003a, p. 25).

[99] ibid., p. 26.

[100] Operations Evaluation Department (2004, Sect. 9).

[101] Notably, a parallel claim was submitted before the Independent Accountability Mechanism of the Inter-American Development Bank, the so-called Investigation Consultation and Investigation Mechanism.

The case is relevant for manifold reasons. First and foremost, the Inspection Panel had the opportunity to express its view on the application of the Bank's remedies when borrower's environmental and social obligations are considered violated, as outlined in OD 13.40 ('Suspension of Disbursements'). Specifically, while Management viewed the remedies as discretionary, allowing flexibility in responding to non-compliance, the Panel offered a different interpretation, aligning with the overarching goals and principles of the Bank's policies by holding that «compliance is not achieved by merely including covenants in Loan Agreements but rather by ensuring that their provisions are implemented in a timely fashion by the borrower and executing entities».[102]

Additionally, from a procedural standpoint, the Panel consolidated the practice of keeping the requester's personal information anonymous, by bringing to the table the Board's acceptance of this practice in the *Arun III* case as a positive ground to counter the risk of reprisals, which «in some countries, cultures or political systems, can be of a significant nature». The Panel also referenced the practice followed in human rights complaints before international bodies like the UN and ILO in this regard, citing these precedents in a footnote to strengthen its argument.[103]

Lastly, it is important to highlight that, as in the *Rondônia* case, the Panel was tasked with overseeing the progress of the remedial Management Action Plan following an additional review. This responsibility enhanced the Panel's role in advocating for actions to bring the project into alignment with environmental and resettlement procedures. In its final report, however, the Panel emphasized that despite its supervisory efforts, the Bank had failed to ensure the continuous involvement of potentially affected people from the very beginning, which was a key element in addressing the issues at hand.[104] In line with this, in 2001, both the internal ICR[105] and the OED's review[106] concluded that the objective of improving environmental management and addressing social aspects was only partially achieved, with significant delays and results of questionable quality.

3.4.1.4 China: Western Poverty Reduction Project (1999)

In 1999, the Panel had to deal with the much-criticized *China: Western Poverty Reduction Project*, whose objective was to reduce the incidence of absolute poverty in remote and inaccessible villages located in three different administrative divisions of China by resettling thousands of multi-ethnic people practicing

[102] Inspection Panel (1996, p. 7).

[103] ibid., Attachment 1, p. 2. The Panel has recently emphasized that «any form of reprisal threatens the integrity of the World Bank's accountability process and that a fundamental premise of the Panel's function is that project-affected persons (PAPs) can access it safely». Inspection Panel (2021, p. 5).

[104] Inspection Panel (1997b, p. 4). See also Treakle and Díaz Peña (2003, p. 69).

[105] The World Bank (2001a, p. 5).

[106] Operations Evaluation Department (2001b, p. 2).

high-altitude rain-fed agriculture into an area affected by the creation of a new irrigation system.

From the outset, the project proved to be very complex. In April 1999, Management conducted an intensive internal review of the environmental and social aspects related to the activities in Qinghai Province. This led to new negotiations with the Chinese government. After agreeing on proposed project modifications, a revised loan package was presented to the Board of Executive Directors for approval.

On 18 June 1999, the Panel became involved in the case after an NGO submitted a complaint on behalf of thousands of individuals from Tibetan and Mongolian ethnic groups. The complaint alleged that, due to the Management's failure to comply with several policies and procedures in the implementation of the Qinghai component, the project could have caused irreversible harm to these people. The main concerns centered around the resettlement process in the move-out area, especially the potential for escalating resource-based tensions.

In the meantime, on 24 June 1999, the Board decided to proceed with the revised project. However, in an unusual move, it stipulated that no work could begin, nor could any funds be disbursed, until further notice. This decision was conditional upon the Panel presenting its findings.[107]

After a thorough investigation, which culminated in 2000 following its first-ever field visit, the Panel made several key statements that are crucial for interpreting the concept of the Bank's compliance with its own policies. In evaluating the Management's actions, the Panel emphasized that compliance should not be limited to a simple verification of adherence to the language of safeguards. Instead, a 'reasonableness' standard of care was required—going beyond merely ensuring that the Bank followed the exact wording of its obligations under the safeguards:

> Most staff at all levels agreed that, in appraising compliance, Management had an obligation to satisfy itself not only that the process and procedures mandated by the policies had been followed, but also that the work under review met professionally acceptable standards of quality. In other words, both process and quality were essential components of compliance.[108]

Delving into the details of the investigation, the Panel found that the Bank had violated several policies, including those related to Environmental Assessment (OD 4.01), by incorrectly classifying the project as category 'B', which failed to account for its high sensitivity, as well as the nature and magnitude of its impact. Other violations included those related to the policies on Involuntary Resettlement (OD 4.30) and Safety of Dams (OP/BP 4.37), among others. Regarding indigenous peoples, the Panel argued that Management had underestimated the presence of various 'ethnic minorities' in both the move-in and move-out areas, each of which required a distinct Indigenous Peoples Development Plan (paras. 16–18). Notably, Management largely agreed with the Panel's findings, recognizing that greater rigor in the application of safeguard standards should have been ensured given the circumstances of

[107] Inspection Panel (2000b, p. xiii).

[108] ibid., p. xv. On this point, see also Passoni et al. (2017).

the project. It thus recommended that the borrower conduct a more thorough environmental analysis to properly classify the project into category 'A', alongside additional consultations with affected communities and the preparation of a separate Indigenous Peoples Development Plan. These actions were to be approved by the Board of Executive Directors before any further disbursements for the Qinghai project component could proceed.[109]

However, following discussions regarding the opportunity to implement these actions, the government of China disagreed with them. As documented by the World Bank's Implementation Completion and Results Report, instead of engaging in the lengthy process required by the implementation of the proposed remedial actions, the borrower decided to dismiss the Qinghai component in order to allow activities in Gansu Province and Inner Mongolia Autonomus Region to proceed.[110] Later on, following a formal restructuring of the project, the Qinghai component was totally removed. In any case, one of its major outcomes was President Wolfensohn's decision to strengthen the Bank's Environment Department in response to the case, marking the first-ever restructuring of the Bank prompted by a Panel investigation.[111]

3.4.1.5 Chad: Petroleum Sector Management Capacity Building Project (2001)

On 22 March 2001, the Panel received another complaint related to the very well-known *Chad: Petroleum Sector Management Capacity Building Project* case (2001). This ambitious development project aimed at drilling oil wells near Doba, in southern Chad, and constructing a 1110-km pipeline to transport the oil to a floating storage and offloading vessel, anchored off the coast of Cameroon. The project was launched in October 2000 and completed in June 2003. The complaint, submitted on 22 March 2001, claimed that the project, both in its design and implementation, constituted an irreversible threat to local communities, their cultural property, and the environment,[112] thus raising non-compliance social concerns with respect to the then-current Operational Directives on Poverty Reduction (OD 4.15), Indigenous Peoples (OD 4.20), and Involuntary Resettlement (OD 4.30), in addition to the Operational Policy Note on Management of Cultural Property (OPN 11.03), among others.

Although in its Investigation Report (17 July 2002) the Panel finally ruled out the applicability of OD 4.20, arguing that the people affected by the project actually constituted the population of southern Chad,[113] this early case is of utmost impor-

---

[109] The World Bank (2000, p. 4).

[110] The World Bank (2007a p. 3), see also Independent Evaluation Group (2007a, Sect. 2).

[111] Inspection Panel (2018, p. 34).

[112] Inspection Panel (2001, para. 2).

[113] Inspection Panel (2002, p. xvi).

tance in terms of its general human rights implications. As the requesters alleged the Bank's infringement of proper governance and human rights principles, the Panel had to carefully consider such claims, which were primarily based on concerns over the lack of compliance with policies on informed and open consultation of affected communities. The Management's response, published on 11 May 2001, acknowledged that instances of poor governance were a significant concern for the Bank, referencing initiatives aimed at addressing them through both the project and broader programs in Chad. While Management recognized the potential relevance of human rights issues to the Bank's work, it limited this to instances where they resulted in direct economic effects, in accordance with the World Bank's Articles of Agreement. Ultimately, it argued that the project had created a platform for dialogue, enabling certain groups to exercise their rights, and therefore dismissed the relevance of human rights concerns in this case.[114]

Notably, at a time when the debate concerning the interpretation of the World Bank's Articles of Agreement in relation to human rights matters was not sufficiently mature yet, the Panel disagreed with the Management's arguments, stating that Bank's policies could not be read in complete isolation from the provisions of core universal human rights instruments, such as the Universal Declaration of Human Rights:

> The Panel appreciates the fact that the frequently imprecise concepts of 'governance' and 'human rights' acquire special significance in the context of the Bank's mandate and operations. Nonetheless, the Panel takes issue with Management's narrow view, and draws attention in this connection to the United Nations Declaration of Human Rights adopted in December 1948, three years after the Bank's Articles of Agreement [...] entered into effect.[115]

It thus recalled that, on the fiftieth anniversary of the adoption of the Declaration, in 1998, the World Bank had expressed its view on the intimate relationship between its mission and human rights, stating that:

> [C]reating the conditions for the attainment of human rights is a central and irreducible goal of development. By placing the dignity of every human being—especially the poorest—at the very foundation of its approach to development, the Bank helps people in every part of the world build lives of purpose and hope. And while the Bank has always taken measures to ensure that human rights are fully respected in connection with the projects it supports, it has been less forthcoming about articulating its role in promoting human rights within the countries in which it operates. This fiftieth anniversary of the Universal Declaration of Human Rights gives us the opportunity to assess our role and to identify areas where we can do even more to reflect the principles enshrined in the Declaration into all of our work.[116]

The Panel finally pointed out that, although it was not within its mandate to assess such matters—especially considering the existence of specialized institutions, including UN bodies, tasked with dealing with these issues—it «felt obliged to examine whether the issues of proper governance or human rights violations in

114 The World Bank (2001b, pp. 46–48).

115 Inspection Panel (2002, p. 62).

116 The World Bank (1998, p. 2).

Chad were such as to impede the implementation of the Project in a manner compatible with the Bank's policies».[117] The main conclusion was that the government's large-scale repression of individuals expressing their opinions in opposition to the Bank-financed project raised important questions of Bank's compliance with its policies on informed and open consultation. Overall, since the situation was far from ideal, the Panel recommended renewed monitoring by the Bank.

The above statements should be read in conjunction with the speech delivered by Edward S. Ayensu, the then Panel Chairperson, which further clarified the Panel's stance on these matters. On 12 September 2002, while presenting the main findings of the Investigation Report to the Board, he broke new ground by declaring that human rights were implicitly embedded in the Bank's policies, thereby arguing that the Panel's consideration of such matters did not exceed the boundaries of its mandate:

> We are convinced that the approach taken in our report, which finds human rights implicitly embedded in various policies of the Bank, is within the boundaries of the Panel's approach to this sensitive subject and has pledged to continue to monitor the developments in this area within the context of the applicable Bank policies.

Consistently, the Panel Chairperson added that the Bank needed to more clearly define its role in promoting human rights within the countries where it operated, once again emphasizing that violations could generally be linked to issues of compliance with the Bank's policies:

> The Panel [...] believes that the human rights situation in Chad exemplifies the need for the Bank to be more forthcoming about articulating its role in promoting rights within the countries in which it operates [...] perhaps this case should lead [...] to study[ing] the wider ramifications of human rights violations as these relate to the overall success or failure of policy compliance in Bank-financed projects.[118]

In response to the Panel's findings, Management, in its report dated 21 August 2002, outlined a series of remedial actions to be implemented independently, in addition to various other actions agreed upon with the borrower regarding the project's failure to achieve its poverty reduction objectives. Regarding human rights issues, Management argued that the affected communities had been provided with the opportunity to express their views. It further stated that, in any case, it would continue its efforts to foster a proper dialogue with civil society. However, Management did not elaborate on any specific remedial actions to be taken regarding these human rights concerns.[119] In its later review, the Independent Evaluation Group held that one of the main objectives of the project, consisting of strengthening Chad's capacity to manage the development of its petroleum resources in an environmentally and

[117] Inspection Panel (2002, p. 62).

[118] Ayensu (2002).

[119] The World Bank (2002, p. 30).

socially sound manner, had been achieved to a modest extent only, with an unsatisfactory performance of both the Bank and the borrower.[120]

As the whole development project of oil fields in Chad's Doba Basin included components to be implemented in Cameroon, it generated another request submitted by a local NGO based in Yaoundé on behalf of residents on 25 September 2002, alleging adverse effects on the people living in the affected areas, including the indigenous *Bakola* and *Bagyeli* communities, due to violations of several Bank's policies. In that case, the Panel found the Bank in compliance with OD 4.20, except for the geographical scope of the analysis contained in both the Environmental Management Plan and the Indigenous Peoples Development Plan, for not having considered the communities' use of a wider area for hunting and gathering activities.[121] In response to the findings, Management agreed with the borrower on discussing appropriate ways to address these issues.[122]

It is worth noting that all project components, including those implemented in Cameroon, underwent a comprehensive evaluation by the IEG. The Program Performance Assessment Report, dated 16 September 2009, rated the overall outcome as unsatisfactory, primarily due to the borrower's performance, with the Bank's performance assessed as moderately unsatisfactory. It also stressed that the World Bank Group's involvement had resulted in stronger environmental and social protection, drawing important lessons to be learned for future Bank's support aimed at achieving more sustainable outcomes in the extractive industry.[123]

3.4.1.6 Colombia: Cartagena Water Supply, Sewerage and Environmental Project (2004)

In this case, the Panel investigated a project involving the construction of a pipeline and submarine outfall designed to carry untreated wastewater (an average of 227,000 cubic meters per day) 20 kilometers north of the city of Cartagena and discharge it into the Caribbean Sea, approximately two and a half kilometers from the coastal fishing villages of Punta Canoa, Arroyo de Piedra, and Manzanillo. The project operations were allegedly harmful to the livelihoods of local communities, whose economies were based on fishing and farming in the involved areas. The request, submitted on 20 April 2004 by a local NGO on behalf of residents of all involved project areas, contended that the Bank-approved assessment of the project was deficient in scope and level of scrutiny, failing to adequately consider the impact on the environment and human health. It also claimed that no consultation had been carried out and that no Indigenous Peoples Development Plan had been prepared, due to the

[120] Independent Evaluation Group (2007b, Sect. 4). See also the Bank's Implementation Completion and Results Report, which rates its own performance as moderately unsatisfactory and that of the borrower as unsatisfactory: The World Bank (2007b, pp. 20–26).

[121] Inspection Panel (2003b, p. 69).

[122] The World Bank (2003b, p. 17).

[123] Independent Evaluation Group (2009, pp. x–xviii).

Bank's failure to detect the presence of Afro-Colombians in the affected area, among other infringements.

In terms of harmful impacts on the environment and human health, the Panel found that, despite some shortcomings in the risk assessment, Bank staff had exercised due diligence in considering alternatives and mitigation measures, thus complying with OD 4.01 ('Environmental Assessment'). However, the potential effects on fishing in the area of influence of the outfall had not been properly addressed.

What makes the case interesting is the identification of the affected people as indigenous inhabitants, which prompted the Panel to take a stance in the debate concerning the use of national legislation in this regard. Despite the Management's response, which argued that, under Colombian legislation, the communities in the northern zone of Cartagena were not recognized as indigenous peoples, the Panel emphasized the importance of the Bank using its own policy as the primary reference point for assessing compliance. The Panel clarified that, regardless of its alignment with national legislation, the Bank was obligated to adhere to its policy due to its binding nature:

> The Panel emphasizes that the issue under investigation is whether the Bank followed OD 4.20 on Indigenous Peoples during the design, appraisal and execution stages of the Project with regards to the Afro-Colombian communities living in the area of the proposed outfall. The classification of certain groups as indigenous peoples under Bank policy OD 4.20 is not necessarily consistent with, or subject to, local legislation, but is still binding on the Bank.[124]

Then, in developing its reasoning, the Panel observed that most of the involved communities met the criteria listed under OD 4.20 ('Indigenous Peoples'), except for 'indigenous language' and, arguably, 'primarily oriented subsistence production'. The report explained that Colombia, and the Americas in general, were historically inhabited by several peoples deracinated from West Africa and penalized by slavery for over 400 years, which led to the loss of their original language. Furthermore, at the time, not all residents relied solely on fishing and farming, despite their strong connection to ocean natural resources and their social and economic marginalization. It thus found that Afro-Colombians living in the project affected area could be regarded as an ethnic minority, broadly falling under the scope of application of Bank's policy on indigenous peoples, and requiring the preparation of an IPDP or similar document to specifically address the impact generated upon them, as well as timely, meaningful, and relevant consultations. However, given the absence of two of the policy criteria, it concluded that the Bank's failure to do so in the specific case could not be deemed non-compliant behavior.

Overall, the Panel's other findings led to major improvements in the final project outcome. The Panel repeatedly emphasized that the social impact assessment, required under OD 4.01, was unsatisfactory, stressing that it lacked both an adequate evaluation and proposals for mitigation measures to protect the livelihoods of the local population, who, regardless of their classification as indigenous peoples or

[124] Inspection Panel (2005, p. 60).

not, had been affected by the project.[125] As a consequence, Management undertook specific actions in response to the findings regarding the social impact assessment.[126] It agreed with the implementing agency Agua de Cartagena, a mixed private-public company established with the Bank's assistance, on carrying out a program to strengthen fishing activities. This led to the organization of training sessions on innovative methods and technologies for the Punta Canoa fishermen, as well as a joint review of the communication and outreach strategies to better engage local communities in the project implementation, as documented in the Management Progress Report to the Board of Executive Directors.[127] In all the subsequent evaluations,[128] including the IEG Project Performance Assessment Report, both the Bank's and borrower's performance were reasonably assessed as satisfactory.[129]

3.4.1.7 Democratic Republic of Congo: TSERO and EESRSP (2005)

A later strand of the Inspection Panel's practice began drawing on international human rights law in a more incisive manner. On 19 November 2005, the Panel received a request regarding the implementation of a development policy loan ('TSERO'), a single-tranche budget support operation aimed at improving governance in the natural resources sector, and an investment loan ('EESRSP') supporting institutional reforms in the forestry sector, respectively. Both operations were related to a new commercial concession system in the rainforest of the Democratic Republic of Congo, where thousands of *Pygmies* had lived for generations. The complaint argued that the use of TSERO had led to the circumvention of safeguard policies. It further alleged that the national institutional strengthening component of EESRSP was undermining the indigenous people's right to use ancestral lands, adversely affecting their cultural property in addition to the world heritage-protected rainforest resources, thereby infringing the Bank's policies on Environmental Assessment (OP 4.01), Poverty Reduction (OD 4.15), Indigenous Peoples (OD 4.20), Forestry (OP/BP 4.36), and Management of Cultural Property (OPN 11.03), among other claims related to project supervision.[130]

As regards TSERO, the Panel ventured the boundaries of its mandate by contesting the choice of a development policy loan to achieve the goal of reforming a sector featuring so many social and environmental complexities. Regarding the other claims, the Panel found that, by failing to perform a proper environmental assessment, Management had not identified the borrower's international obligations stemming from two core environmental treaties signed and ratified by Congo, which,

[125] ibid., pp. 62–63.

[126] The World Bank (2005, pp. 20–22).

[127] The World Bank (2006a, p. 4, 6).

[128] The World Bank (2010a).

[129] Independent Evaluation Group (2011), Independent Evaluation Group (2016a, p. 10).

[130] Vita et al. (2017, p. 14).

according to OP 4.01, paragraph 3, would have compelled the Bank not to finance the project.[131] These treaties, of great importance to indigenous peoples, were: the 1972 UNESCO World Heritage Convention, which designates specific natural and cultural sites to be preserved for present and future generations,[132] and the 1973 Washington Convention on International Trade in Endangered Species of Wild Fauna and Flora, aimed at ensuring that international trade does not threaten the survival of some flora or fauna species.[133]

Thus, the Panel emphasized that the Bank had also failed to recognize the spiritual value of forests to indigenous peoples and, as a result, the appropriate measures to avoid harming areas falling within the definition of cultural property under Bank policy OPN 11.03, the only safeguard explicitly embodying a UN definition in its text to define its scope of application.[134] Furthermore, the Bank had fallen short of achieving the objective of 'sustainable poverty reduction' for not having undertaken any effort to improve the poor's living conditions and their access to health, nutrition and education, in contrast with OD 4.15. In its final remarks, after recognizing that remaining engaged in the forest sector in the Democratic Republic of Congo was important, the Panel stated that it was essential for the Bank to «comply with its social and environmental safeguard policies, as well as its other policies, to ensure that the forests benefit the people in DRC and that they be available for both present and future generations».[135] Notably, this language aligns with the definition of sustainability proposed by the UN Brundtland Commission in 1987,[136] which has been pivotal in shaping the global conversation about sustainable development at the international level since that time.

With respect to the claim concerning OD 4.20 related to the EESRSP component, the Panel held that the Management's failure to trigger the safeguard concerning indigenous peoples for not identifying their presence in the project areas during the early design phase had led to major problems, such as the lack of an Indigenous Peoples Development Plan, with the subsequent infringement of *Pygmies*' rights to consultation, participation and information, as well as a significant negative impact on their collective land rights.[137] In determining whether the *Pygmies* could be considered indigenous peoples, in its Investigation Report dated 31 August 2007, the

[131] Inspection Panel (2007a, p. 93).

[132] UNESCO, *Convention Concerning the Protection of the World Cultural and Natural Heritage*, 17th session, Paris, 16 November 1972 (entered into force on 17 December 1975). DRC ratified the World Heritage Convention on 23 September 1974.

[133] IUCN, *Washington Convention on International Trade in Endangered Species of Wild Fauna and Flora* (CITES), Washington, DC, 3 March 1973 (entered into force on 1 July 1975 and amended in Bonn on 22 June 1979 and in Gaborone on 30 April 1983). Notably, DRC acceded to CITES on 20 July 1976.

[134] The policy has been later replaced by other versions, such as OP/BP 4.11 on Physical Cultural Resources, and ESS-8, which removed this reference.

[135] Inspection Panel (2007a, p. 132).

[136] UN General Assembly (1987).

[137] Inspection Panel (2007a, pp. 63–64).

Panel explicitly relied upon the very well-known approach adopted by the African Commission on Human and Peoples' Rights. Departing from the consideration that, compared to their neighbors, most *Pygmy* people in the project area were more or less marginalized, underprivileged, paid less for their service, had less access to modern health and education facilities, and were much less represented in the political arena, the Panel concluded that, since they conformed to the definition of the 'indigenous' concept in its 'modern analytical form', they were subject to the application of OD 4.20. In support of its analysis, the Panel referenced statements made by the then African Commissioner, Mr. Karnel Rezag Bara, at the fifth session of the UN Permanent Forum on Indigenous Peoples held in New York in May 2006.[138] In an annex to the 2007 Investigation Report ('Note on Ethnographic Background of the Pygmy People in DRC'), the Panel also explicitly held that these statements were particularly relevant to the case.[139]

The referenced statements relied on the main findings of the Working Group of Experts established in 2000 by the AfrCommHPR as a special mechanism to study the implications of the African Charter on Human and Peoples' Rights on the well-being of indigenous communities.[140] In 2005, through the elaboration of these findings,[141] the Working Group developed a comprehensive framework addressing the key issues facing indigenous peoples in Africa, elaborating on concepts such as subordination, marginalization, and discrimination as the primary criteria for identifying them:

> Almost all African states host a rich variety of different ethnic groups, some of which are dominant and some of which are in subordinate positions. All of these groups are indigenous to Africa. However, some are in a structurally subordinate position to the dominating groups and the State, leading to marginalisation and discrimination. It is this situation that the *indigenous* concept, in its modern analytical form and the international legal framework attached to it, addresses. It addresses the root causes of the subordination and it emphasizes the human rights dimension for addressing the issues.[142]

---

[138] The fifth session of the Forum was devoted to the theme 'The Millennium Development Goals and indigenous peoples: Re-defining the Millennium Development Goals'. See UN Permanent Forum on Indigenous Issues (2006).

[139] Inspection Panel (2007a, pp. 57–58, 151).

[140] The Working Group on Indigenous Populations/Communities in Africa was established through a Resolution of the African Commission on Human and Peoples' Rights at its 28th Ordinary Session in Benin in 2000: see African Commission on Human and Peoples' Rights (2000).

[141] The African Commission endorsed the Working Group's findings with a specific Resolution: African Commission on Human and Peoples' Rights (2003).

[142] African Commission on Human and Peoples' Rights (2005, p. 101). As early as 1996, Erica-Irene Daes, the chairperson of the UN Working Group on Indigenous Populations (established by the UN Human Rights Sub-Commission on Prevention of Discrimination and Protection of Minorities in 1982), advocated this understanding outside of Africa. Nevertheless, in doing so, she considered a fourth criterion, that is the voluntary preservation of cultural distinctiveness, encompassing aspects such as language, social organization, religion, modes of production, laws, and institutions. UN Commission on Human Rights (1996).

According to the 2005 framework, early definitions of indigenous peoples primarily focused on aboriginality, referring to peoples still under the political domination of the descendants of colonial settlers.[143] However, this approach was less applicable in the African context than in the Americas or Australia. Given that forms of suppression continued to exist even in independent post-colonial states, a modern definition should address three key criteria: (i) a structural situation of inequality, (ii) self-definition as a distinct collectivity, and (iii) a special attachment to and use of traditional lands.[144]

Since its inception, the framework has attracted a vast array of consensus[145] and is still used as a reference point in UN-level discussions.[146]

It is interesting to note that the framework, in turn, explicitly referenced the World Bank's OD 4.20 of 1991, acknowledging its analogous approach to the matter. According to the policy, in fact, indigenous peoples can be described in light of a structural situation of inequality, as «groups with a social and cultural identity that is distinct from the dominant groups in society and that makes them vulnerable to being disadvantaged in the development process».[147]

The final outcome of the case was the development of a plan in consultation with the indigenous people, as part of the actions undertaken by Management jointly with the borrower to address the Panel's findings.[148] Regular reports were prepared and presented to the Board to detail progress made in implementing the Action Plan. The first report was submitted in March 2009, and the last in March 2011. According to the Bank's Implementation Completion and Results Report, the environmental

[143] In this regard, see also the conclusions of the landmark study of the Special Rapporteur of the Sub-Commission on Prevention of Discrimination and Protection of Minorities: Martínez Cobo (1987), Conclusions, Proposals and Recommendations.

[144] African Commission on Human and Peoples' Rights (2005, pp. 92–93).

[145] In 2009, in the overview report of a research project jointly carried out with the ILO and the Centre for Human Rights of the University of Pretoria to analyze the impact of the legislation of 24 African countries on indigenous peoples' rights, the framework was regarded as an instrument which had «stood the test of time and served national, regional and international audience in the area of indigenous rights, including students, lecturers, researchers, social workers, human rights activists and defenders, the African Union, as well as United Nations agencies». See International Labour Organization and African Commission on Human and Peoples' Rights (2009, p. iii).

[146] See, for instance, the paper submitted by Kanyinke Sena, a Kenyan indigenous lawyer, at the UN International Expert Group Meeting convened in 2010 on the theme 'Indigenous Peoples: Development with Culture and Identity, Articles 3 and 32 of the United Nations Declaration on the Rights of Indigenous Peoples', recommended by the Permanent Forum on Indigenous Issues and endorsed by the Economic and Social Council, which explicitly draws on the framework to elaborate on the understanding of the concept of 'indigenous people': UN Department of Economic and Social Affairs (2010, pp. 3–4). More recently, the African Commissioner Soyata Maiga has presented a paper at the UN Seminar of the Expert Mechanism on the Rights of Indigenous Peoples devoted to the theme 'Right to Land under the UN Declaration on the Rights of Indigenous Peoples: A Human Rights Focus': see Maiga (2019, p. 1).

[147] The World Bank Operations Policy and Country Services (2011, pp. 0–6, para. 3).

[148] The World Bank (2017a, p. 31).

and social aspects of project implementation improved following the implementation of the action plan, in parallel with the national capacity to manage safeguard issues. The ICR rated the overall World Bank's and borrower's performance as moderately satisfactory.[149] The Independent Evaluation Group confirmed the same rating in relation to the Bank's performance and assessed the borrower's performance as moderately unsatisfactory.[150]

3.4.2 Indigenous Peoples Policies as a Reflection of International Human Rights Law (2006–2009)

3.4.2.1 Honduras: Land Administration Project (2006)

In the *Honduras Land Administration* case (2006), the implementation of an adaptable program loan granted in February 1984 by IDA and focused on a comprehensive reform of the land titling system of the country, was raising concern among the members of the indigenous *Garífuna* community, who submitted a request for inspection on 3 January 2006 through a representative organization (Organización Fraternal Negra Hondureña). The request argued that the project component concerning systematic regularization of land to the benefit of local population had not considered the *Garífuna* community's rights in its design, appraisal and implementation, thus infringing OD 4.20 on Indigenous Peoples among other Bank's policies, including OP/BP 4.01 on Environmental Assessment as well as OP/BP 4.04 on Natural Habitats. In particular, it alleged the project failure to address the community's serious concern about the potential impact of a new piece of legislation, enacted by the Congress in June 2004 in furtherance of the project.

According to the requesters, while Chapter III of the Honduran Property Law[151] included an article recognizing the importance of ancestral land rights, it also encompassed some controversial provisions regarding the regularization of property in favor of non-indigenous occupants who had taken possession of the *Garífuna* community's ancestral lands, at times with fraud or violence,[152] thus also infringing the 1989 ILO Convention No. 169 concerning Indigenous and Tribal Peoples, which Honduras signed and ratified on 28 March 1995. Notably, the claim explicitly referred to the Convention, observing that Bank's policies were supposed to be frequently reviewed «so that the Bank, in executing its projects, respects the

[149] The World Bank (2011a, p. v).

[150] Independent Evaluation Group (2013).

[151] Congreso Nacional de Honduras, *Ley de Propiedad*, Decree no. 82 of 2004, in *Diario Oficial La Gaceta 30.428*, 29 June 2004, Article 93.

[152] According to the requesters, while Article 93 of Chapter III of the Honduran Property Law recognized the importance of ancestral land rights, the remaining articles in the Chapter (with special reference to Articles 97, 98, and 100) were highly detrimental to the fulfillment of these same rights.

international rules and standards designed to safeguard the rights of indigenous peoples».[153]

The Panel decided to ask the General Counsel to issue an opinion to clarify whether and to what extent the safeguards incorporated into the project were appropriate to cope with the gaps affecting Honduran legislation concerning the protection of indigenous peoples.[154] Although the opinion, dated 20 December 2006, did not answer the request on the ground that determining the degree of effective protection offered by the project in application of Bank's policies was a task reserved for the Panel, it provided several observations that were analyzed in detail and led to two main considerations.

First, with reference to the statement that OD 4.20 merely required that harm to indigenous peoples resulting from a Bank-funded project be avoided or mitigated—without detailing the exact substantive and procedural contents that local law should contain—the Panel held that «the legal context in which a Project is designed and implemented is very important» and that «Bank policies recognize this».[155] In that particular case, the project had facilitated the enactment of a new piece of legislation detrimental to indigenous people's rights that Management should have taken into consideration in order to include remedies to counter the possible induced negative effects.[156]

Second, the Panel, which in its report placed notable emphasis on the international legal and historical struggle of the community in the pursuit of their rights over ancestral lands, including through petitions filed before the Inter-American Commission on Human Rights ('IACHR'), confirmed that the Bank had failed to take the ILO Convention No. 169 of 1989 into consideration since the early stages of project design. This finding contrasted with Management's view, according to which such an issue was not relevant for the purposes of the application of the Bank's policy, and, as such, should have been raised «within the jurisdictional context of other fora, such as Inter-American Human Rights tribunals».[157] In holding so, the Panel developed an interesting reasoning, arguing that respect for conventional international law by borrowing countries may play a crucial role in influencing the ultimate Bank's decision not to finance a project, even if unrelated to environmental matters, thus proposing an innovative interpretation of OMS 2.20 ('Project Appraisal') adopted in January 1984. In this regard, the General Counsel interpreted

---

[153] See paragraph 3 of the request for inspection submitted by Organización Fraternal Negra Honduras, available at: https://documents.worldbank.org/pt/publication/documents-reports/documentdetail/802551468038149256/honduras-land-administration-project-inspection-panel-notice-of-registration. Accessed 5 May 2025.

[154] The request was made pursuant to paragraph 15 of the Resolution that established the Inspection Panel in 1993, according to which the Panel «shall seek the advice of the Bank's Legal Department on matters related to the Bank's rights and obligations with respect to the request under consideration». The same provision can be found in the latest version of the Resolution (2020) at para. 16.

[155] Inspection Panel (2007b, p. 68, para. 242).

[156] ibid., pp. 68–69.

[157] The World Bank (2006b, p. 14).

OMS 2.20 as limiting the borrower's relevant international obligations to those arising solely from treaties «essentially of an environmental nature». The Panel put on record its concern regarding this interpretation, for different reasons:

(i) According to the Panel, the text of the policy had a broader scope, as it included all the agreements related to people's health and well-being.[158] The policy in fact mentioned those involving the use of international waters, normally not characterized as «essentially of an environmental nature»;
(ii) Another statement issued a few months later, in May 1984, OMS 2.36 ('Environmental Aspects of Bank Work') referred to international environmental agreements in an exclusive way. It included a specific provision, according to which the Bank «will not finance projects that contravene any international environmental agreements to which the member country concerned is a party».[159] Its successor, OP/BP 4.01 ('Environmental Assessment'), adopted in January 1999, explicitly listed all the Operational Manual Statements it replaced in its preamble—none of which included OMS 2.20.

All in all, OMS 2.20 had to be regarded as an autonomous instrument of a more general nature, encompassing international agreements including, but not limited to, environmental matters.

Then, although only in a footnote accompanying the main text (no. 152), the Panel added that the status of both the ILO and the Bank as UN specialized agencies could be regarded as an additional reason for refraining from activities inconsistent with the Convention:

> The Panel notes that both ILO and the World Bank are specialized agencies of the United Nations and this seems to be an additional reason for the World Bank to refrain from financing activities that will not be consistent with the provisions of ILO Convention No. 169.[160]

Finally, in a crucial excerpt of the report, in response to the General Counsel's observation that the Bank's policy on indigenous peoples did not require compliance with the ILO Convention, the Panel fully addressed the issue by holding that, while it was undisputed that the Bank was responsible for compliance with its own policy, it was equally true that this policy mirrored the contents of the Convention:

> [T]he Bank is responsible for compliance with its own policies and procedures. But it also notes that Honduras is a party to ILO Convention No. 169. The General Counsel's Response indicates that OD 4.20 does not require compliance with ILO Convention No. 169. The Panel observes that OD 4.20 broadly reflects the spirit and provisions of ILO Convention No. 169.[161]

---

[158] The statement, dated January 1984, required both Bank staff and borrowers to carry out a specific assessment of the project impact on all involved social groups (later superseded by OP/BP 10.00). See Price (2021, p. 104).

[159] The World Bank, *Operational Manual Statement 2.36, Environmental Aspects of the Bank's Work*, 1984.

[160] Inspection Panel (2007b, p. 72), footnote no. 152.

[161] ibid., para. 256.

The footnote accompanying the main text (no. 153) added that «[t]he Panel was informed that ILO Convention No. 169 was not mentioned in OD 4.20 because at the time the policy was drafted, the Convention had been ratified only by two countries», once again, acknowledging the strong relationship between the contents of the Operational Directive and the ILO Convention.[162] The Panel thus concluded that, although the Bank could not be held responsible for the implementation of the borrower's obligations stemming from a ratified treaty on a general basis, the verification regarding the consistency of a project with such treaty provisions was the object of a specific Bank's obligation aimed at deciding whether to disburse funds or not in project appraisal. A couple of months later, Management formally disagreed with the Panel's findings, arguing that the operational policies could not act as a mechanism capable of settling all land titling disputes in Honduras:

> There is no Bank policy requirement that the "Project rules" force changes in local law to make it fit a Bank-mandated standard. Bank policies, including OD 4.20, require Project compliance with Bank standards, but they do not require national compliance beyond the Project sphere. Hence, it is inconsistent to suggest that the Project serves as a mechanism to settle all land titling disputes in Honduras to the satisfaction of indigenous or Afro-Honduran peoples, or to bring local law in line with ILO 169.[163]

At the same time, Management decided to undertake a series of substantial actions to work with the Honduran government on the update of the IPDP and on the parallel issuance of regulations making the relevant local legal framework conducive to the regularization of ethnic lands. Therefore, it agreed to take the interests of indigenous peoples into account in a manner compatible with relevant Bank's safeguards, as detailed in the Management Progress Report.[164]

Consistently, the ICR rated the Bank's and the borrower's performance as moderately satisfactory. However, the difficulties encountered in the context of safeguards compliance in relation to recognition of indigenous land rights led to a moderately unsatisfactory Bank's performance at entry.[165] The IEG confirmed this assessment with respect to the Bank's performance, due to its underestimation of several risks during project preparation, such as potential delays in consolidating the new legal framework concerning property law. During supervision, although recognizing that the Bank was not proactive in assessing the impact of national legislation on the project, the report emphasized a marked improvement during the second half of the implementation phase. The overall performance was considered moderately satisfactory. By contrast, the borrower's performance was rated as moderately unsatisfactory.[166]

[162] ibid., footnote no. 153.

[163] The World Bank (2007c, p. 32).

[164] The World Bank (2009, p. 9).

[165] The World Bank (2010b, p. 13).

[166] Independent Evaluation Group (2012a).

3.4.2.2 Papua New Guinea: Smallholder Agriculture Development Project (2009)

In relation to a project implemented in Papua New Guinea, aimed at improving the income of targeted smallholders in oil palm production in a sustainable manner, the requester, a local NGO, alleged violations of several policies, including OMS 2.20 on Project Appraisal, in the context of the International Covenant on Economic, Social and Cultural Rights ('ICESCR'),[167] to which Papua New Guinea was a signatory.

First, in its Investigation Report, the Panel clarified that, since the national population was almost entirely composed of indigenous peoples from over 800 distinct ethnic groups, OP/BP 4.10 was broadly applicable to all the projects funded by the Bank in the country. Thus, in examining the claim concerning the violation of OMS 2.20, it clarified that the Covenant «commits its parties to work toward the granting of economic, social, and cultural rights (ESCR) to individuals, including, among others, the right to an adequate standard of living». Furthermore, considering the substantial overlap in terms of contents with OP/BP 4.10, since the policy «covers, and is consistent with, the Treaty's main objectives related to social and cultural rights (insofar as those objectives pertain to indigenous peoples)», it concluded that its compliance analysis could well focus «solely within the parameters of OP/BP 4.10».[168] Once again, OP/BP 4.10 was viewed as reflecting a core international human rights legal instrument, such as the ICESCR.

As no major project activity had been carried out on the ground at the time of the request, much of the focus of the investigation pertained to the design, planning and appraisal phases. By primarily relying on OP/BP 4.10 in its analysis, the Panel found that the failure to include the required «social and economic benefits that are culturally appropriate and gender and intergenerationally inclusive»[169] in the project was a serious shortcoming. Although observing that the policy allows for not preparing an IPDP when indigenous peoples are the sole or the overwhelming majority of direct project beneficiaries, it held that staff's focus should remain on the relevant issues covered by the policy, regardless of their inclusion in the overall design of the project or in a separate plan. It thus openly admitted that such a degree of care from the Bank's side was always due, even when making its task of reviewing project preparation (and supervising its implementation in subsequent phases) more demanding and challenging.[170]

Another significant issue concerned indigenous peoples' consultations, due to the failure to adequately involve local structures of representation, such as clan leaders. In light of previous similar cases, the Panel stressed the importance of

---

[167] UN General Assembly, *International Covenant on Economic, Social and Cultural Rights*, Resolution 2200A (XXI) of 16 December 1966 (entered into force on 3 January 1976), in *UNTS*, Volume 999, p. 171 f., UN Doc. A/RES/2200A (XXI).

[168] Inspection Panel (2011, p. 43).

[169] ibid., p. 89.

[170] ibid.

formulating guidelines for the application of the policy in this regard, showcasing its strong interest in indigenous peoples' welfare. Overall, the inclusion of such statements in its investigation report is a practical demonstration of the pivotal role that the Panel can play in influencing the interpretation of the Bank's operational policies, in spite of the fact that the Board of Executive Directors is the only organ institutionally entrusted with the task of formally amending them:

> Previous Panel investigations have also revealed noncompliance in application of the Bank's Policy on Indigenous Peoples. Again, a significant issue has been shortcomings in consultations with the affected populations, and in particular, failure to adequately account for local structures of representation (for example, Honduras Land Administration Project and DRC forest operations). [...] Hence, it might be useful to formulate clearer guidelines for the application of OP 4.10 to projects where a self-standing IPP is not warranted. The emphasis is on the appropriateness of benefits intended under the project and community support for the project as a whole.[171]

In response to these findings, Management observed that the inclusion of appropriate provisions concerning smallholders' economic and social benefits could be inferred from the analysis of the positive project impact on different levels of their productivity.[172] At the same time, it committed to developing a more adequate consultation process, while also closely monitoring this aspect during the implementation phase.[173] The Board approved the Management Action Plan shortly thereafter.[174] Since then, Management has reported on the successful progress made regarding the required actions twice, in 2014 and 2015. Consistently, the internal ICR report elaborated by the Bank in its self-assessment of overall performance rated it as moderately satisfactory. By contrast, the borrower's performance has been rated unfavorably.[175] The IEG subsequently assessed both performances negatively (as moderately unsatisfactory and unsatisfactory, respectively), citing Management's failure to adequately address important environmental aspects during the design phase,[176] as confirmed by the PARR (2018).[177] Overall, the three reports agreed on the insufficient achievement of the project initial objectives, attributing this to the relatively modest involvement of local inhabitants.

---

[171] ibid., pp. 137–139.

[172] The World Bank (2011b), Annex 1, p. 24.

[173] ibid., p. 20.

[174] See the News Release of the World Bank dated 16 December 2011, available at: https://www.inspectionpanel.org/. Accessed 6 May 2025.

[175] The World Bank (2014a, p. v).

[176] Independent Evaluation Group (2015, p. 9).

[177] Independent Evaluation Group (2018, p. v).

3.4.3 *Interpretation in Light of Regional Human Rights Case Law (2009)*

3.4.3.1 Panama: Land Administration Project (First Request) (2009)

In this case, the Panel took a stance on the issues regarding indigenous peoples' land rights and tenure security in connection with an IBRD loan approved in January 2001, which encompassed a component seeking to advance equitable access to land through private titling, regularization activities and the modernization of the national administration system, and a parallel one aimed at preserving natural resources through demarcation of indigenous territories. In its Investigation Report, the Panel responded to the claims submitted through two separate requests for inspection related to the adverse impact of the same project on two distinct communities.

In the first request, the *Naso* indigenous community contended that the project had failed to facilitate the establishment of a 'comarca', a semi-autonomous reserve—which the national Constitution of Panama allows to create in recognition of collective land rights—in Bocas del Toro Province. According to it, the Bank's financing had facilitated the proposal of a new specific bill of law favorable to indigenous peoples only during the early years of implementation. However, following its rejection by the National Assembly, the project shifted to supporting the adoption of new legislation on 'Collective Lands', without conducting proper consultations.[178] This resulted in undermining *Naso*'s aspirations for autonomy by creating a different, ambiguous legal regime. In response to this request, the Panel found that Management had substantively complied with the key policies and procedures applicable to the project, in favour of the *Naso* community in the initial phases of the project. At a later stage, its decision to support the new legislation was considered a good faith measure undertaken in light of the political instability context consistent with OP/BP 13.05 ('Project Supervision'). At the same time, it found that stronger efforts to ensure clarity on the provisions of the new legislation should have been sought, in addition to adequate consultations. Finally, it positively endorsed the Management's temporary decision to suspend the disbursement of funds for the project activities regarding the *Naso*.

As regards the second request, concerning the inappropriate demarcation of the land area offered to the *Ngäbe* community to expand their rights over the 'áreas anexas', the territories outside their comarca area, which had been formally established by national legislation in 1997, the Panel found several shortcomings in the consultation process related to the areas verification in the project preparation phase, ultimately resulting in hampering *Ngäbe*'s efforts to gain recognition of their lands, in breach of OD 4.20.

---

[178] National Assembly of the Republic of Panama, *Ley sobre tierras colectivas que establece el procedimiento especial para la adjudicación de la propiedad colectiva de tierra de los pueblos indígenas que no están dentro de las comarcas*, Law no. 72 of 2008, in *Gaceta Oficial Digital no. 26193*, 30 December 2008.

Crucially, in reviewing the Bank's compliance with the requirements stated under paragraph 15.a of OD 4.20,[179] prescribing that an IPDP should give particular attention to the right of indigenous peoples to use and develop the lands they occupy—including protection against illegal intruders and access to natural resources vital for their subsistence and reproduction—the Panel used Article 26 of the UNDRIP as a reference point in a footnote.[180] Notably, the provision held that states shall give legal recognition and protection to such lands, territories and resources.

The Panel thus drew critical conclusions regarding the key role the Bank must play in supporting the land rights of indigenous peoples in Panama, emphasizing the importance of remaining engaged on these issues in the country, in line with its operational policies.[181]

It is important to note that, in outlining the general context of both claims, the Panel observed that the struggle for land, in addition to political and cultural autonomy, was a prominent feature of indigenous peoples' history in the Americas. The Panel thus emphasized that the right to the legal recognition of the lands historically occupied by indigenous peoples had been widely recognized by the Inter-American Court of Human Rights, recalling the *Mayagna (Sumo) Awas Tingni Community v Nicaragua* case (2001). This decision was a milestone in acknowledging the significance of such a right, which extends far beyond mere ownership, considering the spiritual value attached to the land, to be fully enjoyed in order to preserve cultural heritage and pass it on to future generations:[182]

> The rights of indigenous peoples were reaffirmed by the Inter-American Court of Human Rights in its judgment of August 31, 2001. The Mayagna (Sumo) Awas Tingni Indigenous Community of the Atlantic Coast of Nicaragua secured recognition of its rights to its ancestral lands in a case presented by the Inter-American Commission on Human Rights (IACHR) to the Inter-American Court, establishing a historical precedent at the international level in the struggle of indigenous peoples for their communal rights [...]. Indigenous peoples, by virtue of their very existence, have the right to live freely on their own lands; the close bond of indigenous peoples with their land should be recognized and understood as an essential element of their cultures, spiritual lives, well-being, and economic survival. For indigenous communities the relationship to land is not merely a question of ownership and production but a material and spiritual element they must enjoy fully, among other reasons to preserve their cultural heritage and pass it on to future generations.[183]

The Panel also cited several other landmark cases decided by the Court, which were extensively referenced in the footnote accompanying the text, such as *Yakye Axa*

[179] The World Bank Operations Policy and Country Services (2011, pp. 0–6, para. 15.a).

[180] Inspection Panel (2010, p. 74), footnote 172.

[181] ibid., p. 90.

[182] Inter-American Court of Human Rights, *Case of the Mayagna (Sumo) Awas Tingni Community v Nicaragua*, Judgment of 31 August 2001 (Merits, Reparations and Costs), Series C, No. 79.

[183] Inspection Panel (2010, pp. 17–18).

Indigenous Community v Paraguay (2005),[184] *Sawhoyamaxa Indigenous Community v Paraguay* (2006),[185] and *Saramaka People v Suriname* (2007).[186]

Notably, in *Saramaka*, the IACtHR interpreted the right to property enshrined in the American Convention in the context of development projects, arguing that such a right could not be restricted by the mining concessions granted by the State of Suriname, which was in fact required to put in place adequate mechanisms to ensure the effective participation of the members of the indigenous community in conformity with their customs and traditions.[187] In support of its view, the Court held that this interpretation was consistent with the text of several international instruments, including the 1989 ILO Convention and the Bank's policy on Indigenous Peoples, OP/BP 4.10, thus giving rise to an interesting case of cross-reference that underscores the positive evaluation made by a regional human rights court with respect to the degree of protection afforded by the Bank's operational framework.

Finally, it is worth reporting that, in response to the Panel's findings, Management proposed an action plan whose main objective was to incorporate the «lessons learned from this Project into the design and implementation of similar projects in the Region, particularly with regard to stakeholder consultations».[188] The plan also committed the Bank to recommend that the government prioritize addressing the land claims of the *Naso*[189] as well as the demarcation of the *Ngäbe* Annex Areas, in Bocas del Toro.[190] However, the Bank self-rated its performance, along with that of the borrower, as moderately unsatisfactory,[191] an assessment later confirmed by IEG.[192]

3.4.4 Recent Cases (2012-Present)

3.4.4.1 Ethiopia: Promoting Basic Services Phase III Project (2012)

This project was initially designed to enhance the quality of services in education, health, agriculture, water supply, sanitation, and rural roads in the Ethiopian Gambella Region. The requesters claimed that a national program implemented in

---

[184] Inter-American Court of Human Rights, *Case of the Yakye Axa Indigenous Community v Paraguay*, Judgment of 17 June 2005 (Merits, Reparations and Costs), Series C, No. 125.

[185] Inter-American Court of Human Rights, *Case of the Sawhoyamaxa Indigenous Community v Paraguay*, Judgment of 29 March 2006 (Merits, Reparations and Costs), Series C, No. 146.

[186] Inter-American Court of Human Rights, *Case of the Saramaka People v Suriname*, Judgment of 28 November 2007 (Preliminary Objections, Merits, Reparations, and Costs), Series C, No. 172.

[187] For a comprehensive analysis of the *Saramaka* case in relation to the collective indigenous peoples' rights to land, see Di Benedetto (2016).

[188] The World Bank (2010c, p. vii).

[189] ibid., p. 14.

[190] ibid., p. 15.

[191] The World Bank (2010d, p. 1).

[192] Independent Evaluation Group (2012b, p. 6).

parallel with the Bank-funded operations and linked to them, which involved the relocation of 4 million people, had resulted in the forced eviction of the *Anuak* indigenous people from their ancestral lands, making them live in refugee camps in South Sudan and Kenya, and entailing systematic human rights abuses, besides lack of assistance at relocation sites and deterioration of their standard of living. Management contended that the Bank had not directly funded the program and that, in any case, the harm described in the request was not attributable to the failure to apply its policies. In this respect, the Panel partially disagreed by holding that there was an operational overlap between the two programs, making them influence each other. The so-called 'Government Villagization Program' of Ethiopia was actually aimed at achieving the same objective of improving basic services for the population in the same region. As part of the program, 60% of households, which were also beneficiaries of the Bank-funded project, had been relocated. Although the Panel ascertained that the project did not support any involuntary resettlement activity, it held that Management should have considered these aspects in its appraisal of risks. It thus found a violation of OMS 2.20 ('Project Appraisal'), and argued that Management should have triggered OP/BP 4.10 to evaluate the impact of the project on *Anuak*'s well-being, including their access to lands and natural resources.[193]

It is interesting to note that, although not in a position to deal with the human rights abuses perpetrated to the detriment of the *Anuak* in any way, the Panel deemed it important to report on the information collected during its investigation, albeit in an informal manner. It also acknowledged their history of conflict in the region, not only with the government, but also with another ethnic group, the *Nuer*.[194] Crucially, it referenced a 2003 report by the United Nations High Commissioner for Refugees ('UNHCR') revealing major outbreaks of violence against the *Anuak*,[195] as well as a 2006 research study by the United Nations Children's Fund ('UNICEF') regarding the general disadvantaged situation of women and children in the whole Gambella Region, due to inter-ethnic and inter-tribal conflicts involving five different groups.[196]

The Panel thus emphasized that during its visit in Ethiopia in 2013, in a meeting organized by the Ministry of Federal Affairs, it had the opportunity to meet with Gambella regional government representatives, who stated that there was no evidence of systemic human rights abuses related to the national program. However, they also revealed that half of the people interviewed prior to implementation did not wish to move to new locations, and that there were reports of some pressure and unmet promises. According to the Panel, the interview of several *Anuak* refugees highlighted a contrasting perspective, as these individuals reported that:

> [T]heir original land had been given to investors after people had moved to the relocation site. [...] The Requesters interviewed by the Panel described concrete incidents of people

[193] Inspection Panel (2015a, p. 37; p. 49).

[194] ibid., pp. 11–12.

[195] UNHCR (2003).

[196] UNICEF (2006).

> who had been beaten, detained and even, in some cases, killed by soldiers or police engaged in overseeing the relocation process when they were showing some resistance. Several of the Requesters stated that they fled because they feared for their lives. They were very concerned about the situation of relatives back home and of the prospects of being able to return to their ancestral lands.[197]

The case led to major developments. Notably, a few weeks after the publication of the investigation report, an NGO disclosed a press release supporting the allegations made by the *Anuak* indigenous people.[198] In response to that, the Panel published its comments clarifying that forced eviction was directly associated with the national Government's Villagization Program only.[199] It also stressed the important role played by Management in response to the investigation findings, which committed to ensuring the consistency of national programs aimed at improving the overall quality of services for people of the Gambella Region, as documented in the progress reports published in 2016,[200] 2017,[201] and 2018.[202] The self-evaluation assessment carried out by the Bank rated its overall performance as satisfactory,[203] acknowledging that a relevant institutional lesson learned from the Panel's inspection practice was that implementation of government budgets financing national programs in connection with Bank-funded projects should entail clearer guidance on staff. The IEG rated it as moderately satisfactory only, due to the shortcomings affecting risks analysis and the Bank's partial adherence to safeguards.[204]

3.4.4.2 Kenya: Natural Resource Management Project (2013)

In this case, the Panel confronted two similar requests for inspection, alleging that the Bank had violated its policies to the detriment of the *Cherangany-Sengwer* indigenous community living in the Cherangany Hills, in the context of a project approved in 2007, intended to support the newly enacted Forests Act (2005). This national legislation prohibited settlement within reserved (gazetted) forests and established the Kenya Forest Service, a state-owned enterprise tasked with co-managing natural resources alongside nearby communities. Bank's activities initially included the demarcation of boundaries in gazetted forests, the identification of partnership models for community participation and benefit sharing, as well as development and implementation of Resettlement Action Plans.

After a major restructuring process occurred in 2011, following the concern expressed by the involved indigenous community on access to land, the project removed the component regarding resettlement activities and replaced it with

[197] Inspection Panel (2015a, p. 20).

[198] Inclusive Development International (2015).

[199] Inspection Panel (2015b).

[200] The World Bank (2016a, p. 6).

[201] The World Bank (2017b, p. 5).

[202] The World Bank (2018a, p. 2).

[203] The World Bank (2019b, pp. 26–30).

[204] Independent Evaluation Group (2020, p. 15).

another one aimed at offering assistance with the resolution of the long-standing historical claims regarding the lands over which the community had lost control between 1895 and 2002. The inclusion of the Cherangany Hills in the project area was then formalized. At the same time, the Restructuring Proposal stressed that a comprehensive resolution of land issues associated with forests, to be eventually addressed as part of a broader dialogue between the government of Kenya and the World Bank, was beyond the remit of the project. While not in a position to find a permanent solution to the plight of the indigenous people living inside gazetted forests, the Bank-funded operations could have actually contributed to the development of suitable IPPs.[205]

Two years later, the requests filed before the Panel presented two distinct sets of claims.

The first set alleged that members of the *Cherangany-Sengwer* community had been forcibly evicted from the forests where they had lived for generations and upon which they relied both economically and culturally, despite the existence of long-standing land claims. This situation was reportedly caused by the Bank-funded project. In addressing it, the Panel noted that the events in question were not directly caused by the project itself, but rather stemmed from circumstances that predated its formal approval.[206] These were to be understood within the broader context of the Kenya Forest Service's institutional powers, which enabled the prosecution of individuals living inside gazetted forests, labeling them as illegal intruders. Additionally, the Panel emphasized the presence of a very challenging national context, marked by ongoing violence targeting certain ethnic groups. This situation was further exacerbated by a national water crisis, prompting the Kenyan government to implement a plan focused on preserving the country's main 'water towers', including the Cherangany Hills, the region most heavily affected by the project's activities. At the same time, the Panel noted that including an area with historical land issues in the project should have triggered an assessment of eviction risks and the development of appropriate mitigation measures through a Resettlement Action Plan. In this regard, the Panel found that the Bank was in non-compliance with OP/BP 4.12 ('Involuntary Resettlement'). Ultimately, the Panel concluded that while the project's goals of resolving the long-standing historical land claims of the indigenous community were ambitious, they were not backed by adequate risk assessments or enough planning to effectively address potential challenges.

As for the second set of claims, the request alleged the Bank's violation of OP/BP 4.10, for having improperly replaced the term 'Indigenous Peoples' with 'Vulnerable and Marginalized Groups' in the IPP. Management contended that the use of this term, requested by the government to align the project with the terminology of the Kenyan Constitution, was not meant to jeopardize the protection provided under the policy in any way. The Panel, which concluded its investigation in

[205] The proposal to restructure (IDA/R2011–0240) was included in a President's Memorandum dated 15 June 2011 (approved by the Board of Executive Directors on 24 June 2011).

[206] In the Embobut Forest, the most notable evictions occurred in 2009, when more than 400 families were displaced, and a significant number of houses, belongings, and crops were destroyed by forest guards and police.

September 2014, supported the view that World Bank's OP/BP 4.10 emphasizes a practical focus on the substantive rights to be protected, regardless of the terminology employed. It also explicitly referenced the approach taken by the African Commission in this regard, citing a passage from a 2006 report that recommended African States adopt a flexible use of the term:[207]

> Whatever the specific term to analyze and describe their situation will be, it is highly important to recognize the issue and to urgently do something to safeguard fundamental collective human rights. Debates on terminology should not prevent such action.[208]

It thus held that the use of a different term did not, in itself, constitute non-compliance with OP/BP 4.10.

The final part of the Panel's analysis dealt with the alleged restriction of indigenous community members' right to «live within their ancestral homes in Kapolet and Embobut Forests while carrying out livelihood activities that promote sustainable conservation and protection of natural resources».[209] In its analysis, the Panel developed an interesting reasoning exploring the main features of indigenous peoples' land and natural resources-based 'customary' rights,[210] described as patterns of long-standing land and resource usage, as governed by customary law, values, and traditions. The Panel emphasized that the borrower needed to pay particular attention to these rights when preparing the IPP, as outlined in paragraph 16 of OP 4.10.[211]

Crucially, the Panel also held that customary rights should be regarded as an expression of the overriding self-determination principle in its internal dimension, as enshrined in Article 7.1 of the 1989 ILO Convention No. 169, which frames it in the context of projects implemented for national development purposes:

> The peoples concerned shall have the right to decide their own priorities for the process of development as it affects their lives, beliefs, institutions and spiritual well-being and the lands they occupy or otherwise use, and to exercise control, to the extent possible, over their own economic, social and cultural development.[212]

It further clarified that they are usually associated with a way of life that is part of a precise cultural identity, referencing General Comment No. 23 (1994) of the UN Human Rights Committee ('HRC')[213] regarding the interpretation of Article 27 of

---

[207] Inspection Panel (2014, pp. 41–42).

[208] African Commission on Human and Peoples' Rights (2006, p. 24).

[209] Inspection Panel (2014, p. 40).

[210] For a comprehensive analysis of indigenous peoples' land rights under international law, see Gilbert (2007).

[211] The World Bank, *Operations Manual, Policy & Procedure Framework, Operational Policy 4.10, Indigenous Peoples*, 2005 (revised in 2013 and 2024), para. 16.

[212] International Labour Organization, *Indigenous and Tribal Peoples Convention*, C169, Geneva, 27 June 1989 (entered into effect on 5 September 1991).

[213] UN Human Rights Committee (1994, para. 3.2).

the International Covenant on Civil and Political Rights ('ICCPR').[214] Finally, it recalled that, as recognized by the UN Special Rapporteur Erica-Irene Daes in 2001,[215] the protection of such rights is also instrumental to the very survival of indigenous peoples, as the land «provides not only material benefits such as food, medicine, fuel, grazing spaces, fish and game, but also non material services such as initiation sites, sacred areas, a connection to ancestors», in addition to spiritual ceremony sanctuaries.[216] In this regard, the Panel determined that the Bank had violated paragraph 21 of OP 4.10, which mandates that restrictions on indigenous peoples' access to legally designated protected areas should be avoided.[217] Furthermore, it concluded that the restructured project was inconsistent with both the spirit and the letter of OP 4.10, as it was developed without an adequate consultation process.

The Panel found that the project had raised expectations regarding land allocation through a long-awaited solution to what the *Cherangany-Sengwer* considered their legitimate claims, but ultimately failed to deliver such a solution. Moreover, it noted that the project had not succeeded in ensuring the indigenous community's participation in the management of forest resources, an approach that could have contributed to achieving the project's goals.[218]

As a result of the investigation, the Bank facilitated dialogue with the government and the affected indigenous people with the aim of addressing legacy issues related to land rights and ownership, as outlined in the Management Progress Report.[219] Upon completion of the project, the Bank rated both its performance and that of the borrower as moderately satisfactory.[220] However, the IEG confirmed this evaluation only with regard to the Bank, acknowledging its proactive stance towards the forceful evictions, which were not attributed to the project. In contrast, the borrower's performance was rated as moderately unsatisfactory due to resettlement issues that arose independently of the activities funded by the Bank.[221]

3.4.4.3 Kenya: Electricity Expansion Project (2014)

On 26 October 2014, the Inspection Panel received a new request for inspection concerning the *Kenya: Electricity Expansion Project*, approved by the World Bank in 2010, and jointly financed by the European Investment Bank and other donor agencies. The project aimed to expand electricity access in various regions. The

[214] UN General Assembly, *International Covenant on Civil and Political Rights*, Resolution 2200A (XXI) of 16 December 1966 (entered into force on 23 March 1976), in *UNTS*, Volume 999, p. 171 f., UN Doc. A/RES/2200A (XXI).

[215] UN Commission on Human Rights (2001).

[216] Inspection Panel (2014, p. 43).

[217] ibid., p. 52.

[218] ibid., p. x.

[219] The World Bank (2015a, p. 2).

[220] The World Bank (2014b, p. v).

[221] Independent Evaluation Group (2016b, pp. 15–16).

complaint was filed by the *Maasai* indigenous community, who had agreed to relocate due to geothermal activities in the Hell's Gate National Park, located in the Rift Valley in Kenya, where they had been living. This relocation was contingent upon the recognition of a communal land title over another area, which had not been secured at the time of the request.

Management contended that the implementation of proper Resettlement Action Plans had adequately addressed the negative impact on the indigenous community associated with the project. Nevertheless, the Panel found serious shortcomings in achieving their inclusive participation in the resettlement activities, which the plans were supposed to ensure. These issues arose from ineffective communication, the failure to use the local language, and the lack of disclosure of relevant documents. The Panel further noted that the failure to recognize the traditional *Maasai* authority structure in the design and implementation of the project was initially overlooked and persisted even after a representative from the 'Elders'—a customary leadership body—was included in the Resettlement Action Plan Implementation Committee, and a Community Advisory Council was established to participate in the grievance mechanism, both intended to enable affected people to seek redress for their losses.

It thus found the Bank in non-compliance with OP/BP 4.12 ('Involuntary Resettlement') and reached the same conclusion regarding OP/BP 4.10 ('Indigenous Peoples'). In this regard, after acknowledging the complexity of indigenous peoples' issues in Kenya and across Africa, the Panel found that during its initial screening to identify indigenous communities in the project area, the Bank primarily focused on hunter-gatherer groups, such as the *Sengwer*, *Ogiek*, *Waata*, and *Boni*, while excluding pastoralist communities like the *Maasai*. The Panel conducted a detailed analysis of the criteria outlined in OP 4.01, and concluded that the *Maasai* met the definition of an indigenous community, based on their collective attachment to the land, the existence of distinct institutions, and the use of an indigenous language.

Regarding the self-identification criterion, which also includes recognition by others as a distinct indigenous cultural group[222] in a broad sense, it observed that the *Maasai* had been represented at meetings for the adoption of the UNDRIP. It added that the African Commission on Human and Peoples' Rights of the African Union had also recognized the *Maasai*,[223] citing a report in which they were regarded as «pastoralists who identify as indigenous peoples».[224] Notably, this report, which emphasizes the importance of international recognition of African indigenous peoples before international *fora* for obtaining protection of their rights, also references the World Bank's Indigenous Peoples policy, in addition to the 1989 ILO Convention No. 169, as positive steps undertaken by UN agencies in this respect.[225]

---

[222] The World Bank, *Operations Manual, Policy & Procedure Framework, Operational Policy 4.10, Indigenous Peoples*, 2005 (revised in 2013 and 2024), para. 4.a.

[223] Inspection Panel (2015c, p. 9).

[224] African Commission on Human and Peoples' Rights (2006, p. 10).

[225] ibid., p. 22.

Upon completing this part of the assessment, the Panel argued that the Bank's failure to apply OP/BP 4.10 was the root cause of all the ensuing shortcomings in the protection afforded to the *Maasai* at different levels. First of all, the Panel noted that the project had not been based on free, prior, and informed consultations to secure the broad community support required by OP/BP 4.10. It ascertained that the interviews with members of the local community had not been conducted in the *Maasai* local language, and that relevant documents had not been translated. As a result, not all members of the indigenous community had the opportunity to express support or objection.

Furthermore, the absence of an Indigenous Peoples Plan for the *Maasai* had deprived them of the opportunity to benefit from the commercial development of natural resources on their lands or territories, in accordance with OP/BP 4.10.[226] Shortly thereafter, Management submitted its Report and Recommendation in response to the Inspection Panel's findings.[227] Given that the European Investment Bank had initiated a mediation process to help resolve the issues raised in the complaint, Management proposed that the Bank participate in its mediation process, instead of addressing remedial actions in parallel. This proposal was later approved.[228] On 28 May 2016, representatives of the *Maasai* community and the Kenyan implementing agency finalized and signed the mediation agreement. The Bank's Management sent to the Board an addendum to its updated action plan incorporating, among other things, measures to identify affected individuals left out of the resettlement process, such as the *Maasai*. It also included plans to improve the physical infrastructure of the resettlement site and support livelihood restoration,[229] with a commitment to report on its main results over the following three years. As part of its self-assessment exercise, in its ICR report, the Bank rated its own performance as moderately satisfactory, acknowledging the successful implementation of the Management's actions as reviewed in light of the mediation agreement.[230] The IEG confirmed this assessment.[231]

3.4.4.4 Bangladesh: Trade and Transport Studies RETF Project (2016)

On 31 August 2016, members of the indigenous *Chakma*, *Marma*, *Tanchangya* and *Lushai* communities in the Chittagong Hill Tracts in Bangladesh, an area legally recognized as a 'tribal-inhabited region' presented a request for inspection. They alleged potential harm from a Bank-funded project component designed to connect

[226] The World Bank, *Operations Manual, Policy & Procedure Framework, Operational Policy 4.10, Indigenous Peoples*, 2005 (revised in 2013 and 2024), para. 18.

[227] The World Bank (2015b).

[228] Inspection Panel (2017, p. 9).

[229] The World Bank (2016b).

[230] The World Bank (2018b, p. 35).

[231] Independent Evaluation Group (2019, p. 22).

the port of the nearby city of Chittagong to the remote Thegamukh area, citing the lack of meaningful engagement with their communities. Furthermore, they raised concern about its impact on their land, forests, cultural sites, and the environment. The Panel conducted extensive due diligence and learned that the project, intended to fund a feasibility study for route options between the two areas, was not going to be appraised as the Bank was not satisfied with the standard of consultations and the quality of the draft study. Management assured the Panel that the Bank would not proceed with any other activity, dropping the component from the main project. The Panel did not register the request, as the component had not yet caused any material adverse effect.[232] This case is significant as it highlights the Bank's commitment to appraising projects only when they comply with the Bank's Indigenous Peoples policy, particularly regarding the consultation process.

3.4.4.5 Bolivia: Santa Cruz Road Corridor Connector Project (San Ignacio—San José) (2022)

On 19 December 2022, the Panel received a request for inspection submitted by four leaders of organizations of the *Chiquitano* indigenous people, claiming the lack of proper engagement with them during the development of a project intended to enhance transport accessibility in Bolivia through the improvement of its primary road network. In their view, the project was ultimately accelerating illegal occupation and confiscation of indigenous lands, thus posing a huge risk to their titling efforts, while also producing an adverse impact on their water sources. Finally, concerns were raised about the sexual exploitation, abuse, and sexual harassment ('SEA/SH') of indigenous women and girls by project workers. While Management argued that the Bank's policies were observed throughout all project phases, the Panel held that the project, classified by the Bank as category 'B', should have included consultations with all affected people and local NGOs, given its potential adverse impacts, in accordance with OP/BP 4.01 ('Environmental Assessment'),[233] and in particular with indigenous peoples, as prescribed by OP/BP 4.10.[234] Overall, the Panel noted that the project failed to meet the required standard for an adequate process of free, prior, and informed consultation. Furthermore, despite the Bank's efforts to address project grievances, including increasing the number of channels available for the community to raise complaints, the Panel found a failure to establish a functioning redress mechanism that could accommodate the customary

---

[232] Inspection Panel (2016).

[233] The World Bank, *Operations Manual, Policy & Procedure Framework, Operational Policy 4.01, Environmental Assessment*, 1999 (revised in 2013 and 2024), para. 14.

[234] The World Bank, *Operations Manual, Policy & Procedure Framework, Operational Policy 4.10, Indigenous Peoples*, 2005 (revised in 2013 and 2024), paras. 6(c) and 10(c); Annex B, para. 2(d).

dispute resolution process used by the affected indigenous community, as originally envisioned in the IPP prepared by the borrower.[235]

The Panel reached similar conclusions regarding other policies, noting that while the Bank complied with OP/BP 4.12 by minimizing resettlements, it failed to ensure compensation payments before the project acquired the affected lands, in violation of the same policy. Additionally, the Bank neglected to pay sufficient attention to the needs of vulnerable groups, such as indigenous peoples, who may not be protected under national land compensation laws.[236] Furthermore, the Bank had not adopted appropriate measures to mitigate the impact of the roadworks on both the environment and the community (OP/BP 4.01).

Finally, the allegations concerning SEA/SH prompted the Panel to analyze the data reported by UN Women with respect to gender-based violence in Bolivia.[237] After noting that SEA/SH incidents were frequently underreported in the country, it held that the project documents correctly recognized the special vulnerability of the *Chiquitano* women in relation to labor discrimination and the inequality stemming from their community's patriarchal system. Overall, it scrutinized the Bank's conduct in light of the measures recommended in previous investigations regarding the same matter, explicitly recalling these past cases:

> This Investigation afforded the Panel an opportunity to assess how the Project is implementing the measures put forward by the Bank following the Panel's Uganda and Democratic Republic of Congo investigations involving GBV cases.[238]

In doing so, it recognized the positive actions taken by the Bank in addressing gender-based violence across all its projects following the issuance of a Good Practice Note on the matter in 2018.[239] This included identifying endemic risks of SEA/SH issues during the early stages of the project and implementing appropriate measures to address them. The Bank was thus found in compliance with the provisions of OP 4.01 concerning the assessment of the social impact of these issues.

Last but not least, the Panel found that, except for SEA/SH issues, Management did not effectively monitor implementation, thus violating the general Bank Policy and Directive on Investment Project Financing.[240] At the same time, it took note of the substantial improvements following the submission of the request, as well as of the various actions taken to address the issues relating to resettlement and other aspects, including through the issuance of a 'Notice of Potential Disbursement Suspension'. The project is still active; in July 2024, the Bank's ICR has rated the progress towards the achievement of its objectives as moderately unsatisfactory.[241]

---

[235] ibid., Annex B, para. 2(h).

[236] ibid., paras. 8 and 10. See also Inspection Panel (2024, p. 55).

[237] Inspection Panel (2024, p. 91).

[238] ibid., p. 125.

[239] The World Bank (2018c).

[240] The World Bank, *Bank Policy, Investment Project Financing*, 2024, Catalogue No. OPS5.03-POL.110, para. 20; The World Bank, *Bank Directive, Investment Project Financing*, 2023, Catalogue No. OPS5.03-DIR.116, para. 44.

[241] The World Bank (2024).

3.5 Interim Conclusions

The analysis presented in this chapter leads to key conclusions that help frame the World Bank's role in advancing indigenous peoples' human rights in the context of development financing. Despite the lack of explicit reference in such terms in its Articles of Agreement, the institution has equipped itself with a set of policies shaping the way investment projects are managed, increasingly engaging with both soft and hard international legal instruments protecting indigenous peoples' rights. This conclusion clearly arises from the analysis of the policy prescriptions, whose revisions have been guided by internal learning reviews that highlight the need to continuously adapt them to the evolving international legal landscape. Following the adoption of its first modern safeguard regulating the matter, introduced in response to the public criticism raised by some of its projects, the Bank has continued elaborating upon its contents, creating a system of norms that can no longer be read in isolation from international human rights law regarding indigenous peoples.[242] This process has ultimately resulted in a full-fledged internal legal system that the organization has committed to following within the context of investment projects, upon the close scrutiny of its Independent Accountability Mechanism, the Inspection Panel.

The analysis of the Panel's practice, which has largely drawn upon human rights legal instruments multiple times, supports this argument.

Crucially, in *Chad: Petroleum Sector Management Capacity Building Project* (2001), the Panel explicitly recognized that human rights are broadly embedded in the Bank's policies, urging the institution to reconsider its role in promoting them in the countries where it operates. Subsequent cases also confirm this view. In *Honduras: Land Administration Project* (2006), the Panel recognized that the policy provisions regarding indigenous peoples mirror those of the ILO Convention No. 169. In *Papua New Guinea: Smallholder Agriculture Development Project* (2009), the Panel held that OP 4.10 covers, and is consistent with, the main objectives of the UN International Covenant on Economic, Social and Cultural Rights, thus regarding it as a reflection of a core international human rights legal instrument. In *Panama: Land Administration (First Request)* (2009), in interpreting the contents of the policy regarding the right of indigenous peoples to use and develop the lands they occupy, the Panel referenced the UNDRIP. In *Kenya: Natural Resource Management Project* (2013), it read the prescriptions enclosed in paragraph 16 of OP 4.10 on land- and natural resources-based rights in light of the ILO Convention No. 169, regarding them an expression of the overriding internal self-determination principle to be framed in the context of development projects. It further clarified that these rights are usually associated with a way of life that is part of

[242] In this regard, in the context of its extensive studies on the fragmentation of international law, the UN International Law Commission observed that the term 'self-contained regime,' often used by and for IFIs to justify their position, is a misnomer, as «no legal regime is isolated from international law». International Law Commission (2006, para. 193), Bonfanti (2012, p. 270), van Genugten (2015, p. 15).

a precise cultural identity, citing the Human Rights Committee's General Comment No. 23 of 1994 on the interpretation of Article 27 of the International Covenant on Civil and Political Rights. Finally, it recalled that, as recognized by the UN Special Rapporteur Erica-Irene Daes in 2001, their protection is instrumental to the very survival of indigenous peoples.

Although the Panel is not formally tasked with the protection of human rights, it is noteworthy that, at the procedural level, in order to counter the risks of reprisals, it often resorted to the introduction of 'due process' elements by keeping the requester's identity confidential, explicitly referring to the procedure followed by international *fora* in handling human rights complaints in this regard, such as the UN and the ILO (*Argentina, Paraguay*: *Yacyretá Hydroelectric Project II*, 1996). Overall, the analysis of its practice displays a variety of general human rights-related considerations, as demonstrated by the concern shown for indigenous peoples' intergenerational well-being, often in a way unrelated to the Bank's financing activities, as in the *Brazil*: *Rondônia Natural Resources Management Project* (1995) and *Colombia: Cartagena Water Supply, Sewerage and Environmental Project* (2004) cases. More recently, in *Ethiopia*: *Promoting Basic Services Phase III Project* (2012), in acknowledging the occurrence of systematic human rights abuses to the detriment of the *Anuak* indigenous people in the country, the Panel cited a UNHCR report and a UNICEF study, while also reporting on the information collected during interviews with displaced individuals, although not allowed to investigate such matters in accordance with its mandate.

Notably, the Panel relied on the practice developed by regional human rights bodies in support of its reasoning on four different occasions. An interesting cross-fertilization phenomenon can be observed here, as the decision of the Inter-American Court of Human Rights rendered in *Saramaka People v Suriname*, cited by the Panel in *Panama: Land Administration (First Request)* (2009), along with the practice developed by the Working Group on Indigenous Peoples of the African Commission on Human and Peoples' Rights, referenced in the *Democratic Republic of Congo: TSERO and EESRSP* (2005) case, all point back to the World Bank's policy. Furthermore, in the 2006 African Commission's report focused on indigenous peoples' rights in the African continent, which is cited by the Panel in both *Kenya*: *Natural Resource Management Project* (2013) and *Kenya: Electricity Expansion Project* (2014), the World Bank's policy is specifically recognized as a positive example of the level of protection afforded by a UN specialized agency in safeguarding indigenous peoples' rights.

Once clarified that the World Bank has a framework in place consisting of a set of internal normative prescriptions embedding international human rights values, it is essential to highlight that this framework holds significant legal implications for borrowers. Since the Bank shapes the way in which funded operations must be executed, the primary effect is that borrowers are obligated to comply with a set of substantive and procedural requirements. These requirements, derived from the Bank's internal policies, effectively translate into practical measures that create a 'safe harbor', ensuring that the project adheres to high standards of protection for indigenous peoples. In many cases, such standards may offer greater safeguards than those provided by the national legal system in the borrowing country.

This approach has been first codified with the formulation of the modern version of the safeguards, which formally establish the prevalence of the Bank's system in all project phases, while also allowing the use of the country's legal and institutional framework only upon the Bank's verification of its equivalence, with a view to improving the borrower's capacity to deal with specific matters beyond individual project settings. The new ESF has finally established that the Bank may use the national environmental and social framework, provided that it is likely to address the risks and impacts of the project and to achieve objectives materially consistent with the Bank's standards.[243] However, in case gaps are identified, an agreement upon the identification of measures aimed at strengthening the national framework is a general necessary precondition.[244] This entails a frequent direct impact of projects on the borrower's legislation in the long term, which, besides being facilitated by the advisory services offered by the Bank, may also potentially arise from the borrower's voluntary actions, as evidenced by recent national trends in related areas.[245] In these cases, therefore, the Bank may even influence the development of national legislative frameworks that are more supportive of indigenous peoples' human rights as a collateral effect of its financing activities.

Delving into the details of the way the Bank protects indigenous peoples' rights in practice, a crucial preliminary step is the identification of their presence in, or collective attachment to, the project area during the screening phase, which is instrumental to trigger the application of its internal normative system to the project settings. Starting from this early phase, the Bank relies on it, especially when national legislation falls short of protecting indigenous peoples' rights. Notably, in *Colombia*: *Cartagena Water Supply, Sewerage and Environmental Project* (2004), the Panel expressed its view on the opportunity to use the borrower's legal framework for identifying affected communities as indigenous peoples, asserting that the Bank was obligated to adhere to its own policy, regardless of its alignment with national legislation.

Following the identification phase, the Bank can resort to various means in order to make the borrowers adhere to its own framework. Prior to the Board of Executive Directors' approval of a loan, during the project design phase, the Bank exerts a *de facto* conditionality that may potentially lead to the decision not to finance a project when the prescribed requirements regarding the initial assessment of all circumstances surrounding the execution of the project are not met by the borrower.

---

[243] The World Bank, *Environmental and Social Framework*, 2017, para. 10.

[244] ibid., para. 23.

[245] This phenomenon has been already observed by Dr. Shihata, who served as General Counsel of the World Bank from 1983 to 1998, with reference to environmental action plans prepared by the borrower in the context of Bank-funded projects, which provided «an important impetus for the development of national environmental law in support of international standards» in all IDA borrowing countries and some IBRD members as well. Shihata (2000b, p. 495).

At this stage, the identification of the international legal obligations arising from environmental treaties to which the borrower must adhere plays an important role. Notably, these specific types of obligations that are relevant to projects with an environmental impact may also acquire a crucial significance for indigenous peoples, since they often inhabit areas that are particularly rich in biodiversity, and their way of life is closely linked to lands and natural resources. The Bank may decide not to finance the project when its operations are likely to contravene these obligations, in light of the 'escape' clause provided by paragraph 3 of OP 4.01. In the *Democratic Republic of Congo: TSERO and EESRSP* case (2005), in the context of a request for inspection filed by representatives of the *Pygmy* people, the Panel found that Management had failed to identify the borrower's international obligations arising from two core environmental treaties signed and ratified by the country. This omission was critical, as recognizing the existence of these obligations would have required the Bank to reconsider proceeding with the project. By refusing to finance such projects, the Bank certainly sends a strong signal of the importance that it attaches to these obligations. It is worth noting that, in this regard, the Bank's new ESF does not contain any explicit provision, with the sole exception of the biodiversity conservation standard, which states that the borrower cannot implement any project activity unless «[a]ll due process required under international obligations or national law that is a prerequisite to a country granting approval for project activities in or adjacent to a critical habitat has been complied with».[246] One may argue that, as part of its due diligence responsibilities, the Bank has to perform the review of the borrower's assessment, which takes into account the international legal obligations applicable to the project under relevant international treaties. As a result, these obligations are no longer limited to those arising from treaties of an environmental nature. While this may be accurate, the impact of such changes must also be considered in light of the approach that the Inspection Panel will decide to adopt on these matters, which has yet to be developed.

Furthermore, the Indigenous Peoples policy, since its formulation in OD 4.20, and in a more articulated way with the introduction of OP/BP 4.10, has specifically required that consultations occur repeatedly throughout the project preparation phase. First, borrowers are required to conduct them in a proper way in order to identify the potential effects of the project as a precondition for being awarded funds. When it is ascertained that the project can generate negative effects, the borrower should also ensure that indigenous peoples broadly support the Bank-funded operations. Shortly thereafter, the Bank reviews the consultations' outcome and does not proceed further if it is unable to ascertain that such support exists. Notably, in *Bangladesh: Trade and Transport RETF Project* (2016), the Bank, not satisfied with the way the consultation process with indigenous communities had been conducted, decided not to proceed with the project. It is worth stressing that the new ESF has introduced some changes in this respect. A key development is the requirement to obtain FPIC in specific circumstances where indigenous peoples may be

[246] The World Bank, *Environmental and Social Framework*, 2017, p. 70.

particularly vulnerable. This requirement aligns with the latest developments recorded in international law in this regard.

The subsequent step that the borrower needs to undertake, in consultation with the affected indigenous communities, is the preparation of the Indigenous Peoples Plan component, to be incorporated into the loan agreement at a later stage, including all the measures envisaged for ensuring that indigenous peoples benefit from project operations or for countering its negative impacts. Against this backdrop, the borrower should pay particular attention to the measures aimed at protecting land- and natural resources-based rights, in accordance with the cultural value that indigenous peoples attach to them, on a general basis and in the context of legally protected areas as well, as the Panel's findings related to *Kenya*: *Natural Resource Management Project* (2013) demonstrate.

The appraisal phase, intended to finally evaluate the appropriateness of the overall project design, is key to ensuring that the borrower adheres to the prescriptions of the Bank's framework. In *China: Western Poverty Reduction Project* (1999), the Panel held that the Bank is required to apply a 'reasonableness' standard of care in appraising compliance, which goes beyond a mere verification of adherence to the safeguards' language. In *Papua New Guinea: Smallholder Agriculture Development Project* (2009), the Panel affirmed the importance of the Bank's role in reviewing project preparation to ensure that the borrower envisages benefits for indigenous peoples' welfare, even if this entails greater challenges for the organization.

Finally, once the Bank appraises the project and an agreement is signed with a member country, the Bank's policy provisions are transfused into specific covenanted provisions that the borrower has to respect while implementing the project. The general Policy (former OP/BP 10.00) on Investment Project Financing specifies that the Bank is entitled to enforce them through the legal remedies envisaged in the agreement, which may result in the suspension of disbursements, or cancellation, of unwithdrawn amounts.[247] The Inspection Panel's practice shows that, during this phase, the Bank needs to properly supervise projects by reacting timely when environmental and social issues arise, and that application of legal remedies in light of the borrower's violation of the obligations covenanted in the legal agreement does not represent a discretionary tool (*Brazil*: *Rondônia Natural Resources Management Project*, 1995). In *Argentina, Paraguay*: *Yacyretá Hydroelectric Project II* (1996), the Panel also clarified that «compliance is not achieved by merely including covenants in Loan Agreements but rather by ensuring that their provisions are implemented in a timely fashion by the borrower and executing agencies».[248] During this phase, any changes to national legislation made to advance a project may still be subject to the Bank's scrutiny to ensure adherence with its safeguard objectives (*Honduras: Land Administration Project*, 2006).

All in all, the Inspection Panel has played a pivotal role in defining the scope of the obligations that the Bank has voluntarily undertaken in managing the adverse risks or impacts produced upon indigenous peoples in its projects.

[247] The World Bank, *Bank Policy*, *Investment Project Financing*, 2024, Catalogue No. OPS5.03-POL.110, para. 29.

[248] Inspection Panel (1996, p. 7).

Although criticisms of the Panel's operating model, particularly its dependence on the Board of Executive Directors, are not central to this discussion—which focuses on the adoption and application of the Bank's policies—it remains important to acknowledge key developments in this area that suggest an evolving interpretation of the Bank's functions. With respect to the final decision establishing whether a case warrants an investigation, it must be noted that, since the adoption of the 1999 Clarifications, the Board's authorization has been intended as granted in all cases, thus conferring a significant degree of independence on the Panel. Furthermore, although the Inspection Panel merely issues fact-finding determinations that are not binding and, as such, cannot be enforced, it has recently begun formally monitoring the progress of the remedial action plan elaborated by Management and the borrower in response to its investigation reports. Pursuant to the latest Resolution (2020) defining the boundaries of the Panel's mandate, the Board of Executive Directors can now assign this important task to it. Notably, this reflects a pattern that the Board had already been following in practice since the *Rondônia* case in 1995. Moreover, one should consider that, to date, the Panel's ability to exert a compliance pull on the Bank has generated unforeseen and groundbreaking effects in multiple ways. Recent experience demonstrates that following a request for investigation, the Bank has recorded a significant improvement in its monitoring activities (*Bolivia*: *Santa Cruz Road Corridor Connector Project*, San Ignacio—San José, 2022). In early cases, the Inspection Panel's findings led to the President's decision to undertake a major institutional restructuring aimed at strengthening the functions of the Environment Department (*China*: *Western Poverty Reduction Project*, 1999), or, in some other instances, to withdraw financial support for the project (*Nepal*: *Arun III Proposed Hydroelectric Project and Restructuring of IDA Credit*, 1994). Last but not least, the Panel's findings in recent cases confirm that a process of consolidation on key issues is gradually taking shape, similar to the way judicial mechanisms develop trends that can be abstracted from individual cases. For instance, in *Bolivia*: *Santa Cruz Road Corridor Connector Project* (San Ignacio—San José) (2022), the Panel has recently scrutinized the Bank's conduct in light of its previous findings related to similar cases dealing with gender-based violence against indigenous women and girls, thereby demonstrating that the authoritative influence it exerts on the Bank can lead to tangible results.

Finally, it must be stressed that, upon closure of the project, the progress on the Management Action Plan is independently assessed by another accountability mechanism, the IEG, which takes into account the overall performance of the project, including the Panel's findings, often emphasizing the need for the Bank to consider the lessons learned from them, which may lead to significant changes in the Bank's conduct through their integration into future strategies developed for the countries it assists. Thus, the combined efforts of the IEG and the Panel mutually reinforce each other.

Table 3.2 Selected Inspection Panel's cases concerning indigenous peoples' rights

1. Nepal: Arun III Proposed Hydroelectric Project and Restructuring of IDA Credit (1994)	
Indigenous peoples	24 ethnic groups within the Arun Basin
Sector	Renewable energy generation
Operation	IDA's credit(s)
Main allegations	Loss of rights over ancestral lands following communities' displacement; deterioration of natural resources and cultural identity
Relevant findings	• In its analysis, the Inspection Panel incorporated indirect human rights considerations, reflecting a strong emphasis on the well-being of indigenous peoples (Report and Recommendation, 16 December 1994) • The Panel expressed the view that the Bank's identification of ethnic groups as indigenous peoples should follow a case-by-case approach, prioritizing the assessment of vulnerability rather than focusing solely on their level of isolation or integration into the dominant society (Investigation Report, 21 June 1995). This perspective reflects modern international legal thinking, which recognizes indigenous peoples' right to self-determination in all its forms, from the right to self-government to the right to decide whether or not to participate in the political, economic, social, and cultural life of the State (as enshrined in Arts. 3–5 of the UNDRIP and the national constitutions of various countries around the world). This also corresponds with the approach adopted in 2010 by the AfrCommHPR that, in a communication regarding the displacement of a community from its traditional lands in Kenya, asserted that the relationship between indigenous peoples and dominant or mainstream groups in society varies from country to country
Final project outcomes	• After receiving the inspection Panel's findings, jointly with the results of an external independent review, the President decided to withdraw financial support for the project. Furthermore, the Bank did not extend any lending to the Nepalese government in the hydropower sector in the following ten years • No final independent review was carried out due to the decision to withdraw the funding
2. Brazil: Rondônia Natural Resources Management Project (1995)	
Indigenous peoples	*Uru-eu-wau-wau*
Sector	Environmental and natural resource management
Operation	IBRD's loan
Main allegations	Damages to livelihoods and cultural heritage; damages to the environment

(continued)

Table 3.2 (continued)

Relevant findings	• The Inspection Panel ventured beyond the boundaries of its mandate as its analysis displayed significant attention towards indigenous peoples' welfare and intergenerational issues based on human rights-related considerations. It also expressed some form of concern about the future provision of health services in the indigenous areas in the Rondônia territory after project completion (Additional Review, 8 December 1995) • The Panel's additional review concluded that there was no evidence that the Bank had considered enforcing the obligations of both the borrower and the implementing agency under the loan documents, as provided in ODs 13.05 ('Supervision') and 13.40 ('Suspension of Disbursements'). In its opinion, such actions and omissions had to be regarded as contributing to the material losses suffered by the requesters • In spite of the Inspection Panel's recommendation for investigation (further reiterated in the Additional Review requested by the Board of Executive Directors), the Board opted for the execution of an Action Plan proposed by Management, jointly with the borrower. Nevertheless, the Board asked the Panel for the first time to play a role in the execution of the Action Plan by monitoring its progress. In this regard, the Panel offered observations primarily focused on the need for institutional strengthening of the implementing agency, in response to the Management's proposal for restructuring the project (Management Progress Report, 25 March 1997)
Final project outcomes	• The project underwent an important restructuring phase which, according to the Bank's Implementation Completion and Results Report, led to mixed results. Although both the Bank's and borrower's performance were assessed as unsatisfactory, the project brought increased promotion of the well-being of the indigenous population, which grew by 10% during the implementation phase (final WB ICR, 30 October 2003) • The Operations Evaluation Department's independent review confirmed these results, stressing that land tenure regularization had resulted in the creation of conservation units covering 20% of the Brazilian national area. However, it also highlighted that the protection of indigenous lands was being hindered by weak or absent management and enforcement procedures (OED ICRR, 21 January 2004)
3. Argentina, Paraguay: Yacyretá Hydroelectric Project II (1996)	
Indigenous peoples	*Mbya*
Sector	Renewable energy generation
Operation	IBRD's loan(s)
Main allegations	Damages to the environment, standards of living, health and economic well-being; communities' displacement
Relevant findings	• The Inspection Panel offered an interpretation of OD 13.40 regarding the Bank's use of legal remedies when a borrower violates environmental and social obligations stipulated in the legal agreement, presenting it as a necessary tool to ensure effective compliance, as in the *Rondônia* case. It also kept requesters' identity confidential based on previous practice (*Arun III*), expressly recalling the procedure followed in human rights complaints before international *fora* in this regard, such as the UN and the ILO (Report and Recommendation, Attachment 1, 26 December 1996) • Once again, the Panel was entrusted by the Board of Executive Directors with the task of assessing the implementation status of the Management Action Plan as in the *Rondônia* case (this procedure was not foreseen at all in the resolution establishing its mandate in 1993)

(continued)

Table 3.2 (continued)

Final project outcomes	• Both the Bank's Implementation Completion and Results Report (WB ICR, 28 June 2001) and the Operations Evaluation Department's independent review (OED ICRR, 13 July 2001) held that the objective of improving environmental management and handling of social aspects was only partially achieved
4. China: Western Poverty Reduction Project (1999)	
Indigenous peoples	Tibetan and other minority ethnic groups
Sector	Environmental and natural resource management
Operation	IDA's credit and IBRD's loan
Main allegations	Damages to wildlife; inappropriate environmental screening; inadequate resettlement plan
Relevant findings	• Before the Inspection Panel was even involved in the case, Management had already carried out an intensive internal review of the environmental and social aspects related to the project activities in Qinghai Province, which later resulted in the presentation of a new loan package to the Board of Executive Directors for approval. Later on, in an unusual move, the Board approved the revised financing operation while holding that no work could be done and no money disbursed until further decision, conditional upon the Panel's presentation of its findings. The Inspection Panel concluded that the Bank had violated several of its own policies. In particular, Management had underestimated the presence of different 'ethnic minorities', each requiring a distinct Indigenous Peoples Development Plan, pursuant to paras. 16–18 of OD 4.20 (Investigation Report, 28 April 2000) • Management widely agreed with the Panel's findings, recommending that the borrower undertake a series of actions to be approved by the Board before further disbursing funds for the implementation of the Qinghai project component, showcasing a substantial commitment towards addressing compliance concerns (Management Report and Recommendation, 13 June 2000)
Final project outcomes	• Following the Management Report and Recommendation, the borrower decided to dismiss the Qinghai component in order to allow activities in Gansu Province and Inner Mongolia Autonomous Region to proceed. The component was then removed after a formal project restructuring (final WB ICR, 26 June 2007 and IEG ICRR, 27 September 2007) • President Wolfensohn's response to the case involved strengthening the role of the World Bank's Environment Department, marking one of the most significant institutional restructurings ever resulting from a Panel's investigation
5. Chad: Petroleum Sector Management Capacity Building Project (2001)	
Indigenous peoples	*Sara* ethnic group
Sector	Oil
Operation	IDA's credit(s) and IBRD's loan
Main allegations	Threats to local communities, cultural property, and the environment
Relevant findings	• The Inspection Panel took a stance on the relevance of governance and human rights considerations to its mandate, stating that Bank's policies cannot be interpreted without regard to core universal human rights instruments, such as the Universal Declaration of Human Rights (Investigation Report, 17 July 2002) • When presenting the main findings of the Investigation Report to the Board, the Panel Chairperson, Edward Ayensu, further held that Bank's policies implicitly embed human rights (Edward Ayensu, 12 September 2002)

(continued)

Table 3.2 (continued)

Final project outcomes	• The Independent Evaluation Group considered that one of the main objectives of the project, consisting of strengthening Chad's capacity to manage the development of its petroleum resources in an environmentally and socially sound manner, had been achieved to a modest extent only (IEG ICRR, 27 September 2007) • The project was also subject to a Program Performance Assessment Report, which rated its overall outcome as unsatisfactory, while stressing that the World Bank Group's involvement had resulted in stronger environmental and social protection. Far from discouraging future funding activities in the extractive industry, it drew important lessons to be learned by the Bank for supporting more sustainable outcomes (IEG PARR, 16 September 2009)
6. Colombia: Cartagena Water Supply, Sewerage and Environmental Project (2004)	
Indigenous peoples	Afro-Colombians living in Punta Canoa, Arroyo de Piedra, and Manzanillo
Sector	Environmental and natural resource management
Operation	IBRD's loan
Main allegations	Damages to human health and the environment
Relevant findings	• The Panel took a stance in the highly controversial debate concerning the use of national legislation in defining indigenous peoples by fully referring to the Bank's internal policy. It thus found that Afro-Colombians living in the project areas could reasonably be considered indigenous peoples. However, due to the absence of two of the policy criteria listed in OD 4.20, para. 5 ('indigenous language' and 'primarily oriented subsistence production'), the Panel determined that the Bank's failure to recognize them as such in the specific case could not be considered a violation of compliance. At the same time, the Panel deemed the social impact assessment unsatisfactory with respect to the analysis of the project impact upon the communities living in the North Zone of Cartagena, as required by OD 4.01. Regardless of whether Afro-Colombians could be classified as indigenous peoples, the Panel concluded that they were affected by the project due to significant exposure to risks, the lack of timely, meaningful, and relevant consultations, and the impact on their fishing activities resulting from marine environmental damage (Investigation Report, 24 June 2005) • The case led to major project improvements. In light of the Panel's findings, Management undertook specific actions to restore compliance with OD 4.01, by agreeing on a series of measures with the national implementing agency Agua de Cartagena, which later resulted in the organization of *ad hoc* training activities for fishermen and the improvement of the communication strategy to the benefit of affected local population (Management Progress Report, 4 September 2006)
Final project outcomes	• Both the Bank's and borrowers' performance were assessed as satisfactory (final WB ICR, 10 June 2010; IEG ICRR, 22 November 2011; IEG PARR, 29 December 2016)
7. Democratic Republic of Congo: TSERO and EESRSP (2005)	
Indigenous peoples	*Pygmy*
Sector	Environmental and natural resource management
Operation	IDA's credit (plus two grants)
Main allegations	Damages to forests; threats to local communities and their rights over ancestral lands

(continued)

Table 3.2 (continued)

Relevant findings	• The Panel ventured the boundaries of its mandate by contesting the choice of a development policy loan to achieve the goal of reforming a sector featuring many social and environmental complexities. Furthermore, it found that Management had not identified the borrower's international obligations stemming from two core environmental treaties signed and ratified by Congo, which, according to OP 4.01, paragraph 3, would have prompted the Bank not to finance the project • It interpreted the UN definition of 'cultural property' embodied in OPN 11.03 in close connection with the spiritual value of forests as perceived by the *Pygmy* people • After recognizing that remaining engaged in the forest sector in the Democratic Republic of Congo was important, the Panel stated that it was essential for the Bank to «comply with its social and environmental safeguard policies, as well as its other policies, to ensure that the forests benefit the people in DRC and that they be available for both present and future generations». Notably, this language aligns with the definition of sustainability proposed by the UN Brundtland Commission in 1987, which has been crucial in shaping the global conversation about sustainable development at the international level since then • In order to identify indigenous peoples, the Panel interpreted OD 4.20 ('Indigenous Peoples') in light of the 2003 approach adopted by the African Commission on Human and Peoples' Rights (Investigation Report, 31 August 2007)
Final project outcomes	• According to the final Bank's ICR, which rated the overall World Bank's and borrower's performance as moderately satisfactory, the environmental and social aspects of the project improved following the Action Plan's implementation; furthermore, the national capacity to manage safeguard issues increased (final Bank ICR, 30 September 2011) • The Independent Evaluation Group confirmed the same ratings in relation to the Bank's performance and assessed the borrower's performance as moderately unsatisfactory (IEG ICRR, 1 February 2013)
8. Honduras: Land Administration Project (2006)	
Indigenous peoples	*Garífuna*
Sector	Environmental and natural resource management
Operation	IDA's credit
Main allegations	Loss of rights over ancestral lands; lack of proper consultations; lack of arrangements to manage or co-manage protected areas
Relevant findings	• The Panel held that changes introduced in the national legislation of the borrowing country during implementation, if detrimental to indigenous peoples' rights, should be subject to the Management's assessment in order to provide remedies to counter their negative effects. It also acknowledged the relevance of ILO Convention No. 169 of 1989, as signed and ratified by the borrower, with respect to the general interpretation of the Bank's policy concerning indigenous peoples and the Bank's appraisal obligation not to finance activities contravening its terms (Investigation Report, 12 June 2007) • Management partly disagreed with the Panel's findings, arguing that the project could not serve as a means to settle all land titling disputes in Honduras to the satisfaction of indigenous peoples, or to bring local law in line with the ILO Convention. At the same time, it undertook a series of specific actions, working with the government on the drafting of new regulations to make the national framework conducive to the recognition of indigenous rights on land (Management Report and Recommendation, 3 August 2007; Management Progress Report, 9 March 2009)

(continued)

Table 3.2 (continued)

Final project outcomes	• The ICR rated the Bank's and the overall borrower's performance as moderately satisfactory (final Bank ICR,18 October 2010) • The IEG confirmed the assessment regarding the Bank's performance, which was rated as moderately unsatisfactory at entry due to the underestimation of several risks during project preparation. By contrast, the borrower's performance was rated as moderately unsatisfactory (IEG ICRR, 2 May 2012)
9. Papua New Guinea: Smallholder Agriculture Development Project (2009)	
Indigenous peoples	Ten indigenous groups living in three provinces of Papua New Guinea
Sector	Urban and rural development
Operation	IDA's credit
Main allegations	Land clearance and associated loss of forestland
Relevant findings	• The Panel considered OP/BP 4.10 to be consistent with the contents and main objectives of the UN International Covenant on Economic, Social and Cultural Rights (insofar as social and cultural rights pertain to indigenous peoples). Furthermore, it affirmed the importance of the Bank's role in reviewing project preparation to ensure that benefits for indigenous peoples' welfare are integrated, even if this entails greater challenges for the Bank. Finally, although not entrusted with the task of amending policies, it recommended the adoption of clearer guidelines for the application of OP/BP 4.10 when indigenous peoples are the direct project beneficiaries (Investigation Report, 19 September 2011) • Management largely accepted the findings regarding the lack of appropriate consultations by developing an action plan and reporting on its successful implementation (Management Report and Recommendation, 31 October 2011; Management Progress Report, 16 January 2014; Second and Final Progress Report, 28 January 2015)
Final project outcomes	• Upon completion of the project, the Bank rated its performance as moderately satisfactory; the borrower's performance was rated as unsatisfactory (final Bank ICR, 29 June 2014) • The IEG rated both performances as unsatisfactory (IEG ICRR, 3 June 2015; IEG PARR, 18 September 2018)
10. Panama: Land Administration Project (First Request) (2009)	
Indigenous peoples	*Naso* and *Ngäbe*
Sector	Public sector management
Operation	IBRD's loan
Main allegations	Loss of rights over ancestral lands

(continued)

Table 3.2 (continued)

Relevant findings	• In interpreting the contents of OP/BP 4.10, the Panel referenced both the UNDRIP and some key cases decided by the Inter-American Court, abundantly cited in the footnote accompanying the text, including *Yakye Axa Indigenous Community v Paraguay* (2005), *Sawhoyamaxa Indigenous Community v Paraguay* (2006), and *Saramaka People v Suriname* (2007) (Investigation Report, 16 September 2010) • Notably, to support the interpretation of the indigenous peoples' right to property in light of the American Convention, the *Saramaka* case explicitly references 'international instruments', such as the 1989 ILO Convention No. 169, and the World Bank's Policy OP/BP 4.10 (Inter-American Court of Human Rights, *Saramaka People v Suriname*, Series C No. 172, judgment of 28 November 2007) • In response to the Panel's findings, the Bank's Management committed to recommending that the government address the land claims of the *Naso* as well as the demarcation of the Annex Areas of the *Ngäbe* (Management Report and Recommendation, 20 October 2010)
Final project outcomes	• In evaluating the final outcome of the project, both the Bank ICR (4 March 2010) and the IEG ICRR (28 October 2010) rated the performance of the organization and the borrower as moderately unsatisfactory
11. Ethiopia: Promoting Basic Services Phase III Project (2012)	
Indigenous peoples	*Anuak*
Sector	Public sector management
Operation	IDA's credit (plus grant)
Main allegations	Loss of rights over ancestral lands; deterioration of livelihoods; lack of adequate assistance following resettlement
Relevant findings	• In this case, the Panel's investigation primarily focused on allegations of systematic human rights abuses perpetrated to the detriment of the *Anuak* indigenous people, who were forcibly evicted from their ancestral lands in the Gambella Region in Ethiopia. Although the report could not include formal findings on these issues, it did present the information gathered during the investigation in an informal manner. In doing so, the Panel acknowledged the *Anuak*'s history of conflict in the region—not only with the government but also with another ethnic group, the *Nuer*. Notably, it referenced a 2003 UNHCR report that highlighted major outbreaks of violence against the *Anuak*, as well as a UNICEF study analyzing the disadvantaged situation of women and children in the region. Additionally, the Panel reported on information gathered through interviews with *Anuak*, revealing episodes of violence and systematic abuses perpetrated against them (Investigation Report, 27 February 2015) • Management took action to ensure better coordination among national programs linked to the Bank's funded-projects, reporting three times on its progress (First Management Progress Report, 11 February 2016; Second Management Progress Report, 23 February 2017; and Third Management Progress Report, 1 February 2018)
Final project outcomes	• The Bank rated its performance as satisfactory, stating that a lesson learned from the Inspection Panel's case was that practical implementation of local government budgets should entail providing Bank staff with clearer guidance (latest Bank ICR, 13 June 2019) • The IEG rated the Bank's performance as moderately satisfactory only, due to shortcomings in risks analysis and limited compliance with the safeguards (IEG ICRR, 28 January 2020)

(continued)

Table 3.2 (continued)

12. Kenya: Natural Resource Management Project (2013)	
Indigenous peoples	*Cherangany-Sengwer*
Sector	Environmental and natural resource management
Operation	IDA's credit
Main allegations	Loss of rights over ancestral lands; lack of consultations
Relevant findings	• In investigating the alleged inadequate protection of the individual and collective right of indigenous peoples to their forests, as outlined in paragraph 16 of the Bank's OP 4.10, the Inspection Panel developed a compelling analysis of its key features in light of international human rights law. It viewed this right as an expression of the broader right to self-determination, to be interpreted in accordance with Article 7.1 of the 1989 ILO Convention, which frames it within the context of national development projects. The Panel further clarified that this right is often linked to a way of life that is integral to a specific cultural identity, referencing the Human Rights Committee's General Comment No. 23 from 1994 on the interpretation of Article 27 of the International Covenant on Civil and Political Rights. Finally, it recalled that, as recognized by the UN Special Rapporteur Erica-Irene Daes in 2001, its protection is also instrumental to the very survival of indigenous peoples (Investigation Report, 22 May 2014)
Final project outcomes	• As a result of the investigation, the Bank facilitated a dialogue with the government and the affected indigenous people to address legacy issues related to land rights and ownership (Management Progress Report, 17 September 2015) • Upon completion of the project, the Bank self-assessed its own performance and that of the borrower, rating them as moderately satisfactory (final Bank ICR, 22 July 2014) • The IEG confirmed this evaluation only with respect to the Bank, noting the Management's proactive stance on the forceful evictions, which were not considered a result of the project. By contrast, the borrower's performance was rated as moderately unsatisfactory due to the presence of resettlement issues (IEG ICRR, 23 February 2016)
13. Kenya: Electricity Expansion Project (2014)	
Indigenous peoples	*Maasai*
Sector	Energy transmission and distribution
Operation	IDA's credit
Main allegations	Damages to livelihoods following resettlement
Relevant findings	• The Panel ascertained that the Bank's failure to include indigenous peoples in project processing was the root cause of the ensuing shortcomings in the implementation of the project. It held that the affected indigenous people met all the requirements prescribed by OP/BP 4.10. With regard to the criterion of self-identification and recognition by others as an indigenous distinct group, it argued that their representatives had taken part in the negotiations leading to the adoption of the UNDRIP, and that the African Commission on Human and Peoples' Rights had recognized them as indigenous pastoralists (Investigation Report, 2 July 2015) • Notably, the report of the African Commission highlighted the significance of international recognition before international *fora*, referencing the World Bank's Indigenous Peoples policy alongside the 1989 ILO Convention as examples of positive actions taken by UN agencies in this regard (African Commission on Human and Peoples' Rights, *Indigenous Peoples in Africa: The Forgotten Peoples?*, 10 June 2006)

(continued)

Table 3.2 (continued)

Final project outcomes	• The Bank rated its own performance as moderately satisfactory, reporting on successful implementation of the majority of the Management's actions (final Bank ICR, 30 June 2018), a result later confirmed by the IEG's independent review (IEG ICRR, 31 January 2019)
14. Bangladesh: Trade and Transport Studies RETF Project (2016)	
Indigenous peoples	Peoples living in the Chittagong Hill Tracts in Bangladesh
Sector	Economic policy
Operation	IDA's credit
Main allegations	Lack of proper consultations
Relevant findings	• Having received a request for inspection from representatives of four indigenous communities residing in a legally recognized 'tribal area' in Bangladesh, who alleged potential harm due to a Bank-funded project, the Panel conducted an extensive due diligence review. It found that the Bank had decided not to appraise the project due to challenges related to the consultation process (Notice of Non-Registration, 18 October 2016)
Final project outcomes	• The project component, which was part of a broader set of operations to be implemented in Bangladesh, was dropped; Management assured the Panel that no other activity would take place
15. Bolivia: Santa Cruz Road Corridor Connector Project (San Ignacio—San José) (2022)	
Indigenous peoples	*Chiquitano*
Sector	Urban and rural development
Operation	IBRD's loan
Main allegations	Lack of proper consultations; sexual exploitation and abuse; sexual harassment
Relevant findings	• In investigating allegations of gender-based violence to the detriment of indigenous women and girls, the Inspection Panel explicitly scrutinized the Bank's conduct in light of previous findings related to other similar cases. Furthermore, it observed a substantial improvement in Management's actions following the request for inspection (Investigation Report, 12 February 2024)
Final project outcomes	• The project is still active; in July 2024, the Bank's ICR rated the progress towards the achievement of its objectives as moderately unsatisfactory

Methodology: Projects selected by first (i) identifying those raising issues concerning indigenous peoples in the request for inspection; and then (ii) isolating those that led to the analysis of issues relevant to international human rights law

Source: Author's own elaboration based on the Inspection Panel's database, available at: https://www.inspectionpanel.org/panel-cases—Cases as of July 2025

References

African Commission on Human and Peoples' Rights (2000) Resolution on the rights of indigenous peoples' communities in Africa. Benin. ACHPR/Res.51(XXVIII)00. https://achpr.au.int/. Accessed 12 May 2025

African Commission on Human and Peoples' Rights (2003) Resolution on the adoption of the 'Report of the African Commission's working group on indigenous populations/communities'. Banjul. ACHPR/Res.65(XXXIV)03. https://achpr.au.int/. Accessed 12 May 2025

African Commission on Human and Peoples' Rights (2005) Report of the African Commission's working group of experts on indigenous populations and communities. https://iwgia.org/. Accessed 12 May 2025

African Commission on Human and Peoples' Rights (2006) Indigenous peoples in Africa: the forgotten peoples? https://iwgia.org/. Accessed 13 May 2025

Ayensu ES (2002) Remarks of the Chairman of the Inspection Panel to the Board of Executive Directors on the Chad–Cameroon pipeline projects. https://www.inspectionpanel.org/news/chairmans-statement-chad-investigation. Accessed 13 May 2025

Barrie G (2024) The 'right' to free, prior and informed consent: evolving customary international law. In: De Villiers B, Isra S, Mohamad Faiz P (eds) Courts and diversity, twenty years of the Constitutional Court in Indonesia. Brill, Leiden, pp 195–227

Bonfanti A (2012) Imprese multinazionali, diritti umani e ambiente. Giuffrè, Milan

Bradlow D (1994) International organizations and private complaints: the case of the World Bank Inspection Panel. Va J Int Law 34(3):533–613

Bradlow D (1996) A test case for the World Bank. Am Univ Int Law Rev 11(2):247–294

Buntaine MT (2015) Accountability in global governance: civil society claims for environmental performance at the World Bank. ISQ 59(1):99–111

Cats-Baril A (2020) Indigenous peoples' rights in constitutions assessment tool. International Institute for Democracy and Electoral Assistance, Stockholm. https://www.idea.int/. Accessed 12 May 2025

Davis SH (2021) The World Bank and indigenous peoples. In: Koch-Weser M, Guggenheim S (eds) Social development in the World Bank, essays in honor of Michael M. Cernea. Springer, Cham, pp 191–204

Di Benedetto S (2016) La funzione ecologica della proprietà collettiva sulle terre ancestrali: un nuovo modello di rapporto tra diritti umani e tutela dell'ambiente? Diritti umani e diritto internazionale 3:587–608. https://doi.org/10.12829/85095

Errico S (2006) The World Bank and indigenous peoples: the operational policy on indigenous peoples (O.P. 4.10). Between indigenous peoples' rights to traditional lands and to free, prior, and informed consent. IJGR 13:367–390

Escher A (1995) World Bank withdraws from Arun III project on Inspection Panel's recommendation. HRB 3(1):5–6

Fox Principi K (2017) United Nations individual complaints procedures - how do states comply? A categorized study based on 268 cases of 'satisfactory' implementation under the follow-up procedure, mainly regarding the UN Human Rights Committee. HRLJ 1:30

Francioni F (2007) The rights of access to justice under customary international law. In: Francioni F (ed) Access to justice as a human right. OUP, Oxford

Gilbert J (2007) Indigenous peoples' land rights under international law, from victims to actors, 2nd edn. Brill, New York

Goodland R (1984) Tribal peoples and economic development: human ecologic considerations. World Bank, Washington, DC

Hunter D (1996) Amazon burning and the World Bank: lessons from the second World Bank Inspection Panel claim. Eco-Notes Environ Law Policy 1(2):1–7

Hunter D (2003) Using the World Bank Inspection Panel to defend the interests of project-affected people. CJIL 4(1):201–211

Inclusive Development International (2015) Bank absolves itself of responsibility and denies redress to victims. https://www.inclusivedevelopment.net/ethiopia/world-bank-whitewashes-ethiopia-human-rights-scandal/. Accessed 15 May 2025

Independent Evaluation Group (2007a) China - Gansu and Inner Mongolia poverty reduction project. Implementation completion and results report review ICRR12759. https://documents1.worldbank.org/. Accessed 13 May 2024

Independent Evaluation Group (2007b) Chad - petroleum sector management capacity building project. Implementation completion and results report review ICRR12757. https://documents1.worldbank.org/. Accessed 14 May 2024

Independent Evaluation Group (2009) The World Bank Group program of support for the Chad-Cameroon petroleum development and pipeline construction. Program performance assessment report 50315. https://ieg.worldbankgroup.org/. Accessed 14 May 2025

Independent Evaluation Group (2011) Colombia - Cartagena water supply & sewerage environment. Implementation completion and results report review ICRR13436. https://documents1.worldbank.org/. Accessed 16 May 2025

Independent Evaluation Group (2012a) Honduras - land administration project. Implementation completion and results report review ICRR13547. https://documents1.worldbank.org/. Accessed 19 May 2025

Independent Evaluation Group (2012b) Panama land administration project. Implementation completion and results report review ICRR13633. https://documents1.worldbank.org/. Accessed 20 May 2025

Independent Evaluation Group (2013) Democratic Republic of Congo emergency economic and social reunification support project. Implementation completion and results report review ICRR14171. https://documents1.worldbank.org/. Accessed 16 May 2025

Independent Evaluation Group (2015) Papua New Guinea, smallholder agriculture development. Implementation completion and results report review ICRR14677. https://documents1.worldbank.org/. Accessed 19 May 2025

Independent Evaluation Group (2016a) Public and private paths to sustainable water supply and sanitation in Colombia (1999-2011). Project performance assessment report 111404. https://ieg.worldbankgroup.org/. Accessed 16 May 2025

Independent Evaluation Group (2016b) Kenya natural resource management project. Implementation completion and results report review ICRR14893. https://documents1.worldbank.org/. Accessed 19 May 2025

Independent Evaluation Group (2018) Papua New Guinea, smallholder agriculture development (IDA-437401). Project performance assessment report 128312. https://ieg.worldbankgroup.org/. Accessed 16 May 2025

Independent Evaluation Group (2019) Kenya - KE-Electricity SIL (2010). Implementation completion and results report review ICRR0021330. https://documents1.worldbank.org/. Accessed 19 May 2025

Independent Evaluation Group (2020) Promoting basic services phase III (P128891). Implementation completion and results report review ICRR0021748. https://documents1.worldbank.org/. Accessed 16 May 2025

Inspection Panel (1994) Nepal: proposed Arun III hydroelectric project and restructuring of the Arun III access road project (Credit 2029-NEP). Report and recommendation on request for inspection. https://www.inspectionpanel.org/. Accessed 9 May 2025

Inspection Panel (1995a) Proposed Arun III hydroelectric project and Credit 2029-NEP. Investigation report. https://www.inspectionpanel.org/. Accessed 12 May 2025

Inspection Panel (1995b) Rondônia natural resources management project (Loan no. 3444-BR). Recommendation of the Inspection Panel on request for inspection. https://www.inspectionpanel.org/. Accessed 13 May 2025

Inspection Panel (1996) Argentina/Paraguay: Yacyretá hydroelectric project. Report and recommendation on request for inspection. https://www.inspectionpanel.org/. Accessed 14 May 2025

Inspection Panel (1997a) Brazil: Rondônia natural resources management project (Loan no. 3444-BR). Report on progress review of implementation. https://www.inspectionpanel.org/. Accessed 14 May 2025

Inspection Panel (1997b) Argentina/Paraguay: Yacyretá hydroelectric project. Review of problems and assessment of action plans. https://www.inspectionpanel.org/. Accessed 14 May 2025

Inspection Panel (2000a) Annual report, 1 August 1998–31 July 1999. https://www.inspectionpanel.org/. Accessed 9 May 2025

Inspection Panel (2000b) The Qinghai project, a component of the China: Western poverty reduction project (Credit no. 3255-CHA and Loan no. 4501-CHA). Investigation report. https://www.inspectionpanel.org/. Accessed 12 May 2025

Inspection Panel (2001) Chad-Cameroon petroleum and pipeline project (Loan no. 4558-CD); petroleum sector management capacity building project (Credit no. 3373-CD); and management of the petroleum economy (Credit no. 3316-CD). Request for inspection. https://www.inspectionpanel.org/. Accessed 13 May 2025

Inspection Panel (2002) Chad-Cameroon petroleum and pipeline project (Loan no. 4558-CD); petroleum sector management capacity building project (Credit no. 3373-CD); and management of the petroleum economy (Credit no. 3316-CD). Investigation report. https://www.inspectionpanel.org/. Accessed 13 May 2025

Inspection Panel (2003a) Accountability at the World Bank: the Inspection Panel, ten years on. https://www.inspectionpanel.org/. Accessed 9 May 2025

Inspection Panel (2003b) Cameroon: petroleum development and pipeline project (Loan no. 7020-CM) and petroleum environment capacity enhancement (CAPECE) project (Credit no. 3372-CM). Investigation report. https://www.inspectionpanel.org/. Accessed 13 May 2025

Inspection Panel (2005) Colombia: Cartagena water supply, sewerage and environmental management project (Loan no. 4507-CO). Investigation report. https://www.inspectionpanel.org/. Accessed 14 May 2025

Inspection Panel (2007a) Democratic Republic of Congo: transitional support for economic recovery grant (TSERO) (IDA Grant no. H 1920-DRC) and emergency economic and social reunification support project (EESRSP) (Credit no. 3824-DRC and Grant no. H 064-DRC). Investigation report. https://www.inspectionpanel.org/. Accessed 14 May 2025

Inspection Panel (2007b) Honduras: land administration project (IDA Credit 3858-HO). Investigation report. https://www.inspectionpanel.org/. Accessed 15 May 2025

Inspection Panel (2010) Panama: land administration project (Loan no. 7045-PAN). Investigation report. https://www.inspectionpanel.org/. Accessed 19 May 2025

Inspection Panel (2011) Independent State of Papua New Guinea: smallholder agriculture development project (IDA Credit no. 4374-PNG). Investigation report. https://www.inspectionpanel.org/. Accessed 16 May 2025

Inspection Panel (2013) India Mumbai urban transport project (first request) (Loan no. 4665-IN; Credit no. 3662-IN). Sixth progress report on implementation of the management action plan in response to the Inspection Panel's report and recommendation. https://www.inspectionpanel.org/. Accessed 7 May 2025

Inspection Panel (2014) Kenya: natural resources management project. Investigation report. https://www.inspectionpanel.org/. Accessed 16 May 2025

Inspection Panel (2015a) Ethiopia: promoting basic services phase III project (P128891). Investigation report. https://www.inspectionpanel.org/. Accessed 15 May 2025

Inspection Panel (2015b) Panel comments to the press release by Inclusive Development International on Ethiopia PBS III investigation. https://www.inspectionpanel.org. Accessed 15 May 2025

Inspection Panel (2015c) Kenya electricity expansion project (P103037). Investigation report. https://www.inspectionpanel.org/. Accessed 16 May 2025

Inspection Panel (2016) Request for inspection, Bangladesh: trade and transport studies RETF project (PI48881); proposed regional connectivity project 1 (P154580). Notice of non-registration. https://www.inspectionpanel.org/. Accessed 16 May 2025

Inspection Panel (2017) Annual report, 1 July 2016–30 June 2017. https://www.inspectionpanel.org/. Accessed 16 May 2025

Inspection Panel (2018) Accountability at the World Bank, Inspection Panel at 25 years. https://www.inspectionpanel.org/. Accessed 13 May 2025

Inspection Panel (2021) Right to be heard: intimidation and reprisals in World Bank Inspection Panel complaints. https://www.inspectionpanel.org/. Accessed 13 May 2025

Inspection Panel (2024) Santa Cruz road corridor connector project (San Ignacio-San José) (P152281). Investigation report. https://www.inspectionpanel.org/. Accessed 23 May 2025

International Labour Organization and African Commission on Human and Peoples' Rights (2009) Overview report of the research project by the International Labour Organization and the African Commission on Human and Peoples' Rights on the constitutional and legislative protection of the rights of indigenous peoples in 24 African countries. https://www.ilo.org/. Accessed 15 May 2025

International Law Association (2004) Accountability of international organizations. Berlin Conference, final report. https://www.ila-hq.org/en/documents/final-conference-report-berlin-2004-1. Accessed 6 May 2025

International Law Commission (2006) Fragmentation of international law: difficulties arising from the diversification and expansion of international law. Report of the study group of the International Law Commission finalized by Martti Koskenniemi. UN Doc. A/CN.4/L.682

Lin W-C (2016) Implementing environmental treaty obligations in project finance activities through an accountability mechanism: an analysis of the World Bank Inspection Panel. CJICL 5:238–271. https://doi.org/10.4337/cilj.2016.02.04

Maiga S (2019) The work and impact of African regional mechanisms in the recognition of indigenous ownership and control of lands. In: Paper presented at the UN Seminar of the Expert Mechanism on the Rights of Indigenous Peoples, Centre for Human Rights, Faculty of Law, Pretoria, South Africa, 30 September–1 October 2019

Martínez Cobo JR (1987) Study of the problem of discrimination against indigenous populations, vol V. UN, New York. UN Doc. E/CN.4/Sub.2/1986/7/Add.4

Oleschak-Pillai R (2010) Accountability of international organisations: an analysis of the World Bank's Inspection Panel. In: Wouters J et al (eds) Accountability for human rights violations by international organizations. Intersentia, Antwerp-Oxford-Portland, pp 401–430

Operations Evaluation Department (2001a) Integrating gender in World Bank assistance. https://documents.worldbank.org/. Accessed 7 May 2025

Operations Evaluation Department (2001b) Yacyretá II. Implementation completion and results report review ICRR11088. https://documents1.worldbank.org/. Accessed 12 May 2025

Operations Evaluation Department (2003a) Implementation of Operational Directive 4.20 on indigenous peoples: an independent desk review. https://documents1.worldbank.org/. Accessed 5 May 2025

Operations Evaluation Department (2003b) Implementation of Operational Directive 4.20 on indigenous peoples: an evaluation of results. https://documents1.worldbank.org/. Accessed 6 May 2025

Operations Evaluation Department (2004) Rondônia natural resources management project. Implementation completion and results report review ICRR11671. https://documents1.worldbank.org/. Accessed 9 May 2025

Passoni C, Rosenbaum A, Vermunt E (2017) Empowering the Inspection Panel: the impact of the World Bank's environmental and social safeguards. JILP 49:921–958

Price S (2021) Social analysis in project lending: writing new rules and changing old practices. In: Koch-Weser M, Guggenheim S (eds) Social development in the World Bank, essays in honor of Michael M. Cernea. Springer, Cham, pp 97–116

Ragazzi M (1995) International Bank for Reconstruction and Development/International Development Association: Inspection Panel operating procedures, including Executive Directors' resolution and explanatory memorandum of the General Counsel. ILM 34(2):503–534

Redwood III J (2002) World Bank approaches to the Brazilian Amazon: the bumpy road toward sustainable development. https://acervo.socioambiental.org/. Accessed 13 May 2025

Salman SMA (2009) The World Bank policy for projects on international waterways. An historical and legal analysis. World Bank, Washington, DC

Sciso E (2017) Appunti di diritto internazionale dell'economia. Giappichelli, Torino

Shihata IFI (1992) The World Bank and the environment: a legal perspective. Mich J Int Law 16(1):1–42

Shihata IFI (2000a) The World Bank Inspection Panel: in practice, 2nd edn. OUP, Oxford-New York

Shihata IFI (2000b) The World Bank in a changing world, vol III. Brill, The Hague-London-Boston

The World Bank (1994) Nepal: Arun III. Management response to request for inspection. https://www.inspectionpanel.org/. Accessed 14 May 2025

The World Bank (1998) Development and human rights: the role of the World Bank. https://documents1.worldbank.org/ Accessed 15 May 2025

The World Bank (2000) China Western poverty reduction project (Credit no. 3255-CHA and Loan no. 4501-CHA). Management report and recommendation on Inspection Panel's findings. https://www.inspectionpanel.org/. Accessed 14 May 2025

The World Bank (2001a) Loan in the amount of 300US$ Million to the Republic of Argentina for the Yacyretá hydroelectric project II P006036. Implementation completion and results report ICR22489. https://projects.worldbank.org. Accessed 13 May 2025

The World Bank (2001b) Chad-Cameroon petroleum and pipeline project (Loan no. 4558-CD); petroleum sector management capacity building project (Credit no. 3373-CD); and management of the petroleum economy (Credit no. 3316-CD). Management response and recommendation. https://www.inspectionpanel.org/. Accessed 14 May 2025

The World Bank (2002) Chad-Cameroon petroleum development and pipeline project (Loan no. 4558-CD); petroleum sector management capacity-building project (Credit no. 3373-CD); and management of the petroleum economy project (Credit no. 3316-CD). Management report and recommendation on Inspection Panel's findings. https://www.inspectionpanel.org/. Accessed 15 May 2025

The World Bank (2003a) Loan in the amount of US$167.0 million to the Federative Republic of Brazil for a Rondônia natural resources management project P006454. Implementation completion and results report ICR26080. https://projects.worldbank.org. Accessed 14 May 2025

The World Bank (2003b) Cameroon: petroleum development and pipeline project (Loan no. 7020-CM) and petroleum environment capacity enhancement (CAPECE) project (Credit no. 3372-CM). Management report and recommendation on Inspection Panel's findings. https://www.inspectionpanel.org/. Accessed 16 May 2025

The World Bank (2005) Colombia: Cartagena water supply, sewerage and environmental management project (Loan no. 4507-CO). Management report and recommendation on Inspection Panel's findings. https://www.inspectionpanel.org/. Accessed 16 May 2025

The World Bank (2006a) Cartagena water supply, sewerage and environmental management project. Progress report on the implementation of the Management's action plan in response to the Inspection Panel's investigation report. https://www.inspectionpanel.org/. Accessed 19 May 2025

The World Bank (2006b) Honduras land administration project (Credit no. 3858-HO). Bank Management response to request for Inspection Panel review. https://www.inspectionpanel.org/. Accessed 20 May 2025

The World Bank (2007a) Loan in the amount of US$46.7 million and a credit in the amount of SDR 73.8 million (US$99.5 million equivalent) to the People's Republic of China for the Gansu and Inner Mongolia poverty reduction project P046564. Implementation completion and results report ICR133. https://projects.worldbank.org. Accessed 16 May 2025

The World Bank (2007b) Credit in the amount of 17.4 million (US$23.7 million equivalent) to the Republic of Chad for a petroleum sector management capacity-building project P048202. Implementation completion and results report ICR553. https://projects.worldbank.org. Accessed 19 May 2025

The World Bank (2007c) Honduras land administration project (Credit no. 3858-HO). Management report and recommendation in response to Inspection Panel's findings. https://www.inspectionpanel.org/. Accessed 20 May 2025

The World Bank (2009) Honduras land administration project (Credit no. 3858-HO). Progress report on the implementation of the Management's action plan in response to the Panel's investigation report. https://www.inspectionpanel.org/. Accessed 20 May 2025

The World Bank (2010a) Loan in the amount of US$85.0 million to the District of Cartagena with the guarantee of the Republic of Colombia for a Cartagena water supply, sewerage and environmental management project P044140. Implementation completion and results report ICR1053. https://projects.worldbank.org. Accessed 19 May 20205

The World Bank (2010b) Credit in the amount of SDR 16.9 million (US$25.0 million equivalent) to the Republic of Honduras for a land administration project in support of the first phase of a land administration program P055991. Implementation completion and results report ICR1445. https://projects.worldbank.org. Accessed 20 May 2025

The World Bank (2010c) Panama land administration project (Loan no. 70-45 Pan). Management report and recommendation in response to Inspection Panel's findings. https://www.inspectionpanel.org/. Accessed 21 May 2025

The World Bank (2010d) Loan in the amount of US$47.9 million to the Republic of Panama for a land administration project P050595. Implementation completion and results report ICR1661. https://projects.worldbank.org. Accessed 22 May 2025

The World Bank (2011a) Grant in the amount of SDR117.0 million (US$164 million equivalent) and a credit in the amount of SDR35.7 million (US$50 million equivalent) to the Democratic Republic of Congo for an emergency economic and social reunification support P081850. Implementation completion and results report ICR1976. https://projects.worldbank.org. Accessed 19 May 2025

The World Bank (2011b) Independent State of Papua New Guinea smallholder agriculture development project, IDA Credit 4374-PNG. Management report and recommendation in response to Inspection Panel's findings. https://www.inspectionpanel.org/. Accessed 20 May 2025

The World Bank (2014a) Credit in the amount of SDR 17.7 million (US$27.5 million equivalent) to the Independent State of Papua New Guinea for a smallholder agriculture development project P079140. Implementation completion and results report ICR2821. https://projects.worldbank.org. Accessed 20 May 2025

The World Bank (2014b) Credit in the amount of SDR 46.0 million (US$68.5 million equivalent) to the Republic of Kenya for a natural resource management project P095050. Implementation completion and results report (IDA-42770 TF-93520) ICR2837. https://projects.worldbank.org. Accessed 21 May 2025

The World Bank (2015a) Kenya natural resource management project (IDA Credit no. 42770-KE). Progress report on the implementation of the Management's action plan in response to the Inspection Panel's investigation report. https://www.inspectionpanel.org/. Accessed 21 May 2025

The World Bank (2015b) Kenya electricity expansion project (Credit no. P103037). Management report and recommendation in response to Inspection Panel's findings. https://www.inspectionpanel.org/. Accessed 22 May 2025

The World Bank (2016a) Ethiopia promoting basic services project (Credit no. 51620). First management progress report on the implementation of the Management's action plan in response to the Panel's investigation report. https://www.inspectionpanel.org/. Accessed 21 May 2025

The World Bank (2016b) Kenya electricity expansion project (Loan no. P103037). Addendum to management report and recommendation in response to the Inspection Panel investigation report. https://www.inspectionpanel.org/. Accessed 22 May 2025

The World Bank (2017a) Democratic Republic of Congo: transitional support for economic recovery grant (IDA Grant no. H 1920-DRC) and emergency economic and social reunification support project (Credit no. 3824-DRC and Grant no. H 064-DRC). Management report and recommendation on Inspection Panel's findings. https://www.inspectionpanel.org/. Accessed 16 May 2025

The World Bank (2017b) Ethiopia promoting basic services project (Credit no. 51620). Second management progress report. https://www.inspectionpanel.org/. Accessed 21 May 2025

The World Bank (2018a) Ethiopia promoting basic services project (Credit no. 51620). Third management progress report. https://www.inspectionpanel.org/. Accessed 21 May 2025
The World Bank (2018b) Credits in the amount of SDR 265.4 million (US$398 million equivalent) and grants from the global partnership on output based aid TF-10097, TF-A2191 in the amount of US$8.15 million to the Republic of Kenya for an electricity expansion project P103037. Implementation completion and results report ICR00004496. https://projects.worldbank.org. Accessed 22 May 2025
The World Bank (2018c) Good practice note on addressing gender based violence in investment project financing involving major civil works. https://ppp.worldbank.org/. Accessed 22 May 2025
The World Bank (2019a) Nordic Trust Fund completion report 2009-2018, 10 years of building knowledge on human rights in the World Bank Group. https://documents1.worldbank.org/. Accessed 9 May 2025
The World Bank (2019b) Credit in the amount of SDR 397.8 million (US$600 million equivalent) on a recipient executed trust fund in the amount of US$32 million to the Federal Democratic Republic of Ethiopia for the promoting basic services phase 3 (PBS3) project P128891. Implementation completion and results report ICR4724. https://projects.worldbank.org. Accessed 16 May 2025
The World Bank (2024) Santa Cruz road corridor connector project (San Ignacio-San José) P152281. Implementation status and results report ISR00975. https://projects.worldbank.org. Accessed 23 May 2025
The World Bank Group (2015) Indigenous Latin America in the twenty-first century. The first decade. https://documents1.worldbank.org/. Accessed 15 May 2025
The World Bank Operations Policy and Country Services (2011) Implementation of the World Bank's indigenous peoples policy, a learning review FY (2006–2008). https://documents.worldbank.org/. Accessed 13 May 2025
The World Bank Operations Policy and Country Services (2012) Investment lending reforms: modernizing and consolidating operational policies and procedures. https://documents1.worldbank.org/. Accessed 12 May 2025
Tomaselli A (2017) The right to political participation of indigenous peoples: a holistic approach. IJGR 24(4):390–427
Treakle K, Díaz Peña E (2003) Accountability at the World Bank: what does it take? Lessons from the Yacyretá hydroelectric project. In: Clark D, Fox J, Treakle K (eds) Demanding accountability, civil society claims and the World Bank Inspection Panel. Rowman & Littlefield, Lanham-Boulder-New York-Oxford, pp 69–92
UN Commission on Human Rights (1983) Study of the problem of discrimination against indigenous populations, final report (last part) submitted by Special Rapporteur, Mr. José R. Martínez Cobo. UN Doc. E/CN.4 Sub.2 /1983/21/Add.8. https://www.un.org/. Accessed 9 May 2025
UN Commission on Human Rights (1996) Standard-setting activities: evolution of standards concerning the rights of indigenous peoples. Working paper by the Chairperson-Rapporteur, Mrs. Erica-Irene A. Daes, on the concept of 'indigenous people'. UN Doc. E/CN.4/Sub.2/AC.4/1996/2. https://docs.un.org/. Accessed 19 May 2025
UN Commission on Human Rights (2001) Indigenous peoples and their relationship to land. Final working paper prepared by the Special Rapporteur of the Sub-Commission on Prevention of Discrimination and Protection of Minorities, Mrs. Erica-Irene A. Daes. UN Doc. E/CN.4/Sub.2/2001/21. https://documents.un.org/. Accessed 21 May 2025
UN Department of Economic and Social Affairs (2010) International expert group meeting. Indigenous peoples: development with culture and identity. Article 3 and 32 of the United Nations Declaration on the Rights of Indigenous Peoples, New York. UN Doc. PFII/2010/EGM. Accessed 15 May 2025
UN General Assembly (1987) Report of the World Commission on environment and development. Note by the Secretary-General. UN Doc. A/42/427. https://docs.un.org/. Accessed 13 May 2025

UN Human Rights Committee (1994) CCPR General Comment No. 23: Article 27 (Rights of minorities). UN Doc. CCPR/C/21/Rev.1/Add.5. https://docs.un.org/. Accessed 16 May 2025

UN Human Rights Council (2009) Promotion and protection of all human rights, civil, political, economic, social and cultural rights, including the right to development. Report of the Special Rapporteur on the Situation of Human Rights and Fundamental Freedoms of Indigenous People, James Anaya. UN Doc. A/HRC/12/34. https://docs.un.org/. Accessed 9 May 2025

UN Human Rights Council (2018) Free, prior and informed consent: a human rights-based approach, Study of the Expert Mechanism on the Rights of Indigenous Peoples. UN Doc. A/HRC/39/62. https://docs.un.org/. Accessed 9 May 2025

UN Permanent Forum on Indigenous Issues (2006) Report on the fifth session (15–26 May 2006). E/C.19/2006/11. https://docs.un.org/. Accessed 14 May 2025

UNHCR (2003) Ethiopia: Gambella situation still tense after killings. https://www.unhcr.org/news/briefing-notes/ethiopia-gambella-situation-still-tense-after-killings. Accessed 15 May 2025

UNICEF (2006) Livelihoods & vulnerabilities study. Gambella Region of Ethiopia. https://allthingspass.com/. Accessed 15 May 2025

van Genugten W (2015) The World Bank Group, the IMF and human rights. Intersentia, Cambridge-Antwerp-Portland

Vita V, Tan R, Panjshiri N (2017) The World Bank Inspection Panel and international human rights law. NYU Law School Clinic on international organizations, New York. https://www.iilj.org/wp-content/uploads/2017/08/The-World-Bank-Inspection-Panel-FINAL-REPORT.pdf. Accessed 12 May 2025

Chapter 4
Relevant Practice Concerning Indigenous Peoples in Private Sector Projects

4.1 The International Finance Corporation's Standard on Indigenous Peoples

Similar to the World Bank, the evolution of IFC's policies has consistently demonstrated significant attention to international human rights legal matters. In January 2003, following a long phase during which IFC's policies closely mirrored those of the World Bank, the Compliance Advisor Ombudsman—its Independent Accountability Mechanism—began to provide feedback on their implementation status, with a view to contributing to their autonomous review. The document recommended adhering to hard and soft international law by explicitly mentioning «international agreements, norms, or standards to which countries and the World Bank Group ascribe» in order to provide helpful context.[1] As the policies were increasingly regarded as best practice models worldwide, the CAO suggested that incorporating such references in the text for clarification could help encourage broader acceptance.

The review process of the IFC's policy framework also greatly benefited from developments in the oil, gas, and mining sectors, which have long presented complex environmental and social challenges for the World Bank Group as a whole. Following the publication of an independent expert's study on extractive industries in 2003,[2] including various recommendations for its future involvement in the

[1] Compliance Advisor Ombudsman (2003a, p. 37).

[2] The initiative was launched by World Bank Group's President James Wolfensohn at the annual meetings in Prague in June 2000 to respond to criticism from the non-governmental community about the organization's involvement in extractive industries with a promise to review its role in this sector. In July 2001, the Extractive Industries Review was launched with the appointment of Dr. Emil Salim, former Minister of the Environment of Indonesia, as an independent expert. See Salim (2003).

S. Solidoro, *Indigenous Peoples in the World Bank Group's Practice*, European Yearbook of International Economic Law,
https://doi.org/10.1007/978-3-032-05147-9_4

sectors, the World Bank Group released its responses and developed a list of time-bound actions aimed at addressing the most commonly faced issues.[3] The document generally indicated the WBG's strong commitment to financing only the projects broadly supported by affected indigenous communities by ensuring that they «receive benefits compensation and rights to due process at least equivalent to what any land owner would be entitled to in the case of commercial development on their land».[4] In the section focused on the private sector, largely drawing upon the assessment conducted by the CAO in April 2003 in relation to the sustainability of extractive industries projects,[5] the Management of both IFC and MIGA acknowledged the relevance of human rights issues from the project appraisal stage, asserting that «appraisal should identify immediate issues that may directly impact project outcomes».[6] In the specific context of extractive industries, it was added that IFC and MIGA would expect new projects to follow specific guidelines on the use of security forces in project sites, in line with the 'Voluntary Principles on Security and Human Rights'.[7]

In 2006, IFC adopted the first version of its Sustainability Framework, which included a Performance Standard specifically devoted to indigenous peoples (PS-7).[8] Shortly thereafter, in 2007, MIGA followed suit. While incorporating most of the content from the corresponding Bank's policy (OP 4.10), adopted just one year earlier, the new Standard presented some autonomous features in light of its relevance to the private sector, as clarified by Guidance Note 7 accompanying its text, updated on 31 July 2007. It is noteworthy that while Guidance Notes cannot substitute for the «sound judgment and discretion used by clients and IFC staff to make project decisions consistent with the Performance Standards»,[9] they are intended to provide context, thus crucially contributing to the way policy prescriptions should be interpreted widely.

A crucial element of the Note is its explanation of how to review the process aimed at identifying the presence of indigenous peoples, a process carried out directly by the client in the case of private sector projects. The Note stated that IFC would consult «with the World Bank from time to time on developments in national and international law and the consistent application of the definition of Indigenous

---

[3] The World Bank Group (2004).

[4] ibid., pp. 20–21. See also MacKay (2004).

[5] Compliance Advisor Ombudsman (2003b).

[6] The World Bank Group (2004), Annex 1, p. 4.

[7] The main purpose of the Principles, developed in 2000 through a multi-stakeholder dialogue process involving the UK and US governments, in addition to extractive industry companies and NGOs, is to guide companies in the assessment of risks related to security operations, with specific emphasis on those having an impact on vulnerable groups. The text of the Principles is available at: https://www.voluntaryprinciples.org/the-principles/. Accessed 26 May 2025.

[8] International Finance Corporation, *International Finance Corporation's Performance Standards on Social & Environmental Sustainability*, 30 April 2006.

[9] International Finance Corporation, *International Finance Corporation's Guidance Notes: Performance Standards on Social & Environmental Sustainability*, 31 July 2007, p. i.

Peoples to [a] particular group or community of people», thus substantially linking the evolving interpretation of PS-7 in this regard to potential relevant international legal developments in the field.[10] The Note also emphasized the existence of various legal instruments governing indigenous peoples' rights at the international level:

> IFC recognizes that the rights of Indigenous Peoples are being addressed under both national and international law. Under international law, key UN human rights conventions [...] form the core of international instruments that provide the rights framework for the world's indigenous peoples. In addition, some countries have passed legislation or ratified other international or regional conventions for the protection of Indigenous Peoples, such as ILO Convention 169.[11]

In this regard, the Note clarified the following:

> While such legal instruments establish responsibilities of states, it is increasingly expected that private sector companies conduct their affairs in a way that would uphold these rights and not interfere with states' obligations under these instruments. It is in recognition of this emerging business environment that IFC expects that private sector projects financed by IFC foster full respect for the dignity, human rights, aspirations, cultures and customary livelihoods of Indigenous Peoples.[12]

It thus framed the emerging concept of corporate 'social' responsibility to respect human rights, as broadly recognized in the 2006 IFC's Policy,[13] within the specific context of projects with an impact on indigenous peoples. The Note also explained that the expectation that private sector operators, besides not interfering with states' obligations arising from ratified treaties, would conduct their affairs in a way capable of upholding indigenous peoples' rights, was gaining increasing ground, and that IFC fully adhered to this expectation.

Clearly, the document drew on emerging developments at the UN level. In 2005, Secretary-General Kofi Annan entrusted Harvard Professor John Ruggie with the mandate of UN Special Representative to address key issues concerning corporate human rights violations.[14] During the early years of his mandate, in 2007—just a few months before the issuance of the Guidance Note—Ruggie submitted a report to the UNHRC for the purpose of mapping the general relevant trends on the matter before delivering his very well-known Guiding Principles on Business and Human Rights ('UNGPs'), one of the most influential soft legal instruments in recent years.[15] Ruggie's report held that the concept of corporate responsibility to respect human rights was increasingly emerging as a result of a series of multi-stakeholder

---

[10] ibid., p. 145.

[11] ibid., pp. 143–144.

[12] International Finance Corporation, *International Finance Corporation's Guidance Notes: Performance Standards on Social & Environmental Sustainability*, 31 July 2007, p. 144.

[13] International Finance Corporation, *Policy on Social and Environmental Sustainability*, 30 April 2006, para. 8.

[14] UN Commission on Human Rights (2005).

[15] UN Human Rights Council, *Guiding Principles on Business and Human Rights: Implementing the United Nations "Protect, Respect and Remedy" Framework*, 21 March 2011, UN Doc. A/HRC/17/31, p. 5.

initiatives, including intergovernmental efforts, with the IFC's Performance Standards serving as a prominent example.[16] It is interesting to note that, according to Ruggie, the Performance Standards required businesses' compliance with a set of prescriptions largely incorporating elements of international human rights law.[17]

If it follows from all the above considerations that IFC, in a way much more explicit than in the case of the World Bank, voluntarily adopted policy instruments widely engaging with international human rights law, the subsequent evolution of PS-7 reinforces this argument.

In 2009, IFC set in motion the process leading to the review of the first version of the Sustainability Framework. In its implementation progress report submitted to the Committee on Development Effectiveness (CODE), IFC held that the relationship between the PSs and human rights would be considered part of the review process. With respect to indigenous peoples, it noted that several groups were advocating for the incorporation of the FPIC requirement into the new Framework, also due to the recent adoption of the UNDRIP (2007):

> IFC anticipates that, in the context of updating the standards, it will analyze, within the parameters of IFC's Articles, the relationship between the Performance Standards and specific human rights. In addition, with the adoption by the UN General Assembly in 2007 of the Declaration on the Rights of Indigenous Peoples, advocacy groups expect multilateral development institutions to adopt a "consent" standard for projects dealing with indigenous peoples.[18]

In 2010, the CAO published an Advisory Note emphasizing the important role IFC was playing in upholding indigenous peoples' rights by ensuring broad support for projects from the affected communities. However, the Advisory Note also argued that uncertainties remained regarding the practical achievement of this goal.[19] During the review process, which also involved extensive external consultations, representatives of indigenous peoples pointed to the symbolic importance of the term 'consent', as, in their view, it was associated with the acknowledgement of their status as groups «with collective rights recognized by the international community».[20] All these instances finally led to the incorporation of FPIC as a requirement for project processing in PS-7.[21] In doing so, the 2012 version of the Sustainability Framework pioneered the approach adopted by IBRD and IDA only at a later stage, with the introduction of ESS-7 in 2016.[22] The most recent version of the Guidance Note 7 (2012) reiterates IFC's commitment to observe the provisions

---

[16] UN Human Rights Council (2007, p. 15).

[17] ibid., pp. 16–17. See also Ruggie (2007, p. 832).

[18] International Finance Corporation (2009, p. 31).

[19] Compliance Advisor Ombudsman (2010a).

[20] International Finance Corporation (2012, p. 9).

[21] International Finance Corporation, *IFC Sustainability Framework, Policy and Performance Standards on Environmental and Social Sustainability*, 2012, pp. 47–51.

[22] For a comparison of the approaches of IFC and OECD to integrating business responsibilities for human rights, with a focus on procedural environmental rights and the right of indigenous peoples to FPIC, see Seck (2016).

arising from the international legal framework governing indigenous peoples' rights,[23] explicitly including the UNDRIP among the listed instruments, alongside the ILO Convention No. 169, the UN Convention on Biological Diversity,[24] and eight other UN Conventions considered particularly relevant to indigenous peoples, such as: (i) the two Covenants; (ii) the International Convention on the Elimination of All Forms of Racial Discrimination;[25] (iii) the Convention against Torture and Other Cruel, Inhuman, or Degrading Treatment or Punishment;[26] (iv) the Convention on the Elimination of All Forms of Discrimination against Women;[27] and (v) the Convention on the Rights of the Child.[28] It is noteworthy that, with a view to enhancing clients' ownership of the project, the Guidance Note does not mention that IFC would review the results of the identification process in consultation with the Bank to take relevant international legal developments into account.[29]

In 2012, following the completion of the update process, as outlined with reference to relevant policy instruments in Table 4.1, IFC conducted two separate studies to assess the degree of convergence between its Sustainability Framework and the then-current status of international human rights law. The first study,[30] which focuses on the UN Guiding Principles, highlights IFC's explicit recognition of the concept of corporate responsibility to respect human rights, to be understood, at a minimum, as those expressed in the International Bill of Human Rights and the eight core Conventions of the ILO.[31] The study also emphasizes the inclusion of human rights-related elements in each of the Performance Standards. In this context, the IFC's due diligence review aimed at verifying clients' observance of these standards is regarded as a critical activity enabling them to address many of the related issues

[23] International Finance Corporation, *International Finance Corporation's Guidance Notes: Performance Standards on Environmental and Social Sustainability*, 2012. See the Guidance Note no. 7 regarding indigenous peoples, pp. 2, 24.

[24] UN General Assembly, *Convention on Biological Diversity*, UN Conference on Environment and Development (Rio Earth Summit), 5 June 1992 (entered into force on 29 December 1993), in *UNTS*, Volume 1760, p. 79 f.

[25] UN General Assembly, *International Convention on the Elimination of All Forms of Racial Discrimination*, Resolution 2106 (XX) of 21 December 1965 (entered into effect on 4 January 1969), in *UNTS*, Volume 660, p. 195 f., UN Doc. A/RES/2106 (XX).

[26] UN General Assembly, *Convention against Torture and Other Cruel, Inhuman or Degrading Treatment or Punishment*, Resolution 39/46 of 10 December 1984 (entered into force on 26 June 1987), in *UNTS*, Volume 1465, p. 85 f., UN Doc. A/RES/39/46.

[27] UN General Assembly, *Convention on the Elimination of All Forms of Discrimination Against Women*, Resolution 34/180 of 18 December 1979 (entered into force on 3 September 1981), in *UNTS*, Volume 1249, p. 13 f., UN Doc. A/RES/34/180.

[28] UN General Assembly, Resolution 44/25 of 20 November 1989 (entered into force on 2 September 1990), in *UNTS*, Volume 1577, p. 3 f., UN Doc. A/RES/44/25.

[29] International Finance Corporation, *International Finance Corporation's Guidance Notes: Performance Standards on Environmental and Social Sustainability*, 2012. See the Guidance Note regarding indigenous peoples, p. 4.

[30] International Finance Corporation (2011a).

[31] International Finance Corporation, *IFC Sustainability Framework, Policy and Performance Standards on Environmental and Social Sustainability*, 2012, p. 5, para. 12.

Table 4.1 Historical evolution of IFC's safeguard policies relevant to projects involving indigenous peoples

	1990	1998—IFC's Board of Executive Directors' decision to adapt the WB safeguards to its use	2006—First version of the Sustainability Framework	2012—Final version of the Sustainability Framework
Environmental assessment	'Procedure for Environmental Review of IFC Projects' (modeled on World Bank's policies and procedures)	New version of the 'Procedure for Environmental and Social Review of Projects'; adoption of WB's 'Environmental Health and Safety Guidelines'; adoption of WB's OP 4.01 ('Environmental Assessment')	PS-1	PS-1
Natural habitats	As above	As above; adoption of WB's OP 4.04 ('Natural Habitats')	PS-1	PS-1
Indigenous peoples	As above	As above; adoption of World Bank's OD 4.20 ('Indigenous Peoples'), at the time under review for conversion into its safeguard format	PS-7	PS-7
Involuntary resettlement	As above	As above; adoption of World Bank's OD 4.30 ('Involuntary Resettlement'), at the time under review for conversion into its safeguard format	PS-5	PS-5

Source: Author's own elaboration

encountered in projects. Notably, in relation to indigenous peoples, the study highlights the alignment of the provisions of PS-7 concerning FPIC with UNGP 18, which requires meaningful consultations with potentially affected groups and other relevant stakeholders so as to «assess any actual or potential adverse human rights impacts with which they may be involved either through their own activities or as a result of their business relationships».[32] Additionally, the study emphasizes how PS-7 aligns with UNGP 23, particularly the provision that mandates clients to «comply with applicable national law, including those laws implementing host country obligations under international law».[33]

[32] International Finance Corporation (2011a, pp. 6–7).

[33] Cf. International Finance Corporation, *IFC Sustainability Framework, Policy and Performance Standards on Environmental and Social Sustainability*, 2012, p. 47, footnote 1.

The second study,[34] which assesses the alignment of the Sustainability Framework's provisions with those of the International Bill of Human Rights, confirms the broad human rights coverage of the Performance Standards across a wide range of issues. With regard to PS-7, the study underscores the adherence of the general provisions regarding the client's engagement process with affected communities to the right to equality before the law enshrined in the Universal Declaration of Human Rights (Article 7) and the International Covenant on Civil and Political Rights (Article 26). Moreover, the requirements prescribing that FPIC should be obtained in relation to project operations affecting their right to land, resource rights, critical cultural heritage, or involving their relocation, are seen as consistent with the right to own property (UDHR, Article 17), among others. Notably, these provisions also correspond with the right to self-determination under the International Covenant on Economic, Social and Cultural Rights (Article 1).

It is noteworthy that the document reports that, in light of its main findings, IFC decided not to create a separate standard on human rights, instead choosing to strengthen the environmental and social requirements of PSs within their existing structure.[35]

4.2 Peculiarities of the Compliance Advisor Ombudsman's Mandate

Within the World Bank Group, the CAO serves as the Independent Accountability Mechanism responsible for assessing compliance by IFC (and MIGA as well) with the Sustainability Framework on a case-by-case basis. Like the Inspection Panel, the CAO is accountable to, and reports directly to, the respective Boards of Executive Directors, while also providing regular updates on its activities to the CODE. What distinguishes the CAO from the Inspection Panel are several unique features.[36] Its work is supported by a Strategic Advisors Group composed of experts from the private sector, civil society, academia, and specialists in dispute resolution, all of whom contribute to ensuring the CAO's independence. This group is tasked with assessing the effectiveness of the CAO's work and promoting best practices.[37] Additionally, while the Inspection Panel can assess compliance with all World Bank's policies, excluding only guidance and good practice notes, the CAO's mandate is narrower, focusing specifically on verifying compliance with the policies

[34] International Finance Corporation (2011b).

[35] ibid., p. 1.

[36] Although still relatively underexplored, a recent strand of international legal literature has shown growing interest in the CAO, both independently and in comparison to the Inspection Panel. See Saper (2012), Marrella and Vettorel (2017, p. 42), Ta and Graham (2019, p. 120), and Reif (2020, pp. 105–110).

[37] Compliance Advisor Ombudsman, *Terms of Reference*, 2013, p. 3. The group meets twice a year to discuss and provide advice on current issues and cases important to the CAO.

related to environmental and social aspects, thus making its role highly specialized. Furthermore, the CAO can initiate *ex officio* appraisals to determine whether an investigation is warranted in some specific cases,[38] and it may also accept complaints from single individuals.

Beyond its compliance role, from the outset, the CAO has also performed an ombudsman function to address grievances of project-affected communities through dispute resolution. Notably, more explicitly than in the case of the Inspection Panel, the ombudsman function, together with its compliance role, aims at facilitating access to remedy for project-affected people,[39] herein intended as a core tenet of the UNGPs, as outlined in the latest version of the CAO's Policy: «[i]n executing its mandate, CAO facilitates access to remedy for Project-affected people in a manner that is consistent with the international principles related to business and human rights included within the Sustainability Framework».[40]

Overall, the CAO's functioning highlights a distinctive emphasis on the ombudsman role, which is regulated by a well-established set of rules that apply to each case as a first step. This stands in contrast to public sector projects, where the Accountability Mechanism offers a dispute resolution option only after the Inspection Panel has recommended that an investigation be conducted. Apart from these differences, the procedure followed by the CAO to handle complaints is similar to the one applied to public sector projects.

Upon receiving a complaint, the process always begins with the CAO conducting an eligibility screening, which takes no more than 15 business days. If the CAO needs to receive clarification either from the complainant or from IFC, the term can be extended for an additional period of up to 20 days. The complaint is deemed eligible if it is ascertained that (i) it refers to an active project; (ii) the issues raised are related to environmental or social matters pertaining to the CAO's mandate; (iii) the complainant is, or could potentially be, affected by harm. Upon this phase, the CAO may make an exception to such a general rule by deeming eligible a complaint submitted up to 15 months after the project closure when it ascertains that (i) there were compelling reasons preventing the complainant from submitting the request at an earlier stage; (ii) the complaint meets all other eligibility criteria; and (iii) accepting the complaint would be consistent with its mandate, after consulting with Management. The following phase, the so-called assessment, is aimed at developing a thorough understanding of the issues raised in the complaint. Nevertheless, it does not entail any judgment on the merits. This phase needs to be completed within 90 business days from the date of determination of eligibility, with a possible extension of 30 business days, when there is potential for dispute resolution. An assessment typically involves the review of project files, site visits, and meetings with interested stakeholders. Notably, it gives an opportunity to the complainants, the legal entities

---

[38] Seatzu (2008, p. 350).

[39] MacKay (2010, p. 296).

[40] Compliance Advisor Ombudsman, *IFC & MIGA Independent Accountability Mechanism (CAO) Policy*, 23 June 2021 (effective 1 July 2021), para. 5.

representing the beneficiary of the investment, as well as IFC, to ask questions to CAO staff. During the assessment phase, when the parties agree to do so, they may engage directly with each other to solve the issues raised in the complaint without the direct involvement of the CAO. If the issues are resolved, the CAO issues an assessment report to close the case.

On a more general basis, during the assessment phase, the parties may agree on initiating either a dispute resolution or compliance process. Internally, the decision-making process, in both functions, typically involves several staff members, in addition to the CAO Director (or General Director).

It is important to note, however, that when there is no agreement, the complaint is transferred to the compliance function. In the absence of such an agreement, the CAO undertakes a mediation role in dispute resolution, encouraging the parties to engage directly in dialogue and negotiations to address the issues raised in the complaint. Notably, in this case, the Policy states that the final agreement should not violate any provision of applicable international law: «[i]n pursuit of a resolution, CAO will not knowingly support agreements that would coerce one or more Parties, be contrary to IFC/MIGA policies, or *violate applicable* domestic laws or *international law*» [*italics added*].[41]

At the end of the dispute resolution process, the CAO monitors the agreement to ensure that all the commitments are implemented to the mutual satisfaction of the parties. If the parties do not reach a full agreement or fail to implement its terms, the CAO inquires whether complainants wish to transfer the case to its compliance function. In the absence of such explicit consent, it closes the case.

Once triggered, the compliance process follows different steps. It starts with appraisal, which determines whether a case warrants an investigation. Under specific circumstances, the CAO may initiate an appraisal based on an internal request from its Director General, the World Bank Group's President, the Board of Executive Directors, or even the IFC's Management. In this respect, the Policy provides that this type of internal requests can be made only when it is deemed necessary to review environmental and social compliance issues of systemic importance to IFC. Furthermore, there should be concern regarding severe harm associated with the project. As a remaining option, there should be fear that project-affected people may be subject to reprisals, preventing them from lodging a complaint with the CAO.[42]

At this stage, Management needs to provide its comments on the issues raised in the complaint within ten business days from the date of acknowledgment of the transfer of a complaint to the compliance function for appraisal, which can be extended to up to ten days in exceptional circumstances. In parallel with that, the CAO will have to complete its appraisal report within 45 business days from the date of the transfer of the complaint, which does not lead to a definitive assessment

[41] ibid., para. 67. A similar provision can be found in both the 2013 and 2007 versions of the CAO's Operational Guidelines, which were recently replaced by the 2021 Policy.

[42] ibid., paras. 81–84.

of IFC's compliance with environmental and social policies or related harm in any case. Once a decision is made to investigate the case, the CAO prepares the terms of reference to define the scope of the investigation.

Even at this time, there may be room for a further attempt to settle the case by allowing Management to address the alleged issues directly. When the allegations of harm appear to be amenable to early resolution and the Management's response includes specific commitments that are commensurate with them, the CAO may defer the decision to investigate. The deferral can lead to, alternatively: (i) the closure of the case, once all issues have been addressed; (ii) the extension of the deferral period, which is possible when there exists a high likelihood of the issues being resolved within a defined extension period; or (iii) the resumption of the decision to proceed to the investigation. Furthermore, at any time during the deferral period, if the CAO assesses that the conditions have materially changed, or that making progress is unlikely or unfeasible, it may conclude the deferral period to commence a compliance investigation.

Notably, the 2021 CAO's Policy introduced a significant change regarding the decision to investigate. It allows Management, in exceptional circumstances, to request a review of the decision by the Board if it believes that any of the technical review criteria the CAO is required to follow have not been met. In any case, this review is based solely on an examination of technical criteria, as no judgment can be made «on the merits of the complaint or on considerations that require the exercise of discretion by the CAO».[43]

Within one year from the circulation of the appraisal report, the CAO sends the draft investigation report to Management to obtain its factual review and comments, and the complainants as well, on the general condition that appropriate measures are in place to safeguard the confidentiality of the draft report prior to public disclosure. As in the case of the Inspection Panel, the compliance function cannot formally aim to evaluate the adequacy of environmental and social policies.

When non-compliance and related harm are found, the CAO makes recommendations to IFC on developing a Management Action Plan that may relate to remediation and prevention of future non-compliance in the final version of the report. In the case of a project where IFC's exit from investment operations has occurred, recommendations take into account the implications of the exit. After receiving comments from IFC and the complainants, the CAO finalizes the investigation report. Within 50 days of receiving it, Management will be required to prepare a response including a plan to be approved by the Board stating a series of time-bound remedial actions proposed in response to the CAO's findings, after consulting with the parties. Actions involving the clients must be agreed upon with them before inclusion. The document should also include a reasoned response in relation to the CAO's findings or recommendations regarding non-compliance or related harm that IFC is unable to address in the plan. At this stage, the CAO first provides comments on the proposed plan to the Board of Executive Directors, and then starts monitoring the

[43] ibid., paras. 107–109.

implementation of the remedial actions approved as part of it. From its side, Management is required to send progress reports to the Board periodically. The case is closed once the CAO determines that actions outlined in the plan have been implemented, or when the Board determines that there are no further expectations for additional actions.

Finally, by gathering insights from dispute resolution and compliance cases, the CAO provides independent advice to the Management of IFC and MIGA and to their Boards. The advisory function primarily addresses systemic social or environmental issues. In this capacity, the CAO has crucially contributed to both the conversion process of the IFC's safeguard policies into the Sustainability Framework and to its latest review,[44] with final better outcomes in terms of adherence to international legal developments.[45] Advice from the CAO may also be requested from the Management of IFC, MIGA, or the World Bank Group. The CAO determines whether to accept such a request by assessing the potential value and relevance of the advice sought. In each of its three roles, the CAO seeks to maximize disclosure of findings, reports, assessments, and recommendations.

4.3 Protection of Indigenous Peoples' Rights in the Compliance Advisor Ombudsman's Practice

Since 1999, the CAO has handled a total of 35 cases involving indigenous peoples' rights, out of which ten have shown specific relevance to the present analysis. Due to the presence of sensitive corporate data, there are no publicly available post-implementation evaluations of IFC's projects. While, unlike the Bank, this limits an understanding of IEG's assessment of how the original project objectives were met with regard to indigenous peoples, it is still possible to evaluate the direct impact of IFC's policies on the ground by virtue of the CAO's findings, which have enforced them. In this regard, a distinction can be made between older and more recent cases, based on the main issues that have clearly come to the forefront. Notably, early cases (2002–2011) prompted self-reflection within IFC on the robustness of its internal policies, leading to significant internal developments. These included the issuance of a note interpreting the implications of the ILO Convention of 1989 on private sector projects and the elaboration of a full-fledged internal strategy aimed at coping with the issues posed by investments in the palm oil sector, which had been long criticized for generating inequitable benefit-sharing with indigenous peoples. On the other hand, the more recent practice highlights the CAO's ability to resolve disputes that facilitate indigenous peoples' access to remedy (2012–2014). Finally, its compliance cases (2014–2018) show significant attention towards the correct supervision of the process aimed at obtaining FPIC, reflecting a greater

[44] Arp (2018, p. 187).

[45] McBeth (2009, p. 1151).

emphasis on ensuring that it is conducted in an adequate manner in the context of the projects funded by IFC. Against this backdrop, Table 4.2 highlights the main project outcomes and related developments for each case.

4.3.1 *Early Cases (2002–2011)*

4.3.1.1 Chile: Empresa Eléctrica Pangue SA-02/Upper Bío-Bío Watershed (2002) (Closed) (Dispute Resolution)

This very much criticized and well-known hydroelectric project aimed at building a complex of dams on the upper Bío-Bío River in Chile, home to the indigenous *Pehuenche* community, is very significant as it was at the root of the very establishment of the CAO. A first dam, completed in 1996, was built by Empresa Eléctrica Pangue S.A. ('Pangue'), a Chilean company owned 97.5% by Empresa Nacional de Electricidad S.A. ('ENDESA') and 2.5% by IFC, following an equity investment made in October 1993. Furthermore, IFC arranged loans totaling $170 million for the project upon the request of ENDESA. As part of the loan agreement stipulated with ENDESA, an institution called the 'Pehuen Foundation' was created to mitigate the impacts of the building of the first Pangue dam over the *Pehuenche* community living in the project area.[46] In particular, the foundation was supposed to share benefits from the dam project with the local indigenous community. Nevertheless, the dam flooded hundreds of hectares of land, displacing 53 people. In the same period, ENDESA started planning to build a second and bigger dam, Ralco, which raised a great deal of controversy, especially among NGOs. In May 1995, IFC hired anthropologist Theodore Downing to conduct an interim analysis assessing whether the Pehuen Foundation had met its original goals. The original version of the analysis, according to which the foundation was being used to subsidize the building of the second dam, was not fully disclosed.[47]

In September 1995, the project generated a request for inspection from a Chilean NGO before the Inspection Panel, alleging IFC's violation of policies regarding dam and reservoir projects, indigenous peoples, and environmental assessments. Furthermore, the NGO argued that funds allocated to Pangue were used for the Ralco project in clear violation of the loan agreement concluded by IFC with ENDESA. The request was rejected on the grounds that it did not concern an IBRD- or IDA-financed project.[48] In May 1996, the World Bank Group's President, James Wolfensohn, decided to appoint ecologist Jay Hair to conduct a review to investigate IFC's compliance with the loan agreement stipulated with ENDESA.[49] Its main results were never disclosed in full. In July 1997, a heavily censored version of the report was made publicly available. The review found gross non-compliance with

[46] Nesti (2002, p. 9).

[47] Downing (1996, para. 28).

[48] Inspection Panel (1995).

[49] Shihata (2000, p. 115).

relevant applicable environmental and social standards and noted the failure of IFC to adequately supervise the project, becoming the focus of several activist movements advocating for greater accountability from the institution. As a result, IFC started embarking on an internal process of reform. This included a substantial increase in staff (from two to 80 people) in charge of the environmental clearance process. It also provided impetus for the creation of the CAO itself in 1999.[50]

In July 2002, municipalities flooded by water releases from the Pangue dam's reservoir during heavy rain, together with a group of *Pehuenche* indigenous women, lodged a complaint with the newly established Independent Accountability Mechanism to resolve the outstanding issues arising from IFC's involvement in the Pangue/Ralco project. The complaint was the first one ever received by the CAO. It alleged inappropriate social and environmental mitigation measures as well as the lack of adequate compensation for the individuals already affected by Pangue and threatened by Ralco. In particular, it claimed that the damages caused by the project, as already detailed in the complaint presented before the World Bank's Inspection Panel in November 1995, far from being avoided or mitigated, had increased. That happened in spite of the introduction of social and environmental covenants into the original loan agreement and the reports produced by independent experts in 1996 (Downing report) and 1997 (Hair report). The complaint thus requested the full disclosure of all relevant project documentation, including the reports. In the meantime, a few days after receiving the complaint, IFC totally divested its equity stake from the Pangue company. The CAO decided to accept the complaint, although concerning a closed project, based on the role IFC had played in its launching and implementation over a number of years.

The CAO's assessment, completed in May 2003, acknowledged that «to the extent environmental and social commitments between a sponsor and IFC are covenanted in investment agreements, details of these should be disclosed in some form».[51] Furthermore, it recommended the disclosure of the two independent reports in full, also formulating several systemic-level recommendations regarding IFC's approach to transparency. In particular, it emphasized that IFC should have used the Hair report as a tool to guide its future involvement in projects having an impact on indigenous peoples. Finally, it supported the view that a revision of the then-current version of the policies concerning IFC's due diligence of environmental and social aspects was necessary.

The case immediately triggered a wide process of deep institutional reform within IFC, with a view to expanding the scope of its due diligence. In 2004, the institution published a report summarizing the main lessons learned from the case, stating that issues concerning land in large development projects would be systematically addressed at appraisal, particularly in situations where weak land registration systems exist or indigenous or other vulnerable groups live in the project area.[52]

---

[50] Orellana (2005, p. 517).

[51] Compliance Advisor Ombudsman (2003c, p. 28).

[52] International Finance Corporation (2004).

In the meantime, in 2005, the CAO committed to providing funds for a local development capacity-building program intended to support the *Pehuenche* community. Through participatory consultations, the community requested training sessions to equip its members with the skills needed to engage productively in the regional development activities. After identifying Educational Corporation Universidad Mapuche as the most qualified institution for the delivery of a two-year program, in March 2006, a settlement agreement was reached.

In an unusual move, then, the CAO entered the agreement directly, accepting to engage with the community to ensure that the *Pehuenche* benefit from a positive, lasting impact, based on a commitment made by the President James Wolfensohn in this respect. The CAO continued monitoring the settlement on an annual basis by working with local and indigenous organizations until 2010, based on the quarterly reports on the activities of the project provided by the institution in charge of delivering the training sessions. The CAO's final report emphasizes that an indigenous community center was created in 2008. The center allowed the creation of communal greenhouses for the cultivation of vegetables, which, by generating income, made the indigenous community self-sustainable, while also strengthening bonds among and within families. A second initiative included the organization of fairs in which artisanal goods made by the indigenous community, particularly by women, could be sold to the public. Besides encouraging economic activity, fairs were intended to serve as a meeting point for traditional artisans to come together and embrace their cultural heritage.[53] As a result, the community gained greater self-confidence in its abilities and was empowered to strengthen its cultural identity.

4.3.1.2 Guatemala: Marlin-01/Sipacapa (2005) (Closed) (Assessment)

The case arose from the operations of a gold and silver mine acquired when it was at the early stages of its development, in 2002, by the local company Montana, a 100% subsidiary of Glamis Gold Ltd., based in Toronto. The development of the mine, located in an area inhabited by indigenous groups, was funded by IFC, which provided a loan of $45 million. Montana began conducting consultations with the indigenous groups and obtained the required exploitation license from the government of Guatemala in 2003.

In March 2005, the CAO received a complaint from the civil society organization Madre Selva on behalf of the inhabitants of the municipality of Sipacapa, who were mainly members of the *Maya* indigenous people, alleging that the mining activities were exacerbating social tensions, violence, and insecurity. The complaint also raised concerns about the reduced access to local water supplies and their contamination, in addition to the lack of adequate consultations in the presence of the national government. In particular, it contended that the indigenous people had not been involved in the design and evaluation of mining exploration plans, nor

[53] Compliance Advisor Ombudsman (2010b, p. 2).

properly consulted on their priorities, in violation of the ILO Convention No. 169. This resulted in the government not legitimately granting the exploration license, with the consequence that the company was not operating legally. The complainants finally asked IFC to withdraw its financial support in order to cease the mining operations. The CAO appraised and accepted the complaint. In the meantime, in June 2005, a popular referendum was held in the municipality of Sipacapa, and residents voted against the continuation of mining activities. As the Guatemalan Constitutional Court ultimately ruled that the results of the consultation were not binding, the legal status of the referendum remained unresolved. At the same time, some NGOs' allegations created a strong opposition movement against the project, which resulted in a reduction of the company's ability to carry out its activities.

Shortly thereafter, on 7 September 2005, the CAO delivered its assessment report. First, it noted that the national context surrounding the Marlin mine was particularly challenging as Guatemala had ended a 36-year civil war involving extreme violence in rural and indigenous areas of the country. As part of the peace process, the country had both signed the Agreement on the Identity and Rights of Indigenous People in 1995,[54] and ratified the ILO Convention No. 169 in 1996, thus conferring significant rights to indigenous peoples in the management of natural resources, which, however, did not extend to sub-surface minerals. As regards the issues concerning the exploration license, allegedly issued by the government illegitimately, the CAO asserted that, in the absence of specific government regulations governing the matter,[55] the project had developed its own protocols mainly based on the company's own assessment, ultimately resulting in a high degree of uncertainty on the right procedure to be followed. Therefore, the CAO expressed the view that Montana should have found better ways of engaging with local community groups, while also creating a fair grievance mechanism to solve the encountered issues, and therefore addressed a set of recommendations regarding disclosure and consultation to the company directly. Finally, the CAO concluded that the results of the review, upon which IFC had based its determination of adequacy of the consultation process during appraisal, were not entirely clear, due to the lack of relevant documentation. It broadly recommended that IFC provide greater clarity in illustrating the benefits deriving from indigenous consultation to its clients, in the context of future projects involving similar issues.

The CAO also took a stance on the threats of intimidation perpetrated by Montana's security personnel against indigenous groups, maintaining that the lack of a clear policy on human rights and management of security forces represented a significant oversight on the part of IFC. In particular, it formulated the

[54] The 'Agreement on Identity and Rights of Indigenous People' (*Acuerdo sobre la Identidad y los Derechos de los Pueblos Indígenas*), stipulated between the government of Guatemala and the Unidad Revolucionaria Nacional Guatemalteca, was signed at Mexico City on 31 March 1995. As part of the Peace Accords that officially ended the Guatemalan Civil War (1960–1996), it took note of the historical marginalization of indigenous groups in Guatemala and sought to provide a legal framework for protecting their rights.

[55] Spalding (2023, p. 108).

recommendation that IFC «systematically consider potential risks to human rights at the project level, take appropriate steps to mitigate them, and provide clearer guidance to clients on both of these aspects»,[56] and that the company implement the US/UK Voluntary Principles on the Management of Security Forces, reiterating the observations formulated in its 2003 report contributing to the WBG Extractive Industry Review. Finally, it made comments of a more systemic nature on the level of due diligence required by IFC in high-risk projects in the extractive sector:

> IFC experience in the extractive industry (EI) sector, of which the Marlin project is a part, has shown that when the IFC supports high-risk EI projects, a high level of due diligence is required in order to ensure these investments lead to development benefits and the fulfillment of the IFC's mandate.[57]

Overall, based on the conclusion that the project was not likely to affect the indigenous people involved in relation to the environmental risks illustrated in the complaint, it recommended that a group representing the complainants, leaders from Sipacapa, and a delegation from Montana engage in a participatory process of dialogue in pursuit of conflict resolution, intended to promote enhanced participation by local communities in all subsequent project-related decisions, such as those regarding exploration activities, benefits distribution, as well as environmental monitoring. In the meantime, in October 2005, IFC published its observations on the report, stating its commitment to implementing the CAO's project-level recommendations.[58] In response to the recommendation for creating a participatory plan to publicly monitor the project's environmental performance, it was noted that a dedicated committee had already been established.[59]

Crucially, in December 2005, the World Bank Group's President and several staff members met in Washington, DC, with the CSO Madre Selva, national and international NGOs, as well as the Council of Indigenous Authorities of the Western Highlands of Guatemala to discuss potential options to address the ongoing concerns raised by the project. As the President requested the CAO to facilitate the process, the latter undertook a field visit in Guatemala, finding that neither the complainants nor the company were willing to engage in a dialogue process led by 'outsiders', such as the World Bank Group.[60] The CAO was thus unable to further contribute to the resolution of the issues originally raised in the complaint, and, although remaining available to the parties for re-engagement in dispute resolution at their request, it closed the case. Nonetheless, it advised IFC to persist in providing updates on the progress made with respect to its recommendations. It also expressed the view that WBG as a whole should have considered playing a catalytic role by supporting the people of Sipacapa in participating more effectively in existing regional and municipal development processes. In addition, it encouraged the

[56] Compliance Advisor Ombudsman (2005, p. 40).

[57] ibid., p. 39.

[58] International Finance Corporation (2005, p. 1).

[59] ibid., p. 1.

[60] Compliance Advisor Ombudsman (2006, p. 3).

relevant government ministries to strengthen their technical capacity to regulate the mining industry in a way respectful of the interests of those directly affected, as well as the broader population of Guatemala.[61]

It is interesting to note that the case led to further developments at the regional and international levels. In 2009, consistent with the findings of the CAO report, the ILO Committee of Experts on the Application of Conventions and Recommendations called for the suspension of the Marlin mining activities, observing that the government was granting exploration licenses without properly consulting the indigenous people concerned, in violation of the ILO Convention No. 169.[62] In May 2010, in response to a 2007 petition lodged before the Inter-American Commission by 13 indigenous communities against the government of Guatemala, alleging violations of several provisions of the American Convention on Human Rights, the mining operations were suspended as a precautionary measure.[63] Nevertheless, the Guatemalan government chose not to comply with the IACHR's request for interim measures, despite continued opposition and growing evidence of potential environmental contamination. In 2011, the United Nations Special Rapporteur on the Rights of Indigenous Peoples, James Anaya, in his report on the situation of Guatemala, explicitly referenced the CAO's findings to conclude that in the case of the Marlin Mine no consultation had been conducted pursuant to applicable international standards such as the UN Declaration on the Rights of Indigenous Peoples.[64] Finally, in 2014, the Inter-American Commission on Human Rights determined that the petition of the Sipacapa communities against Guatemala was admissible on the basis of violations of their rights to, *inter alia*, consultation, equal protection, and the progressive development of economic, social, and cultural rights.[65] The Marlin's mining activities actually ceased only in May 2017.

Within IFC, although the case was closed without substantial resolution, it nonetheless spurred significant policy developments. In 2007, IFC followed up on the CAO's recommendations by issuing an explanatory policy document clarifying the implications of the ILO Convention No. 169 for both governments and business enterprises, particularly in the context of private sector projects in countries that have ratified the Convention, with particular emphasis on their potential impact on indigenous peoples' rights. The document, which explicitly drew on the experience

---

[61] ibid., p. 14.

[62] ILO Committee of Experts on the Application of Conventions and Recommendations (2009, p. 680).

[63] The Commission has the authority to grant precautionary measures in situations where it is persuaded that urgent action is necessary while assessing a pending case. Inter-American Commission on Human Rights, *Communities of the Maya People (Sipakepense and Mam) of the Sipacapa and San Miguel Ixtahuacán Municipalities in the Department of San Marcos, Guatemala*, Precautionary Measure 260–07, 20 May 2010.

[64] UN Human Rights Council (2011, p. 28).

[65] Inter-American Commission on Human Rights, *Communities of the Sipakepense and Mam Mayan People of the Municipalities of Sipacapa and San Miguel Ixtahuacán, Guatemala*, Report No. 20/14, Petition 1556–07, 3 April 2014.

documented in the Marlin case, provides guidance on interpreting the Performance Standards, and in particular of PS-7, in light of the principles enshrined in the Convention. With regard to business enterprises, it illustrates the benefits associated with the spontaneous observance of the Convention, formally addressed to governments only:

> While private companies do not have any direct obligations under the Convention, it has clear implications for their activities and operations [...] Compliance with the Convention will not only protect indigenous and tribal peoples' rights, but will promote the interests of private business by laying the groundwork for a positive and socially responsible investment environment.[66]

Crucially, it formulates a series of observations that remain relevant today, explaining that, while private businesses' direct legal obligations can only arise from national law, at the same time, they face a «reputational imperative arising from the perceived duties of companies to be seen to act in a way that is compliant or consistent with international law».[67] It adds that in countries like Guatemala, in the absence of government regulations on consultations with indigenous peoples to ensure compliance with the Convention, business enterprises need to play a proactive role in the design and implementation of consultations with the participation of the government to add credibility to the process.[68]

Furthermore, the document highlights the key role governments must generally play in promoting human rights, asserting that the obligations arising from the ratification of the Convention cannot be deemed fulfilled simply by regulating the behavior of businesses. It states that governments remain «ultimately responsible for ensuring that indigenous and tribal peoples affected by private sector projects benefit from them and are properly consulted and compensated».[69] In this regard, it refers to the observations made in 2004 by the ILO Committee of Experts. According to these observations, «the obligation to ensure that consultations are held in a manner consistent with the requirements established in the Convention is an obligation to be discharged by governments, not by private persons or companies».[70]

The IFC's document further clarifies the way in which governments can impose obligations on private businesses, specifying that the necessary requirements have to be introduced through general legislation or administrative regulations, as in the case of the licenses typically granted for exploitation purposes in extractive projects. Indeed, when governments retain ownership of extractive resources, the ILO Convention No. 169 recognizes that they have the ultimate right to dispose of such resources through licensing concessions. However, the Convention also mandates that indigenous and tribal peoples should have a say in how these resources are

[66] International Finance Corporation (2007, pp. 1, 3).

[67] ibid., p. 3.

[68] ibid., p. 10.

[69] ibid., p. 4.

[70] ILO Committee of Experts on the Application of Conventions and Recommendations (2005, para. 6).

exploited; without their involvement, there is a real risk that the license could be deemed unlawful:

> It is a responsibility of government to consult indigenous peoples prior to any project going ahead, and to ensure that the peoples concerned can participate in the benefits of exploitation of natural resources and also receive fair compensation for any damage they may sustain as a result of these activities [...]. In cases where there has been a failure on the part of the State to carry out its obligations directly [...] there is a risk that a company could find its license or concession in jeopardy.[71]

4.3.1.3 Indonesia: Wilmar-01/West Kalimantan (2007), Wilmar-02/Sumatra (2008), Wilmar Group-03/Jambi (2011) (Closed) (Dispute Resolution and Compliance)

The case originated from a complaint lodged on 18 July 2007 by 19 representatives of CSOs, led by the Forest Peoples Programme (*Wilmar-01/West Kalimantan*), which raised concerns on IFC's financial support provided through various investments in the Wilmar Group, one of the world's largest processors and merchandisers of palm oil in Indonesia. In particular, complainants alleged that the Wilmar Group's subsidiaries had destroyed forests in clearing land for palm oil plantations in West Kalimantan Province, including areas customarily used by indigenous communities, while also displacing local residents in violation of IFC's policies. Regarding the allegations about the impact of Wilmar Group's plantations on indigenous communities, the parties agreed to enter a dialogue process mediated by the CAO. After six rounds of negotiations, a settlement agreement was reached between over 1000 members of indigenous communities and the Wilmar Group, which was announced in late 2008. Notably, it involved the company's return of 1699 hectares of forest lands, in addition to compensation to two communities.[72] The Wilmar Group also committed to providing investment funds for collective benefits, as well as to adopting improved operational standards consistent with those promoted by the Roundtable on Sustainable Palm Oil, a global non-profit organization.[73] In order to ensure implementation of the agreement, a joint monitoring and evaluation team, including representatives from the CAO, indigenous communities, and the Wilmar

[71] International Finance Corporation (2007, pp. 5–6).

[72] Compliance Advisor Ombudsman (2009a, pp. 2–3).

[73] The Roundtable on Sustainable Palm Oil was established in 2004 on a voluntary basis by a group of stakeholders, including representatives from business enterprises operating in the palm oil industry, environmental organizations, social groups, and other interested parties. Its main objective is to set standards for palm oil production that are environmentally and socially responsible and minimize negative impacts on ecosystems, human rights, and local communities. Its standards place strong emphasis on respecting land tenure rights, especially for indigenous communities, while seeking to prevent the destruction of forests. In particular, the organization has recently required that business enterprises respect the rights of indigenous peoples and their traditional lands by obtaining FPIC before initiating projects. See Roundtable on Sustainable Palm Oil (2022).

Group, was established. The CAO also remained engaged with the parties to help address any other concern.

Meanwhile, unresolved allegations regarding the IFC's lack of due diligence in deciding whether to finance the project were addressed separately through the transfer to the CAO's compliance process. In September 2008, based on the findings of the appraisal, the CAO determined that an investigation was necessary to examine whether IFC had fully complied with its operational framework.

In August 2009, the CAO released its investigation report. It found that IFC had been aware for over 20 years of the significant environmental and social risks associated with the oil palm sector in Indonesia. However, it also found that no general strategy had been prepared to counter such risks in relation to this type of investments. Therefore, the CAO formulated a series of systemic observations concerning IFC's commitment to sustainable development in the sector:

> The CAO finds this approach counter-productive to IFC's mission of reducing poverty and improving lives, when it was clear from the earliest project documentation that IFC was fully aware of the significance of its engagement with the Wilmar Group, and the challenges that existed within the Indonesian palm oil sector.[74]

Notably, IFC acknowledged the shortcomings identified by CAO in its official response, developing an action plan aimed at addressing them. As part of the plan, it committed to developing a new comprehensive strategy for oil palm investments. It is noteworthy that, immediately after the disclosure of the CAO report, in June 2009, IFC withdrew its funding from another similar project, the Bertin Cattle Ranching in the Brazilian Amazon, which was attracting a great deal of criticism for deforesting indigenous peoples' lands in order to be implemented.[75]

As the CAO's findings began to attract international media attention, in August 2009, the World Bank Group's President instructed that financing for oil palm projects be suspended until a new strategy was developed. In 2010, IFC launched a series of global consultations involving a wide range of stakeholders, such as environmental and social NGOs, farmers, indigenous communities, business enterprises, and governments. A new WBG framework and IFC strategy for the palm oil sector were released in March 2011. The document prioritizes initiatives to foster benefit sharing with rural communities, while also adopting a new approach to ensure that IFC's review of proposed projects considers the country context, as well as all key issues typically associated with the sector. Specifically, it emphasizes the crucial relevance of land use rights, social and human rights aspects, indigenous peoples' rights, and environmental concerns, such as deforestation and biodiversity loss. The document also includes an annex interpreting the requirements prescribed by each Performance Standard in relation to the palm oil sector, generally holding that they all «incorporate many schemes of internationally recognized human rights, but phrased in project operational language». Regarding indigenous peoples, it requires IFC to review the way clients address relevant matters, such as

[74] Compliance Advisor Ombudsman (2009b, pp. 27–28).

[75] Herbertson et al. (2010, p. 15).

identification, traditional ownership or customary use of lands and natural resources, livelihood activities, vulnerability, and similar concerns, in addition to appropriate mitigation, restoration, or compensation measures.[76] Furthermore, in 2012, IFC began to deliver various advisory services programs in Indonesia, focused on diagnostics and good practices in the palm oil sector.[77]

In its second monitoring report, issued in April 2013, the CAO acknowledged that IFC was properly addressing the issues analyzed during the investigation, thereby closing the case.

Notably, while the investigation process was still ongoing, IFC made a fourth loan to the Wilmar Group, despite strong protests from the complainants to the IFC's Board of Executive Directors, which led to another complaint being filed with the CAO in December 2008 (*Wilmar-02/Sumatra*). The new complaint reported 17 other cases of land conflict between local communities, including indigenous groups in Jambi Province, and Wilmar Group's subsidiaries. In response, the CAO did not formally convene another dispute resolution process. Instead, it chose to support two independent mediation processes in which the Wilmar Group and the communities decided to spontaneously engage. While an agreement was reached with local communities in Riau Province in June 2010, the *Suku Anak Dalam* indigenous people inhabiting Jambi Province did not find a satisfactory solution and, as a result, filed a third complaint in November 2011 (*Wilmar Group-03/Jambi*). In May 2016, the CAO released its investigation examining IFC's actions in relation to investment supervision in the period following the finalization of the first investigation report of June 2009. The new investigation made a number of non-compliance findings in relation to IFC's disbursement, supervision, and disclosure of information regarding the loans to the Wilmar Group. While the IFC's response did not propose any project-specific actions to address the CAO's findings, it did acknowledge the need for a more rigorous and systematic approach to due diligence and supervision of the palm oil supply chain. IFC also noted that its policies and practices had notably evolved, with many improvements made as a result of the CAO's first investigation report. In its final monitoring report, the CAO noted that no new palm oil investment had been processed during the monitoring period, as IFC had terminated its contractual relationship with the Wilmar Group in the meantime. The case was closed in June 2018.[78]

4.3.1.4 The Philippines: Ambuklao-Binga Hydroelectric Power-01/Binga (2008) (Closed) (Dispute Resolution)

In June 2008, members of the *Iowak* and *Ibaloi* indigenous communities in the Philippines, along with a group of residents, lodged a complaint with the CAO regarding a $100 million loan provided by IFC to the company SN Aboitiz

[76] The World Bank Group (2011, p. 82).

[77] Compliance Advisor Ombudsman (2013, p. 44).

[78] Compliance Advisor Ombudsman (2018a, p. 8).

Power-Benguet, Inc., aimed at both privatizing and rehabilitating the Ambuklao and Binga hydroelectric power plants. The indigenous communities alleged that they had been displaced from the original project site by a decision of the government since the late 1950s, and that their claims had never been fully settled before the planned privatization of the project in 2008. After deeming the complaint eligible, the CAO sent staff to conduct a field visit and meet with all concerned stakeholders in July 2008. It was found that the unresolved land claims had been a source of tension in the region for decades. While national courts had ruled in favor of land expropriation in the 1970s, the government had partly compensated affected families with both judicial and out-of-court settlement arrangements. However, resettlement of displaced families in inhospitable areas had led to the persistence of some claims, which remained largely unaddressed at the time when the plant was privatized.[79] For many years, the affected communities had sought to regain land ownership through legal means, but the process was difficult to navigate and ultimately unsuccessful.

Against this backdrop, the CAO acknowledged the parties' willingness to seek a collaborative solution, thus proposing a three-step approach intended to facilitate dialogue: (i) a first stage to support stakeholders in presenting their claims; (ii) a second stage to provide training on how to effectively express their views; and (iii) a final stage devoted to engaging all parties in the dialogue process.[80] The process culminated in a formal historical agreement between the company, indigenous organizations, and the local government regulating land-use rights in May 2009.[81] One of its most significant achievements was the creation of a Cultural Heritage site, which granted indigenous communities the right to manage the areas not included in the privatization of the power plants.[82] The agreement also included provisions for benefit-sharing from corporate social responsibility funds and local government revenues, and enhanced livelihood opportunities for indigenous communities through specific protection programs. Before closing the case, the CAO monitored the implementation of the agreement for 12 months, in order to ensure the full satisfaction of the parties. Notably, as reported by the CAO itself, the national Ministry of Energy regarded this solution as a new model for addressing complex land-related issues in project development.[83] Specifically, the Ministry viewed this approach as a shift from focusing solely on land ownership to emphasizing the cultural and economic significance of land for indigenous peoples in the Philippines, who had been seeking legal resolution of their issues for nearly 60 years.

[79] Compliance Advisor Ombudsman (2015a, p. 20).

[80] Compliance Advisor Ombudsman (2008, pp. 4–5).

[81] Compliance Advisor Ombudsman (2010c, pp. 130–131).

[82] Compliance Advisor Ombudsman (2009c, p. 3).

[83] ibid., p. 2.

4.3.1.5 The Philippines: Mindoro Resources-01/Jabonga (2011) (Closed) (Appraisal)

The case dealt with IFC's equity investment made in 2010 to support Mindoro Resources Ltd., a mining exploration company headquartered in Canada, which held various permits for the extraction of nickel, copper, and gold in the Philippines. In September 2011, two *Mamanwa* indigenous groups from the Dinarawan and Bunga settlements lodged a complaint with the CAO, claiming that IFC had failed to identify them as indigenous peoples. Furthermore, they alleged that the company's mining activities were taking place in their ancestral lands although no proper consultation process had been carried out. The CAO found the complaint eligible for further assessment. Its team traveled to the field in December 2011 and February 2012 to meet with relevant stakeholders and explore options for addressing the alleged issues. During the assessment process, indigenous community members indicated that they were not interested in pursuing a dispute resolution process, prompting the CAO to transfer the case to its compliance function.

A compliance appraisal was carried out in 2012 to determine whether an investigation was warranted. The resulting report, which organized its analysis around the various phases of the project cycle in chronological order, identified significant environmental and social shortcomings. In particular, it highlighted that, according to the Sustainability Policy, in the pre-commitment phase, IFC is required to review the identification of the project area of influence to properly assess the environmental and social impacts of its investment operations on affected communities.

Regarding the company's obligation to conduct free, prior, and informed consultations, the CAO noted that this requirement was correctly included in the Environmental and Social Action Plan, as part of the subscription agreement formalizing the conditions of IFC's purchase of shares. However, in reviewing the implementation activities, the CAO noted that the 2011 Mindoro Annual Monitoring Report described the approach to consultations in overly generic terms. This was deemed inadequate to meet the requirements of PS-7 regarding engagement with indigenous peoples whose traditional or customary lands are likely to be impacted by the project. Furthermore, the CAO found no evidence that IFC had conducted a proper review of the company's compliance with the requirements set out in the subscription agreement during supervision.[84] Additionally, in the response provided after receiving the complaint, IFC clarified that it had largely relied on the company's assertions to ensure that the investment was being carried out in compliance with the Performance Standards. The CAO broadly noted that extractive industry projects involve highly sensitive aspects, which can have a significant impact on indigenous peoples even at the exploration stage, particularly when sites of religious or cultural importance are affected.

[84] Compliance Advisor Ombudsman (2012, p. 12). On the standard of care required by IFC when lending for projects involving environmental and social issues, see Morrow (2020, pp. 765–766).

Meanwhile, as Mindoro decided to suspend activities in the affected project area, the CAO determined that a compliance investigation was unnecessary. It considered the suspension a substantial mitigation measure against the risks of adverse outcomes for the complainants. The CAO subsequently closed the case, noting concerns about the effectiveness of policies managing the risks associated with early-stage mining investments, and recommended a review by IFC to provide clearer guidance for staff.

4.3.2 Facilitating Access to Remedy Through Dispute Resolution (2012–2014)

4.3.2.1 Mongolia: Oyu Tolgoi-01 (2012), Oyu Tolgoi-02/Khanbogd (2013) (Closed) (Dispute Resolution)

The case involved a project aimed at establishing a copper and gold mine in the Southern Gobi Region of Mongolia to be developed by Oyu Tolgoi, a company jointly owned by Turquoise Hills Resources, a Canadian company, and Erdenes Oyu Tolgoi, LLC, a Mongolian state-owned company, funded with the support of IFC for up to $4.4 billion and a MIGA's guarantee of up to $1 billion. In October 2012, a group of local nomadic herders engaged in livelihood activities near the project site lodged a complaint with the CAO, alleging that the project's use of land and water was disrupting their nomadic lifestyle, while also threatening their culture. Furthermore, the complainants, who identified themselves as indigenous peoples, contended that they had not been relocated and compensated appropriately. In February 2013, a second group of herders lodged a further complaint, arguing that the project's plan to divert a river, as part of the development activities, could negatively affect a site they considered sacred. They also raised concerns about the drying up of water sources, the deterioration of pastureland, and the reduced water supply to forests.

The CAO found both complaints eligible. Shortly thereafter, a CAO team visited Mongolia multiple times between 2012 and 2013. Following discussions with the parties, both groups of complainants and the Oyu Tolgoi company agreed to address relevant issues through a voluntary dispute resolution process mediated by the CAO. In March 2013, the CAO began facilitating meetings between the parties, who agreed to engage an independent expert panel to assess the project impacts through a fact-finding process. Notably, the CAO has employed this approach multiple times, helping the parties address issues in a way that fosters mutual trust and a shared understanding of the facts. The process generally includes access to previously confidential information, a thorough review of its credibility, and the generation of new insights through scientific investigation.

At that point, the parties agreed to request the participation of the government in the dispute resolution process. After two years of negotiations, in June 2015, a Tripartite Council was established. The Council, constituted with equal representation from the herders, the company, and the government, was tasked with addressing all the issues originally raised in the complaint. Its mandate encompassed facilitating the exchange of information between the parties, offering recommendations, and overseeing the implementation of any agreements that were reached. In July 2015, the parties engaged in a second joint fact-finding collaborative process intended to evaluate the project impacts on the herders' livelihoods and the adequacy of compensation to resettled people. The process involved a multidisciplinary team of researchers and laid the foundations for resolving the issues raised in the complaint through two final agreements reached in May 2017.

As a result, the Oyu Tolgoi company acknowledged the inadequacy of the resettlement process and agreed to work to resolve the related issues with the Tripartite Council, which was concurrently entrusted with the responsibility of assessing the validity of compensation claims submitted by displaced herders based on a mutually agreed-upon set of criteria. Furthermore, Oyu Tolgoi agreed to implement both short- and long-term measures for collective compensation for herders. These measures encompassed the provision of sustainable livelihood support initiatives, coverage of school tuition for the children of herders, health services, and other forms of support.

Finally, the parties established that the «resolution of issues raised in the original complaints would be subject to the complete, effective, and satisfactory implementation of commitments in the agreements by all the parties».[85] Upon the signing of the final agreements governing the resolution of all outstanding issues, the CAO concluded its mediation phase and began monitoring implementation for 12 months. After this period, members of the Tripartite Council reported that over 70% of agreed actions had either been completed or were in the process of being implemented. They also acknowledged the benefits of the dispute resolution process.[86]

The case was closed with a formal meeting convened by the Tripartite Council, together with the CAO, in Mongolia in March 2019. In its conclusion report, the CAO acknowledged that, although the primary parties in a dispute resolution process are typically the complainants and the project private operator, other stakeholders may need to be invited to participate in order to effectively resolve the issues. Furthermore, IFC provided a list of important lessons learned from the case, which were included in the CAO's final report.[87] In this regard, IFC underscored the importance of the joint fact-finding process in generating mutually credible data. It also stated that future projects should design compensation programs tailored to the specific needs of affected communities.

The CAO's role in facilitating access to remedy for affected communities is evident in this case. Specifically, the CAO supported the Oyu Tolgoi company in establishing, and participating in, the Tripartite Council, an operational-level grievance mechanism designed to provide remedies quickly and directly to affected

[85] Compliance Advisor Ombudsman (2020a, p. 4).

[86] The joint statement of the Tripartite Council of Khanbogd Soum was issued in 2018.

[87] Compliance Advisor Ombudsman (2020a, p. 8).

stakeholders, in accordance with the meaning and objectives of Article 29 of the UN Guiding Principles on Business and Human Rights.[88] In this regard, in 2024, the United Nations Office of the High Commissioner for Human Rights ('OHCHR'), a key body within the United Nations system responsible for promoting the dissemination and implementation of the Guiding Principles, has released an interpretive guide clarifying that, regardless of whether these mechanisms are developed with the Guiding Principles in mind, they should «provide a readily accessible means through which grievances can be quickly identified and resolved, preventing harms from compounding and grievances from escalating».[89] It further stipulates that for a mechanism to be classified as 'operational-level', it must address grievances with human rights implications arising from business operations on a non-judicial basis.

It is also noteworthy that, in fulfilling its advisory role, the CAO published a note in 2023 outlining how dispute resolution processes can contribute meaningfully to remedy. The note emphasizes that the principle of remedying adverse impacts on project-affected people is enshrined in the Sustainability Framework and also forms a foundational objective of the CAO itself.[90] It further asserts that, following the UN Guiding Principles, remedy cannot be solely seen as an outcome, but as a process that actively seeks to restore the dignity of the affected individuals whose rights were compromised by harm. The note remarks that the UN Guiding Principles inform the CAO's remedy mandate, with a core principle guiding its work being consistency with good practice, including the responsibility of businesses to respect human rights, as outlined in paragraph 10(g) of its Policy.[91] In this context, the Oyu Tolgoi case is cited as a key example of a dispute resolution process that facilitates remedy, leading to the establishment of company-community engagement structures designed to persist beyond the CAO's involvement to address emerging concerns as they arise.[92]

4.3.2.2 Cambodia: Veil II-01/Ratanakiri Province (2014), TPBank and VPBank-01/Ratanakiri (2019) (Open) (Dispute Resolution)

The case originated from IFC's investment of $16.4 million in the Vietnam Enterprise Investments Ltd., a private equity fund operating since 1995, aimed at acquiring publicly and privately issued securities of companies. The fund, managed by Dragon Capital Management Ltd., a subsidiary of Dragon Capital Group, invested in the Vietnamese company Hoang Anh Gia Lai ('HAGL'), whose main activity consisted of running rubber plantations through various subsidiary

[88] For a comprehensive analysis of the key functions of operational-level grievance mechanisms, see Knuckey and Jenkin (2015), Scheltema (2023, p. 224).

[89] UN Office of the High Commissioner for Human Rights (2024, p. 74).

[90] In this regard, see Altholz and Sullivan (2017, p. 73).

[91] Compliance Advisor Ombudsman (2023a, p. 4).

[92] ibid., p. 5.

companies in Cambodia. In February 2014, local residents from 17 villages in Ratanakiri Province, living close to the project site and largely belonging to the *Khmer* ethnic group, which self-identified as indigenous, lodged a complaint with the CAO with the support of five local NGOs. The complaint raised both environmental and social concerns about HAGL's operations, including impact on water and fish resources, loss of ancestral lands, illegal forest clearance, lack of compensation, lack of information disclosure, insufficient consultation with indigenous peoples, and threats to spiritual, cultural, and indigenous practices. During the assessment of the complaint, the parties agreed to engage in a voluntary dispute resolution process. At that point, HAGL committed to ceasing further land clearing to allow the dialogue process to advance; both parties sought support from the Cambodian government. The CAO began to conduct pre-mediation sessions in preparation for dialogue. Starting from 2015, various agreements were reached, including one regarding the return of land to the affected people.[93] In the meantime, HAGL committed to halting further activities, which paved the way for the conclusion of the so-called Siem Reap Agreements.[94] Crucially, these agreements stipulated that if the company needed to use land belonging to villagers, it would provide compensation to them. In the event of refusal, the company would not only return the land but also assist the village inhabitants in securing their ownership rights.[95] On 13 November 2015, in order to facilitate the implementation of the agreements, all the parties, including representatives of the government and the CAO, participated in a spiritual ceremony. In recognition of the impact caused by the rubber plantation project, HAGL offered its apologies to the villages.[96]

The land demarcation activities, deemed essential to the mediation process, took place between January 2016 and March 2018 with the support of a Working Group established by the government. This group participated in the dispute resolution process to help both parties reach an amicable solution. Following the conclusion of the demarcation process, HAGL agreed to return 20 spirit mountains and two burial grounds to the control of the villages.[97] Nevertheless, villagers expressed their expectation for the return of all identified indigenous areas overlapping with the rubber plantations. In the meantime, the Working Group prepared a report stating that the total indigenous area amounted to 169 hectares. It then addressed a communication to the Ministry of Agriculture, recommending that the land be returned to the affected people. However, the company did not consent, as most of that area had already been planted, thus withdrawing from the dispute resolution process and expressing a preference for the government to resolve the issues. The CAO remained involved in its monitoring role to assist the government in implementing the land return agreement.

[93] Compliance Advisor Ombudsman (2015b).

[94] Compliance Advisor Ombudsman (2015c).

[95] ibid., p. 2.

[96] Compliance Advisor Ombudsman (2020b, p. 4).

[97] ibid., p. 4.

In 2019, the same complainants lodged a further request with the CAO, alleging adverse environmental and social impact related to HAGL's operations, as well as the failure to obtain the indigenous people's free, prior, and informed consent. This time, they contended that IFC was exposed to HAGL's operations due to the activities of two other financial intermediary clients, VP and TP Bank, who were actively investing in the company at the time. The complaint was deemed eligible for assessment. In the meantime, the company agreed to re-engage in the dispute resolution process. Given the overlap in both the parties involved and the issues at hand with the first complaint, the CAO decided to merge the two cases and handle them jointly.[98] In June 2024, the parties finally signed a Memorandum of Understanding, incorporating an agreement for the return of over 700 hectares of land to the affected indigenous people, in addition to provisions for resolving remaining disputes over additional hectares. The process is ongoing.

4.3.3 Free, Prior, and Informed Consent in Recent Compliance Cases (2014–2018)

4.3.3.1 Guatemala: Real LRIF-01/Coban (2014) (Open) (Compliance)

The case originated from IFC's approval in 2012 of a $15 million equity investment in Latin Renewables Infrastructure Fund L.P. ('LRIF'), a private equity fund established to invest in infrastructure projects in the renewable energy sector in Latin America and the Caribbean. The fund soon acquired a local company, Hidroeléctrica Santa Rita, S.A., managing a small-scale project aimed at building an open canal to channel water from a dam to two electric turbines in a very remote area. From the outset, the project faced strong opposition from local communities, predominantly composed of people from the *Q'eqchi'*. Between 2010 and 2012, at least 20 communities organized their own consultations and communicated to the municipal government their rejection of the project. Despite this open conflict, in July 2013, construction began at the dam site. Almost immediately, the communities set fire to machinery and erected a roadblock, resulting in the suspension of the project activities. The conflict also led to the murder of indigenous community members, including children living in the area. In October 2014, two local organizations filed a complaint before the CAO on behalf of several people residing downstream and upstream of the project area. The complaint raised a wide range of environmental and social issues in connection with the project, such as impacts on local water sources and livelihood activities, potential displacement issues, and the failure to comply with FPIC requirements, in light of the newly approved version of PS-7. In particular, the complainants indicated that the government or the company should have obtained the indigenous people's consent prior to the commencement of

[98] Compliance Advisor Ombudsman (2020c, p. 5).

project operations, while also contending that consultation and information sharing were not adequate from the beginning.[99] In November 2014, following the eligibility phase, the CAO conducted its assessment. Since the complainants chose not to pursue a CAO-facilitated dispute resolution process, the case was transferred to the compliance function. In July 2015, the CAO completed its compliance appraisal and decided to initiate an investigation. In the course of the same year, LRIF decided to halt the project.

The CAO published its investigation report in October 2017, confirming that IFC had recognized the significant risks associated with its investment, including impacts on local communities, particularly the indigenous people concerned. In its view, however, IFC's pre-investment review was not commensurate with the risks raised by the project, as it failed to give sufficient consideration to the challenges that could arise in implementing the recently revised PS-7 requirement.

Regarding supervision, which began with IFC's first disbursement to the fund in July 2012 and ended with the project closure, the CAO found that IFC had failed to identify key project shortcomings in the environmental and social due diligence carried out by LRIF, which, in its role as a financial intermediary, was directly responsible for the sub-project it was supporting. In spite of a number of agreed mitigation measures, IFC had not correctly reviewed LRIF's assessment of project impacts on water and existing land use, while also overlooking the correct application of the requirements set out in PS-7, particularly in relation to FPIC:

> IFC's review was not sufficient to ensure that the Fund had correctly assessed the application of Performance Standard 7 to the project, in particular the requirement for Free Prior Informed Consent for projects impacting land and natural resources under traditional ownership or customary use.[100]

Finally, the investigation concluded that IFC had not even sufficiently engaged with the financial intermediary to address the rising tensions, violent incidents, and serious allegations raised by the complainants in relation to the project.

In its Management's Response, IFC noted that it had consulted two different social specialists during the review; both of whom concluded that FPIC was not applicable because the impact was limited and did not meet the criteria set out in the Performance Standard.[101] IFC also emphasized that supervision had been properly carried out, confirming that LRIF was addressing the situation appropriately, particularly following its decision to halt the project in 2015 as a result of the complaint lodged with the CAO. IFC also argued that, since the plant was never constructed, any potential impact from the project never materialized. Nevertheless, since IFC partly disagreed with the CAO's findings, it did not commit to any specific project-level actions with the financial intermediary regarding the issues raised in the complaint. Nevertheless, it decided to strengthen its internal procedures for managing

[99] Compliance Advisor Ombudsman (2015d, p. 10).

[100] Compliance Advisor Ombudsman (2017, p. 46).

[101] International Finance Corporation (2017, p. 5).

environmental and social risks in future appraisals and supervision of projects managed by private equity funds.

In August 2019, the CAO published its first monitoring report.[102] After speaking with the complainants, it found that substantial concerns remained, particularly regarding the land status of the project. The report noted that the complainants requested the return of the lands to be managed by their ancestral authorities, in addition to the permanent cancellation of the project. Furthermore, the CAO recommended that IFC advise the financial intermediary, which still owned Hidroeléctrica Santa Rita, S.A., to draft a public statement clarifying its position. Since IFC still held a controlling share in LRIF, the CAO decided to keep the investigation open for monitoring purposes.

Notably, the monitoring report prompted IFC to commission an independent analysis to address all outstanding issues. However, as emphasized in the second CAO's monitoring report published in May 2024, a key weakness in the preparation of this analysis was the failure to consult with the complainants and local communities. After renewing its recommendation that LRIF clarify its position regarding the project, the CAO has recently decided to continue monitoring the case. This decision was based not only on the repeated assertions made by the complainants regarding unresolved land tenure issues, but also on their concerns that the project might resume with IFC's involvement.[103]

Notably, in an advisory note published in 2023 to illustrate the main takeaways of complex compliance cases like this one, the CAO acknowledges the multiple challenges it faces in fulfilling its functions. It highlights that, in several cases, the harm caused to individuals by the negative impacts of projects remains unaddressed by IFC, MIGA, or their clients, including all types of financial intermediaries, resulting in a regrettable 'remedy gap'. The note adds that, given the responsibility IFC and MIGA bear towards the communities who raise concerns through complaints, they should commit to addressing this gap. The CAO recommends that both institutions review all past cases to identify those with significant unaddressed issues and propose solutions to resolve them.[104]

4.3.3.2 Guatemala: CIFI-01/Hidro Santa Cruz (2015) (Open) (Compliance)

Another case involving a sub-project managed by a financial intermediary concerned an equity investment and two loans made in 2008 by IFC in Corporación Interamericana para el Financiamiento de Infraestructura ('CIFI'), a non-banking financial institution supporting small and medium infrastructure projects in Latin America and the Caribbean. In 2011, CIFI directly invested in a project to be

[102] Compliance Advisor Ombudsman (2019).

[103] Compliance Advisor Ombudsman (2024a, pp. 69–70).

[104] Compliance Advisor Ombudsman (2023b, p. 25).

developed by the company Hidro Santa Cruz, S.A., a subsidiary of the Spanish company Hidralia Energía. The project aimed to build a hydropower plant in the Canbalam River Basin, located outside the town of Santa Cruz Barillas in Huehuetenango, Guatemala.

In July 2015, residents living near the project site, mainly *Q'anjob'al* indigenous people, who strongly opposed its development, filed a complaint. A central issue in their rejection of the project was the cultural significance of the Canbalam River and its close connection to their land rights, which depended on physical access to the riverbed. The complaint alleged that the project did not meet IFC's requirements for free, prior, and informed consultations. It also raised concerns regarding the transparency of the land acquisition process and alleged that opponents of the project had faced violence, intimidation, and repression. Notably, in 2012, one individual was shot and killed, and two others were injured, with one of the perpetrators allegedly being a security guard hired by the company. A few months later, in November 2015, CIFI ended its financial relationship with Hidro Santa Cruz S.A., which officially abandoned the project in December 2016.

The CAO found the complaint eligible and conducted an assessment visit. Since the complainants chose not to pursue a CAO-facilitated dispute resolution process due to unresolved social conflicts, the case was transferred to the compliance function in May 2016. In August 2016, the CAO concluded its appraisal and determined that, although CIFI had withdrawn its investment, an investigation was warranted in response to the complaint, as it raised substantial concerns about the social outcomes of the project.[105] This decision was in line with the 2013 version of the Operational Guidelines defining the CAO's mandate, which were still in force at the time.[106]

In its investigation report, dated 2018, the CAO first provided contextual background to the case. It emphasized that the project was being developed in a region with one of the highest incidences of land disputes in Guatemala, and a history of violence during the civil war. Since the 1966 Peace Accords, Guatemala had made progress in consolidating democratic institutions. Nevertheless, the country was still facing significant challenges in addressing economic and social issues, including crime and violence. The CAO thus specifically cited a report by the

---

[105] Compliance Advisor Ombudsman (2016, p. 11).

[106] Compliance Advisor Ombudsman, *Operational Guidelines*, 2013, p. 22. The Guidelines used to be prepared by the CAO itself, in consultation with different stakeholders, and periodically updated. The 2013 version of the Guidelines (together with the Terms of Reference, established by the World Bank Group's President to define the CAO's role and responsibility) has been replaced by the new comprehensive CAO Policy in 2021. The Policy, approved by IFC's and MIGA's Board of Executive Directors, has provided detailed rules for cases where the appraisal is concluded during the process of exit of IFC or MIGA from the project. In particular, para. 92(a) stipulates that the CAO will consider "[f]or any Project or Sub-Project where an IFC/MIGA Exit has occurred at the time CAO completes its compliance appraisal, whether an investigation would provide particular value in terms of accountability, learning, or remedial action despite an IFC/MIGA Exit". See Compliance Advisor Ombudsman, *IFC & MIGA Independent Accountability Mechanism (CAO) Policy*, 23 June 2021.

Inter-American Commission on Human Rights, according to which the main obstacle to ensuring indigenous property rights in Guatemala was «the failure to recognize historical use and occupation as the basis of indigenous peoples' and communities' collective rights to the land, territory, and natural resources».[107] The CAO also acknowledged that the project had been temporarily suspended in 2012 due to violent riots, which prompted the President of Guatemala to declare a state of siege in the area, as reported by the United Nations High Commissioner for Human Rights.[108]

The CAO then presented its main findings regarding the different phases of the sub-project cycle, assessing IFC's compliance with the 2006 version of the Sustainability Framework, which was applicable at the time.[109] In doing so, it clarified IFC's role in relation to sub-projects managed by financial intermediaries, stating that the institution should ensure that the client has an appropriate Environmental and Social Management System in place, in accordance with the Performance Standards. However, it also noted that IFC is not specifically involved in the appraisal and monitoring of individual sub-projects in which the financial intermediary may invest:

> When investing through a financial intermediary such as CIFI, IFC's responsibility is to ensure that the client is implementing an appropriate Environmental and Social Management System (ESMS) and applying the IFC Performance Standards to the higher risk projects that it finances. Where there are shortcomings in the client's ESMS, IFC's role is to ensure that these are addressed. IFC is generally not involved in the appraisal and monitoring of individual projects that the client is financing.[110]

Against this backdrop, the CAO found IFC generally non-compliant with its policies for failing to properly review CIFI's management system during the pre-investment phase. The CAO concluded that IFC had not adequately identified crucial shortcomings in CIFI's implementation capacity prior to the final disbursement decision, such as its limited ability to oversee higher-risk projects and to ensure that the agreed-upon risk mitigation measures were being implemented.

More specifically, regarding the complaint allegations concerning lack of consultations, the CAO determined that the shortcomings affecting the process were due to the project developer's failure to conduct a proper social impact assessment study. Additionally, the financial intermediary was unable to reach sound conclusions on compliance with Performance Standards, particularly regarding the assessment of project social impact (PS-1), the specific requirements related to indigenous peoples (PS-7), and those concerning management of security risks (PS-4), all before the project was developed. In this regard, it held that IFC had not met the requirements

---

[107] Inter-American Commission on Human Rights (2015, p. 191).

[108] UN Human Rights Council (2013).

[109] The former version of the Sustainability Framework was applicable to all IFC's projects approved after 30 April 2006.

[110] Compliance Advisor Ombudsman (2018b, p. 3).

set out in the Sustainability Policy regarding supervision for not addressing CIFI's non-compliance with the Performance Standards.

The CAO also noted that, in the context of the riots occurred in 2012, once notified of the violent incident resulting in the murder of an individual, IFC had not engaged with CIFI to investigate the allegations of unlawful acts committed by the project security personnel, as required by paragraph 15 of PS-4 ('Community Health, Safety and Security').[111] Furthermore, the CAO noted that serious, unaddressed residual impacts stemming from the project remained, including escalation of social conflicts, as well as limitations on access to land and natural resources due to the construction of a perimeter fence around the project site. On this specific point, the CAO found IFC non-compliant with the Sustainability Policy for failing to assess, reduce, mitigate, or appropriately compensate for these residual impacts. Finally, it emphasized that, at a systemic level, IFC's policies did not provide adequate protection in response to serious environmental and social incidents associated with financial intermediary investments. In light of all these findings, it decided to keep the investigation open to monitor IFC's response.

For its part, IFC's Management agreed that CIFI's environmental and social due diligence could have been better documented in the pre-investment review. It also admitted that closer and more timely monitoring of CIFI would have been beneficial to risks management. Furthermore, it agreed to develop guidance for financial intermediaries to better respond to incidents occurring in the context of projects and to review its policies for withdrawing from an investment, as well as to define an approach to 'responsible exit'. However, it did not commit to taking any specific project-level actions,[112] as it did in the *Guatemala*: *Real LRIF-01/Coban* case.

In 2020, the CAO published its monitoring report. After acknowledging CIFI's withdrawal from financing Hidro Santa Cruz in 2015, it noted that IFC had also sold its equity investment in the financial intermediary in 2019. The report further stated that the complainants continued to assert that the initial development of Hidro Santa Cruz power plant had caused impacts on them that had yet to be addressed. The CAO concluded that, since IFC had not committed to any specific project-level remedial measures, there was no reasonable expectation of further action by IFC to address residual impacts. Consequently, the CAO decided to close the project-level monitoring of the case, while keeping it open in relation to systemic-level commitments.[113]

It is noteworthy that IFC's approach to exiting investments was the subject of a 2023 CAO's Advisory Note, which analyzes it in light of the complaints received over a decade, from 2013 to 2022, to identify the challenges that typically restrict IFC's ability to adhere to its commitments under its Sustainability Policy. The note finds that exits during active CAO's cases are common and can be quite

[111] Under the new version of the Framework, the provision has been replaced by para. 14 with no substantial changes.

[112] International Finance Corporation (2020).

[113] Compliance Advisor Ombudsman (2024b, p. 8).

controversial, specifically citing the Hidro Santa Cruz case as an example. It further observes that, while exits are a normal part of the investment life cycle and can occur at various points during a project, they often leave project-affected people without remedy when handled irresponsibly, ultimately making them bear the unintended costs of development projects.[114] Shortly thereafter, in October 2024, IFC released its long-awaited statement detailing the 'Approach to Responsible Exit'. The document, which builds on the Sustainability Policy, outlines five key principles to guide IFC in determining whether and how to exit a project responsibly. The principles aim to ensure that IFC considers not only the development impact but also the potential environmental and social consequences of its exit, in addition to other factors such as reputational risks and legal liability.[115]

4.3.3.3 Panama PL IV-01/Multi-locations (2018) (Open) (Compliance)

In 2017, IFC began to advise a state-owned company, Empresa de Transmisión Eléctrica S.A. ('ETESA'), on structuring a public-private partnership intended to finance, construct, and operate a 330-km transmission line project in Panama. On 18 June 2018, the CAO received a complaint filed on behalf of the indigenous communities living inside the *Ngöbe-Buglé* comarca, a government-recognized indigenous territory, as well as those living outside it in the Norte de Santa Fé region of Veraguas Province. The complaint alleged serious concerns regarding the FPIC process carried out by the company ETESA in relation to the transmission line. As the parties decided not to pursue a dispute resolution process following the assessment phase, the case was transferred to the CAO compliance function. In December 2019, the CAO completed its appraisal, affirming that a key requirement for IFC advisory services projects is to provide advice consistent with the requirements of the Performance Standards. Therefore, in light of the resulting adverse impact of the project on involved communities, it determined that a compliance investigation in response to the complaint was warranted.

The investigation report found that the preliminary FPIC process was not fully aligned with the general requirements concerning stakeholders' engagement, and with PS-7 in particular. In the CAO's view, the lack of IFC's proper advice on these aspects had contributed to the main shortcomings regarding the consultations carried out by ETESA, leading to limited involvement of the traditional authorities, representatives of indigenous communities living in the comarca, as well as the exclusion of those living outside it, in addition to a general limited involvement of women.

[114] Compliance Advisor Ombudsman (2023c, p. 5). The CAO's approach to this matter is cited in a report authored by OHCHR, which signals the growing attention of international financial institutions to the issue. The report extensively analyzes situations in which a business enterprise may decide to exit a project due to particularly challenging contexts that threaten human rights through the lens of the UN Guiding Principles. See UN Office of the High Commissioner for Human Rights (2023, p. 14).

[115] International Finance Corporation (2024).

According to the CAO, this could also result in a broader negative impact upon their cultural, economic, and customary rights.[116] Finally, the report considered the historical opposition to infrastructure development in the region, noting that the lack of FPIC could lead to increased social tension.

Shortly thereafter, Management developed its plan in response to the findings, including a series of actions to be implemented in order to ensure proper indigenous communities' engagement, such as the delivery of ongoing advice to ETESA on how to develop the project in accordance with the Performance Standards.

Crucially, the IFC's Board of Executive Directors approved the MAP on condition that additional commitments were made, such as updating the CAO on further actions to address the systemic recommendations from the investigation report, and, in particular, on the development of guidance for staff to better understand the IFC's role when providing advice on projects with specific risks or impacts involving FPIC or land acquisition. In welcoming such efforts, the CAO Director General had a chance to stress the critical role played by the FPIC as enshrined in the IFC Sustainability Framework for ensuring the legitimacy of projects with an impact on indigenous peoples' rights: «FPIC is enshrined in IFC's policies and is critical to the legitimacy of projects impacting the ancestral lands, customs, and resources of Indigenous Peoples».[117]

In December 2022, Management presented its first report on the progress of implementing the MAP regarding both project-level and systemic actions.[118] In its monitoring report, dated May 2023, the CAO noted that, in spite of good progress concerning systemic recommendations, FPIC shortcomings continued to occur, particularly in relation to the indigenous communities outside the comarca. Therefore, the CAO recommended that IFC take additional measures to ensure that ETESA makes every effort to apply the Performance Standards. The CAO also determined that, if ETESA continued to act inconsistently with its obligations under the project agreement, IFC would need to consider its reputational risks.[119] Shortly thereafter, the CAO conducted a monitoring mission to deepen its understanding of the implementation of IFC's MAP. After meeting with members of the indigenous communities and other relevant stakeholders, it became apparent that ETESA had made no progress on planning or implementing the FPIC process, as also acknowledged by IFC.[120] In May 2024, the CAO reiterated its concern regarding this issue, noting that ETESA had not yet implemented IFC's advice on the matter. It also emphasized that IFC had not engaged with the complainants since July 2023, despite its commitment to doing so every six months.[121] The case remains under compliance monitoring for project-level actions.

[116] Compliance Advisor Ombudsman (2022, p. 3).

[117] International Finance Corporation (2022a).

[118] International Finance Corporation (2022b).

[119] Compliance Advisor Ombudsman (2023d, p. 11).

[120] International Finance Corporation (2023, p. 5).

[121] Compliance Advisor Ombudsman (2024c, p. 9). Notably, while in May 2025 the CAO has recognized IFC's efforts to course-correct, no concrete progress has been made by ETESA yet.

4.4 Interim Conclusions

The evolution of IFC's policies demonstrates how the institution has drawn upon the latest developments occurred in international human rights law to shape the way its supported operations uphold the rights of indigenous peoples. Notably, the studies accompanying the most recent version of the Sustainability Framework reveal its significant alignment with the UN Guiding Principles on Business and Human Rights and the International Bill of Human Rights. Furthermore, the Guidance Note complementing Performance Standard-7 on indigenous peoples clarifies that project requirements incorporate elements of the 1989 ILO Convention No. 169, as well as several relevant UN Conventions and international declarations, including the UNDRIP. Against this backdrop, it is not surprising that the practice of the CAO, the IFC's Independent Accountability Mechanism, refers less explicitly to international human rights law.

As in the case of IBRD and IDA, IFC requires that proposed projects align with the Performance Standards, and jointly identifies with the client any action needed to address compliance gaps during the pre-appraisal phase.[122] Additionally, during the monitoring phase of client's operations—after funds have been disbursed and project requirements have become legally binding through incorporation into the legal agreement—the client must also comply with the specific conditions outlined in the action plan, as well as with relevant provisions on environmental and social reporting and supervision visits by IFC staff or representatives. In case of non-compliance, IFC may exercise its rights and remedies, as appropriate.[123] Notably, the Sustainability Framework also repeatedly emphasizes that, in addition to meeting the requirements set out in the Performance Standards, clients must comply with applicable national laws, including those that implement the host country's obligations under international law.[124] Other relevant provisions concern the role played by the client in obtaining FPIC for projects involving relocation of indigenous peoples from lands and natural resources subject to traditional ownership or under customary use. In such cases, recognizing the applicant's full ownership of the project, PS-7 explicitly provides that the client does not proceed with the project unless FPIC has been obtained.[125] Nevertheless, at this stage, IFC retains critical due diligence and supervisory responsibilities. In *Guatemala: Marlin-01/Sipacapa* (2005), the CAO stressed that IFC must verify the adequacy of the consultation process conducted by its clients starting from appraisal. In *The Philippines*: *Mindoro Resources-01/Jabonga* (2011), the CAO identified several shortcomings in IFC's supervisory activities concerning the client's compliance with the requirements set out in PS-7.

---

[122] International Finance Corporation, *Environmental and Social Review Procedures Manual*, 2025, para. 4.26.

[123] International Finance Corporation, *IFC Sustainability Framework, Policy and Performance Standards on Environmental and Social Sustainability*, 2012, p. 5, para. 24. See also Morgera (2020, pp. 247–248).

[124] International Finance Corporation, *IFC Sustainability Framework, Policy and Performance Standards on Environmental and Social Sustainability*, 2012, pp. 17, 47.

[125] International Finance Corporation, *IFC Sustainability Framework, Policy and Performance Standards on Environmental and Social Sustainability*, 2012, p. 50, para. 15.

Overall, in a manner far more evident than in the case of public sector projects, IFC applies a form of conditionality specifically designed to protect the human rights of indigenous peoples in the business operations that it supports, as the CAO's practice demonstrates.

In this respect, in its very first case, the much-criticized *Chile*: *Empresa Eléctrica Pangue SA-02/Upper Bío-Bío Watershed* case (2002), the CAO expressed the view that a revision of the then-current version of the policies concerning IFC's due diligence on environmental and social aspects was necessary. The case, which arose from a complaint lodged by representatives of the *Pehuenche* indigenous community flooded by water releases of a dam reservoir, is very significant as it ultimately led to a wide process of deep institutional reform within IFC, with a view to expanding the scope of its responsibilities. In 2004, the institution released a report highlighting key lessons from the case, emphasizing that land-related issues in large development projects should undergo thorough examination during the appraisal phase, especially in countries with weak land registration systems.

In *Indonesia: Wilmar-01/West Kalimantan* (2007), the CAO found in its investigation report that IFC, despite being aware of the risks associated with investments in the palm oil sector in the country, had not developed a comprehensive strategy to address them. The CAO criticized this approach, noting that IFC was undermining its mission to reduce poverty and improve people's standards of living. In response to the CAO's findings, IFC not only acknowledged these shortcomings and developed an action plan but also withdrew its funding from another controversial project that was being implemented in Brazil, which was associated with deforestation. Finally, in 2011, IFC released its new strategy for the palm oil sector, primarily focused on sharing benefits with rural communities and addressing key issues such as land use, human rights, and environmental concerns. Notably, it included significant statements concerning the incorporation of internationally recognized human rights into the Performance Standards.

A more recent strand of the CAO's practice has focused on compliance with the requirements regarding the process for obtaining FPIC. In *Guatemala: Real LRIF-01/Coban* (2014), as a consequence of the complaint lodged with the CAO, the private equity fund directly involved in the project decided to halt the related activities. The CAO found IFC out of compliance for not having conducted the pre-investment review and the supervision of environmental and social aspects properly. In particular, it noted that IFC's review was not sufficient to ensure the financial intermediary's proper assessment of the FPIC requirement for projects impacting land and natural resources under traditional ownership or customary use. Notably, by partly disagreeing with the findings, IFC did not commit to any specific project-level action, although it decided to strengthen its internal procedures for managing environmental and social risks in future appraisal and supervision of projects managed by private equity funds. In *Guatemala: CIFI-01/Hidro Santa Cruz* (2015), the CAO found IFC non-compliant with its policies for not having adequately reviewed and supervised the issues related to the lack of consultations with the indigenous people concerned and the lack of transparency in the land acquisition process. In response to the investigation findings, IFC committed to systemic-level actions, including the adoption of a proper approach to responsible exit from investments, which has been released in October 2024. In the recent *Panama PL IV-01/Multi-locations* case (2018), in the context of a project intended to provide advisory services to a state-owned enterprise, the CAO had a chance to reflect on the general role played by FPIC as enshrined in the IFC's Sustainability Framework in ensuring «the legitimacy of projects impacting the ancestral lands, customs, and resources of Indigenous Peoples». Crucially, in its investigation report, the CAO observed that non-compliance with the requirements set out in PS-7 may result in a broader negative impact on the cultural, economic, and territorial rights and interests of affected indigenous communities.

Lastly, it is worth noting that, in execution of its mandate, the CAO facilitates access to remedy for harm suffered by project-affected communities, in alignment with the international business and human rights principles embedded in the IFC's Sustainability Framework. The practice related to the exercise of its dispute resolution functions has made significant contributions to this objective in various ways. Typically, the CAO supports the resolution of allegations raised by complainants in an indirect manner, as a mediator. In *The Philippines: Ambuklao-Binga Hydroelectric Power-01/Binga* (2008), the CAO mediated a dispute resolution process that culminated in a formal historical agreement regulating land-use rights in 2009, which was stipulated between the involved business enterprise, the indigenous communities, and the local authorities. One of the most significant achievements of the agreement was the creation of a Cultural Heritage site. The agreement also included provisions for benefit-sharing from corporate social responsibility funds and local government revenues, along with improved livelihood opportunities for indigenous communities through specific protection programs. In *Cambodia: Veil II-01/Ratanakiri Province* (2014), as a result of the CAO-mediated dispute resolution process, a company managing rubber plantations on the ancestral lands of an ethnic group in Ratanakiri Province, whose members self-identified as indigenous, agreed to return 20 spirit mountains and two burial grounds to them. Although the company withdrew from the process at a later stage, refusing to return the areas already planted, a few years later, after another complaint was lodged by the same people, it agreed to re-engage in CAO-facilitated dialogue. As a result, it signed a Memorandum of Understanding that provided for the return of several hectares of ancestral lands (*Cambodia: TPBank and VPBank-01/Ratanakiri*, 2019). Notably, the CAO has also encouraged the establishment of operational-level grievance mechanisms directly managed by business enterprises, aimed at providing indigenous peoples with prompt and effective access to remedy in a way consistent with the meaning and objectives of Article 29 of the UN Guiding Principles, which describes how such mechanisms should work. In *Mongolia: Oyu Tolgoi-01* (2012), *Oyu Tolgoi-02/Khanbogd* (2013), which involved a project causing the displacement of local nomadic herders, the CAO supported a dialogue process that resulted in the establishment of a Tripartite Council. Composed of representatives from the involved company, the herders, and the government, the Council was tasked with resolving compensation claims related to the project. The CAO concluded its mediation phase only after a final agreement was reached and remained involved in monitoring its implementation.

Table 4.2 Selected Compliance Advisor Ombudsman's cases concerning indigenous peoples' rights

1. Chile: Empresa Eléctrica Pangue SA-02/Upper Bío-Bío Watershed (2002) (Closed) (Dispute Resolution)	
Indigenous peoples	*Pehuenche*
Business Enterprise	Empresa Eléctrica Pangue S.A.
Sector	Renewable energy generation
Financial exposure	IFC's equity investment (2.5%); IFC's loan ($170 million)
Main allegations	Lack of appropriate social and environmental mitigation measures; lack of adequate compensation
Relevant project outcomes	• The case is relevant as, in response to the first informal allegations concerning the project, the then-President of the World Bank Group commissioned an independent review that led to the establishment of the CAO. A few days after the complaint was lodged, IFC dismissed its investment in the company involved in the building of a complex of dams which had allegedly harmed the indigenous community living near the project site • In its assessment report, the CAO provided systemic-level recommendations to IFC so that it could improve transparency and its future involvement in projects with similar features • As the *Pehuenche* indigenous community expressed the will to be provided with appropriate skills to contribute to the development activities in the region, the CAO directly funded a development program aimed at helping strengthen their cultural identity and self-sufficiency. In an unusual move, the CAO also formally stipulated (and monitored the implementation of) a settlement agreement with the educational institution selected to provide training programs, with noteworthy results (Conclusion Report, 1 June 2010)
Further developments	• The case triggered a wide process of deep institutional reform within IFC, with a view to expanding the scope of its environmental and social due diligence activities
2. Guatemala: Marlin-01/Sipacapa (2005) (Closed) (Assessment)	
Indigenous peoples	*Maya*
Business Enterprise	Montana
Sector	Mining
Financial exposure	IFC's loan ($45 million)
Main allegations	Lack of consultations in the presence of the national government

(continued)

Table 4.2 (continued)

Relevant project outcomes	• In the context of a mining project funded by IFC, inhabitants of the municipality of Sipacapa in Guatemala, who were mainly *Maya* indigenous people, lodged a complaint alleging that the mining activities were exacerbating social tensions, while also raising concerns about the reduced access to local water supplies and their contamination, in addition to the lack of adequate consultations in the presence of the national government, in violation of the ILO Convention No. 169 • The CAO acknowledged the difficult context in which the project was being implemented, emphasizing that, in the absence of national regulations concerning consultations, the project had developed its own protocols. At the same time, it noted that the involved company should have found better ways of engaging with the local community groups, providing direct recommendations in this regard. Finally, the CAO determined that the basis on which IFC had considered the company's consultation practices adequate during the appraisal phase was not clear (Assessment Report, 7 September 2005)
Further developments	• Based on the conclusion that the project was not likely to significantly impact the involved indigenous people in relation to the environmental risks asserted in the complaint, the CAO recommended that a group representing the complainants and a delegation from the mining company Montana engage in a participatory process of dialogue in pursuit of conflict resolution. However, the parties were not willing to engage in the process and the CAO had to close the case • In 2007, IFC drew upon the experience recorded in this case to clarify the implications of the ILO Convention on both governments and private companies • Although the CAO had to close the case, subsequent developments emerged in the practice of the ILO supervisory system, demonstrating a significant alignment with the CAO's findings. In 2009, the Committee of Experts on the Application of Conventions and Recommendations recommended the suspension of the mining activities, observing that the government was granting exploration licenses without properly consulting the indigenous people in violation of the ILO Convention No. 169. Furthermore, in 2011, in a report concerning the situation of the rights of indigenous peoples in Guatemala in relation to extractive projects, the UN Special Rapporteur James Anaya explicitly endorsed the CAO's assessment to conclude that the company had conducted the consultation process in violation of the UNDRIP. Despite further allegations brought by various NGOs before the Inter-American Commission on Human Rights, the mine only ceased its activities in May 2017

(continued)

Table 4.2 (continued)

3. Indonesia: Wilmar-01/West Kalimantan (2007), Wilmar-02/Sumatra (2008), Wilmar Group-03/Jambi (2011) (Closed) (Dispute Resolution and Compliance)	
Indigenous peoples	Indigenous communities living in West Kalimantan and Sumatra; *Suku Anak Dalam*
Business Enterprise	Wilmar Group
Sector	Palm oil
Financial exposure	IFC's loan (approx. \$17.5 million); IFC's guarantee (approx. \$33.3 million)
Main allegations	Devastation of forests; communities' displacement
Relevant project outcomes	• In *Wilmar-01/West Kalimantan*, in its dispute resolution function, the CAO facilitated an agreement providing the return of 1699 hectares of forest lands to *Senujuh* and *Sajingan Kecil* communities, in addition to compensation. The company also committed to providing investment funds for collective benefits, and to adopting improved operational standards for future investments in the sector (Conclusion Report, 1 October 2009) • The case was transferred to the compliance function in response to allegations concerning IFC's lack of due diligence in deciding whether to finance the project, later resulting in an investigation. In response to the CAO's investigation report, the World Bank Group committed to developing a comprehensive strategy for oil palm investments, which was launched in 2011. The document highlights that IFC must review how clients manage key sensitive matters in projects involving indigenous peoples. It also remarks that each Performance Standard incorporates international human rights legal elements that are phrased in operational language
Further developments	• The operations supported by IFC gave rise to a second complaint (*Wilmar-02/Sumatra*), lodged in December 2008, which resulted in partly satisfactory agreements. In November 2011, the *Suku Anak Dalam* indigenous people filed a third complaint (*Wilmar Group-03/Jambi*), which led to a further investigation, released by the CAO in May 2016. Although the IFC's response did not propose any project-specific actions, the CAO acknowledged that no new palm oil investment had been processed during the monitoring period before closing the case

(continued)

Table 4.2 (continued)

4. The Philippines: Ambuklao-Binga Hydroelectric Power-01/Binga (2008) (Closed) (Dispute Resolution)	
Indigenous peoples	*Iowak* and *Ibaloi*
Business Enterprise	SN Aboitiz Power-Benguet, Inc.
Sector	Renewable energy generation
Financial exposure	IFC's loan ($100 million)
Main allegations	Unresolved ownership land claims
Relevant project outcomes	• The CAO facilitated a dialogue process that culminated in a formal historical agreement between the company, the indigenous communities, and the local government, regulating land-use rights. One of the most significant achievements was the creation of a Cultural Heritage site, which granted indigenous communities the right to manage the areas not included in the privatization of the power plants (Conclusion Report, 1 August 2009)
Further developments	• As reported by the CAO, the national Ministry of Energy of the Philippines regarded the creation of the site as a new model for resolving complex land issues in project development
5. The Philippines: Mindoro Resources-01/Jabonga (2011) (Closed) (Appraisal)	
Indigenous peoples	*Mamanwa*
Business Enterprise	Mindoro Resources Ltd.
Sector	Mining
Financial exposure	IFC's equity investment ($9.5 million)
Main allegations	Failure to identify the presence of indigenous peoples; lack of consultations
Relevant project outcomes	• In its compliance appraisal, the CAO determined that IFC had not properly reviewed the consultation strategy engaging the *Mamanwa* indigenous community, which had been developed by the mining company and included as a covenant in the subscription agreement formalizing IFC's purchase of shares (Appraisal Report, 2 October 2012). Since the company decided to suspend the mining activities in the affected project area as a result of the CAO's compliance investigation, with a substantial reduction of the adverse impact on complainants, the CAO closed the case
Further developments	• The CAO concluded that the case had raised serious concerns about the effectiveness of IFC's policies in managing the risks associated with early-stage investments in mining, recommending a comprehensive policy review to provide clearer guidance for staff

(continued)

Table 4.2 (continued)

6. Mongolia: Oyu Tolgoi-01 (2012), Oyu Tolgoi-02/Khanbogd (2013) (Closed) (Dispute Resolution)	
Indigenous peoples	Nomadic pastoralists living in Khanbogd Soum
Business Enterprise	Oyu Tolgoi
Sector	Mining
Financial exposure	IFC's loan ($4.4 billion); MIGA's guarantee ($1 billion)
Main allegations	Disruption of nomadic lifestyle and indigenous culture through the inappropriate use of land and water; lack of adequate resettlement plan and compensation
Relevant project outcomes	• In its role as a mediator in dispute resolution, the CAO facilitated the parties' efforts leading to the establishment of an operational-level grievance mechanism, the Tripartite Council. This Council, composed of representatives from the involved company, affected nomadic herders, and the Mongolian government (Conclusion Report, May 2020), was tasked with addressing the resettlement issues arising from the project. Notably, it provided access to remedy for those impacted by the project, in accordance with the meaning and objectives of Article 29 of the UN Guiding Principles, which mandates that business enterprises establish or participate in non-judicial operational mechanisms to address grievances promptly and provide direct remediation. The mediation phase concluded when the parties reached an agreement on the herders' compensation claims. The CAO remained engaged in the subsequent monitoring phase
Further developments	• The CAO explicitly referenced the case in its advisory note concerning the role of dispute resolution in access to remedy, a significant contribution aimed at elucidating its role in advancing one of the core tenets of the UN Guiding Principles
7. Cambodia: Veil II-01/Ratanakiri Province (2014), TPBank and VPBank-01/Ratanakiri (2019) (Open) (Dispute Resolution)	
Indigenous peoples	Inhabitants of 17 villages in Ratanakiri Province belonging to the *Khmer* ethnic group
Business Enterprise	Hoang Anh Gia Lai through the private equity fund Vietnam Enterprise Investments Ltd. (equity financing)
Sector	Financial intermediation
Financial exposure	IFC's equity investment ($16.4 million)
Main allegations	Impact on water and fish resources; loss of ancestral lands; illegal deforestation; lack of information disclosure and consultations; lack of compensation; threats to spiritual, cultural, and indigenous practices

(continued)

Table 4.2 (continued)

Relevant project outcomes	• As a result of the CAO-facilitated dispute resolution process, the Vietnamese company Hoang Anh Gia Lai, which managed rubber plantations on the ancestral lands of an ethnic group in Ratanakiri Province, whose members self-identified as indigenous, agreed to return specific areas to them, including 20 spirit mountains and two burial grounds (Conclusion Report, 1 January 2020). However, at a later stage, the company withdrew from the process, due to the existence of other intractable disputes. Following a further complaint lodged by the same people, the company re-engaged in the process facilitated by the CAO by signing a Memorandum of Understanding that provided the return of several hectares of ancestral lands to the ethnic group
Further developments	• The case is ongoing, with the CAO consistently remaining engaged to monitor the implementation of all agreements already reached with the involved complainants
8. Guatemala: Real LRIF-01/Coban (2014) (Open) (Compliance)	
Indigenous peoples	*Q'eqchi'*
Business Enterprise	Hidroeléctrica Santa Rita, S.A. through the private equity fund Latin Renewable Infrastructure Fund LP (equity financing)
Sector	Financial intermediation
Financial exposure	IFC's equity investment ($15 million)
Main allegations	Impact on water and indigenous peoples' livelihood; communities' displacement; lack of FPIC
Relevant project outcomes	• In 2014, local communities mainly composed of *Q'eqchi'* indigenous people who strongly opposed the implementation of the Hidroeléctrica Santa Rita project in Guatemala, lodged a complaint with the CAO, expressing their concerns on a wide range of environmental and social issues, including the failure to comply with FPIC. In 2015, as a consequence of the complaint, LRIF, the financial intermediary involved in the implementation of the project, decided to cease the related activities, although it never divested the shares held in the company managing the project • IFC was found non-compliant for not having carried out a proper review and supervision of the project activities (Investigation Report, 30 October 2017). In response to the findings, IFC decided to strengthen its internal procedures for managing environmental and social risks in future appraisal and supervision of projects managed by private equity funds. However, it did not commit to any specific project-level actions
Further developments	• In 2024, with the release of its second monitoring report, the CAO decided to continue monitoring the case, in light of the repeated assertions made by the complainants regarding unresolved land tenure issues and their concerns about the potential resumption of the project with IFC's involvement. To date, the financial intermediary has not clarified its position regarding a possible future continuation of the project

(continued)

Table 4.2 (continued)

9. Guatemala: CIFI-01/Hidro Santa Cruz (2015) (Open) (Compliance)	
Indigenous peoples	*Q'anjob'al*
Business Enterprise	Hidro Santa Cruz, S.A. through the non-banking financial institution Corporación Interamericana para el Financiamiento de Infraestructura
Sector	Financial intermediation
Financial exposure	IFC's equity investment ($10 million); IFC's loan(s) ($68.5 million)
Main allegations	Lack of consultations; lack of transparency of the land acquisition process
Relevant project outcomes	• The case originated from a complaint lodged in July 2015 in the context of a project intended to build a hydropower plant that faced strong opposition from local residents, mainly *Q'anjob'al* indigenous people, from the outset. A few months later, in November 2015, the financial intermediary ended its financial relationship with the company implementing the project. In December 2018, the CAO found IFC out of compliance with its 2006 Sustainability Policy for not having properly reviewed and supervised the performance of the financial intermediary in managing the environmental and social aspects related to the sub-project implemented by Hidro Santa Cruz, S.A. (Investigation Report, 30 October 2017)
Further developments	• In 2019, IFC sold the equity owned in the financial intermediary. As IFC did not commit to any specific project-level action in response to the investigation findings, the CAO continues to monitor systemic-level actions only • In October 2024, IFC finally adopted its long-awaited Approach to Responsible Exit
10. Panama PL IV-01/Multi-Locations (2018) (Open) (Compliance)	
Indigenous peoples	Indigenous communities living in the *Ngöbe-Buglé* comarca and in the Norte de Santa Fé region
Business Enterprise	Empresa de Transmisión Eléctrica
Sector	Advisory
Financial exposure	Not available
Main allegations	Shortcomings affecting the FPIC process
Relevant project outcomes	• The CAO Director General stressed the critical role of FPIC in ensuring the legitimacy of projects with an impact on indigenous peoples' rights. In its investigation report, the CAO found that the lack of IFC's proper advice had contributed to the shortcomings affecting the consultation process carried out by the state-owned enterprise ETESA (Investigation Report, 10 June 2022)
Further developments	• The IFC's Board of Executive Directors approved the MAP on condition that specific commitments were met, such as regularly updating the CAO on actions to address the systemic recommendations included in the investigation report. To date, significant progress has been achieved on these actions

Methodology: Projects selected by first (i) identifying those raising issues concerning indigenous peoples in the request for inspection; and then (ii) isolating those that led to the analysis of issues relevant to international human rights law

Source: Author's own elaboration based on the Compliance Advisor Ombudsman's database, available at: https://www.cao-ombudsman.org/cases—Cases as of July 2025

References

Altholz R, Sullivan C (2017) Accountability & international financial institutions: community perspectives on the World Bank's office of the Compliance Advisor Ombudsman. International Human Rights Law Clinic, Berkeley. https://www.law.berkeley.edu/. Accessed 18 June 2025

Arp B (2018) Integrating human rights into the work of the World Bank Group: the International Finance Corporation's Compliance Advisor/Ombudsman. In: Piernas CJ (ed) New trends in international economic law, from relativism to cooperation. Institut Suisse de Droit Comparé, Genève-Zurich-Bâle, pp 175–202

Compliance Advisor Ombudsman (2003a) A review of IFC's safeguard policies. Core business: achieving consistent and excellent environmental and social outcomes. https://www.cao-ombudsman.org/. Accessed 3 June 2025

Compliance Advisor Ombudsman (2003b) Extracting sustainable advantage? A review of how sustainability issues have been dealt with in recent IFC & MIGA extractive industries projects. https://www.cao-ombudsman.org/. Accessed 3 June 2025

Compliance Advisor Ombudsman (2003c) Assessment by the office of the Compliance Advisor/Ombudsman in relation to a complaint filed against IFC's investment in ENDESA Pangue S.A. Assessment report. https://www.cao-ombudsman.org/. Accessed 6 June 2025

Compliance Advisor Ombudsman (2005) Assessment of a complaint submitted to CAO in relation to the Marlin mining project in Guatemala. Assessment report. https://www.cao-ombudsman.org/. Accessed 9 June 2025

Compliance Advisor Ombudsman (2006) Follow-up assessment, Guatemala, complaint regarding the Marlin mining project. Follow-up assessment. https://www.cao-ombudsman.org/. Accessed 9 June 2025

Compliance Advisor Ombudsman (2008) Stakeholder assessment and framework, regarding the SN Aboitiz Power Ambuklao-Binga project. Assessment report. https://www.cao-ombudsman.org/. Accessed 11 June 2025

Compliance Advisor Ombudsman (2009a) Resolving land dispute in the palm oil sector through collaborative mediation, CAO Ombudsman intervention in Sambas, Indonesia - Wilmar Group. Conclusion report. https://www.cao-ombudsman.org/. Accessed 10 June 2025

Compliance Advisor Ombudsman (2009b) CAO Audit of IFC's investments in: Wilmar Trading (IFC no. 20348), Delta-Wilmar CIS (IFC no. 24644), Wilmar WCap (IFC no. 25532), Delta-Wilmar CIS Expansion (IFC no. 26271). Audit report. https://www.cao-ombudsman.org/. Accessed 10 June 2025

Compliance Advisor Ombudsman (2009c) Ambuklao-Binga hydroelectric power project, Philippines. Conclusion report. https://www.cao-ombudsman.org/. Accessed 11 June 2025

Compliance Advisor Ombudsman (2010a) Review of IFC's Policy and Performance Standards on social and environmental sustainability and Policy on disclosure of information. https://www.cao-ombudsman.org/. Accessed 6 June 2025

Compliance Advisor Ombudsman (2010b) The CAO's first case: Pangue hydroelectric project, Chile. Conclusion report. https://www.cao-ombudsman.org/. Accessed 9 June 2025

Compliance Advisor Ombudsman (2010c) CAO at 10, annual report FY2010 and review FY2000-10. https://www.cao-ombudsman.org/. Accessed 11 June 2025

Compliance Advisor Ombudsman (2012) IFC investments in Mindoro Resources Limited, Philippines, complaint from members of indigenous communities of Barangay San Pablo and Barangay Bunga, Agusan del Norte. Appraisal report. https://www.cao-ombudsman.org/. Accessed 11 June 2025

Compliance Advisor Ombudsman (2013) Annual report. https://documents1.worldbank.org/. Accessed 10 June 2025

Compliance Advisor Ombudsman (2015a) Advisory series lessons from CAO cases: land. https://documents.worldbank.org/. Accessed 10 June 2025

Compliance Advisor Ombudsman (2015b) Dispute resolution process between HAGL company and its subsidiaries and 17 affected villages. Joint statement. https://www.cao-ombudsman.org/. Accessed 13 June 2025

Compliance Advisor Ombudsman (2015c) Dispute resolution process between HAGL company and its subsidiaries and affected indigenous villages. Joint statement. https://www.cao-ombudsman.org/. Accessed 13 June 2025

Compliance Advisor Ombudsman (2015d) CAO assessment report, complaint regarding IFC investment in Real LRIF (Project 31458), Cobán, Guatemala. Assessment report. https://www.cao-ombudsman.org/. Accessed 16 June 2025

Compliance Advisor Ombudsman (2016) Summary of results, IFC investment in CIFI - Hidro Santa Cruz (IFC Project 26031) Guatemala. Compliance appraisal report. https://www.cao-ombudsman.org/. Accessed 17 June 2025

Compliance Advisor Ombudsman (2017) CAO investigation of IFC environmental and social performance in relation to: Latin Renewables Infrastructure Fund, Latin America region, as related to Hidroeléctrica Santa Rita complaint. Investigation report. https://www.cao-ombudsman.org/. Accessed 16 June 2025

Compliance Advisor Ombudsman (2018a) Monitoring of IFC's response to: CAO investigation of IFC investment in Delta-Wilmar (no. 25532 and 26271), complaint 03. Compliance monitoring report. https://www.cao-ombudsman.org/. Accessed 10 June 2025

Compliance Advisor Ombudsman (2018b) IFC investment in Corporación Interamericana para el Financiamiento de Infraestructura, S.A. (Project 26031). Compliance investigation report. https://www.cao-ombudsman.org/. Accessed 16 June 2025

Compliance Advisor Ombudsman (2019) IFC investment in Latin Renewables Infrastructure Fund (LRIF), Latin America region, as related to the Hidroeléctrica Santa Rita complaint project no. 31458. First monitoring report. https://www.cao-ombudsman.org/. Accessed 13 June 2025

Compliance Advisor Ombudsman (2020a) CAO dispute resolution conclusion report - Oyu Tolgoi 01 & 02/Southern Gobi. Conclusion report. https://www.cao-ombudsman.org/. Accessed 12 June 2025

Compliance Advisor Ombudsman (2020b) CAO progress report, Cambodia Veil II-01/Ratanakiri Province. Progress report. https://www.cao-ombudsman.org/. Accessed 13 June 2025

Compliance Advisor Ombudsman (2020c) CAO assessment report regarding concerns in relation to IFC's investment in TPBank and VPBank (37920, 41043, 38038, 39020) in Cambodia. Assessment report. https://www.cao-ombudsman.org/. Accessed 13 June 2025

Compliance Advisor Ombudsman (2022) Compliance investigation of IFC's environmental and social performance in relation to its advisory services to Empresa de Transmisión Eléctrica, S.A. in Panama. Compliance investigation report. https://www.cao-ombudsman.org/. Accessed 18 June 2025

Compliance Advisor Ombudsman (2023a) Insights on remedy: the role of dispute resolution in remedy. Advisory note. https://www.cao-ombudsman.org/. Accessed 12 June 2025

Compliance Advisor Ombudsman (2023b) Insights on remedy, the remedy gap: lessons from CAO compliance and beyond. Advisory note. https://www.cao-ombudsman.org/. Accessed 17 June 2025

Compliance Advisor Ombudsman (2023c) Responsible exit, insights from CAO cases. Advisory note. https://www.cao-ombudsman.org/. Accessed 18 June 2025

Compliance Advisor Ombudsman (2023d) Omnibus case report: Q4, 2023. Compliance monitoring report. https://www.cao-ombudsman.org/. Accessed 18 June 2025

Compliance Advisor Ombudsman (2024a) Compliance monitoring, omnibus case report: Q4, FY2024. Second monitoring report. https://www.cao-ombudsman.org/. Accessed 16 June 2025

Compliance Advisor Ombudsman (2024b) Compliance monitoring, omnibus case report: Q4, FY2024. First monitoring report. https://www.cao-ombudsman.org/. Accessed 17 June 2024

Compliance Advisor Ombudsman (2024c) Omnibus case report: Q4, FY2024. Compliance monitoring report. https://www.cao-ombudsman.org/. Accessed 18 June 2025

Downing TE (1996) A participatory interim evaluation of the Pehuen Foundation (IFC 20671). https://teddowning.com/wp-content/uploads/2019/04/Downing-Peheun-report-English.pdf. Accessed 9 June 2025

Herbertson K, Thompson K, Goodland R (2010) A roadmap for integrating human rights into the World Bank Group. World Resources Institute, Washington, DC

ILO Committee of Experts on the Application of Conventions and Recommendations (2005) Observation, Indigenous and Tribal Peoples Convention, 1989 (No. 169), Bolivia, 2004, 93rd ILC session. https://normlex.ilo.org/dyn/nrmlx_en/f?p=NORMLEXPUB:13100:0::NO::P13100_COMMENT_ID%2CP13100_COUNTRY_ID:2243444%2C102567. Accessed 9 June 2025

ILO Committee of Experts on the Application of Conventions and Recommendations (2009) Report III (Part 1A), general report and observations concerning particular countries, 6 March 2009, 98th session. https://www.ilo.org/resource/report-iiia-report-committee-experts-application-conventions-and. Accessed 6 June 2025

Inspection Panel (1995) Chile: financing of hydroelectric dams in the Bío Bío River. Summary of decision not to register. https://www.inspectionpanel.org/. Accessed 6 June 2025

Inter-American Commission on Human Rights (2015) Situation of human rights in Guatemala: diversity, inequality and exclusion. 31 December 2015. OEA/Ser.L/V/II, Doc. 43715

International Finance Corporation (2004) Lessons learned: Pangue hydroelectric. https://www.ifc.org/. Accessed 6 June 2025

International Finance Corporation (2005) CAO assessment report: complaint regarding Marlin mining project in Guatemala. Assessment report. https://www.ifc.org/. Accessed 9 June 2025

International Finance Corporation (2007) ILO Convention 169 and the private sector, questions and answers for IFC clients. https://documents.worldbank.org/. Accessed 10 June 2025

International Finance Corporation (2009) IFC's Policy and Performance Standards on social and environmental sustainability and Policy on disclosure of information: report on the first three years of application. https://documents1.worldbank.org/. Accessed 6 June 2025

International Finance Corporation (2011a) UN Guiding Principles on business and human rights and IFC Sustainability Framework. https://www.ifc.org/. Accessed 9 June 2025

International Finance Corporation (2011b) The International Bill of Human Rights and IFC Sustainability Framework. https://www.ifc.org/. Accessed 9 June 2025

International Finance Corporation (2012) IFC's Sustainability Framework: from policy update to implementation. https://www.ifc.org/. Accessed 6 June 2025

International Finance Corporation (2017) IFC Management's response to the CAO investigation report on Latin Renewables Infrastructure Fund, as related to the Hidroeléctrica Santa Rita complaint (Project 31458). Management response and action plan. https://www.cao-ombudsman.org/. Accessed 16 June 2025

International Finance Corporation (2020) CAO compliance investigation report, Latin America and Caribbean, Corporación Interamericana para el Financiamiento de Infraestructura, S.A. (Project 26031). Management response. 23 April 2020. https://www.cao-ombudsman.org/. Accessed 17 June 2025

International Finance Corporation (2022a) IFC Board approves action plan in response to CAO investigation of IFC's advisory services to Panama's state electricity transmission company, ETESA. Press release. https://www.ifc.org/. Accessed 18 June 2025

International Finance Corporation (2022b) Implementation of the management action plan in response to the CAO investigation report for the Panama electricity transmission line IV project no. 602084. First management progress report. https://www.cao-ombudsman.org/. Accessed 18 June 2025

International Finance Corporation (2023) Implementation of the management action plan for Panama electricity transmission line IV, Panama, Latin American and the Caribbean, Project no. 602084. Second management progress report. https://www.cao-ombudsman.org/. Accessed 18 June 2025

International Finance Corporation (2024) IFC's approach to responsible exit. https://www.ifc.org/. Accessed 17 June 2025

Knuckey S, Jenkin E (2015) Company-created remedy mechanisms for serious human rights abuses: a promising new frontier for the right to remedy? Int J Hum Rights 19(6):801–827

MacKay F (2004) Indigenous people's right to free, prior and informed consent and the World Bank's extractive industries review. Sustain Dev Law Policy 4(2):43–65
MacKay F (2010) Indigenous peoples and international financial institutions. In: Bradlow D, Hunter D (eds) International financial institutions and international law. Wolters Kluwer, Alphen aan den Rijn, pp 287–320
Marrella F, Vettorel A (2017) Banca Mondiale e diritti umani: il ruolo dell'Inspection Panel. In: Manderieux L, Vellano M (eds) Éthique globale, bonne gouvernance et droit international économique. Giappichelli, Torino, pp 39–55
McBeth A (2009) Transnational corporate responsibility for the 21st century. A right by any other name: the evasive engagement of international financial institutions with human rights. Geo Wash Int Law Rev 40(4):1101–1156
Morgera E (2020) Corporate environmental accountability in international law. OUP, Oxford
Morrow KE (2020) Development disasters: accountability and remedy in international development projects. Am Univ Law Rev 70(2):725–772
Nesti L (2002) The Mapuche-Pehuenche and the Ralco dam on the Biobío River: the challenge of protecting indigenous land rights. IJGR 9(1):1–40
Orellana MA (2005) Indigenous peoples, energy and environmental justice, the Pangue/Ralco hydroelectric project in Chile's Alto BíoBío. JERL 23(4):511–528. https://doi.org/10.1080/02646811.2005.11433418
Reif LC (2020) Ombuds institutions, good governance and the international human rights system, 2nd edn. Brill, Leiden-Boston
Roundtable on Sustainable Palm Oil (2022) RSPO free, prior and informed consent (FPIC) guide. https://rspo.org/wp-content/uploads/RSPO-Free-Prior-and-Informed-Consent-FPIC-Guide-2022_RSPO-GUI-T08-002-V2-ENG.pdf. Accessed 10 June 2025
Ruggie JG (2007) Business and human rights: the evolving international agenda. AJIL 101(4):819–840
Salim E (2003) Striking a better balance, the World Bank Group and extractive industries, the final report of the extractive industries review, vol I. World Bank, Washington, DC
Saper BM (2012) The International Finance Corporation's Compliance Advisor/Ombudsman (CAO): an examination of accountability and effectiveness from a global administrative perspective. NYU JILP 4:1279–1329
Scheltema M (2023) Guiding Principle 29: non-state-based grievance mechanisms; role of business. In: Choudhury B (ed) The UN Guiding Principles on business and human rights: a commentary. Edward Elgar, Cheltenham-Northampton, pp 224–231
Seatzu F (2008) Il Panel di ispezione della banca mondiale. Contributo allo studio della funzione di controllo nelle banche internazionali di sviluppo. Giappichelli, Torino
Seck SL (2016) Indigenous rights, environmental rights, or stakeholder engagement? Comparing IFC and OECD approaches to implementation of the business responsibility to respect human rights. MJSDL 12(1):57–97
Shihata IFI (2000) The World Bank Inspection Panel: in practice, 2nd edn. OUP, Oxford-New York
Spalding RJ (2023) Breaking ground: from extraction booms to mining bans in Latin America. OUP, Oxford
Ta LMG, Graham BAT (2019) Can quasi-judicial bodies at the World Bank provide justice in human rights cases? Geo J Int Law 50:113–142
The World Bank Group (2004) Striking a better balance, the World Bank Group and extractive industries: the final report of the extractive industries review, World Bank Group Management response. https://documents1.worldbank.org/. Accessed 3 June 2025
The World Bank Group (2011) The World Bank Group framework and IFC strategy for engagement in the palm oil sector. https://www.ifc.org/. Accessed 10 June 20245
UN Commission on Human Rights (2005) Human rights and transnational corporations and other business enterprises. Resolution 2005/69 of 20 April 2005. UN Doc. E/CN.4/RES/2005/69. https://docs.un.org/. Accessed 4 June 2025

UN Human Rights Council (2007) Report of the Special Representative of the Secretary-General (SRSG) on the issue of human rights and transnational corporations and other business enterprises. UN Doc. A/HRC/4/035. https://documents.un.org/. Accessed 6 June 2025

UN Human Rights Council (2011) Report of the Special Rapporteur on the Situation of Human Rights and Fundamental Freedoms of Indigenous People, James Anaya. Addendum. Observations on the situation of the rights of the indigenous people of Guatemala with relation to the extraction projects, and other types of projects, in their traditional territories. UN Doc. A/HRC/18/35/Add.3. https://docs.un.org/. Accessed 9 June 2025

UN Human Rights Council (2013) Annual report of the United Nations High Commissioner for Human Rights. Addendum. Report of the United Nations High Commissioner for Human Rights on the activities of her office in Guatemala. UN Doc. A/HRC/22/17/Add.1. https://docs.un.org/. Accessed 12 June 2025

UN Office of the High Commissioner for Human Rights (2023) Business and human rights in challenging contexts. Considerations for remaining and exiting. https://www.ohchr.org/. Accessed 17 June 2025

UN Office of the High Commissioner for Human Rights (2024) Access to remedy in cases of business-related human rights abuse: an interpretive guide. UN, New York-Geneva. https://www.un-ilibrary.org/. Accessed 12 June 2025

Chapter 5
The World Bank Group's International Legal Obligations Regarding Indigenous Peoples' Rights

The analysis conducted in the previous chapters certainly points to the conclusion that the World Bank and IFC (hereinafter 'the World Bank Group') have developed a relevant body of consistent practice in the field of indigenous peoples' human rights. This conclusion is drawn from the examination of two key elements: (i) the way the organization shapes the design of its investments and monitors the progress of funding recipients in achieving the primary project objectives in both the public and private sectors; and (ii) the comprehensive review of the findings of its Independent Accountability Mechanisms that are tasked with assessing the organization's compliance with its own policies.

To date, the significance of this approach within the context of international human rights law has been explored to a very limited extent only, with or without reference to indigenous peoples' rights. The limited body of existing international legal literature posits that the World Bank Group is bound by human rights obligations, yet it has done so only based on approaches that are not tenable for various reasons. Specifically, the arguments that are commonly put forward are twofold: they infer its subjection to either the obligations stemming from the treaties ratified by its member countries or from the UN Charter. Since each of these arguments warrants separate examination, an in-depth analysis of both will be provided. Against this backdrop, a third, more theoretically robust thesis will be explored in order to evaluate the extent to which the World Bank Group may be considered bound by international law. Based on an inductive rationale that emphasizes the significance of the role it plays as an autonomous actor in the international order capable of developing relevant practice, the final part of the analysis will offer a new perspective through which the debate on the interpretation of its mandate may continue to evolve.

S. Solidoro, *Indigenous Peoples in the World Bank Group's Practice*, European Yearbook of International Economic Law,
https://doi.org/10.1007/978-3-032-05147-9_5

5.1 Attribution of Member States' Treaty Human Rights Obligations: Criticism

Based on the general theory of functional substitution, some scholars argue that international organizations, in their capacity as agents of their member states, would bear the human rights obligations that are relevant for the exercise of their powers,[1] obligations derived from the treaties ratified by those member states.[2] In other words, since international organizations are created by states for the purpose of carrying out specific functions on their behalf, they would take on the obligations directly linked to their mandate, including those related to human rights. In the case of the World Bank Group, this would support the argument that, for projects involving indigenous peoples, the organization must adhere to binding instruments such as the ILO Convention No. 169 of 1989, the two UN Covenants, and the UN Convention on the Elimination of All Forms of Racial Discrimination ('ICERD') of 1965, among others. Nevertheless, although this approach may be desirable, it is not tenable for two main reasons.

First, since human rights treaty obligations vary widely across states, it would be extremely difficult to determine the obligations an international organization should adopt in performing its functions. In fact, it would need to continuously assess and adapt to each member state's commitments under international human rights law, which would create significant complexity in its operations.[3]

Second, if such a rule existed, it might even deter states from joining international organizations as their act of accession would entail the indirect acceptance of the consequences stemming from treaties concluded by other members.[4] In this regard, Article 11 of the Vienna Convention of 1969 ('Means of expressing consent to be bound by a treaty') clearly provides, on a general basis, that treaties can bind only states that have given their consent, as expressed in various means, including through «signature, exchange of instruments constituting a treaty, ratification, acceptance, approval or accession».[5] The consent requirement originates in states' sovereign equality, a corollary of which is the *pacta tertiis nec nocent nec prosunt* rule, whereby treaties do not create rights or obligations for third states without their consent in writing, as outlined in Articles 34 ('General rule regarding third States') and 35 ('Treaties providing for obligations for third States').[6]

Notably, these arguments, which carry considerable weight on a practical level, are overlooked by that strand of the doctrine that argues that international organizations should be bound by the human rights treaty obligations of their member states,

---

[1] Schreuer (1995, p. 237).

[2] Cogen (1992, pp. 387–388).

[3] Neuman (2019, p. 4).

[4] Zagel (2018, p. 80).

[5] UN Conference on the Law of Treaties, *Vienna Convention on the Law of Treaties*, Vienna, 23 May 1969, in *UNTS*, Volume 1155, p. 331 f.

[6] Fitzmaurice (2002), Singer (1995, p. 58).

asserting that their abstention from becoming parties to such treaties cannot necessarily be interpreted as the desire not to be bound:

> International organizations cannot participate in the creation of new rules of international law in the same way as states. Hitherto they have been accepted as parties to multilateral law-making treaties only exceptionally. Their general abstention from becoming such parties cannot therefore be interpreted as a desire not to be bound. In considering the question of whether an international organization is subject to the rules of treaty law, one cannot start from the hypothesis that this is not the case unless the organization has expressly bound itself. It will often be necessary to search for the rules of international law that bind an international organization, irrespective of its will.[7]

This would suggest that the consent requirement does not apply to international organizations, based on the primary argument that they cannot participate in the creation of new rules in the same way as states, because they derive their powers from them.

In this regard, it is worth noting that the text of the so-called Vienna II Convention of 1986 concerning the law of treaties concluded between states and international organizations or between international organizations,[8] although not yet in force, provides a negative answer to the question of whether organizations can incur obligations from treaties to which they are not parties (so-called 'third-party' issue), unless they have explicitly accepted these obligations in writing (Articles 34 and 35).

More generally, international organizations have a direct role in treaty-making, as they possess the capacity to, and frequently do, become parties to treaties in their own right, within the limits of their competences. In the very well-known advisory opinion on *Reparation for Injuries Suffered in the Service of the United Nations* of 1949, the International Court of Justice determined that the UN carried out functions and held rights that could only be understood by acknowledging its international legal personality. One of the considerations on which the Court based this conclusion was that, according to the UN's practice, in particular the conclusion of conventions to which it was a party, the organization occupied a «position in certain aspects in detachment from its Members».[9] As a consequence, affirming that the human rights obligations of an international organization are automatically the same as those of its member states, insofar as they pertain to the exercise of the organization's powers, does not appear to be theoretically tenable. Overall, the theories mentioned above overlook the fact that, as autonomous subjects with distinct international legal personality, international organizations possess the capacity to

---

[7] Schermers and Blokker (2011, pp. 996–997).

[8] UN Conference on the Law of Treaties between States and International Organizations or between International Organizations, *Vienna Convention on the Law of Treaties between States and International Organizations or between International Organizations*, Vienna, 21 March 1986 (not yet entered into force), UN Doc. A/CONF.129/15. For a comparison of the 1986 Convention with its 1969 counterpart, to which it bears a strong resemblance, see Elias (2020).

[9] International Court of Justice, *Reparation for Injuries Suffered in the Service of the United Nations*, Advisory Opinion of 11 April 1949, in *ICJ Reports 1949*, p. 174 f., p. 179. According to Crawford, since the issuance of the Advisory Opinion, «international organizations have joined states as a recognized category of legal persons»: Crawford (2019, p. 106).

independently decide whether to enter into agreements.[10] In the case of IBRD, IDA, and IFC,[11] evidence of the capacity to act independently in this regard is reflected in their core activities, including the agreements they enter into with Member States when providing loans or advisory services. This capacity is also demonstrated by the agreements they have concluded with the UN to formalize their status as specialized agencies.

A more appropriate view is the one that recognizes the direct consequences of the general obligations undertaken by states through the treaties they have ratified within the context of the mission pursued by international organizations. Without a doubt, international organizations cannot create obstacles to their member states' compliance with the international obligations to which they are bound. This is also confirmed by the World Bank Group's practice regarding how projects need to be designed and implemented. The modern version of the policy framework applicable to public sector projects provides that the assessment prepared by the borrower to evaluate the risks and adverse impacts of the project proposed for financing takes into account the «obligations of the country, pertaining to project activities, under relevant international environmental treaties and agreements»,[12] an approach reiterated in the 2016 version of the Environmental and Sustainability Framework.[13] The

[10] Notably, an alternative approach has simply doubted that the consent requirement would apply to international organizations, based on the argument that their legal personality would not necessarily be identical with that of states. See Klein (1998, p. 331).

[11] Although the discussion regarding the requirements to establish the existence of international legal personality for international organizations falls outside the scope of this discussion, it is worth noting that many scholars agree that, based on the elements outlined in the 1949 Reparation Advisory Opinion, the key elements for recognizing it in an objective way should be as follows: (i) to be an entity with organs and assigned special tasks; (ii) to possess legal capacity, privileges, and immunity within the territory of its members; (iii) to be able to conclude agreements with members; (iv) to be able to conclude conventions to which the organization itself is a party; (v) to be able to remind members of certain obligations; and (vi) to occupy a position 'in certain respects in detachment from its Members'. Finally, (vii) the intention of the founders to give the organization the capacity to perform activities on its own in the international legal sphere may also be relevant. With regard to the World Bank Group, in relation to the first and the second requirements, the Articles of Agreement of the various entities forming part of the World Bank Group define their structure and contain several different provisions regarding their privileges and immunities (IBRD: Article VII, sections 4-9; IDA: Article VIII, sections 4-9; IFC: Article VI, sections 4-9). In addition, these entities can clearly conclude international agreements with Member States when providing loans (in the case of IBRD and IDA) or advisory services (in the case of IFC), as well as with the UN, which are all governed by international law (third and fourth requirements). Furthermore, they can intervene to remind members of their obligations, when necessary (fifth requirement) and they operate distinctly from them (sixth requirement). Finally, regarding the notion of the founders' intention, although the Articles of Agreement did not grant these entities international legal personality in an explicit way, the history of their creation and subsequent evolution strongly supports this interpretation. As a result, it seems reasonable to assert that IBRD, IDA, and IFC all have international legal personality. In this regard, see Skogly (2001, pp. 64–68), Gazi (2005, pp. 102–106), Bradlow (2023, pp. 72–80).

[12] The World Bank, *Operations Manual, Policy & Procedure Framework, Operational Policy 4.01, Environmental Assessment*, 1999 (revised in 2013 and 2024), para. 3.

[13] The World Bank, *Environmental and Social Framework*, 2017, p. 19, para. 26.

2012 version of the IFC's Sustainability Framework contains an analogous provision in the Standard concerning indigenous peoples explicitly stating that «[i]n addition to meeting the requirements under this Performance Standard, clients must comply with applicable national law, including those laws implementing host country obligations under international law».[14]

Nevertheless, while this may be the only collateral effect reasonably linked to the obligations of Member States in relation to the World Bank Group, it remains to be determined what obligations are directly incumbent upon the organization itself.

5.2 Obligations Arising from the Relationship Agreement with the UN: Criticism

Another widely cited theory asserting that the World Bank Group bears human rights obligations under international law relies on the status of its entities as UN specialized agencies, as outlined in Chapter IX of the UN Charter ('International Economic and Social Cooperation'). Some scholars argue that, based on Article 59, which specifies that the purpose of specialized agencies is the implementation of the UN goals enshrined in Article 55, their activities should be consistent with the mission of promoting «universal respect for, and observance of, human rights and fundamental freedoms for all without distinction as to race, sex, language, or religion».[15] In particular, this argument has been advanced with reference to the IMF:

> A reasonable inference would be that the purposes set forth in article 55 are the raison d'être of any specialized agency created under article 57 or article 59. Interpreted in this manner, the IMF is under an obligation to fulfill the human rights purposes set forth in article 55 of the U.N. Charter.[16]

If accepted, this reasoning should apply to the different entities constituting the World Bank Group as well. Nevertheless, this theory appears overly optimistic in its attempt to deduce the existence of a World Bank Group's duty to uphold human rights from the principles of cooperation animating Chapter IX of the Charter. Furthermore, it raises the challenge of determining the precise scope of the human rights enshrined in the UN Charter, from which the corresponding obligations of the World Bank Group are supposed to derive. While there are some broad references that pervade the Charter like a common thread that can be found in its preamble, as well as in the provisions concerning the organization's purposes and principles (Article 1.3) and the powers of its main organs (Articles 13.1, 62.2, 68), their exact interpretative scope is not totally clear. In this respect, an authoritative strand of the debate, looking at the 1948 Universal Declaration of Human Rights as the most

---

[14] International Finance Corporation, *IFC Sustainability Framework, Policy and Performance Standards on Environmental and Social Sustainability*, 2012, p. 2, para. 5.

[15] De Feyter (2004, p. 65).

[16] Rajagopal (1993, pp. 93–94).

authoritative source of interpretation of the Charter,[17] argues that the World Bank Group would be bound to uphold the human rights enshrined in all the subsequent body of international human rights law building on it.[18] In addition to the Covenants,[19] this may include the ILO Convention No. 169, which explicitly draws on the contents of the UDHR, as well as the United Nations Declaration on the Rights of Indigenous Peoples, which is also firmly anchored in the purposes and principles of the UN Charter.

Nevertheless, although the reasoning behind this thesis is noteworthy, it ultimately lacks persuasiveness, as it fails to consider the crucial factor of the independence of the various entities constituting the World Bank Group from the UN, as explicitly codified in the Relationship Agreements separately stipulated with IBRD, IFC, and IDA.[20] In essence, there exist different levels of ties with the UN, with the World Bank Group standing out among those international organizations that exhibit a certain degree of independence in the UN family.[21]

Against this backdrop, the manner in which various UN specialized agencies are required to act in relation to the Security Council's decisions under Articles 41 and 42 of the UN Charter is in fact very different. The existence of a much closer connection with the UN is very evident in the case of the Relationship Agreement stipulated with the ILO,[22] whose mandate explicitly addresses human rights concerns in the context of labor matters. The agreement plainly states that the organization will provide assistance «in carrying out decisions of the Security Council for the maintenance or restoration of international peace and security» (Article VI). By contrast, the corresponding provision in the IBRD's Relationship Agreement, on which those stipulated by IDA and IFC are also based, draws a subtle distinction between the obligations assumed by its Member States, as also UN members, to carry out the Security Council's decisions «through their action in the appropriate specialized agencies», of which it takes note, and the conduct of its own activities, specifying that it will have 'due regard' to such decisions (Article VI.1).[23]

[17] In international legal literature, it is commonly held that the drafting history of the UN Charter indicates an intention to adopt a comprehensive human rights instrument separately, under the auspices of the new organization. See Sohn (1977, p. 132), Jhabvala (2009).

[18] Darrow (2003, p. 128).

[19] Coomans (2007, p. 369).

[20] Dann (2013, pp. 270–272).

[21] The Commentary to Article 57 of the UN Charter emphasizes that, in terms of their relationship with the UN, the entities constituting the World Bank Group «differ institutionally from other specialized agencies (weighted voting and the resulting dominance of developed states). Their relationship agreements with the UN limit UN competences to a minimum». See Waibel (2024, p. 2117).

[22] UN and International Labour Organization, *Protocol concerning the entry into force of the Agreement between the United Nations and the International Labour Organization*, New York, 19 December 1946, in *UNTS*, Volume 1, p. 183 f.

[23] UN and International Bank for Reconstruction and Development, *Protocol concerning the entry into force of the Agreement between the United Nations and the International Bank for*

In this respect, former World Bank's General Counsel Ibrahim F. Shihata emphasized that this state of affairs is perfectly consistent with Article 103 of the UN Charter, according to which members' obligations under the Charter prevail over any other international treaty, including the IBRD's Articles of Agreement. However, the fact remains that IBRD, rather than fully committing to a regime of cooperation with the United Nations, limits itself to giving due regard to the decisions of the Security Council:

> If the Bank were to ignore such decisions, it would in fact be asking its members to act within the Bank inconsistently with their obligations under the UN Charter. This would not be correct, from a legal viewpoint. Members' obligations under the UN Charter prevail over their obligations under any other treaty to which they are parties, including the Bank's Articles. What is required of the Bank in this respect is to pay due regard to the Security Council decisions, without substituting itself for such a political body.[24]

This argument gains further strength when examining the approach to recommendations. According to Article IV of the ILO Relationship Agreement, the organization agreed to «enter into consultation with the United Nations upon request» and to report in due course to the UN on «the action taken, by the Organization or by its members» to give effect to recommendations issued by the General Assembly or the ECOSOC (Article IV.2).

In the case of the different entities constituting the World Bank Group, the Relationship Agreements provide instead for their full independence from the UN in financing decisions. In essence, such provisions recognize that the World Bank Group's entities hold a specialized mandate and expertise and that, while they should consult with and be respectful of the United Nations, they are not bound to comply with any instructions from it. As the two unsettled disputes in South Africa and Portugal have shown, when the UN General Assembly requested IBRD to refrain from assistance of any kind to countries with a poor human rights record, the General Counsel invoked these provisions of the Relationship Agreement, maintaining that neither organization is entitled to «present any formal recommendation to the other without reasonable prior consultation» (Article IV.2), also arguing that «the action to be taken by the Bank on any loan is a matter to be determined by the independent exercise of the Bank's own judgment in accordance with the Bank's Articles of Agreement», as recognized by the United Nations (Article IV.3).

Overall, in light of the considerations discussed above, while it is certainly true that the World Bank Group must respect its members' Charter-based human rights obligations, it seems untenable to assert that it bears obligations on its own in the field of human rights solely due to its relationship with the UN. For this reason, the subsequent analysis will focus on the viability of alternative approaches.

Reconstruction and Development, New York, 15 April 1948, in *UNTS*, Volume 16, p. 341 f. See also De Sena (2011, p. 831).

[24] Shihata (2000, p. 169). See also McInerney-Lankford (2010, pp. 281–282).

5.3 The Way Forward

Another intriguing thesis posits that international organizations, as autonomous subjects of international law, are generally bound by customary rules.[25] At this stage, one may contend that, given that customs arise from the practice of states, international organizations should not be subject to the application of rules in the creation of which they did not participate. Christian Tomuschat argued against this view, holding that:

> [I]nternational organizations may be characterized as common agencies operated by States for the fulfilment of certain common tasks. Now, if States acting individually have been subjected to certain rules thought to be indispensable for maintaining orderly relations within the international community, there is no justification for exempting international organizations from the scope *ratione personae* of such rules. International organizations cannot have more or more extended rights than States.[26]

The Committee on Economic, Social and Cultural Rights ('CESCR') has also supported this argument in 2016, citing an advisory opinion of the International Court of Justice (1980) regarding the interpretation of an agreement between the WHO and Egypt,[27] according to which international organizations are «bound by any obligations incumbent upon them under general rules of international law, under their constitutions or under international agreements to which they are parties».[28]

From a theoretical perspective, this is certainly the most defensible thesis among those that attempt to attribute direct obligations to the World Bank Group.[29] However, the problem with this argument is that, since in the field of human rights it is widely accepted that only core standards form part of customary law, particularly those qualifying as *jus cogens*,[30] such obligations would only pertain to the most heinous forms of violation. Accordingly, the organization would not be allowed to finance projects that contribute to genocide, an argument which is totally agreeable, although hardly likely to occur in reality.[31] Yet it is increasingly claimed that other instruments have come to be regarded as part of customary international law, such as the UDHR, or at least significant portions of it.[32] In this regard, it is noteworthy to observe that the same claim has been advanced in relation to another declaration with a more explicit focus on the protection of indigenous peoples. This line of reasoning will be discussed in the course of the analysis thereof.

---

[25] Daniel Bradlow (1996, p. 63).

[26] Tomuschat (2001, pp. 134–135).

[27] International Court of Justice, *Interpretation of the Agreement of 25 March 1951 between the WHO and Egypt*, Advisory Opinion of 20 December 1980, in *ICJ Reports 1980*, p. 73 f., pp. 89–90.

[28] UN Committee on Economic, Social and Cultural Rights (2016, para. 7).

[29] Reinisch (2001, p. 136); Daugirdas and Schuricht (2020, pp. 58–59).

[30] Brownlie (2008, pp. 562–564).

[31] In the same vein, De Sena (2011, p. 830).

[32] Buergenthal (1999, p. 96).

5.3.1 Obligations Arising from Customary International Law

Clearly, the UN Declaration on the Rights of Indigenous Peoples, adopted as a General Assembly resolution in 2007, stands as a highly influential document in the international arena. Despite its tumultuous drafting history, which also saw the direct involvement of indigenous peoples as early as 1982,[33] it ultimately gained widespread consensus among attending states, receiving significant support with 143 votes in favor and 11 abstentions. Broadly, it is acknowledged that, although not possessing binding legal authority, such resolutions of the UN General Assembly would enjoy at least persuasive weight and that, as an expression of the views of a large number of states, in some cases they may represent significant evidence of *opinio juris*, with all due caution,[34] as so recognized by the International Court of Justice in 1986.[35]

Nevertheless, since its adoption, the UNDRIP has sparked intense debate regarding the international legal status of its provisions. To contribute to this discussion, the International Law Association ('ILA') decided to involve its newly established Committee on the Rights of Indigenous Peoples[36] in analyzing such matters through the delivery of an expert commentary. The aim of this effort was to provide authoritative clarification, elucidation, and guidance concerning the provisions of the UNDRIP, including their development, context, and standing in international law, particularly given the uncertainty surrounding whether certain provisions had evolved into customary law.[37] In the course of its work, the Committee was initially chaired by James Anaya (2006–2008), and subsequently, following his appointment as UN Special Rapporteur on the Situation of Human Rights and Fundamental Freedoms of Indigenous People, by Siegfried Wiessner (2008–2012). Through a Resolution adopted in 2012, the Committee affirmed that certain provisions of the Declaration could be regarded as reflecting existing customary international law:

---

[33] The original version of the Declaration was promulgated by the UN Working Group on Indigenous Populations in 1993 for the first time, after more than a decade of discussions between states and indigenous groups from all over the world.

[34] Lepard (2010, pp. 209–210). Nevertheless, in this context, it is crucial to consider the doctrinal perspective that rejects the idea that General Assembly resolutions such as the UNDRIP may have any direct impact on customary international law. According to Voyiakis, «the adoption of Resolutions such as the Declaration on the Rights of Indigenous Peoples should not be taken to have an intrinsic impact on customary international law, but rather to function as an inspiration for future practice and as an occasion for individual States to make collateral statements that clarify their attitude with regard to the customary law of indigenous rights». See Voyiakis (2011, p. 222).

[35] International Court of Justice, *Military and Paramilitary Activities in and against Nicaragua (Nicaragua v United States of America)*, Judgment of 27 June 1986, in *ICJ Reports 1986*, p. 14 f., pp. 99–100.

[36] Established just a year before the adoption of the UNDRIP, the Committee's mandate was to clarify existing «international norms of indigenous rights by conducting a study of relevant treaties, other instruments, and international practice». See International Law Association (2008, p. 2).

[37] ibid., p. 3.

> The 2007 United Nations Declaration on the Rights of Indigenous Peoples (UNDRIP) as a whole cannot yet be considered as a statement of existing customary international law. However it includes several key provisions which correspond to existing State obligations under customary international law.[38]

The Resolution was grounded in an extensive survey that demonstrates the existence of international and domestic practice, in addition to the element of *opinio juris*. This survey, included in the 2010 ILA's Interim Report, clarified that a specific set of indigenous peoples' rights, derived from the foundational collective right to self-determination and corresponding to specific states' obligations to respect, protect, and fulfill, had crystallized within the realm of customary international law.[39] These include:

(i) The right to autonomy or self-government (Article 3 of the UNDRIP), in matters relating to indigenous peoples' internal and local affairs within their lands (Article 4 of the UNDRIP). This encompasses the right to organize their social, economic, and political life according to their customary laws (Article 34 of the UNDRIP), and also to establish, maintain, and develop their own legal and political institutions. At the same time, indigenous peoples retain their right to fully participate, should they so choose, in the political, economic, social, and cultural life of the State (Article 5 of the UNDRIP), which is consistent with the international human rights law principle that all citizens are entitled to political participation rights on the basis of equality;

(ii) The right to be consulted in relation to states' rule-making processes that may affect them (Article 18 of the UNDRIP), as also reflected in Article 6 of the ILO Convention No. 169. This right is closely related to the right that legislative or administrative measures with a significant impact on indigenous peoples cannot be carried out without their free, prior, and informed consent (Article 19 of the UNDRIP). However, this should not be interpreted as establishing a general right of *veto* for the indigenous communities concerned;

(iii) The right to cultural identity, in all its elements, including the right not to be subjected to genocide (which amounts to a rule of *jus cogens*) and all the prerogatives necessary to secure the preservation and transmission of cultural heritage to future generations (Articles 11–13, 31, and 34 of the UNDRIP), as also reflected in Article 27 of the ICCPR, Article 15 of the ICESCR, and Article 5(e)(vi) of the ICERD. Against this backdrop, indigenous languages would represent an exception, as the legal evolution «occurred in this respect has probably not yet reached the point of leading to the existence of a rule of customary international law dictating a *positive* State obligation», merely meaning that «States are bound not to create any obstacles to the efforts and activities carried out by indigenous peoples in order to preserve their own languages»,[40]

[38] International Law Association (2012a). For an overview of the path leading to the Committee's resolution, see Koivurova et al. (2022, pp. 96–101).

[39] International Law Association (2010, p. 43).

[40] International Law Association (2012b, p. 15). See also Wiessner (1999).

which remains a vital and increasingly endangered element of their culture. Consistently, indigenous peoples should not be denied the right to speak and teach their own language (Article 16 of the UNDRIP);

(iv) The right to traditional lands, territories, and resources, also in recognition of the spiritual value attached to them, including demarcation, titling, and equivalent forms of legal recognition of such resources (Article 36 of the UNDRIP), as reflected in a very similar way in various treaties, such as the ILO Convention. This also includes the indigenous peoples' right to be allowed to manage their lands autonomously and according to their customary rules;

(v) As a corollary of all the previous rights, the right to reparations and redress for wrongs resulting from a breach of a right that is itself part of customary international law, in particular in relation to lands confiscated, taken, occupied, used or damaged without their free, prior, and informed consent (Article 28 of the UNDRIP), as also reflected in Article 16 of the ILO Convention.

First and foremost, the ILA emphasized the possibility of observing a form of 'universalization' of these rights, drawing from relevant international practice developed by UN human rights institutions and specialized agencies. In particular, the Interim Report examined the interpretation provided in relation to various treaty provisions, ranging from those included in instruments that broadly address human rights or cultural heritage to those specifically devoted to indigenous peoples, such as the ILO Convention No. 169.

In several instances, indeed, UN human rights treaty bodies have implicitly or explicitly used the UNDRIP as a benchmark to characterize certain general rights in relation to indigenous peoples. In 2009, the CESCR affirmed that the right of everyone to take part in cultural life as enshrined in Article 15 of the Covenant on Economic, Social and Cultural Rights must be realized «in a way that is pertinent and suitable to a given cultural modality or context, that is, respectful of the culture and cultural rights of individuals and communities, including minorities and indigenous peoples».[41] It also held that indigenous peoples have the right «to maintain and strengthen their spiritual relationship with their ancestral lands and other natural resources traditionally owned, occupied or used by them, and indispensable to their cultural life»,[42] and to participate «in the design and implementation of laws and policies that affect them. In particular, States parties should obtain their free and informed prior consent when the preservation of their cultural resources, especially those associated with their way of life and cultural expression, are at risk».[43]

Notably, in relation to ILO Convention No. 169, the ILO Committee of Experts on the Application of Conventions and Recommendations frequently expressed concerns about actions taken by States parties that could jeopardize indigenous land rights. Specifically, it called on them to adopt measures addressing the displacement

[41] UN Committee on Economic, Social and Cultural Rights (2009, para. 16.e).

[42] ibid., para. 49.d.

[43] ibid., para. 55.e.

of indigenous peoples caused by dam development projects[44] and to ensure fair compensation for the harm caused to indigenous communities by the exploitation of natural resources in their traditional territories.[45]

Against this backdrop, the ILA's Interim Report also highlighted the significance of the initiatives undertaken by the World Bank Group through the adoption of its operational policies, serving as evidence of the «special concern of the international community for the rights of indigenous peoples».[46]

At the regional level, the ILA's Interim Report gave utmost consideration to the practice of the bodies of the Inter-American System of Human Rights of the OAS, reporting that, in a lawsuit against Nicaragua, the Inter-American Commission had explicitly asserted that «there is an international customary international law norm which affirms the rights of indigenous peoples to their traditional lands».[47] In that instance, although Nicaragua produced a large body of defense arguments to deny having violated the rights of the *Awas Tingni* community, it did not counter this argument.

Furthermore, the Interim Report clarified that the number of countries where a corresponding practice had developed in affirming the recognition and protection of such rights was remarkably large at the policy, legislative (including constitutional) and jurisdictional levels.[48] This consolidated body of state behavior, read alongside the judicial and para-judicial international practice that was never disputed by concerned States on the merits, constituted a direct manifestation of the «belief that this practice is rendered obligatory by the existence of a rule of law requiring it»,[49] thus amounting to indisputable evidence of both the elements required to establish that indigenous peoples' rights fall within the scope of customary international law. Finally, with regard to the exact contents of the rights, the Interim Report added that it was unnecessary to examine whether the relevant rules of customary international law precisely aligned with the provisions of the UNDRIP in their exact formulation. In the view of the ILA Committee, UNDRIP represents a declaration of principles and thus, even though its content partially reflects general international law, it

---

[44] ILO Committee of Experts on the Application of Conventions and Recommendations (1997, para. 11).

[45] ILO Committee of Experts on the Application of Conventions and Recommendations (2006, para. 9).

[46] International Law Association (2010, p. 49).

[47] Inter-American Court of Human Rights, *Case of the Mayagna (Sumo) Awas Tingni Community v Nicaragua*, Judgment of 31 August 2001 (Merits, Reparations and Costs), Series C, No. 79, para. 140(d).

[48] International Law Association (2010, pp. 49–50). These countries include Argentina, Australia, Bangladesh, Belize, Bolivia, Botswana, Brazil, Cambodia, Canada, Chile, Colombia, Costa Rica, Ecuador, India, Japan, Laos, Malaysia, Mexico, New Zealand, Nicaragua, Norway, Paraguay, Peru, the Philippines, South Africa, Taiwan, the United States of America, and Venezuela.

[49] International Court of Justice, *North Sea Continental Shelf Cases (Federal Republic of Germany v Denmark; Federal Republic of Germany v Netherlands)*, Judgment of 20 February 1969, in *ICJ Reports 1969*, p. 3 f., p. 44.

inherently carries a driving force that is intended to promote the development of its subject matter over time.[50]

As a comprehensive study based on the authoritative opinion of prominent legal scholars,[51] the ILA's commentary received positive recognition, as evidenced by the fact that an ICSID Arbitral Tribunal, constituted under Chapter 11 of the North American Free Trade Agreement ('NAFTA'), referred to it in the *Grand River Enterprises Six Nations, Ltd., et al v United States of America* award, in relation to the likely existence of a «principle of customary international law requiring governmental authorities to consult indigenous peoples on governmental policies or actions significantly affecting them».[52]

Nevertheless, the commentary also raised significant objections within the international legal academic community, especially at the outset, particularly due to the lack of endorsement of UNDRIP by the States that had voted against it, which also represented those with larger indigenous populations than most other States. In this regard, Stephen Allen in fact argued that «[t]he doctrine of customary international law attaches considerable weight to the views and practices of those States that would be 'specially affected' by the formation of new customary norms».[53] Given that the so-called CANZUS States—Canada, Australia, New Zealand and the United States—opposed the text of the Declaration from the earliest drafting stages, it is likely that they could be considered persistent objectors. At the same time, it must be argued that all four eventually changed their position over time,[54] albeit to varying degrees.

In this regard, Federico Lenzerini argued that the contentious debate denying the existence of indigenous peoples' rights under customary international law is mostly rooted in an epistemological misunderstanding. According to Lenzerini, recognizing a customary international legal status to these rights does not entail «an obligation for States to ensure the realisation of the rights in point *in all circumstances*—with no exception possible».[55] As a consequence, all other values, and especially those essential to the national society of the State in question, would not be unconditionally

[50] International Law Association (2010, p. 51).

[51] In 2016, following closely the language of paragraph 1(d) of Article 38 of the Statute of the International Court of Justice, the UN International Law Commission asserted that teachings of the most highly qualified publicists of the various nations «may serve as a subsidiary means for the determination of rules of customary international law», attributing such status to its own proceedings and those of the ILA. See UN General Assembly (2016, pp. 111–112).

[52] International Centre for Settlement of Investment Disputes, *Grand River Enterprises Six Nations, Ltd., et al v United States of America*, Award of 12 January 2011, Washington, DC, ICSID Case No. ARB/10/5, IIC 481 (2011), p. 53, footnote 55.

[53] Allen (2011, p. 228).

[54] See the information concerning the historical overview of the UN Declaration on the Rights of Indigenous Peoples available on the website of the UN Department of Economic and Social Affairs: https://social.desa.un.org/issues/indigenous-peoples/united-nations-declaration-on-the-rights-of-indigenous-peoples. Accessed 23 June 2025. See also International Law Association (2010, p. 5).

[55] Lenzerini (2019, p. 53).

and *a priori* sacrificed for the sake of indigenous peoples' rights. Such a strict approach would, in fact, only apply to the very narrow category of *jus cogens* rules. In contrast, obligations under 'ordinary' customary international law rules can be subject to exceptions and may be weighed against other norms that protect goods or values of equal or greater significance. In this context, determining which conflicting goods or values should take precedence in a specific situation must be assessed on a case-by-case basis. In other words, an undeviating practice is not required for a rule of customary international law to be established, as confirmed by the International Court of Justice in the case of *Military and Paramilitary Activities in and against Nicaragua*:

> The Court does not consider that, for a rule to be established as customary, the corresponding practice must be in absolutely rigorous conformity with the rule. In order to deduce the existence of customary rules, the Court deems it sufficient that the conduct of States should, in general, be consistent with such rules, and that instances of State conduct inconsistent with a given rule should generally have been treated as breaches of that rule, not as indications of the recognition of a new rule.[56]

Based on this premise, Lenzerini concluded that the ILA's work, supported by abundant evidence of *opinio juris* and state practice, reveals the existence of a specific set of rules of customary international law regarding indigenous peoples' rights. Furthermore, he noted that it remains difficult to determine whether any or all of these rules have reached the level of customary international law provisions before or after the UNDRIP.

Should the opposing argument be accepted, it would follow that indigenous peoples' rights are not yet part of customary international law. In this case, their protection would rely on treaty law, which applies only to certain states, with all the limitations this entails. Furthermore, such an argument would exclude the World Bank Group from the purview of international legal actors bound by the relevant obligations. However, in this case, as outlined in the ILA's commentary, the use of the UNDRIP by various UN human rights treaty bodies as a benchmark to interpret these obligations certainly keeps open the possibility for the legal status of its provisions to evolve over time.[57]

This approach is embraced by other prominent scholars who, by emphasizing the significance of the UNDRIP's impact over time, maintain that some of its provisions «can be looked to for evidence of the content of customary international law»,[58]

[56] International Court of Justice, *Case concerning Military and Paramilitary Activities in and against Nicaragua* (*Nicaragua v United States of America*), Judgment of 27 June 1986, in *ICJ Reports 1986*, p. 14 f., para. 186.

[57] In this regard, Barelli argued that «in the light of the context in which it has been established and its very normative content, the Declaration has important legal effects and generates reasonable expectations of complying behaviour». Barelli (2009, p. 960).

[58] See Mensi (2023, p. 149). Furthermore, at the time of the adoption of the Declaration, Wiessner had already supported this argument in a short note accompanying the text of the Declaration that appears on the UN's website, asserting that the «UNDRIP is a solemn, comprehensive and authoritative response of the international community of States to the claims of indigenous peoples, with which maximum compliance is expected. Some of the rights stated therein may already form part

without excluding the more cautious possibility that they are instead currently in the process of emerging as new customary rules.[59] In 2016, the Special Rapporteur on the Rights of Indigenous Peoples, Victoria Tauli-Corpuz, endorsed this view, advocating for «the emergence of customary international law in the area of indigenous peoples' rights». She reached this conclusion by noting that UN human rights bodies systematically use the Declaration as the most comprehensive interpretative guide to assist States in fulfilling their obligations under both the Covenants and in the ICERD. This suggests the near-universal applicability of the UNDRIP and helps explain how its provisions are contributing to the development of a customary legal regime regulating indigenous peoples' rights.[60]

This perspective, deemed preferable in the present analysis due to its more prudent nature, is particularly significant in relation to the World Bank Group for two main reasons. First and foremost, it supports the conclusion that there is an emerging customary international legal regime imposing human rights obligations on the organization concerning indigenous peoples, extending beyond mere non-interference or abstention, as previously reflected in the restrictive interpretation of its Articles of Agreement. Moreover, it aligns with the manner in which the World Bank Group currently operates when providing financing for projects in both the public and private sectors. Indeed, the analysis presented in the preceding chapters reveals the existence of a unified body of practice demonstrating that its core activities are conducted in accordance with international human rights law.

In particular, it is noteworthy that, in public sector projects, the World Bank, as early as 2005 with the adoption of the first version of its modern safeguard (OP 4.10), employed a number of identification criteria for the concept of 'indigeneity' that largely overlap with those listed in the ILA's reports. These criteria, which must be evaluated on a case-by-case basis due to the absence of a universal definition of 'indigenous peoples', align with the contemporary understanding of the term as advanced in various international *fora*. Notably, in project operations implemented in African countries, the Inspection Panel adopted the AfrCommHPR's approach,[61] focusing on aspects such as subordination, marginalization, and dispossession to adapt these criteria to the regional context.

Furthermore, the Inspection Panel emphasized multiple times that the World Bank's policies mirror the provisions of key international legal instruments, such as the ILO Convention No. 169,[62] and are consistent with the objectives related to the social and cultural rights enshrined in the ICESCR, insofar as these objectives pertain to indigenous peoples.[63] In some other instances, the Panel analyzed the negative

of customary international law, others may become the *fons et origo* of later-emerging customary international law». See Wiessner (2007).

[59] Lagoutte (2016, p. 210). See also Stavenhagen (2011, pp. 151–152).

[60] UN Human Rights Council (2016, p. 5).

[61] Inspection Panel (2007a, pp. 57–58, 151).

[62] Inspection Panel (2007b, p. 72), footnote no. 152.

[63] Inspection Panel (2011, p. 43).

impact produced by projects upon indigenous peoples, based on the failure to conduct proper consultations, and, in particular, to adequately account for indigenous local structures of representation,[64] consistent with the provisions of the UNDRIP.

In addition, the Panel interpreted indigenous peoples' rights by giving utmost consideration to the relevant international practice developed by UN human rights treaty bodies and regional human rights courts in this regard. For instance, in clarifying the contents of indigenous peoples' lands- and natural resources-based rights, it held that these rights are associated with a way of life that is part of their cultural identity, consistent with HRC's General Comment No. 23 of 1994 on Article 27 of the ICCPR regarding the treatment of minorities.[65] In another case dealing with the demarcation of the *Ngäbe* territories in Panama, the Inspection Panel explicitly referenced Article 26 of the UNDRIP to clarify that paragraph 15.a of OD 4.20 requires the borrower to prepare a specific project component that should include a national legal assessment of indigenous peoples' ability «to use and develop the lands that they occupy, to be protected against illegal intruders, and to have access to natural resources (such as forests, wildlife, and water) vital to their subsistence and reproduction».[66] In the same case, it also referenced the milestone decision of the Inter-American Court in *Mayagna (Sumo) Awas Tingni Community v Nicaragua* (2001), which acknowledges the significance of land rights far beyond the mere ownership relationship, in consideration of the spiritual value attached to the land. Finally, in a recent case involving resettlement, the Panel found that the Bank's failure to ensure compensation payments prior to the project acquisition of indigenous peoples' lands[67] violated its policies. These policies require, in fact, particular attention to the most vulnerable groups among those displaced, who may not be protected by national land compensation legislation.[68]

As for private sector projects, starting in 2006, IFC adopted the same approach as the World Bank regarding the flexible criteria to identify indigenous peoples. It is also significant that the 2012 Guidance Note, which clarifies the main contents of the latest version of the IFC's Performance Standard on indigenous peoples, recognizes the existence of an international legal framework protecting their rights. This framework includes the UNDRIP, the ILO Convention No. 169, and several UN Conventions that are acknowledged to be particularly relevant. Considering the direct incorporation of these instruments into IFC's policies, the CAO's practice is very assertive in relation to cases concerning projects implemented without obtaining indigenous peoples' FPIC.[69] It is also noteworthy that, in its dispute resolution role, the CAO has facilitated the conclusion of agreements providing for the

---

64 Among other cases, see Inspection Panel (2007a, pp. 63–64); Inspection Panel (2011, pp. 137–139).

65 Inspection Panel (2014, pp. 42–43).

66 Inspection Panel (2010, p. 74), footnote 172.

67 Inspection Panel (2024, p. 55).

68 The World Bank, *Operations Manual, Policy & Procedure Framework, Operational Policy and Bank Procedure 4.12, Involuntary Resettlement,* 2001 (revised in 2013 and 2024), para. 8.

69 Among other cases, see Compliance Advisor Ombudsman (2012, p. 12).

resolution of land issues in cases dealing with resettlement, ultimately aimed at ensuring collective compensation.[70]

All in all, by incorporating relevant international legal instruments into its policies and interpreting them in light of related international practice, the World Bank Group has voluntarily committed to shaping its activities in a way that upholds the specific indigenous peoples' rights that the ILA considers part of customary international law. This approach ultimately ensures that the World Bank Group's actions do not contribute to a causal chain that could potentially lead to violations of these rights, whether through a project implemented by a state or a private entity. The organization in fact refrains from financing projects that may violate such rights before the appraisal phase and can withhold funding at a later stage, while monitoring the project's progress, for the same reason. Against this backdrop, arguing that the World Bank Group is bound by an emerging customary international legal obligation to respect, protect, and fulfill indigenous peoples' rights on par with states[71] would be based not only on a deductive rationale but also on an inductive one. Overall, its practice provides empirical support for the thesis that extends the potential applicability of customary law (including *jus cogens*) to the organization in its capacity as an international legal actor, making this the most viable approach to be pursued in light of the preceding analysis.

5.3.2 *Obligations Arising from General Principles of International Law*

The main argument put forward by the ILA is that the existence of abundant international and state practice, accompanied by the necessary element of *opinio juris*, demonstrates that some of the UNDRIP's provisions have acquired the status of customary international law.

An alternative approach argues that the universal application of the UNDRIP serves as evidence that many of the rights it enshrines, and in particular those related to collective ownership, consultation, and redress, have now become established general principles of international law.[72]

In 2002, the Inter-American Commission on Human Rights articulated this view in relation to some provisions of the then-draft American Declaration on the Rights

---

[70] Compliance Advisor Ombudsman (2020, pp. 3–4).

[71] For an overview of the contents of these obligations, see Letnar Černič (2013, pp. 1148–1158).

[72] Mensi (2023, p. 2). This is also the position supported by James Anaya in 2008, who stated: «Albeit clearly not binding in the same way that a treaty is, the Declaration relates to already existing human rights obligations of States, as demonstrated by the work of United Nations treaty bodies and other human rights mechanisms, and hence can be seen as embodying to some extent general principles of international law. In addition, insofar as they connect with a pattern of consistent international and State practice, some aspects of the provisions of the Declaration can also be considered as a reflection of norms of customary international law». See UN Human Rights Council (2008, p. 13).

of Indigenous Peoples,[73] which, in its preamble, explicitly draws upon the progress achieved at the international level in recognizing indigenous peoples' rights, particularly through the ILO Convention No. 169 and the UNDRIP. Specifically, the Commission argued that Article XVIII of the American Declaration, which addresses the collective right of indigenous communities to land, territories, and resources, can be seen as a reflection of evolving general international legal principles that extend beyond the regional framework within which they were initially conceived:[74]

> Article XVIII of the Draft American Declaration on the Rights of Indigenous Peoples [...] provides for the protection of traditional forms of ownership and cultural survival and rights to land, territories and resources. While this provision [...] has not yet been approved by the OAS General Assembly and therefore does not in itself have the effect of a final Declaration, the Commission considers that the basic principles reflected in many of the provisions of the Declaration, including aspects of Article XVIII, reflect general international legal principles developing out of and applicable inside and outside of the inter-American system and to this extent are properly considered in interpreting and applying the provisions of the American Declaration in the context of indigenous peoples.[75]

According to the Commission, such principles would encompass not only «the right of indigenous peoples to legal recognition of their varied and specific forms and modalities of their control, ownership, use and enjoyment of territories and property» but also «the right to fair compensation in the event that such property and user rights are irrevocably lost».[76] Later on, in a report published in 2010, the Commission extended the same approach to the indigenous peoples' right to restitution of the lands taken without their consent:

> The IACHR considers the right to restitution of the lands and territories of which peoples have been deprived without their consent as one of the international principles appertaining to indigenous peoples' rights over their lands, territories and natural resources.[77]

In 2012, the Inter-American Court developed a similar reasoning in relation to the indigenous peoples' right to consultation in decisions concerning their communal property as enshrined in relevant provisions contained in international instruments, explicitly referencing the ILO Convention No. 169 and the UNDRIP. In *Kichwa Indigenous People of Sarayaku v Ecuador*, the IACtHR in fact noted that the judicial decisions and the domestic legislation of several OAS Member States, even including those that had not ratified the ILO Convention, recognize this right in relation to administrative or legislative measures that directly affect indigenous peoples, and with regard to the exploitation of natural resources on their territory.

---

[73] The Declaration was adopted by the OAS General Assembly only in 2016, following negotiations that had lasted for more than 25 years. Organization of American States, *American Declaration on the Rights of Indigenous Peoples*, 15 June 2016, AG/RES.2888 (XLVI-O/16).

[74] Schabas (2021, p. 189).

[75] Inter-American Commission on Human Rights, *Mary and Carrie Dann v United States*, Case 11.140, Report No. 75/02, Merits, 27 December 2002, para. 129.

[76] ibid., para. 130.

[77] Inter-American Commission on Human Rights (2010, p. 53).

Based on these arguments, it reached the conclusion that there exists 'a general principle of international law' prescribing a corresponding obligation of states to ensure indigenous peoples' consultation.[78]

Against this backdrop, the case of Belize is particularly interesting as, in 2007, when ruling on a case regarding the recognition of customary land rights of the *Maya* communities living in the southern part of the country, the Supreme Court explicitly cited Article 26 of the UNDRIP, affirming that this provision, together with Article 14 of the ILO Convention No. 169, embodies general principles of international law.[79]

The implications of this perspective are particularly noteworthy. Although distinguishing general international principles from customary international law is not always straightforward, a tentative approach regards such principles as an autonomous source of human rights law stemming directly from the international sphere, which would «percolate down into domestic fora, instead of being elevated from the domestic level to that of international law».[80] In this regard, renowned scholars further contend that these principles are not based on the traditional elements of state practice and *opinio juris*, but rather on the widespread recognition and general consensus within the international community, which considers them as a reflection of shared international legal values.[81] Recently, in 2018, the International Law Commission ('ILC') has embraced this approach and has commenced discussing the existence of a second category of general principles of law under Article 38, paragraph 1(c) of the Statute of the International Court of Justice, which may be formed within the international legal system.[82] As explained in the latest version of the draft conclusions provisionally adopted by the Commission on first reading in May 2023, determining their existence requires ascertaining that the community of nations has recognized them as intrinsic to the international legal system (Conclusion 7).[83] The commentary clarifies that the term 'intrinsic' should be understood as specific to the international legal system, reflecting and regulating its fundamental features. Regarding the methodology for identifying the principles, the commentary emphasizes the need to analyze the existing rules of the international legal system, as they may reflect or underlie the principles. It further notes that the analysis «must take into account all available evidence of the recognition of the principle[s] in

[78] Inter-American Court of Human Rights, *Case of the Kichwa Indigenous People of Sarayaku v Ecuador*, Judgment of 27 June 2012 (Merits and Reparations), Series C, No. 245, p. 45.

[79] Supreme Court of Belize, *Cal (on behalf of the Maya Village of Santa Cruz) and Others & Coy (on behalf of the Maya Village of Cenejo) and Others v Attorney General of Belize and Minister of Natural Resources and Environment*, 18 October 2007, Claims no. 171 and 172, para. 131.

[80] Simma and Alston (1992, p. 102).

[81] Pisillo Mazzeschi (2020, pp. 37–38).

[82] The International Law Commission decided to include the topic 'General Principles of Law' in its program of work at its 70th session in 2018 and appointed Mr. Marcelo Vázquez Bermúdez as Special Rapporteur. The General Assembly subsequently took note of the decision of the Commission in para. 7 of its resolution 73/265 of 22 December 2018.

[83] UN General Assembly (2023, pp. 13–35).

question by the community of nations», including through international instruments reflecting the principles, such as resolutions adopted by international organizations. The issue is currently the subject of considerable debate, which makes it difficult to reach definitive conclusions. However, if the argument for the existence of such principles is accepted, it would be hard to overlook the fact that their foundation rests on the recognition of their 'intrinsic' nature by the international community. In this regard, it is noteworthy that, according to some scholars, the term 'international community' should be understood at large, so as to include not only states, but also international organizations. According to this line of reasoning, the manner in which the World Bank Group operates when providing its core financing activities would gain direct significance, as contributing to the very emergence of these principles. Therefore, this argument suggests that the World Bank Group is not only obligated to uphold the principles enshrined in the UNDRIP in a passive capacity, but also plays an active role in fostering their advancement.

5.4 Interim Conclusions

All the considerations presented thus far indicate that the arguments put forth by the limited existing literature on the subject, which assign direct positive obligations to the World Bank Group in the realm of human rights based either on the obligations of its Member States or the status of its entities as UN specialized agencies, are untenable for various reasons. However, it can be argued that, as an autonomous international legal actor, the organization can be considered bound by an emerging body of rules and principles of general international law upholding indigenous peoples' rights. This argument is strongly supported by the World Bank Group's established track record in its financing operations, as outlined in the previous chapters. Its approach reflects a *de facto* commitment in this field by incorporating relevant international legal instruments into its policies and interpreting them in light of related international practice. Undoubtedly, this ensures that the World Bank Group's actions do not become part of a causal chain that could lead, through its financing activities, to violations of indigenous peoples' rights, whether in projects carried out by a state or a private entity. Furthermore, these considerations offer valuable insights into the ongoing debate concerning the World Bank Group's mandate, particularly as the strict interpretation of the formal prohibition on engaging in 'political affairs' of its member countries—an interpretation the organization has relied upon to distance itself from pressures by the UN, civil society, and academia to commit explicitly to human rights—can now be seen as outdated.

Overall, the World Bank Group's reliance on the international legal framework governing indigenous peoples underscores the necessity of reassessing its role in relation to human rights within this domain. Should this lead to the recognition of specific international legal obligations incumbent upon the organization, it would also require concurrent efforts to more precisely articulate its international responsibility.[84] In this regard, it is noteworthy that the role of the Independent Accountability Mechanisms in scrutinizing the World Bank Group's conduct and recommending corrective actions to restore compliance with its policies *vis-à-vis* project-affected indigenous peoples is becoming increasingly significant. In line with the Compliance Advisor Ombudsman's model, in fact, the Inspection Panel has progressively been granted greater independence from the Board of Executive Directors in determining whether a case warrants investigation. Similarly, the recent establishment of a monitoring function for the Panel, designed to ensure proper implementation of the Management's action plans in response to its recommendations, has enhanced its effectiveness, notwithstanding its quasi-judicial nature. Given the current conceptual and practical difficulties in establishing the organization's international responsibility, such mechanisms, if further strengthened in their functioning, may provide a viable alternative for ensuring compliance with human rights standards.[85]

Last but not least, the analysis of the World Bank Group's practice brings forth another crucial consideration. By shaping the way public funding recipients engage with indigenous peoples, its operational policies may have another relevant effect. The implementation of the World Bank Group's 'high' standards may, in fact, lead to substantial changes in member countries' domestic legislation, potentially resulting in the legal recognition of ownership, occupation, or usage rights in relation to land, or ensuring prompt and effective compensation in involuntary resettlement cases, to name just a few examples. This effect is further reinforced by the fact that, following the model of the World Bank Group, most Multilateral Development Banks have adopted similar operational policies and tend to interpret them in a consistent manner. By relying on such instruments, these international organizations not only align their own conduct with international law but also foster an increased awareness among states of the necessity to implement and adhere to it. As a result, over time, this dynamic may encourage the emergence of new patterns of state behavior that could eventually evolve into customary international law.

References

Allen S (2011) The UN Declaration on the Rights of Indigenous Peoples and the limits of the international legal project. In: Allen S, Xanthaki A (eds) Reflections on the UN Declaration on the Rights of Indigenous Peoples. Hart Publishing, Oxford-Portland, pp 225–256

Barelli M (2009) The role of soft law in the international legal system: the case of the United Nations Declaration on the Rights of Indigenous peoples. ICLQ 58:957–983

[84] Bradlow and Hunter (2010, p. 393). In this regard, the International Law Commission, which decided to include the topic concerning the responsibility of international organizations in its program of work in 2002, has adopted the latest version of a project of articles at its 63rd session, in 2011. See UN General Assembly (2011).

[85] Ong (2021, p. 122), Lorenzo (2024, p. 212).

Bradlow D (1996) The World Bank, the IMF, and human rights. J Transnatl Law Contemp Prob 6:47–90

Bradlow D (2023) The law of international financial institutions. OUP, Oxford

Bradlow D, Hunter D (2010) Conclusion: the future of internal law and international financial institutions. In: Bradlow D, Hunter D (eds) International financial institutions and international law. Wolters Kluwer, Alphen aan den Rijn, pp 387–397

Brownlie I (2008) Principles of public international law, 7th edn. OUP, Oxford

Buergenthal T (1999) The World Bank and human rights. In: Weiss EB et al (eds) The World Bank, international financial institutions, and the development of international law: a symposium held in honor of Dr. Ibrahim F.I. Shihata. American Society of International Law, Washington, DC, pp 95–101

Cogen M (1992) Human rights, prohibition of political activities and the lending policies of World Bank and International Monetary Fund. In: Chowdhury SR, Denters MG, de Waart PJIM (eds) The right to development in international law. Brill, Dordrecht, pp 379–396

Compliance Advisor Ombudsman (2012) IFC investments in Mindoro Resources Limited, Philippines, complaint from members of indigenous communities of Barangay San Pablo and Barangay Bunga, Agusan del Norte. Appraisal report. 2 October 2012. https://www.cao-ombudsman.org/. Accessed 11 June 2025

Compliance Advisor Ombudsman (2020) CAO dispute resolution conclusion report - Oyu Tolgoi 01 & 02/Southern Gobi. Conclusion report. May 2020. https://www.cao-ombudsman.org/. Accessed 12 June 2025

Coomans F (2007) Application of the International Covenant on Economic, Social and Cultural Rights in the framework of international organisations. Max Planck Ybk UN Law 11:359–390

Crawford JR (2019) Brownlie's principles of public international law, 9th edn. OUP, Oxford

Dann P (2013) The law of development cooperation. A comparative analysis of the World Bank, the EU and Germany. CUP, Cambridge

Darrow M (2003) Between light and shadow: the World Bank, the International Monetary Fund and international human rights law. Hart Publishing, Oxford

Daugirdas K, Sachi Schuricht S (2020) Breaking the silence: why international organizations should acknowledge customary international law obligations to provide effective remedies. In: Quayle P (ed) The role of international administrative law at international organizations, vol 3. Brill Nijhoff, Leiden-Boston, pp 54–87

De Feyter K (2004) The international financial institutions and human rights: law and practice. Hum Rights Rev 6:56–90

De Sena P (2011) Fondo monetario internazionale, Banca mondiale e rispetto dei diritti dell'uomo. In: Ligustro A, Sacerdoti G (eds) Problemi e tendenze del diritto internazionale dell'economia: Liber Amicorum in onore di Paolo Picone. Editoriale Scientifica, Napoli, pp 829–858

Elias O (2020) Who can make treaties? International organizations. In: Hollis DB (ed) The Oxford guide to treaties, 2nd edn. OUP, Oxford, pp 98–115

Fitzmaurice M (2002) Third parties and the law of treaties. Max Planck Ybk UN Law 6:37–137

Gazi B (2005) The IMF, the World Bank and the question of human rights. Transnational Publisher Inc., Ardsley, New York

ILO Committee of Experts on the Application of Conventions and Recommendations (1997) Direct request, Indigenous and Tribal Peoples Convention, 1989 (No. 169), Paraguay, 1996, 85th ILC session. https://normlex.ilo.org/dyn/nrmlx_en/f?p=1000:13100:0::NO:13100:P13100_COMMENT_ID,P13100_COUNTRY_ID:2156362,102796. Accessed 3 July 2025

ILO Committee of Experts on the Application of Conventions and Recommendations (2006) Observation, Indigenous and Tribal Peoples Convention, 1989 (No. 169), Bolivia, 2005, 95th ILC session. https://normlex.ilo.org/dyn/nrmlx_en/f?p=1000:13100:0::NO:13100:P13100_COMMENT_ID,P13100_COUNTRY_ID:2260622,102567. Accessed 3 July 2025

Inspection Panel (2007a) Democratic Republic of Congo: transitional support for economic recovery grant (TSERO) (IDA Grant no. H 1920-DRC) and emergency economic and social reunification support project (EESRSP) (Credit no. 3824-DRC and Grant no. H 064-DRC). Investigation report. 31 August 2007. https://www.inspectionpanel.org/. Accessed 14 May 2025

Inspection Panel (2007b) Honduras: land administration project (IDA Credit 3858-HO). Investigation report. 12 June 2007. https://www.inspectionpanel.org/. Accessed 15 May 2025
Inspection Panel (2010) Panama: land administration project (Loan no. 7045-PAN). Investigation report. 16 September 2010. https://www.inspectionpanel.org/. Accessed 19 May 2025
Inspection Panel (2011) Independent State of Papua New Guinea: smallholder agriculture development project (IDA Credit no. 4374-PNG). Investigation report. 19 September 2011. https://www.inspectionpanel.org/. Accessed 16 May 2025
Inspection Panel (2014) Kenya: natural resources management project. Investigation report. 22 May 2014. https://www.inspectionpanel.org/. Accessed 16 May 2025
Inspection Panel (2024) Santa Cruz road corridor connector project (San Ignacio-San José) (P152281). Investigation report. 12 February 2024. https://www.inspectionpanel.org/. Accessed 23 May 2025
Inter-American Commission on Human Rights (2010) Indigenous and tribal peoples' rights over their ancestral lands and natural resources, norms and jurisprudence of the Inter-American Human Rights System. 30 December 2009. OEA/Ser.L/V/II, Doc. 56/09
International Law Association (2008) Rights of indigenous peoples. First report, Rio de Janeiro Conference. https://www.ila-hq.org/. Accessed 27 June 2025
International Law Association (2010) Rights of indigenous peoples. Interim report, Hague Conference. https://www.ila-hq.org/. Accessed 2 July 2025
International Law Association (2012a) Rights of indigenous peoples. Resolution no. 5/2012, Sofia Conference. https://www.ila-hq.org/. Accessed 27 June 2025
International Law Association (2012b) Rights of indigenous peoples. Final report, Sofia Conference. https://www.ila-hq.org/. Accessed 2 July 2025
Jhabvala F (2009) The drafting of the human rights provisions of the UN Charter. NIRL 44(1):1–31
Klein P (1998) La responsabilité des organisations internationales dans les ordres juridiques internes et en droit des gens. Bruylant, Brussels
Koivurova T, Lenzerini F, Wiessner S (2022) The role of the ILA in the restatement and evolution of international and national law relating to indigenous peoples. In: Karjalainen K, Tornberg I, Pursiainen A (eds) International actors and the formation of laws. Springer, Cham, pp 89–112
Lagoutte S (2016) The role of soft law in the progressive development of indigenous peoples' rights. In: Lagoutte S, Gammeltoft-Hansen T, Cerone J (eds) Tracing the roles of soft law in human rights. OUP, Oxford, pp 185–212
Lenzerini F (2019) Implementation of the UNDRIP around the world: achievements and future perspectives. The outcome of the work of the ILA Committee on the implementation of the rights of indigenous peoples. Int J Hum Rights 23:51–62
Lepard BD (2010) Customary international law. A new theory with practical applications. CUP, Cambridge
Letnar Černič J (2013) State obligations concerning indigenous peoples' rights to their ancestral lands: lex imperfecta? Am Univ Int Law Rev 28(4):1129–1171
Lorenzo JAP (2024) Accountability mechanisms of multilateral development banks and the law of international responsibility. ICLQ 73(1):209–245
McInerney-Lankford S (2010) International financial institutions and human rights: select perspectives on legal obligations. In: Bradlow D, Hunter D (eds) International financial institutions and international law. Wolters Kluwer, Alphen aan den Rijn, pp 239–285
Mensi A (2023) Indigenous peoples, natural resources and permanent sovereignty. Brill Nijhoff, Leiden-Boston
Neuman GL (2019) International organizations and human rights - the need for substance. In: Paper presented at YTL Law and Justice Centre Forum on Human Rights and Non-State Actors, King's College, London, 1 June 2018
Ong D (2021) Shared responsibility or institutional accountability? Continuing conceptual and enforcement issues for grievance mechanisms of public and private international finance institutions. In: Barnes R, Long R (eds) Frontiers in international environmental law: oceans and climate challenges. Essays in honour of David Freestone. Brill Nijhoff, Leiden-Boston, pp 106–138

Pisillo Mazzeschi R (2020) Diritto internazionale dei diritti umani. Teoria e prassi. Giappichelli, Torino

Rajagopal B (1993) Crossing the Rubicon: synthesizing the soft international law of the IMF and human rights. Boston Univ Int Law J 11(1):81–107

Reinisch A (2001) Securing the accountability of international organizations. Glob Gov 7(2):131–149

Schabas WA (2021) The customary international law of human rights. OUP, Oxford

Schermers HG, Blokker NM (2011) International institutional law: unity within diversity, 5th edn. Brill, Leiden-Boston

Schreuer C (1995) Die Bindung Internationaler Organisationen an völkerrechtliche Verträge ihrer Mitgliedstaaten. In: Ginther K et al (eds) Völkerrecht zwischen normativem Anspruch und politischer Realität: Festschrift für Karl Zemanek zum 65. Geburstag. Duncker & Humblot, Berlin, pp 223–250

Shihata IFI (2000) The World Bank in a changing world, vol III. Brill, The Hague-London-Boston

Simma B, Alston P (1992) The sources of human rights law: custom, jus cogens, and general principles. AYBIL 12(1):82–108

Singer M (1995) Jurisdictional immunity of international organizations: human rights and functional necessity concerns. Va J Int Law 36(1):53–166

Skogly S (2001) The human rights obligations of the World Bank and the International Monetary Fund. Cavendish Publishing Limited, London-Sydney

Sohn L (1977) The human rights law of the Charter. Tex Int Law J 12:129–140

Stavenhagen R (2011) Making the Declaration on the Rights of Indigenous Peoples work: the challenge ahead. In: Allen S, Xanthaki A (eds) Reflections on the UN Declaration on the Rights of Indigenous Peoples. Hart Publishing, Oxford, pp 147–170

Tomuschat C (2001) International law: ensuring the survival of mankind on the eve of a new century. General course on public international law. Martinus Nijhoff Publishers, The Hague-Boston-London

UN Committee on Economic, Social and Cultural Rights (2009) General Comment No. 21, right of everyone to take part in cultural life. 21 December 2009. UN Doc. E/C.12/GC/21. https://www.refworld.org/. Accessed 2 July 2025

UN Committee on Economic, Social and Cultural Rights (2016) Public debt, austerity measures and the International Covenant on Economic, Social and Cultural Rights. 22 July 2016. UN Doc. E/C.12/2016/1. https://digitallibrary.un.org/. Accessed 1 July 2025

UN General Assembly (2011) Report of the International Law Commission, 63rd session. 26 April-3 June and 4 July-12 August 2011. UN Doc. A/66/10. https://docs.un.org/. Accessed 4 July 2025

UN General Assembly (2016) Report of the International Law Commission, 68th session, 2 May-10 June and 4 July-12 August 2016. UN Doc. A/71/10. https://docs.un.org/. Accessed 3 July 2025

UN General Assembly (2023) Report of the International Law Commission, 74th session. 24 April-2 June and 3 July-4 August 2023. UN Doc. A/78/10. https://docs.un.org/. Accessed 4 July 2025

UN Human Rights Council (2008) Report of the Special Rapporteur on the Situation of Human Rights and Fundamental Freedoms of Indigenous People, S. James Anaya. 11 August 2008. UN Doc. A/HRC/9/9. https://docs.un.org/. Accessed 8 July 2025

UN Human Rights Council (2016) Report of the Special Rapporteur on the Rights of Indigenous Peoples, Note by the Secretariat. 11 August 2016. UN Doc. A/HRC/33/42. https://docs.un.org/. Accessed 7 July 2025

Voyiakis E (2011) Voting in the General Assembly as evidence of customary international law? In: Allen S, Xanthaki A (eds) Reflections on the UN Declaration on the Rights of Indigenous Peoples. Hart Publishing, Oxford, pp 209–224

Waibel M (2024) Article 57. In: Simma B et al (eds) The Charter of the United Nations: a commentary, 4th edn. OUP, Oxford, pp 2107–2120

Wiessner S (1999) Rights and status of indigenous peoples: a global comparative and international legal analysis. Harv Hum Rights J 12:57–128

Wiessner S (2007) United Nations Declaration on the Rights of Indigenous Peoples, introductory note. Available via Audiovisual Library of International Law of the UN. https://legal.un.org/avl/ha/ga_61-295/ga_61-295.html. Accessed 7 July 2025

Zagel GM (2018) International organisations and human rights: the role of the UN Covenants in overcoming the accountability gap. Nord J Hum Rights 36(1):74–90. https://doi.org/10.1080/18918131.2018.1453586

Chapter 6
Final Remarks

6.1 The Emergence of a Spontaneous Commitment to Uphold Indigenous Peoples' Rights

Surprisingly, the question of whether the World Bank Group is required to uphold indigenous peoples' rights has not gained significant traction in contemporary legal scholarship. Nevertheless, the issue remains highly relevant as the WBG, while formally operating outside the conventional framework of international human rights treaties, exerts a direct and often profound impact on indigenous communities. As this book argues, even in the absence of a clear-cut legal obligation, the World Bank Group has demonstrated a *de facto* commitment to indigenous peoples' rights through its operational policies and related interpretative practice. This evolution suggests that the WBG, as an autonomous actor within the international legal order, is progressively aligning its institutional conduct with an emerging *corpus* of rules and principles of general international law concerning the rights of indigenous peoples. In this regard, it has been observed that, while only core human rights norms, recognized as *jus cogens*, are traditionally seen as customary international law, there is growing recognition that a specific set of indigenous peoples' rights as articulated in the UN Declaration on the Rights of Indigenous Peoples has crystallized within this body of law.

In contrast, the limited legal scholarship on the topic tends to assume that the World Bank Group bears direct legal obligations based on two main theoretical approaches.

The first theory, building on the general concept of functional substitution, argues that international organizations, as agents of their member states, should bear the obligations arising from human rights treaties ratified by those states, particularly when executing functions associated with their competences. Notably, this would imply that the World Bank Group must adhere to the binding human rights

S. Solidoro, *Indigenous Peoples in the World Bank Group's Practice*, European Yearbook of International Economic Law,
https://doi.org/10.1007/978-3-032-05147-9_6

instruments ratified by the borrowing country, such as the UN Covenants, ILO Convention No. 169 as well as ICERD, when financing projects involving indigenous peoples. However, this approach faces two major challenges: the diversity of human rights obligations across states would create operational complexity for the organization. Furthermore, it could even deter states from joining international organizations due to the unintended legal consequences of their membership.

The second theory posits that the World Bank Group's obligations arise from its status as a UN specialized agency, as outlined in Chapter IX of the Charter. According to this perspective, the World Bank Group's activities should align with the UN's mission to promote «universal respect for, and observance of, human rights and fundamental freedoms» (Article 55 of the UN Charter). Therefore, by virtue of its affiliation with the UN, the World Bank would be implicitly bound by a broad array of legal instruments—both binding and non-binding—that derive their authority from the purposes and principles of the Charter. This would encompass not only core human rights treaties but also instruments such as the UNDRIP.

However, even this argument falls short, not only because it struggles with the complexity of defining the precise scope of the human rights obligations arising from the Charter in the context of the World Bank Group's activities, but also because it overlooks the distinct legal status of the latter and its relative independence from the UN, as explicitly outlined in the Relationship Agreements with its constituent entities—IBRD, IFC, and IDA.

Overall, rather than relying on formalistic assumptions tied to the obligations of Member States or the World Bank Group's status as a UN specialized agency, this analysis proposes a more autonomous line of reasoning. By attributing independent legal significance to the WBG's institutional practice, it identifies a more tangible basis on which to assess whether, and to what extent, the organization is bound by international legal standards concerning indigenous peoples' rights. This perspective allows for a shift from theoretical speculation to an evidence-based understanding rooted in the WBG's own policies and operational conduct.

6.2 The Normative Weight of the World Bank Group's Institutional Practice

The gradual, yet increasingly deliberate, emergence of the World Bank Group's spontaneous commitment to uphold indigenous peoples' rights was initially catalyzed by external pressure from CSOs, indigenous peoples' movements and the UN, which created a demand for greater transparency and human rights compliance in development financing.[1] As a result, the organization has been pushed towards a partial redefinition of its operations in connection with indigenous peoples' rights. This process has taken place due to three fundamental drivers. First and foremost,

[1] Clark (2002, p. 206).

its operational policies have gradually reflected and drawn upon global soft and hard legal instruments, such as the UNDRIP and the ILO Convention No. 169. Secondly, the WBG has subjected its operations to scrutiny regarding their consistency with such policies. In doing so, both the Inspection Panel and the Compliance Advisor Ombudsman have contributed to the internalization of indigenous peoples' rights considerations within the framework governing public and private sector operations. Specifically, they have explicitly referenced relevant international practice developed by UN human rights treaty bodies and regional human rights courts, using them to apply the operational framework and clarify the contents of the policies. Finally, this has also had substantial effects on how the World Bank Group measures the outcomes of its projects. Both the World Bank and IFC currently incorporate qualitative benchmarks against which project performance is assessed to compare results with original objectives. Crucially, such benchmarks consider not only projects' success in terms of financial outcomes but also in relation to their impact on indigenous peoples.

Overall, the World Bank Group's spontaneous adherence to international human rights law illustrates that the organization does not operate within a self-contained regime.[2] In this context, it is argued that its operational framework incorporates a normative dimension, positioning it as a functional subsystem of international law in the area of indigenous peoples' rights. This evolution also calls for a reassessment of the organization's mandate, which can no longer be seen as confined to traditional financial or economic objectives. Rather, the commitment to upholding indigenous peoples' rights must be recognized as essential to the attainment of sustainable development and poverty reduction.

Broadly, the evidence gathered throughout the analysis carried out in this book indicates that, over the years, the World Bank has significantly shifted its role from one of non-interference, in line with a restrictive interpretation of the political prohibition clauses included in the Articles of Agreement, to a more proactive and engaged stance in relation to indigenous peoples' rights. In both the World Bank and IFC policies, the borrower is in fact required to prepare a consultation strategy as well as to elaborate a dedicated plan that extends beyond the core objectives of the main project.[3] The plan involves various measures aimed at avoiding, minimizing or compensating for the adverse impacts generated by the project on indigenous peoples, while ensuring the equitable sharing of benefits from commercial development of lands and natural resources traditionally owned, used, or occupied by them. In this context, the WBG undertakes early-stage screening and categorization of projects based on the scale and nature of potential social and environmental impacts,

[2] Bonfanti (2012, pp. 270–271).

[3] In this regard, the operational policy governing the operations of IBRD and IDA specifies that when indigenous peoples are the sole or the overwhelming majority of direct project beneficiaries, the elements of the plan should be included in the overall project design. See The World Bank, *Operations Manual, Policy & Procedure Framework, Operational Policy 4.10, Indigenous Peoples*, 2005 (revised in 2013 and 2024), para. 12; The World Bank, *Environmental and Social Framework*, 2017, p. 78, para. 15.

ensuring that high-risk projects undergo more intensive scrutiny.[4] Moreover, ongoing monitoring and supervision mechanisms are crucial to ensure that commitments made in project plans are effectively implemented.

In this regard, it is worth noting that, following the adoption of the Environmental and Social Framework applicable to the operations financed by IBRD and IDA, the institutional practice related to the public sector has become even more aligned with that of IFC for two main reasons. First, the new Framework has harmonized the terminology used to define the Bank's role in reviewing the borrower's actions, consolidating it under the concept of 'due diligence' throughout the project cycle. Second, the Framework has introduced the requirement of Free, Prior, and Informed Consent in specific circumstances. Both of these developments mirror the IFC's Sustainability Framework, contributing to a more unified and coherent institutional practice across the World Bank Group as a whole.

Based on the analysis of such practice, it has been claimed that, although the World Bank Group is not, strictly speaking, a human rights enforcer, its operational framework is designed to ensure that its actions are not part of a causal chain that could lead to human rights violations—whether through a project implemented by a state or a private actor.

The WBG can in fact resort to various means in order to obtain such a result. Prior to the approval of a loan by the Board of Executive Directors, the Bank may decide to withhold financing if the borrower fails to meet the established requirements for the preliminary assessment of all relevant circumstances surrounding the project's implementation. In contrast, the language adopted by IFC is more nuanced in this regard. Nonetheless, it consistently emphasizes that clients must demonstrate their ability to meet the Performance Standards and other applicable requirements within a reasonable timeframe, as a condition for proceeding with the investment.

Furthermore, specific provisions exist regarding compliance with the FPIC requirement during the early stages of the project cycle. As previously noted, both the World Bank's Environmental and Social Framework and the IFC's Sustainability Framework currently identify three circumstances under which FPIC must be obtained: (i) when the project has adverse impacts on land and natural resources subject to traditional ownership or customary use (including occupation in the case of the Bank); (ii) when it causes the relocation of indigenous peoples; or (iii) when it has significant impacts on their cultural heritage. Both frameworks explicitly state that, in cases involving relocation from communally held lands or natural resources under traditional ownership or customary use, the funding recipient must not proceed with the project unless FPIC has been obtained.[5] This reflects the particularly serious nature of such impacts. In addition, the World Bank's ESF includes a broader safeguard: if the Bank cannot ascertain that FPIC has been obtained, the

[4] On this point, see McBeth (2006, pp. 396–397).

[5] The World Bank, *Environmental and Social Framework*, 2017, p. 82, para. 31; International Finance Corporation, *IFC Sustainability Framework, Policy and Performance Standards on Environmental and Social Sustainability*, 2012, p. 50, para. 15.

components of the project affecting indigenous peoples will not be processed further.[6] This general clause reinforces the binding nature of FPIC within the Bank's operational decision-making beyond the specific context of relocation.

Notably, once disbursement has occurred and the requirements set forth by the operational framework have become binding as part of the agreement concluded with the public or private entity, both the Bank and IFC have the authority to exercise their rights and remedies, including suspension, withdrawal, or cancellation of undisbursed funds. Even at this stage, the alignment between the operational frameworks of the Bank and IFC reflects a unified commitment. Specifically, it involves ensuring that projects move forward only when strong environmental and social safeguards are consistently upheld throughout the implementation phase.

6.3 The Impact on State Practice

Against this backdrop, it is important to recognize that the WBG's operational framework has not evolved in isolation. Indeed, a significant driver of normative convergence is the growing degree of harmonization of indigenous peoples' policies among Multilateral Development Banks. In particular, several of these institutions have adopted internal operational frameworks that are structurally and substantively aligned with the World Bank Group's safeguards. For instance, the Environmental and Social Standard 7 of the Asian Development Bank, issued in 2024, which applies to both public and private sector projects, recognizes the UNDRIP as the most comprehensive international instrument in this area and affirms that indigenous peoples «have the right to determine and develop priorities and strategies for exercising their right to development».[7] In the case of the Inter-American Development Bank, the most recent version of its Environmental and Social Policy Framework for public sector operations (2020) states that the requirements set out in the Standard devoted to indigenous peoples «have been guided in part by international conventions and instruments, including those of the International Labour Organisation (ILO) and the United Nations», such as the ILO Convention No. 169, the UNDRIP, as well as the OAS Declaration on the Rights of Indigenous Peoples, as further specified in the footnote accompanying the main text.[8] This is echoed by the policy adopted in the same year by IDB Invest, the private sector arm of the Inter-American Development Bank, which promotes the responsibility of businesses to respect human rights, requiring its clients to «have in place an approach to assess potential human rights risks and impacts, respect human rights, avoid

[6] The World Bank, *Environmental and Social Framework*, 2017, p. 80, para. 27.

[7] Asian Development Bank, *Environmental and Social Framework*, 2024, p. 101, para. 3.

[8] See Inter-American Development Bank, *Environmental and Social Policy Framework*, 2020, p. 85, footnote 161.

infringement on the human rights of others, and address adverse human rights risks and impacts in IDB Invest-supported project[s]».[9]

Equally, the 2023 Vision for Sustainable Development of the African Development Bank affirms that financed activities in both the public and private sectors support the realization of human rights as expressed in the Universal Declaration of Human Rights, the UN Charter, and the African Charter on Human and Peoples' Rights.[10] Furthermore, the Environmental and Social Operational Safeguard no. 7 ('Vulnerable Groups') holds that its requirements aim at encouraging borrowers to «observe international human rights norms, standards, and best practices».[11]

Broadly, this convergence—facilitated through project co-financing, peer institutional learning, and other coordinated efforts among these organizations—is contributing to the emergence of a cross-institutional normative consensus, which is leading to the consolidation of globally shared operational standards that uphold indigenous peoples' rights.

It is noteworthy that by applying such standards to borrowing countries—without eliciting formal contestation from them—Multilateral Development Banks require that indigenous peoples' rights are upheld in a way that may have significant implications for national legal systems, thus extending beyond the scope of individual projects. As borrowing countries are frequently compelled to adopt or amend their domestic legislation in accordance with the Banks' standards to secure and retain access to funding, a new pattern of state practice may emerge over time, especially if consistently applied across various projects and regions. As a result, this process may ultimately further solidify the obligation to uphold indigenous peoples' rights as part of rules and principles of general international law, thereby reinforcing the global legal framework that binds both states and international organizations, in line with the analysis presented in Chap. 5.

This dynamic is exemplified by the policy concerning environmental assessments. Since it was introduced in 1989 by the Bank, it has served first as a model for other Multilateral Development Banks, such as the Inter-American Development Bank,[12] and later for the legislation of many countries.[13] As emphasized in 2000 by Dr. Ibrahim F. Shihata, who served as General Counsel of the World Bank from 1983 to 1998, although the World Bank was not initially envisaged as a vehicle for the progressive development of international environmental law, through its policy dialogue and loan operations, it has provided «incentives for observance of international environmental obligations both under existing treaties and by virtue of new

[9] IDB Invest, *Environmental and Social Sustainability Policy*, 2020, p. 7, para. 17.

[10] African Development Bank, *An African Vision for Sustainable Development, African Development Bank Group's Integrated Safeguards System*, 2023, pp. 6–7, paras. 8, 11.

[11] ibid., p. 94, para. 1.

[12] Boisson de Chazournes (2000, p. 299).

[13] For an analysis of the effects of World Bank's policies regarding the Environmental Impact Assessment on the domestic legal framework of selected Sub-Saharan African countries, see Bekhechi and Mercier (2002, p. 7).

provisions in the agreements with its members which also constitute treaties governed by international law».[14]

A distinct analysis is warranted regarding the International Finance Corporation. While its Performance Standards, as interpreted by the Compliance Advisor Ombudsman, play a pivotal role in strengthening soft law instruments that govern the conduct of business enterprises in relation to indigenous peoples' rights, thereby fostering a corporate compliance culture, they may also contribute to the implementation and consolidation of international obligations voluntarily undertaken by host countries where IFC-supported projects are executed. As stated in the common introductory section to the Performance Standards, in addition to adhering to the provisions set forth within them, clients are obligated to comply with the applicable national laws, including those that implement host country obligations under international law.[15]

Although this may appear to be a modest effect—one that is also common to public sector projects—it should be emphasized that Performance Standard 7 ('Indigenous Peoples') further specifies that, since governments often play a central role in the handling of indigenous peoples' issues, «clients should collaborate with the responsible authorities in managing the risks and impacts of their activities».[16] Therefore, by stressing the importance of collaboration to meet compliance requirements, the Standard contributes to fostering greater national awareness of their relevance.

Furthermore, it is important to note that when the regulations of the host country diverge from the levels and measures outlined in the IFC's Environmental, Health, and Safety Guidelines, which describe the performance thresholds applicable to all industry sectors that are normally acceptable to IFC, clients are expected to adopt the more stringent of the two. In instances where less stringent measures are deemed appropriate due to the specific circumstances of the project, a comprehensive and substantiated justification for any proposed alternatives must be provided as part of the environmental assessment, with the potential effect of encouraging adherence to stronger standards in the private sector (and beyond).[17] Notably, although the Guidelines primarily focus on the protection of human health and the environment, they also contain provisions that highlight the importance of community engagement and risk management, particularly in projects involving the use of hazardous materials that could affect local communities, including indigenous peoples.[18]

Finally, it is noteworthy that the CAO's mediation function typically results in outcomes that address harm suffered by indigenous peoples through legal

[14] Shihata (2000, pp. 514–515).

[15] International Finance Corporation, *IFC Sustainability Framework, Policy and Performance Standards on Environmental and Social Sustainability*, 2012, p. 15, para. 5.

[16] ibid., p. 47, para. 2.

[17] See International Finance Corporation, *Environmental, Health, and Safety General Guidelines*, 2007, p. 1.

[18] ibid., pp. 44–45.

settlements,[19] which may lead to compensation, access to land, livelihood support, or the restoration of territorial rights. As such settlements often require cooperation with state authorities for implementation, they may further contribute to shaping patterns of state practice that reflect a growing engagement with indigenous peoples' rights, thus reinforcing convergence with evolving international norms.

6.4 The Multifaceted Nature of World Bank Group's International Legal Obligations

The analysis carried out so far demonstrates that the World Bank Group as a whole has voluntarily committed to upholding the rights of indigenous peoples in the performance of its core activities. Although the organization cannot be regarded as a human rights enforcer, it has nonetheless integrated these rights into its decision-making processes, particularly when assessing whether to authorize, maintain, or withdraw its financial engagement.

Notably, its institutional practice may be further understood through the analytical framework traditionally applied to state obligations under international human rights law, namely through the tripartite approach of respect, protection, and fulfillment.[20] While this framework is primarily developed in relation to states, its comparative application to international organizations, particularly Multilateral Development Banks such as the World Bank Group, is increasingly recognized in academic discourse.[21]

Without a doubt, the World Bank Group can be seen as engaging in actions that correspond to the duties to respect and protect indigenous peoples' rights. Respect is primarily demonstrated through the avoidance of harm. Due diligence procedures are designed to ensure that the operations it supports do not interfere with indigenous peoples' ability to fully enjoy their rights. A paradigmatic example is provided by the circumstance in which, before approving a project, the World Bank Group ascertains whether FPIC has been obtained in relation to activities that could negatively impact upon indigenous peoples' lands, natural resources, and cultural heritage, or cause their relocation, potentially denying funding if this condition is not

[19] On this aspect, see Guidi (2014, p. 244).

[20] The tripartite typology of state obligations to respect, protect, and fulfill human rights originates in the practice of the UN Committee on Economic, Social and Cultural Rights. It was first systematically articulated in General Comment No. 12 (1999) on the right to adequate food, where the Committee distinguished these three core duties as the framework through which states should implement socio-economic rights. This structure was further elaborated in General Comment No. 14 (2000) on the right to the highest attainable standard of health, which applied the same tripartite analysis to the right to health as enshrined in Article 12 of the International Covenant on Economic, Social and Cultural Rights. See UN Committee on Economic, Social and Cultural Rights (1999, p. 5, para. 15); and UN Committee on Economic, Social and Cultural Rights (2000, p. 9, para. 33). Cf. Tomuschat (2014, p. 142).

[21] Darrow (2003, pp. 131–133), Lehane (2018, p. 200).

met. Respect, in this context, refers to how the WBG operates to avoid contributing to indigenous peoples' rights violations, with the result of refraining from funding activities that could potentially lead to such violations from the outset of a project. Protection, on the other hand, involves proactive oversight to prevent third parties, particularly funding recipients, from violating those rights by using WBG's support. In other words, the role of the organization does not end with the decision to fund or not fund a project, as it also seeks to avoid becoming complicit in potential human rights violations at a later stage. Thus, the duty to protect is operationalized via the WBG's monitoring tasks throughout project implementation to ensure that indigenous peoples' rights are upheld. In both cases, the underlying objective remains the same: to avoid becoming part of the causal chain that could lead to the infringement of indigenous peoples' rights, either by abstaining from supporting the project during the initial phase, or by influencing the conduct of funding recipients throughout the project's lifespan.

Yet the World Bank Group's engagement sometimes extends beyond this dimension of respecting and protecting. Specifically, in the context of technical or financial support provided by IBRD and IDA to Member States, whether through specific projects or as separate initiatives, Environmental and Social Standard 7 allows for the direct promotion of the well-being of indigenous peoples, upon governments' request. Such activities may encompass: (a) strengthening local legislation that recognizes customary or traditional land tenure arrangements; (b) addressing gender and intergenerational issues within indigenous communities; (c) protecting indigenous knowledge, including intellectual property rights; (d) enhancing indigenous peoples' capacity to participate in development planning and programs; and (e) improving the ability of government agencies to deliver services that benefit them.[22] In these instances, the World Bank assumes a role that aligns more closely with the duty to fulfill human rights. Indeed, it contributes directly to the realization of these rights—not merely by protecting them, but by supporting the institutional, social, and material conditions necessary for their enjoyment through the preparation of strategies that are implemented by borrowers.[23]

Similarly, in the case of IFC, Guidance Note 7, which accompanies the Performance Standard dedicated to indigenous peoples, specifies that, while addressing negative project impacts is a mandatory requirement, providing broader development support to private recipients is encouraged as a good practice, especially in large-scale projects, where the client may offer a wider range of development benefits. Notably, recommended development programming, to be designed

---

[22] The World Bank, *Environmental and Social Framework*, 2017, p. 82, para. 35.

[23] In addition, there exist also World Bank's recent initiatives that provide direct financing to indigenous peoples through multi-donor trust funds, enabling them to take a more active and direct role in environmental protection and climate action. Notable examples are the Forest Carbon Partnership Facility Capacity Building Program (2009–2022), together with the Enhancing Access to Benefits while Lowering Emissions initiative (launched in 2020), as well as the Dedicated Grant Mechanism (launched in 2010). Detailed information is available on the World Bank's website at: https://www.worldbank.org/en/topic/indigenouspeoples#2. Accessed 21 July 2025.

and implemented in consultation with indigenous communities, includes a list of examples that largely align with those outlined in the World Bank's Environmental and Social Standard 7.[24]

Accordingly, looking ahead, the World Bank Group's operational framework, along with its interpretative practice, is likely to assume an increasingly normative function in relation to indigenous peoples' rights. This reflects a broader engagement with the full spectrum of international human rights obligations: not only to respect and protect but also to fulfill. In this context, the WBG is gradually shifting from being viewed as a neutral financial actor to emerging as a global institution whose actions carry significant legal implications under international law. As a result, it is positioned to play a pivotal role in advancing the international legal discourse regarding indigenous peoples.

References

Bekhechi MA, Mercier JR (2002) The legal and regulatory frameworks for environmental impact assessments. A study of selected countries in Sub-Saharan Africa. World Bank, Washington, DC

Boisson de Chazournes L (2000) Policy guidance and compliance: the World Bank operational standards. In: Shelton D (ed) Commitment and compliance: the role of non-binding norms in the international legal system. OUP, Oxford-New York, pp 281–303

Bonfanti A (2012) Imprese multinazionali, diritti umani e ambiente. Giuffrè, Milan

Clark D (2002) The World Bank and human rights: the need for greater accountability. HHRJ 15:205–226

Darrow M (2003) Between light and shadow: the World Bank, the International Monetary Fund and international human rights law. Hart Publishing, Oxford

Guidi M (2014) The protection of indigenous peoples' concerns in World Bank-funded projects. In: Sacerdoti G et al (eds) General interests of host States in international investment law. CUP, Cambridge, pp 237–262

Lehane G (2018) Human rights at the World Bank Group. In: Radi Y (ed) Research handbook on human rights and investments. Edward Elgar, Cheltenham-Northampton, pp 186–219

McBeth A (2006) Breaching the vacuum: a consideration of the role of international human rights law in the operations of the international financial institutions. Int J Hum Rights 10(4):385–404

Shihata IFI (2000) The World Bank in a changing world, vol III. Brill, The Hague-London-Boston

Tomuschat C (2014) Human rights: between idealism and realism. OUP, Oxford

UN Committee on Economic, Social and Cultural Rights (1999) General Comment No. 12: the right to adequate food, Art. 11 of the Covenant. UN Doc. E/C.12/1999/5. https://docs.un.org/. Accessed 21 July 2025

UN Committee on Economic, Social and Cultural Rights (2000) General Comment No. 14: the right to the highest attainable standard of health, Art. 12. UN Doc. E/C.12/2000/4. https://docs.un.org/. Accessed 21 July 2025

[24] International Finance Corporation, *International Finance Corporation's Guidance Notes: Performance Standards on Environmental and Social Sustainability*, 2012. See the Guidance Note no. 7 regarding indigenous peoples, pp. 19–20.